BIBLIOTHECA SCHOENBERGENSIS

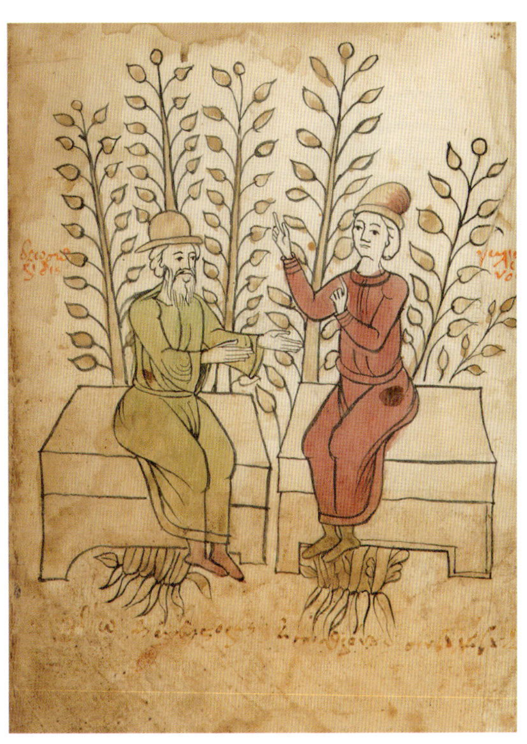

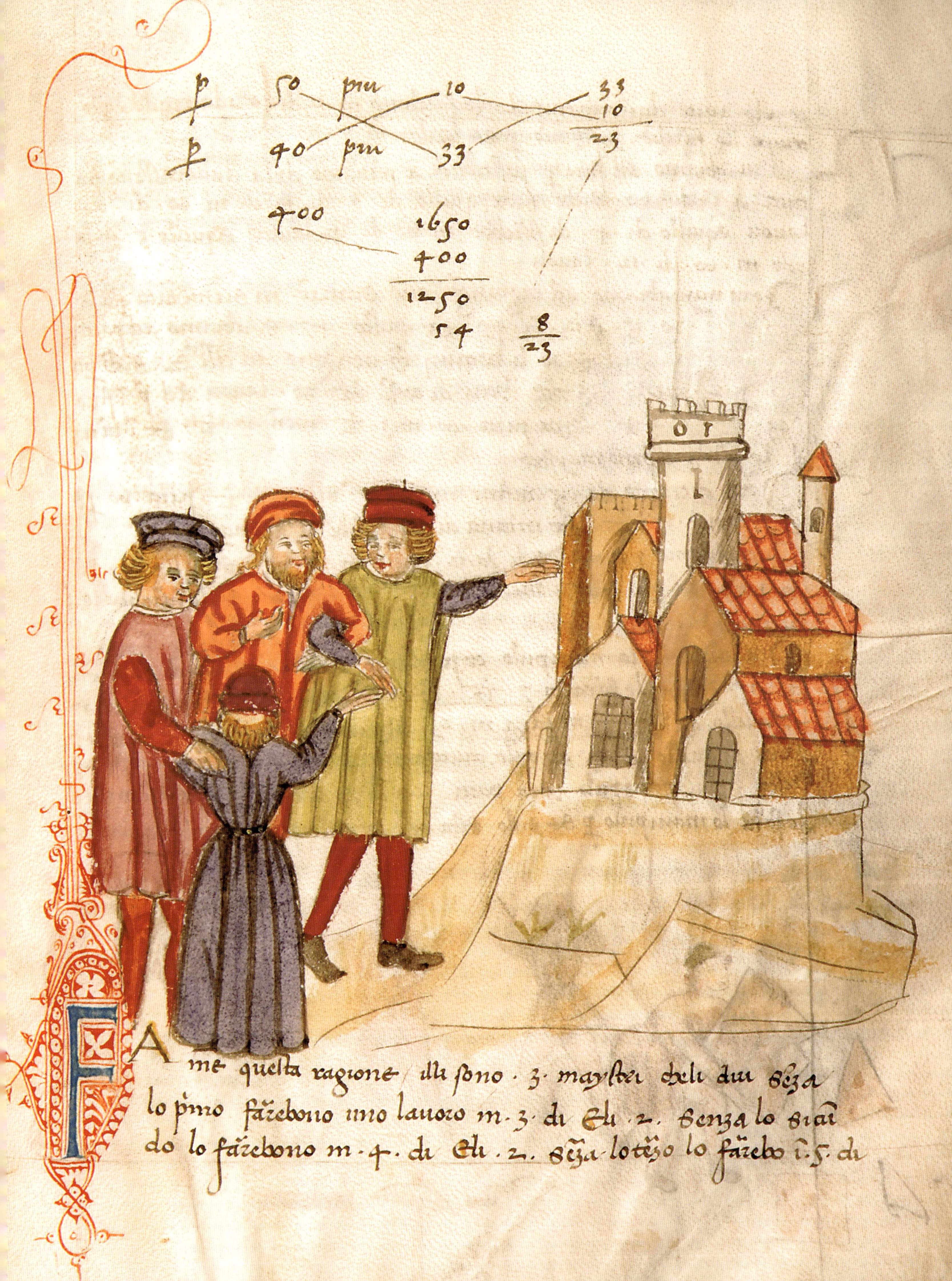

A me questa ragione / elli sono . 3 . maystri cheli dui senza
lo primo farebono uno lauoro in . 3 . di eli . 2 . senza lo terzo
do lo farebono in . 4 . di eli . 2 . senza lotezo lo farebo in . 5 . di

Transformation of Knowledge

Early Manuscripts from the Collection of

Lawrence J. Schoenberg

Edited by Crofton Black

Paul Holberton publishing, London

ISBN 1 903470 50 1 [9781903470503]
British Library Cataloguing in Publication Data
A catalogue record for this book is available from the British Library

Library of Congress Control Number 2006931851

Produced by Paul Holberton publishing, 37 Snowsfields, London SE1 3SU
www.paul-holberton.net

Designed by Roger Davies
rogerdaviesdesign@btinternet.com

Photographs by Phototech, Total Image Systems, Sarasota FL
www.photo-tech.com

Printed in Italy by Graphic Studio, Bussolengo, Verona

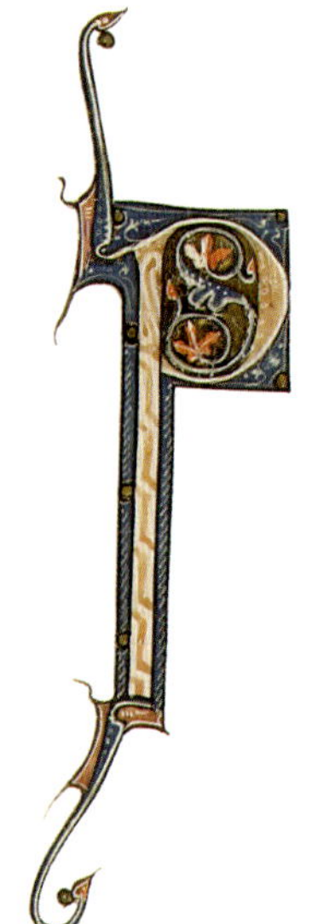

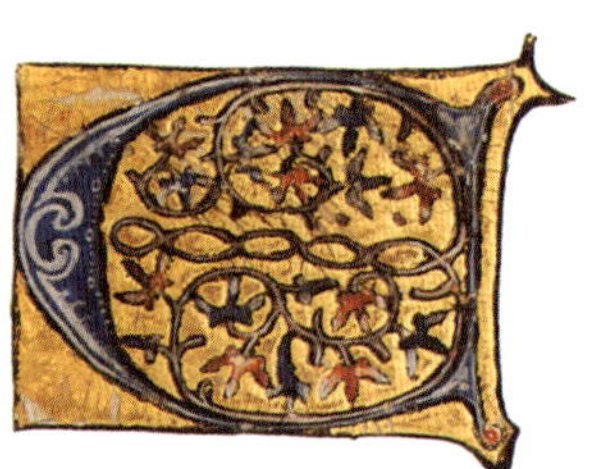

The following manuscripts are represented on the cover:
Front, top row, from left: LJS 49, f. 16v (V, no. 15); 184, f. 1r (IX, no. 2); 445, p. 114
(IV, no. 35); 235, f. 8v (II, no. 3); bottom row, from left: LJS 264, f. 3r (IX, no. 6);
419, f. 28r (V, no. 40); 37, f. 16v (III, no. 6); 64, f. 8r (IV, no. 12)
Back, top row, from left: LJS 226, f. 3r (IV, no. 26); 50, f. 137v (IX, no. 8); 434, f. 4r
(IV, no. 40); 449, f. 23v (IV, no. 29); bottom row, from left: LJS 423, p. 128
(III, no. 24); 198, f. 19r (V, no. 23); 278 (V, no. 42); 47, f. 40v (II, no. 2)

Half title: LJS 62, f. 3v, Galen discoursing with Dioscorides (V, no. 38; Herbal)
Frontispiece: LJS 27, f. 58r (III, no. 18; Pietro Paolo Muscarello, Algorismus, 1478)

Contents

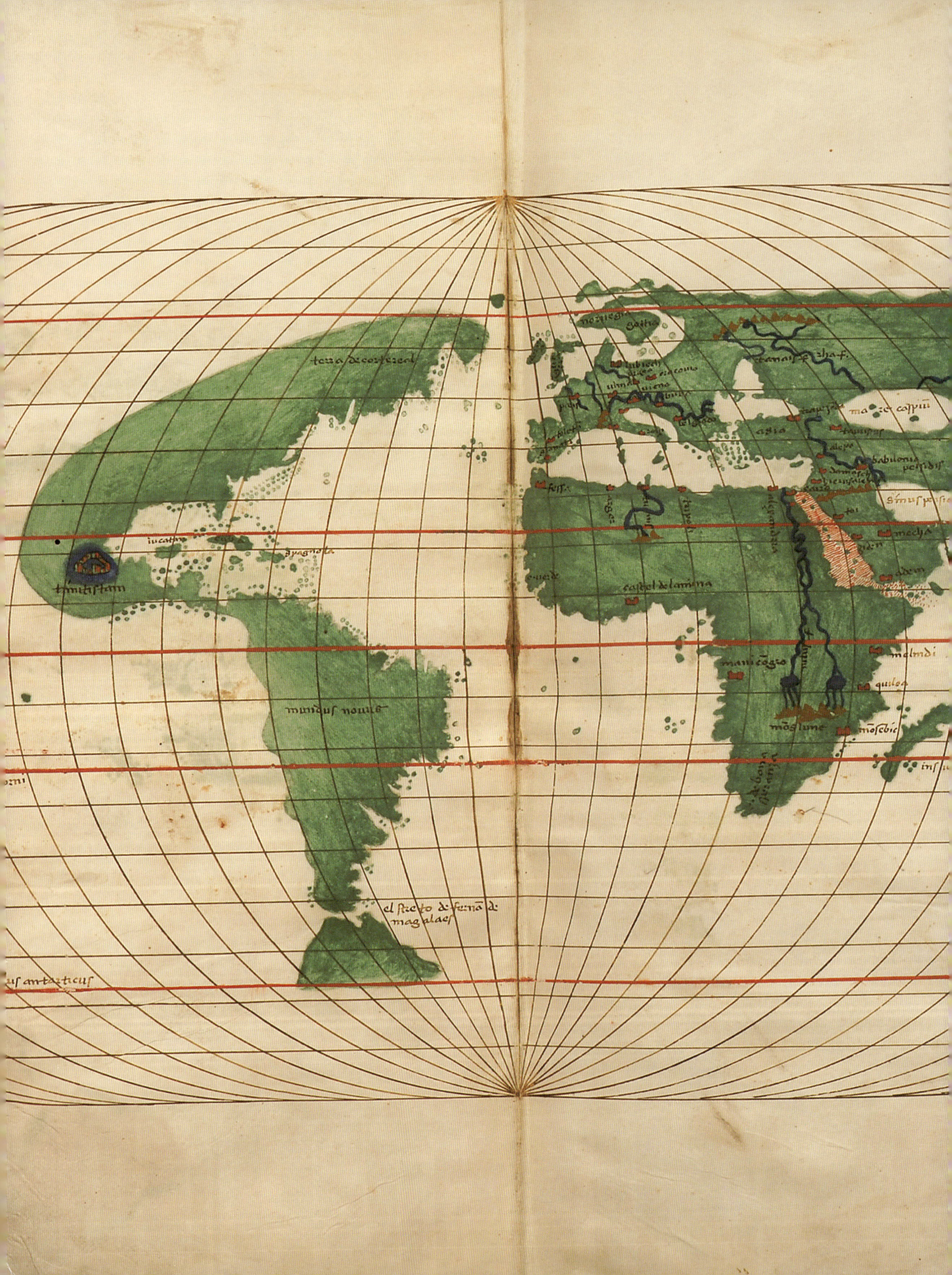
terra de cortereal
norvegia
gothia
lubiech
ciacouo
vilna
uiena
buda
oceanus ghaf.
asia
mare caspiu
tauris
alepo
babulonia
persidis
damasch
hierusale
cauro
sinus persi.
fess
mare caspiu
medya
aden
iucatan
spagnola
timistitan
e. uerde
casbel de la miena
mani congo
melindi
quiloa
moglume
mosebic
insu
mundus nouus
de bon speransa
el streto de fernã de
magalaes
us antarticus

PREFACE

CHRISTOPHER DE HAMEL

Lawrence Schoenberg would probably have got on very well in the court of Rudolf II of Bohemia (1576–1612). In Prague, the emperor gathered a circle of exceptional scholars, collectors and scientists, looking at the Copernican universe in a new way and sometimes also in very old ways indeed, for they practised alchemy and the arts of magic. Larry is primarily a logician and an early innovator of computer software and is a successful businessman, philanthropist, an international tennis and chessplayer, and a tireless traveller. He is also agreeably unconventional. There is a whiff of the medieval magician about Larry Schoenberg, whose mind sparkles in unexpected directions, lateral-thinking, wise-cracking, fast-talking, as mischievous and as unpredictable as Mephistopheles. He probably never sleeps. His extraordinary collection of early manuscripts has no modern parallel, for it comprises not only the jaw-dropping illuminated highspots, which have graced the various public exhibitions to which selections have often been lent, but also the unexpected and quirky, and the strange and exotic. Many collectors simply buy fine books, as opportunity allows. The theme of Larry Schoenberg's library – secular texts, especially science and mathematics – might seem to narrow the field to a few great and well-charted authors. There they all are, of course, Aristotle, Ptolemy, Euclid, and Boethius, among others, but as well as these there are the unexpected. Here too are astrology, algebra, botany, astronomy in Hebrew, anatomy in Arabic, the *Wonders of Creation* in Persian; here are the *Algorismus* of Sacrobosco, the *Isagoge* of Gerbert of Auvergne, Dioscorides, Pomponius Mela, al-Biruni, al-Tusi, Avicenna, William of Conches, Gauthier de Metz, Alfonso the Wise, Albertus Magnus, Regiomontanus. The names are as resonant as incantations, and they conjure up a spirit world of heresy, magic, alchemy and human genius across all cultures.

Many of Larry's friends probably think him very odd, or perhaps they simply have no idea that this genial, relaxed and sun-tanned sportsman from Florida possesses one of the most fascinating and most intellectually remarkable libraries in the world. Probably even fewer have ever looked at the *Schoenberg Database of Manuscripts* and, if they did, they might seriously doubt their friend's sanity, for this is no more than a brilliantly organized index, mostly entered by Larry himself, of well over 80,000 different medieval manuscripts which have been sold at auction or have changed hands, anywhere in the world, in the last two hundred and fifty years. For 99.9% of humankind, this would doubtless seem monumentally pointless, but for the remaining 0.1% of us (and I am proud to be among them), this is probably the most revolutionary and important medieval manuscript website ever devised. It allows one to track and to trace countless manuscripts which none of us knew existed, and to follow the journeys and wanderings of this very itinerant class of art back and forth across the world, into libraries and frequently out again, often invisible except from their footsteps through the salerooms. There are more manuscripts on the Schoenberg Database than in any of the largest national libraries in the world. It has the potential to transform medieval studies and the history of taste and economics, and it has already revolutionized auctioneers' sale catalogues.

My own involvement with Larry Schoenberg was initially through Sotheby's, where he has been a regular participant in major sales for almost thirty years. He is a thoughtful and unusually self-controlled viewer of manuscripts. He will make decisions, and will often bid far beyond an estimate and then, when we least expect it, stop. What he has bought is truly phenomenal. What he has underbid is probably even more extraordinary and the auction houses always fail to give enough credit to this crucial class of sale participants, who in fact create the market and are unremembered after the event, even in the Schoenberg Database. If Sotheby's could give honorary knighthoods, Larry Schoenberg would have one. One day, however, when we had invited him to a dinner at Sotheby's in New York, he asked if he might bring a friend too, Barbara Brizdle, their first date, where she must have listened appalled to the excited talk of manuscripts, through which she charmed us all. Later he married her, and this catalogue was her idea and her initiative.

Corpus Christi College, Cambridge

LJS 26, f. 7v-8r (VII, no. 11; Battista Agnese, Portolan, Venice, *c.* 1535–38)

I NTRODUCTION

LAWRENCE J. SCHOENBERG

I have been asked many times just how I became a collector of medieval and Renaissance Manuscripts. I cannot point to one seminal moment. It was a combination of at least three events.

The first occurred in 1948 when I was in high school and I was doing a paper on the elections of 1908 and 1912 and Theodore Roosevelt. My father, then a Principal in the New York City public school system, arranged for me to have access to the New York Public Library's reference room – something that was not usually granted to high-schoolers. The librarians brought me from the stacks original election handbills directed at the various ethnic communities of New York City. They were in many languages and quite simplistic but provided a wonderful insight into the fractured nature of New York politics. What particularly struck me was that I was looking at material that had not been referenced in the forty years since the time of the election. The tactile sense of being the first to touch the past in such a direct way was a moving moment. Thus a collector was born.

The second one involved a research project on Modigliani that I undertook in 1957 for an art historian named Alfred Werner. While working for him – as a moonlighter since I had a full time job at IBM – I began collecting monographs on Modigliani and subsequently on other artists. As time passed, I looked for earlier and earlier monographs, which often had woodcuts and engraved illustrations – some of which were created specifically for the book. Buying these books led me to Benjamin Swann, the then proprietor of Swann Auction Galleries, who encouraged me to look at medieval manuscripts.

The first medieval manuscript that I bought was LJS 12, a copy of the *Office for the Reception of Novices*. I didn't even know what the text was but I was intrigued by the decorated initials, which had been painstakingly pasted into the text. I was intrigued by the idea that someone had created a production line for drawing, cutting and then pasting the initials into the manuscripts as decoration. The purchase of this manuscript, with its painted illustrations, formed the third influencing event in my collecting life.

Over the years, three additional events had a significant influence on my collecting scope and focus.

The first was when I met Christopher de Hamel some twenty-five years ago. It was his knowledge, enthusiasm and focus that re-ignited my interest and led to my changing my collection orientation from the art or aesthetics, which is where I started, to the texts themselves and the context in which they were created.

Then some ten years ago, under Christopher's leadership, we visited the Bodmers in Geneva. Seeing the non-traditional organization of their collection – the intermixing of manuscripts with armour and other artefacts – reinforced my interest in having a subject and time-line structure. I now felt comfortable in breaking the chains of classical organization – traditionally by chronology, country, culture or material – to structure my own collection in a different way and still have a coherent presentation.

Lastly, in 1997, I was able to acquire the manuscript collection of John Stanitz, whose far-reaching collection of scientific manuscripts was both substantial and relevant to my focus.

Today, my collection, *Bibliotheca Schoenbergensis*, consists of medieval and Renaissance secular manuscripts with an emphasis on mathematics and science and the application of that knowledge to everyday life. It reflects the transformation of man's knowledge about the world around him from simple observation to recognition, to documenting and analysis, and then to the application and interpretation of that learning.

As such, I am tracing this transformation of knowledge from magic to science, astrology to astronomy, alchemy to chemistry, numerology to mathematics, remedies to pharmacology, and wonders to natural science particularly as it moved back and forth between cultures in the Golden Crescent and across various languages from Greek and Latin, to Arabic and Hebrew, to the Romance languages. I am more interested in the interconnection between manuscripts than in each as an individual codex.

During the forty-plus years of my collecting, the availability of manuscripts which have both aesthetic and textual purity has become close to non-existent. I was led to collect those texts that were available, often copies made by students for use during their studies. This has resulted in less than perfect copies of codices but also in ones which provide the opportunity to study the process of learning. Where else could you find, in one volume, the various texts used for medical study in the Middle Ages?

Collectors have often been guided in their acquisitions by the desire to create a set of 'high spots'. They do this to demonstrate their appreciation and understanding of what is the best in the area of their collection. It is still desirable, if quite unachievable, to search for the finest materials, but the consequential creation of a physical site where the material could be viewed at one time has become less significant. While once this stand-alone approach had validity because of the great difficulty in getting to any particular collection site, the availability of scanned materials on the internet has reduced that value considerably.

In 1996, I founded the *Schoenberg Center for Electronic and Text Imaging* (SCETI) at the University of Pennsylvania. Penn was already a leading force in building scanned and digitized materials so the match was a natural one for both of us. My starting motive was to make my collection more easily available to scholars although many did not find it unpleasant to visit us in Florida, to see and feel the actual codex.

By 1999, however, I was amazed to discover how difficult it was for most researchers to find material that was available on the internet. It was not enough to make my collection – or any manuscript material – available electronically on the web; it was desirable to build a comprehensive database of all manuscript descriptions, not just those I owned, to serve as an online equivalent of the old library card catalogue. Academics and collectors as well as dealers are able both to research specific manuscripts or to use this *Schoenberg Database of Manuscripts* as a virtual library. Variant spellings, languages, measurements, etc. make this a daunting task but one that I am consumed by.

This collecting life would not have been possible without the efforts of my number-one dealer and friend Sam Fogg, under whose guidance this catalogue is being produced, and of the late Bernard Breslauer, Stéphane Clavreuil, Seth Fagen, Mary Ann and Roland Folter, Jörn Günther, Sandra Hindman, Richard Linenthal, Umberto Pregliasco, Francesco Radaeli, Fiammetta Soave, Kay Sutton, Heribert Tenschert, and many other dealers and academics.

I offer fond thanks to my fellow collectors and travel companions Martin Schøyen of Norway, Henri Schiller of France, the late Sion Segre-Amar of Italy, Roger de Kesel and Germain Desmet of Belgium, and Jack Lunzer of England, whose enthusiasm and competitive instincts have furthered my collector's spirit.

This catalogue is dedicated to Christopher de Hamel, whose contagious passion for medieval materials changed the direction of my interests for the last twenty-five years, and to my wife, Barbara Brizdle, the progenitor of this catalogue, whose passion for life has made it a wonderful voyage.

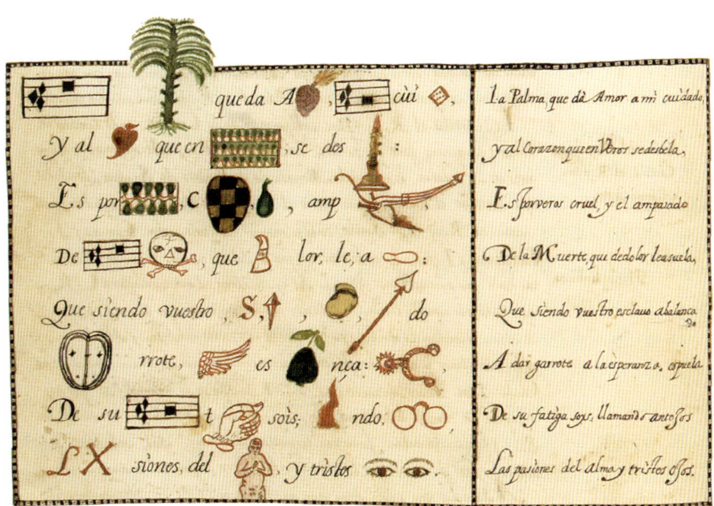

LJS 423, p. 26 (III, no. 24; Anon., *De zifras*, Spain, *c.* 1600)

OVERVIEW

CROFTON BLACK

Many remarkable records of human endeavour sit side by side in the Schoenberg Collection. The purpose behind this catalogue is not only to give their particulars but also to sketch their role in the history of ideas. The reflection of this history in the material gathered here spans over four thousand years, from the practice of arithmetic in Babylon in the third millennium BC to a report on submarine detection experiments in 1919. Its particular concentration, however, is on the 'early modern' era, running approximately from the thirteenth to the eighteenth centuries.

Knowledge has many facets. The arrangement of the first half of this catalogue is inspired by the medieval pedagogic scheme of the seven liberal arts – grammar, rhetoric, dialectic, music, arithmetic, geometry and astronomy. In the second half, this standard framework is complemented by records of other ways in which people interacted with their environment – medicine, alchemy and chemistry, technology, agriculture and the legal system.

The focus of the catalogue is almost entirely secular. Nonetheless, behind most of the works presented here stand the intertwined traditions of the three great near-eastern monotheist faiths, Judaism, Christianity and Islam. All of the cultures which coalesced around these religions were profoundly influenced by the intellectual developments of pagan antiquity. With a few exceptions this religious framework delineates the geographical scope of this selection of material – from Europe to North Africa, to the Middle East and central Asia, following the silk route as far as Samarqand.

In the first place, this catalogue traces the reception of a number of ancient authorities of central importance, Aristotle, Euclid, Ptolemy and Galen among others. Reception encompasses reading, translating, copying, abridging, commentating and criticizing. By studying it we can plot the lives of these works in parallel and successive cultural contexts; we can determine how they were read and misread, how they were attacked and defended. From this combat none of them survives unscathed, but their longevity is remarkable. In this catalogue we find Aristotle still underpinning university study in 1666; we observe Ptolemy's sun, still revolving around the earth in 1680; and we encounter Galen's theory of humours, still requiring refutation at the end of the seventeenth century.

The longevity of these authorities is the result of their transformation, as the title of this catalogue makes clear. As they shift from Greek to Arabic and Hebrew, to Latin, or move between Islam, Judaism and Christianity, each culture realigns them into its own frame of reference. This process of assimilation can be harmonious; or, as the host culture attempts to digest a body of alien thought, it can prove bitterly controversial.

Waiting in the wings, meanwhile, are those whose works will eventually lead to the downfall of these eminent ancients – Copernicus, Descartes, Newton and Leibniz. For this catalogue is also a record of innovation. To these names must be added several less well known. Here is Nastulus, inventor of astrolabes; al-Khazini, who perfected the hydrostatic balance; al-Zahrawi, devisor of medical instruments. In their illustrious company are a number of other figures, the success or failure of whose projects remains undocumented: here we may note the presence of Don Antonio de' Medici's recipe for limitless wealth and the fish-shaped submarine of Adamandus.

Beyond the demarcation of these intellectual highlights a particularly valuable aspect of this collection is the light it casts on more typical, but less studied, records of thought. These include university textbooks and theses, necessary to define the norm against which exceptional achievements are measured. The collection therefore helps us not only to glimpse the intellectual peaks of the period but also to survey the plateaux from which they emerge. Ghostly figures, overlooked by mainstream historical narrative, can regain some semblance of flesh and blood.

Manuscripts, properly speaking, are not rare; they are unique. Each one provides a snapshot of one or more individuals – some celebrated, others unknown or anonymous – grappling with the intellectual problems of their time. The aim of this catalogue is to present each item in a way which reflects both its individuality and its links with longstanding, constantly transforming tradition.

Opposite: Details from LJS 449, f. 9 (IV, no. 29; Anthology of medical and astronomical texts, south-west Germany, *c.* 1446)

TRANSFORMATION OF KNOWLEDGE

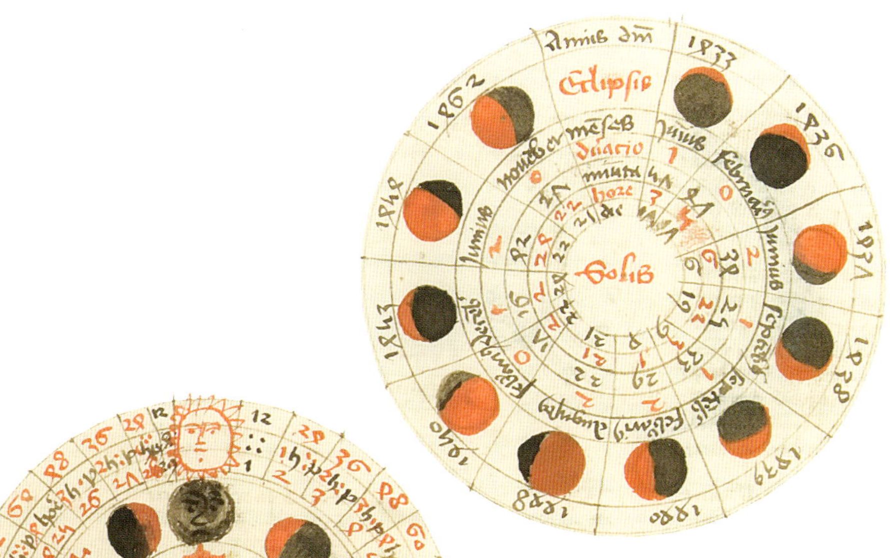

Editorial Note

Full descriptions of all manuscripts in the Schoenberg
Collection, and a number of complete facsimiles, are
available online at www.library.upenn.edu/ljschoenberg.

The present catalogue is based on these existing
descriptions. Additional brief contextual notes have been
provided for the majority of manuscripts: their aim is to focus on
the role of each in the transmission of ideas within and across four
principal intellectual traditions – Greek, Latin, Arabic/Persian and Hebrew.
Bibliographical references used in these notes are listed at the end of the book.

Also at the end of the book, in the Concordance, the catalogue entries are
correlated to the *Schoenberg Database of Manuscripts* (SDBM). This Web-based
database includes bibliographic material culled from over 8,300 catalogues
issued by more than a thousand dealers and auction houses since the late
eighteenth century, augmented by inventories and catalogues from private
and institutional libraries. It encompasses more than 82,000 entries of
manuscripts consisting of five or more leaves dating from before 1600.

I Responses to Aristotle

In 1929, Alfred North Whitehead made his subsequently celebrated and much-quoted remark that "the safest general characterization of the European philosophical tradition is that it consists of a series of footnotes to Plato". In the Middle Ages, however, Plato was a footnote to his student Aristotle. Aristotle's logical texts – as digested into Latin by Boethius – constituted (along with the study of rhetoric and grammar) the trivium, the first three of the seven liberal arts and the foundation of the educational curriculum. Many of the following manuscripts were evidently used as textbooks and directly or indirectly for teaching. Aristotle's philosophy remained a vital point of reference throughout the Middle Ages and Renaissance. One result of this pervasiveness was that his name became attached to other works bearing no relation to his philosophy (see Pseudo-Aristotle, LJS 459 [no. 7] and 456 [no. 8]). In the Renaissance, however, his hegemony was challenged by new translations and rediscoveries of other ancient philosophers, some of which feature here – Plato, Lucretius, whose *On the Nature of Things* was an exposition of atomism, and the sceptic Sextus Empiricus (LJS 438 [no. 23], 179 [no. 24] and 380 [no. 22]).

Boethius, *De interpretatione*
Central France (perhaps Saint-Benoît-sur-Loire), 9th and 11th centuries

Most of this manuscript comprises one of the earliest surviving copies of a commentary by Boethius on Aristotle's *Peri hermēneias* (On interpretation). Boethius translated the *Peri hermēneias* from Greek into Latin around 516; the beginning of his translation is found on f. 1v of this manuscript. Around the same time he produced two commentaries on it, the shorter of which is included here. His translation and commentaries were not widely known until the end of the ninth century. By the twelfth century, however, the translation had become one of the core elements of the *logica vetus*, or 'old logic' curriculum; as such, it and its commentaries were an essential part of the university syllabus.

Most of this manuscript dates from the ninth century and therefore precedes the period when these texts were widely copied. Evidently by the eleventh century its beginning and end were missing and had to be recopied. The manuscript was probably written and illustrated at the Carolingian abbey of Fleury (Saint-Benoît-sur-Loire). Fleury was famous for its library at the time this manuscript was copied. By the seventeenth century it had become well-known to collectors; the original abbey was demolished in 1790.

Also included here are several other grammatical, rhetorical and logical texts.

DESCRIPTION Parchment, 64 folios, 205 x 180 mm, in Latin (with some Greek words); ff. 5-44 (9th century) upright Carolingian minuscule, yellow-brown ink, with 4 large diagrams; ff. 1-4 and 45-64 (11th century) fine late Carolingian minuscule, dark brown ink, red and blue initials, one large decorated initial and diagram. 19th-century English binding.
PROVENANCE Abbey of Fleury; James Taylor; Sir Thomas Phillipps, ms. 2179; William H. Robinson Ltd; H.P. Kraus; Beck collection, ms. 3; Sotheby's, London, 16 June 1997, lot 3
BIBLIOGRAPHY PL 64, 293-392; Lacombe 266

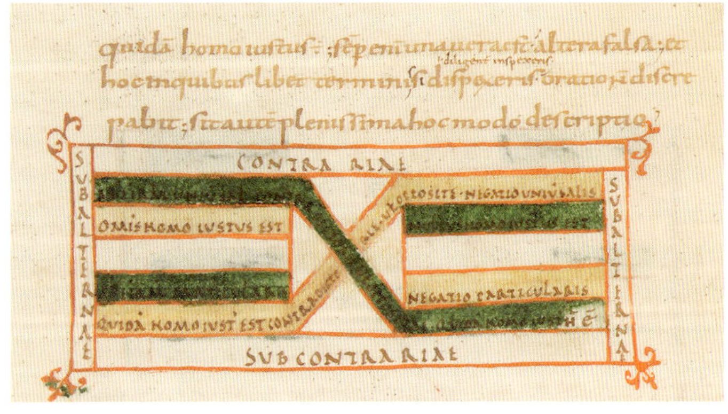

LJS 101
f. 36v

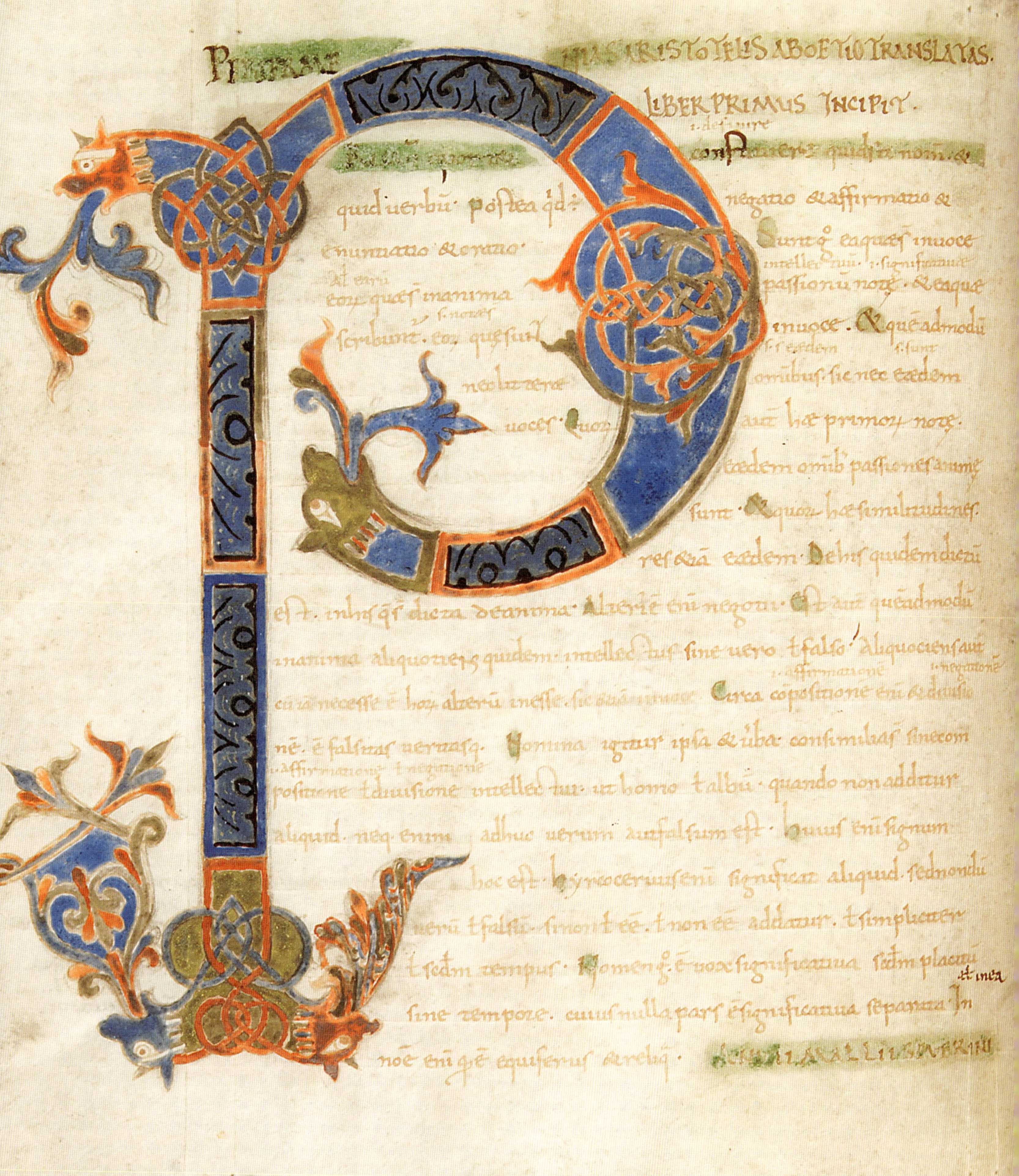

PERIERMENIAS ARISTOTELIS A BOETIO TRANSLATAS. LIBER PRIMUS INCIPIT.

Primum oportet constituere (.i. definire) quid sit nomen et quid verbum, postea quid sit negatio et affirmatio et enuntiatio et oratio. Sunt ergo ea quae sunt in voce earum quae sunt in anima passionum notae, et ea quae scribuntur eorum quae sunt in voce. Et quemadmodum nec litterae omnibus eaedem, sic nec eaedem voces; quorum autem hae primorum notae, eaedem omnibus passiones animae sunt, et quorum hae similitudines, res etiam eaedem. De his quidem dictum est in his quae sunt dicta de anima, alterius enim negotii est.

Est autem, quemadmodum in anima aliquotiens quidem intellectus sine vero vel falso, aliquotiens autem cui iam necesse est horum alterum inesse, sic etiam in voce. Circa compositionem enim et divisionem est falsitas veritasque. Nomina igitur ipsa et verba consimilia sunt sine compositione et divisione intellectui, ut homo vel album, quando non addatur aliquid; neque enim adhuc verum aut falsum est. Huius enim signum hoc est: hircocervus enim significat aliquid, sed nondum verum vel falsum, si non esse vel esse addatur, vel simpliciter vel secundum tempus. Nomen ergo est vox significativa secundum placitum sine tempore, cuius nulla pars est significativa separata. In nomine enim quod est equiferus et reliqua.

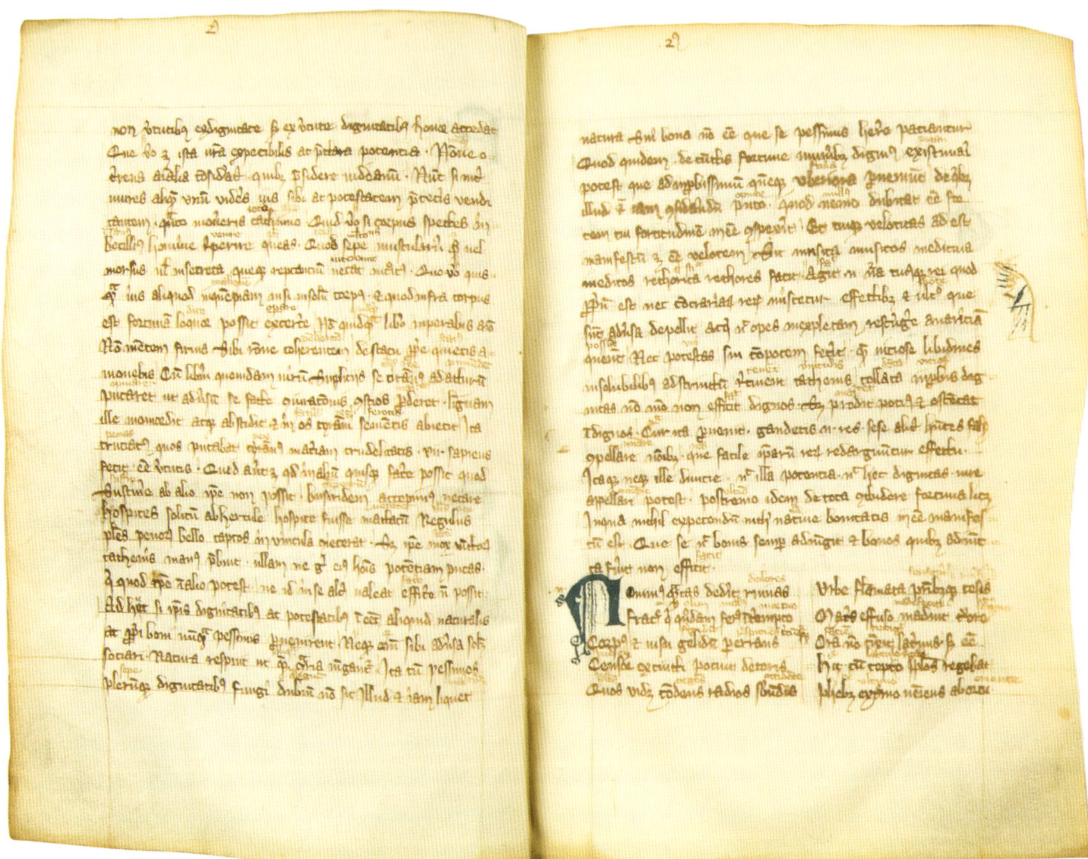

LJS 347, ff. 1v-2r

2   LJS 347

Boethius, *De consolatione philosophiae*
England, 14th century

The role of Boethius as commentator and transmitter of
Aristotle's texts (see LJS 101 [no. 1]) is complemented by his
Consolation of Philosophy. This he wrote in prison, where he
had been sent on the orders of King Theodoric, just prior to
his execution (523–24). The circumstances of its composition
form the frame of the narrative, in which Lady Philosophy
visits a prisoner and instructs him in the nature of fortune,
good, evil and the attainment of happiness.

The *Consolatio* had an extremely wide influence from late
antiquity to the Renaissance and gave rise to a large number
of commentaries and vernacular translations. Two
translations were made into English, by King Alfred the Great
(*c.* 900) and by Geoffrey Chaucer (*c.* 1380), with whose life
this manuscript, in Latin, is approximately contemporary. It
contains a gloss, on f. 1v, of the Latin *sustinere* as English
'suffre'; presumably it was used as a school text.

DESCRIPTION Parchment, 43 folios, 202 x 137 mm, in Latin, English
cursive script, dark brown ink, some rubrics in blue, many
interlinear glosses; 12 painted initials in blue. 19th century English
half dark blue morocco binding, marbled boards.
PROVENANCE Armorial bookplate of Lord Henry Maxwell
Farnham, 7th Baron (1799-1868); Sotheby's, 7 December 1999, lot 33
BIBLIOGRAPHY Marenbon; DSB II 228-36

3   LJS 385

Boethius, *De consolatione philosophiae*, Book I, ch. 1, and
other texts
Italy, *c.* 1500

The beginning of Boethius's *Consolation of Philosophy* is found
in this compilation of classical works, which was presumably
intended as a school textbook. Also included are the first
book of Cicero's *De officiis*, two plays by Terence, a section
from Virgil's *Aeneid* and various verses and recipes.

DESCRIPTION Paper, 102 folios, 210 x 140 mm, in Latin, various
hands, brown ink, some sections with rubrics in red, initials and

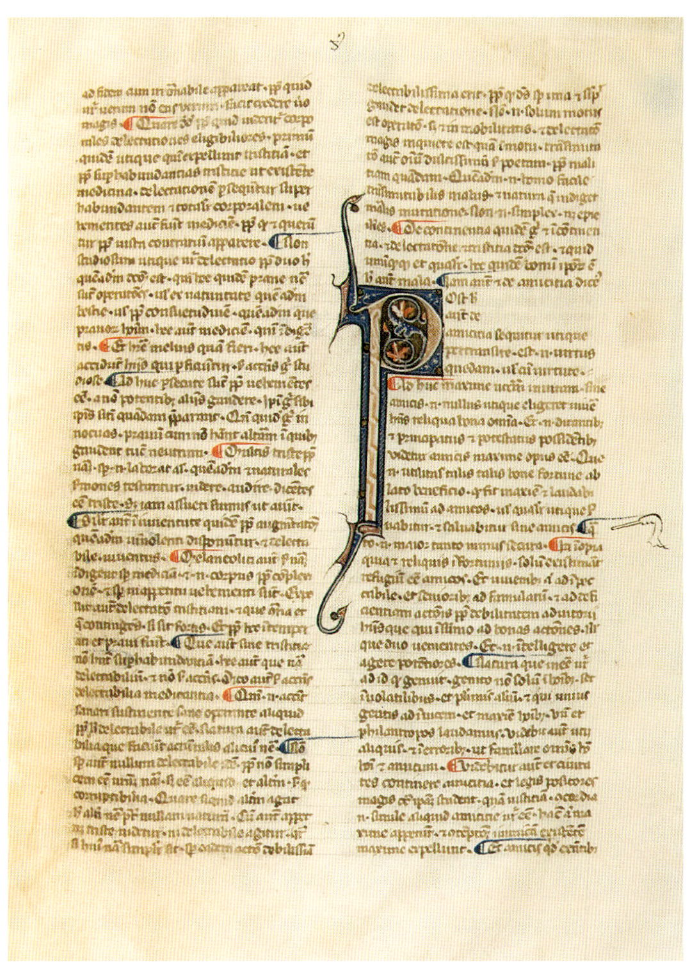

which lacked Book XI; William revised this, making a new translation, from Greek, of Book XI, as well as of Book XIV and sections from Book XIII which were apparently missing from the manuscript of the *translatio anonyma* he used. His new text was widely copied and a large number of variant readings entered the tradition. The majority of extant copies attest a tradition based on the text used at the University of Paris, the predominant centre for Aristotelian studies in the Middle Ages. The version of the *Metaphysics* contained in this manuscript, though incomplete, provides valuable evidence for a different, independent tradition of textual transmission.

Also included here is William's translation of Aristotle's *Ethica*, copied in a different hand. The manuscript once also contained the *translatio Durandi* of Aristotle's *Economica*, but only the first folio of this remains.

DESCRIPTION Parchment, 80 folios, 307 x 218 mm, in Latin, Gothic script, in two hands, brown ink, capitals touched in red, running titles and some paragraph-marks in red or blue, early marginal notes; 2-line initials in red or blue with contrasting penwork extending far into margins; eight illuminated initials (mostly 4- to 5-line), polychrome and gold. Late 15th or early 16th-century Florentine binding, pale tanned leather over wooden boards, stamped.
PROVENANCE Latin inscription, partly in code, dated 1368; Sotheby's, London, 10 December 1980, lot 79
BIBLIOGRAPHY Vuillemin-Diem; Beullens; Brams; DSB IX 434-40

capitals touched with red or green, marginal and interlinear annotations; 2-line initials in red, occasional sketches. Original binding, wooden boards with brown leather spine.
PROVENANCE Giovanni Angelo, Duke of Altemps (died 1620); Henry Allan; Samuel Allan, County Antrim; William Foyle; Christie's, London, 11 July 2000, lot 83

5   LJS 439

Al-Kindi, Treatise on science, religion and cosmology
Andalusia, 14th century

4   LJS 25

Aristotle, *Metaphysics,* translated by William of Moerbeke
Italy, 13th century

Late medieval Latin translations of Aristotle and his commentators, exemplified by William of Moerbeke's *Metaphysics* (see LJS 25 [no. 4]), were to a large extent dependent on the wave of translation of Greek philosophical works into Arabic which began in the ninth century. The reception of this foreign body of knowledge into Islam provoked considerable debate, and is the subject of this work by the eminent scholar and philosopher Abu Yusuf al-Kindi (*c.* 801–866), relatively few of whose many compositions have survived. This is a previously unknown text by al-Kindi which considers one of the central issues in Islamic thought in his

Although Boethius provided a valuable digest of Aristotelian learning, relatively few Greek philosophical texts were directly available to the Latin West in the early centuries of the Middle Ages. Translations of Aristotle into Latin became more widely available in the twelfth and thirteenth centuries. The version of Aristotle's *Metaphysics* by William of Moerbeke (*c.* 1230–*c.* 1286) provided the scholastic tradition with one of its central texts. It was based on an existing *translatio anonyma,*

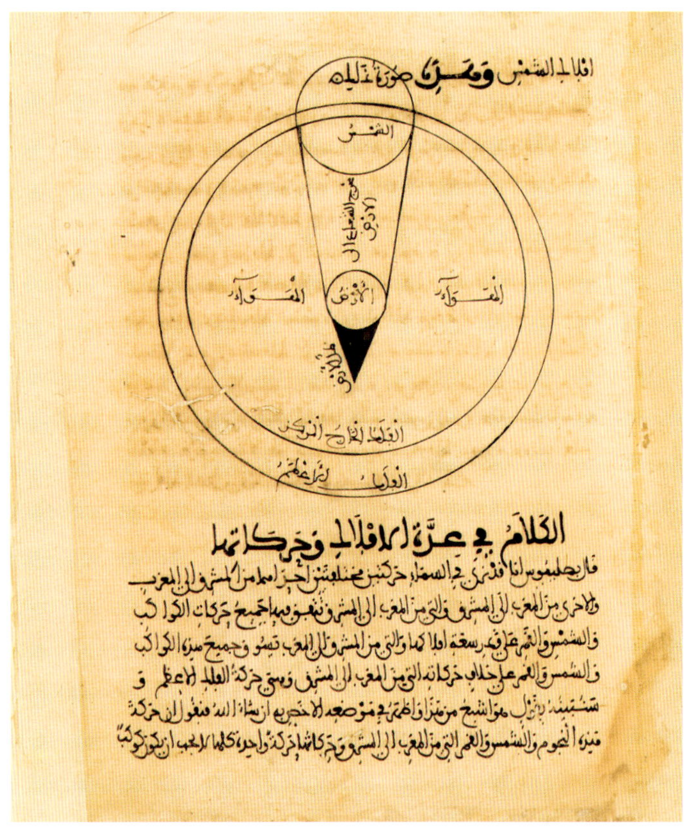

time, the relationship of philosophy to religion. In it, al-Kindi argues that the Greek scientific model – which he conceived as a combination of the Aristotelian and Platonist traditions – was in accordance with the tenets of Islam. In the best-known expression of his philosophical credo, al-Kindi argued that "the science of things and their true nature" was identical to the message of the Prophets. He was opposed by traditionalists, who viewed his writings as "wrongful innovation" (*bid'a*).

This text also deals with such subjects as cosmology and physics and contains a number of illustrations showing the structure of the universe, the phases of the moon and eclipses. Although the manuscript is anonymous, the attribution to al-Kindi is justified by its content; the calligraphic style suggests an Andalusian provenance of the fourteenth century, possibly Seville.

DESCRIPTION Paper, 25 folios, 235 x 165 mm, in Arabic, Andalusian maghrebi script, dark brown ink; 18 diagrams. Modern brown morocco binding.

PROVENANCE Sam Fogg, October 2002

BIBLIOGRAPHY EI V 122-23

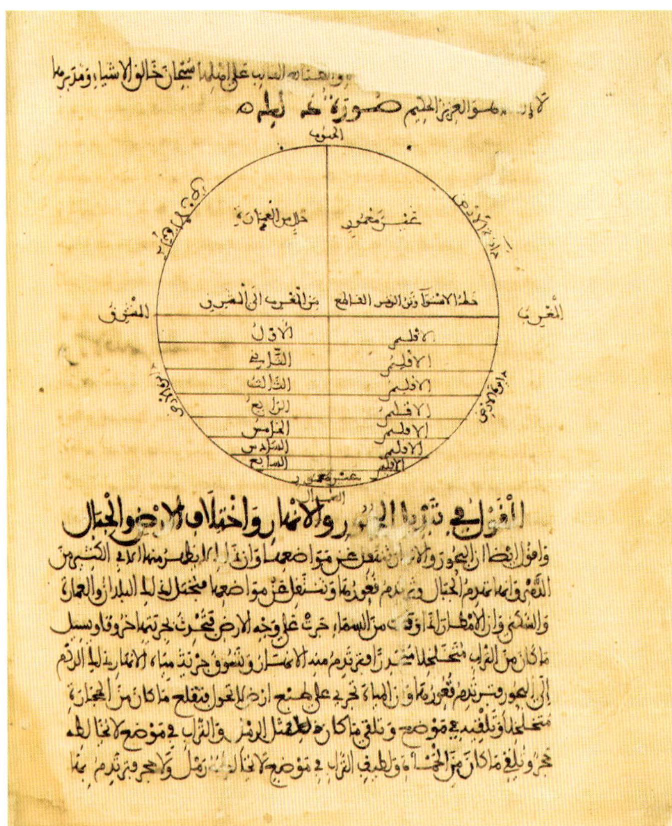

6 LJS 440

Al-Razi, *Lubab isharat wa'l-tanbihat*
Anatolia, 16 Shawwal 603 / 15 May 1207

The insertion of Aristotle into the Arabic tradition continued with the works of Ibn Sina (980–1037; known in the Latin West as Avicenna). He composed a philosophical work in four parts, dealing with logic, physics, metaphysics and Sufism, entitled *Kitab al-isharat wa'l-tanbihat* (Book of directives and remarks). This was commented on, and then summarized, by the Persian theologian and exegete Fakhr al-Din al-Razi (1149–1209); the present manuscript contains the summary, which dates to the last years of al-Razi's life.

DESCRIPTION Paper, 58 folios, 254 x 165 mm, in Arabic, bold and elegant naskh script, occasional marginalia. Contemporary brown morocco binding, blind-tooled.

PROVENANCE Sam Fogg 2002

BIBLIOGRAPHY EI II 751-53, III 942-43; Inati

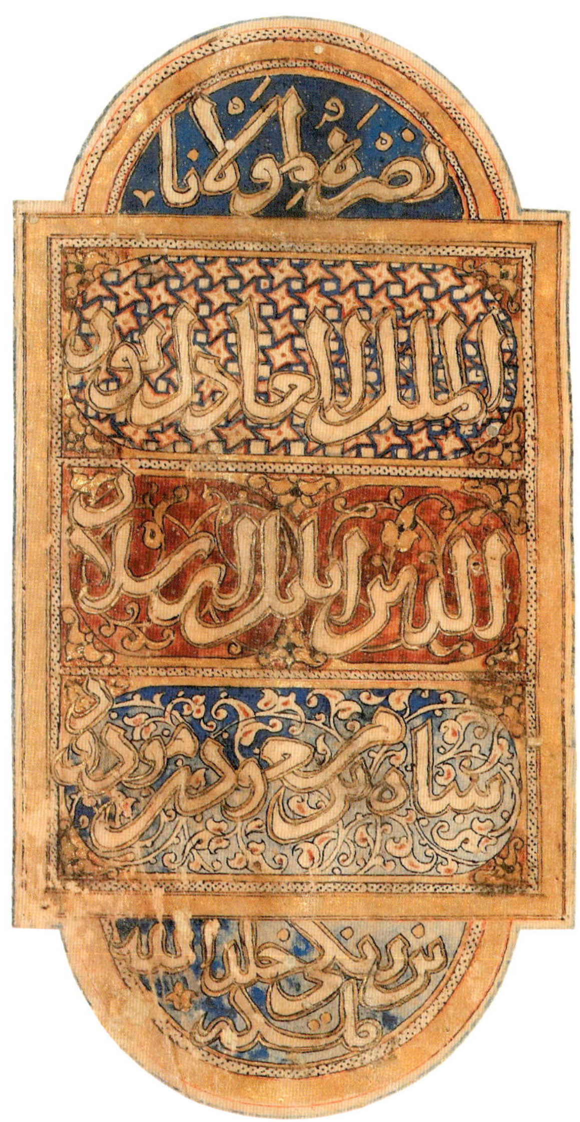

LJS 459
f. 1r

Pseudo-Aristotle, *Kitab sirr al-asrar* ('Secret of Secrets') Probably Mosul, Iraq, *c.* 1200

As Aristotle's works became more widely known in the Middle Ages, so did a large and heterogeneous corpus of texts erroneously attributed to him. The most widely circulated of all these was the *Secret of Secrets*, a compilation of information on a variety of matters including medicine, alchemy, magic and astrology, framed within a letter of advice from Aristotle to his pupil Alexander the Great. The work went through a long and complex period of evolution. It claims to have been translated from Greek into Arabic in the ninth century by the famous translator Yahya ibn-al-Bitriq. It seems more likely, however, that it was originally written in Arabic. The dates of its composition remain a matter of debate; although part of it dates back to 941, the complete treatise in the form in which it is now known appears to have been finalized considerably later. Another recension of the work is found below (LJS 456 [no. 8]).

The present manuscript is among the earliest known copies of the complete work. It was made for Nur al-Din Arslan Shah, Turkmen ruler of Mosul between 1193 and 1211, whose name is found on the illuminated title page.

In the mid-twelfth and early thirteenth centuries the work was translated into Latin. Versions of it were also made in Hebrew and in about a dozen European vernaculars. It proved influential in a number of fields, including political theory, moral philosophy, alchemy and physiognomy.

DESCRIPTION Paper, 128 folios, 190 x 130 mm, in Arabic, clear naskh script, dark brown ink, headings in red or dark brown, vocalization in a different hand, occasional later marginal comments; opening illuminated panel and invocation, one illustration and several charts in colours. Fifteenth-century brown morocco binding with flap, blind-stamped.
PROVENANCE Nur al-Din Arslan Shah, Zangid ruler 1193-1211; Sam Fogg, *Islamic Calligraphy*, no. 25 (2003)
BIBLIOGRAPHY Ryan and Schmitt; Manzalaoui; EI XI 246

8   LJS 456

Pseudo-Aristotle, *Kitab al-siyasa fi tadbir al-riyasa*
Andalusia, AH 797 / 1394 AD

Another recension of the previous work (LJS 459 [no. 7]),
under a different title.

DESCRIPTION Paper, 22 folios, 256 x 190 mm, in Arabic, maghrebi
script, sepia ink, titles in red or blue. 19-century binding with flap.
PROVENANCE Christie's, London, 14 October 2003, lot 23

9   LJS 234

Albertus Magnus, *Physica*
Northern France (Flanders), 14th century

The thirteenth century saw a marked increase in interest in
Aristotle among Christian scholars, inspired by new
translations of his writings and reception of the works of his
Arab commentators, particularly Averroes (Ibn Rushd; see
LJS 453 [no. 12]). Albertus Magnus (*c.* 1193–*c.* 1206) was at the
forefront of this attempt to assimilate the influx of new
material into the existing Christian philosophical model. The
present text is an example of his project to make the
Aristotelian corpus "intelligible to the Latins": it is a
commentary on Aristotle's *Physics,* heavily influenced by that
of Averroes, which had become available in a Latin
translation in the mid-thirteenth century. Albertus's work
is divided into eight books, which consider, among other
things, nature, causes, infinity and eternity, time, place and
motion.

 The present copy can be dated to the middle of the
fourteenth century: according to a note on the inside of the
upper board, it was bought on 7 October 1349 from a certain
"Benost", for 4 pounds.

DESCRIPTION Parchment, 95 folios, 323 x 230 mm, in Latin, littera
notularis textualis script, brown ink, two columns, red rubrics, blue
and red headings; large gold, red and blue decorative initial on f. 1r,
numerous smaller initials in various colours. Contemporary leather
over wooden board binding, blind-tooled.
PROVENANCE Bought 7 October 1349 from "Benost"; by 1355 in
northern Italy, according to various notes on the inside of lower

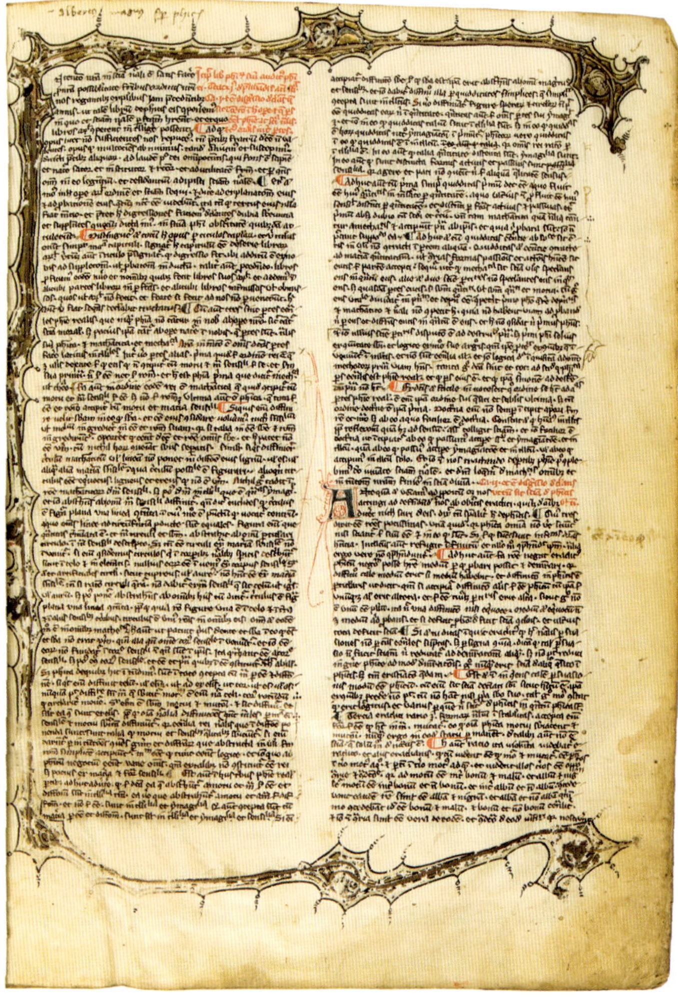

LJS
f. 1

board and on f. 94v; Sotheby's, 2 May 1979, lot 1093; Sam Fogg,
February 1997
BIBLIOGRAPHY Hossfeld; ODCC 34

10   LJS 252

Folio from Aristotle's *Physics,*
England, *c.* 1300

This folio, formerly used as a pastedown, contains a Latin
translation of *Physics* Book V, chapters 6 and 7.

DESCRIPTION Parchment, 1 folio, 316 x 160 mm, in Latin, Gothic
script, black ink, headers in red and blue, 4 large paragraph marks in
red and blue, 2-line initial in red and blue extending into margin.
PROVENANCE Maggs Bros., cat. 1249 (1998), no. 6

11 LJS 482

Albertus Magnus, Commentaries on Aristotle's *De generatione et corruptione* and *Meteora*
Southern France, possibly Toulouse, late 13th century

Two further commentaries by Albertus Magnus (see LJS 234 [no. 9]), on Aristotle's 'On Generation and Corruption' and 'Meteorology'.

DESCRIPTION Parchment, 104 folios, 301 x 223 mm, in Latin, small gothic bookhand, dark brown ink, many medieval annotations; headings in red, paragraph marks in red or blue, decorated initials, mostly 2-line, in red or blue with contrasting penwork; one historiated initial. Bound in paper boards with parchment spine.
PROVENANCE Sotheby's, London, 6 July 2006, lot 56

12 LJS 453

Ibn Rushd, Commentaries on Aristotle
Probably Germany, 1446

Abu'l-Walid Muhammad ibn Rushd (1126–1198), known as Averroes to the Latins, was the foremost medieval Arabic commentator on Aristotle. His works were translated into both Latin and Hebrew; the Hebrew tradition is represented in this manuscript. Contained here are commentaries on *De caelo et mundo* (translated by Solomon ibn Ayub, 1259), on *De generatione et corruptione* and on the *Meteora* (both translated by Kalonymus ben Kalonymus of Arles, d. 1316) and on Book XI of *De animalibus* (translated by Jacob ben Machir, 1302). There is also present a translation by Solomon ben Moses of Melgueil supposedly of Aristotle's *De somno et vigilia*, although it has been suggested that the text in question is actually by Avicenna. In addition, the manuscript contains a commentary on the Song of Songs by the renowned scientist Abraham ibn Ezra (1089–1164) and a letter to the Jews of Yemen (Iggeret Teiman) by Maimonides (Moses ben Maimon, 1135–1204).

A detailed colophon (f. 250v) records that the book was copied by Judah ben Jacob for Jehiel Katz on 13 Shevat 5206 (1446 AD).
DESCRIPTION Paper, 269 folios, 303 x 201 mm, in Hebrew, Ashkenazi semi-cursive script, headings in square script, some marginal notes. Modern red morocco binding.

PROVENANCE Jehiel Katz; London, Beth Din, 19th century; Christie's, New York, 23 June 1999, lot 13
BIBLIOGRAPHY HUM 128-29, 131, 143-46, 284; EJ III 950-53

13 LJS 229

Ibn Rushd, Commentaries on Aristotle and Porphyry
Provence or Spain, 2nd half 15th century

This manuscript contains three texts by ibn Rushd (Averroes; see previous) relating to the Aristotelian logic tradition – two commentaries on Aristotle entitled (in their Hebrew translations) *Sefer ha-ma'amarot* (The book of sayings) and *Sefer ha-meliza* (Book of praise), and *Sefer ha-mavo*, the epitome of Porphyry's *Isagoge* (see LJS 203 [no. 21]) or introduction to Aristotle's logical works.

DESCRIPTION Paper, 118 folios, 205 x 143 mm, in Hebrew, Sephardic cursive script, brown ink. Residue of contemporary or near-contemporary blind-stamped calf binding.
PROVENANCE Early ownership inscriptions in Latin and French; Comites Latentes collection, 1974; National Library, Jerusalem, ms. 129; Sotheby's, London, 2 December 1997, lot 88
BIBLIOGRAPHY HUM §17

14 LJS 483

Disputed Questions from Aristotle's *Physics*
Ingolstadt, *c.* 1480

The practice of "disputing questions" to resolve apparent contradictions was a standard pedagogic technique in the Middle Ages. The present manuscript was used by a number of friar-scholars active at the University of Ingolstadt.

DESCRIPTION Paper, 240 folios, 210 x 158 mm, in Latin, several cursive hands, black ink, underlinings in red, many marginal annotations. Original wooden board binding, with brown leather cover and brass fittings.
PROVENANCE Ingolstadt, probably the study library of the Franciscans, with contemporary usage inscriptions; Erik Wirén; exhibited at the Röhsska Konstlöjdsmuseet in Göteborg, Sweden, in 1954 (cat. no. 19); Sam Fogg, July 2006

Paul of Venice, *Logica parva*
Probably northern Italy, 1420 and earlier

Early medieval teaching of logic revolved around Aristotle's *Organon* and Porphyry's *Isagoge* (see LJS 203 [no. 21]), as translated by Boethius. The twelfth century saw a rapid expansion of this field of study, partly on account of the influx of Arabic philosophy into the Latin West, and partly in the wake of new translations of Aristotle. This expansion, and the rise of the universities, created a new demand for textbooks of logic, which remained a cornerstone of university study both as a theoretical discipline and as a practical tool for use in disputations.

Of these, one of the most influential was the *Logica parva* of Paul of Venice (*c.* 1370–1429), composed around 1400. Intended as "a useful compendium for young students", it considers the composition of discourse from propositions (which themselves are made up of terms) and the ways in which propositions can relate to meaning (including such categories as suppositions and inferences). Its success is attested not only by the several commentaries written on it during the fifteenth century but also by the later humanist reaction against it. It was printed in 1472, and by the end of the fifteenth century was a required text at the universities of Venice, Padua and Ferrara.

This manuscript was written, in part, by Johannes Beylarius of Cologne, who dated it 6 April 1420. Paul of Venice was at this time at the height of his career: he had taught at Padua for several years, and would go on to lecture at Siena, Perugia, Rome and Bologna.

DESCRIPTION Parchment and paper, 48 folios, 212 x 145 mm, in Latin, highly abbreviated Italian Gothic cursive script, dark brown ink, paragraph marks in red; one large and many small decorated initials. Limp vellum binding.
PROVENANCE H.P. Kraus, cat. 91 (1993), no. 41
BIBLIOGRAPHY Perreiah 1984, 1986 and 2002; DSB X 419-21; REP V 746-59

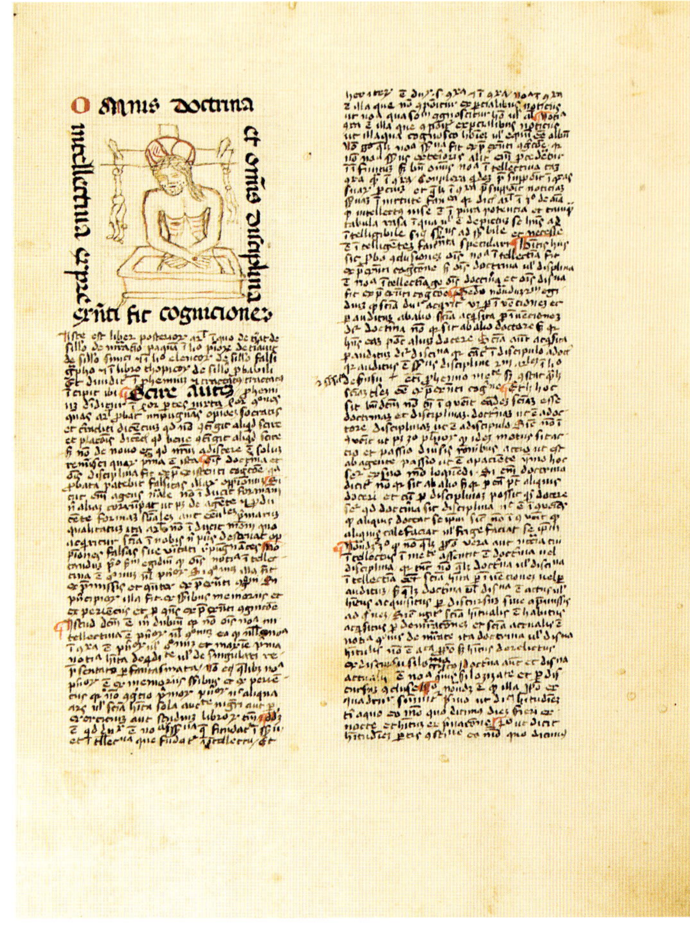

LJS
f. 1r

Paul of Venice, *Expositio in libros Posteriores Aristotelis*
Italy (possibly Verona), mid-15th century

Paul of Venice's well-known *Logica parva* (see LJS 56 [no. 15]) was complemented by a series of commentaries on works by Aristotle. Among these are commentaries on the *Ethics*, the *Politics*, *De generatione et corruptione*, the *Metaphysics*, *De anima*, and the present text, a commentary on the *Posterior Analytics* composed in about 1407. The *Posterior Analytics* builds on the theory of the syllogism contained in the *Prior Analytics*: specifically, it applies syllogistic reasoning to scientific disciplines, in order to demonstrate the truth of their axioms.

As a part of the *Organon*, the *Posterior Analytics* played a fundamental role in basic education throughout the Middle Ages. Commentaries such as this demonstrate that, despite the demand in the fourteenth and fifteenth centuries for new textbooks on university-level logic such as Paul of Venice's

Logica parva, continued attention to Aristotle was still a vital part of the curriculum.

An early inscription on this manuscript states that it was owned by Brother John of the Chapel of Verona.

DESCRIPTION Paper, 152 folios, 286 x 217 mm, in Latin, written by at least three scribes, highly abbreviated Gothic cursive, brown ink; initials throughout in red and blue; seven geometric diagrams at beginning and sketch of Christ in tomb. Contemporary half-cover over board binding.

PROVENANCE Brother John of the Chapel of Verona; Butterfield and Butterfield, 21 October 1997, lot 3750

BIBLIOGRAPHY REP v 687-88; Perreiah 1986, 41-42

17   LJS 457

Paul of Venice, *Logica parva*; Paul of Pergula, *Tractatus de sensu composito et diviso*
Perugia, 1475

As well as Paul of Venice's *Logica parva* (see LJS 56 [no. 15]) this manuscript contains a short work on logic by his pupil, Paul of Pergula, who taught in Venice from 1421 until his death (*c.* 1451), 'On compounded and divided sense'.

According to the colophon on f. 86, the manuscript was copied by an otherwise unrecorded scribe, Franciscus Alexandri de Callio, in the abbey of the Hermits of Saint Augustine in Perugia, Italy.

DESCRIPTION Paper, 89 folios, 230 x 160 mm, in Latin, slanted cursive script in two columns, light brown ink, rubrics and paragraph marks in red, numerous marginal annotations; two initials in red, one 5-line initial in pink and gold with gold decoration extending into margin, spaces left for other initials; 2 diagrams in green and yellow wash. Late 16th- or early 17th-century parchment binding, with arms and initials.

PROVENANCE Copied by Franciscus Alexandri de Callio in the Abbey of the Hermits of Saint Augustine in Perugia, Italy, 1475; Library of the Jesuit Collegium Germanicum; Les Enluminures, October 2003

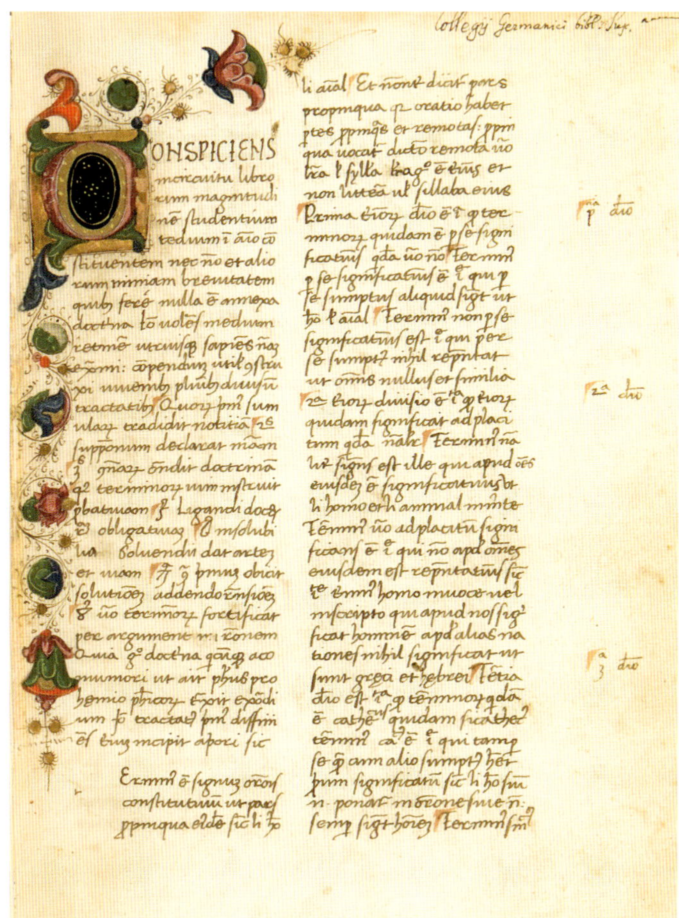

LJS 457
f. 1r

18   LJS 325

Brunetto Latini, *L'ethica d'Aristotile ridotta in compendio*
Printed text, Lyons 1568, with 16th-century manuscript collation

This discussion of Aristotle's *Ethics* is drawn from an Italian translation of the *Livres dou tresor*, an encyclopaedic text composed between 1260 and 1266 by the Florentine notary and politician Brunetto Latini. It was printed in 1568 and is accompanied by a sixteenth-century collation made against a manuscript of the same work belonging to the humanist and bibliophile Giovanni Vincenzo Pinelli (1535–1600).

DESCRIPTION Printed text: paper, 185 pages, 212 x 150 mm, in Italian; manuscript: paper, 16 folios, in Italian, cursive script, brown ink.

PROVENANCE Bookplate of Noel Pinelli; Christie's, South Kensington, 10 September 1999, lot 4

BIBLIOGRAPHY Baldwin and Barrette; Rivolta

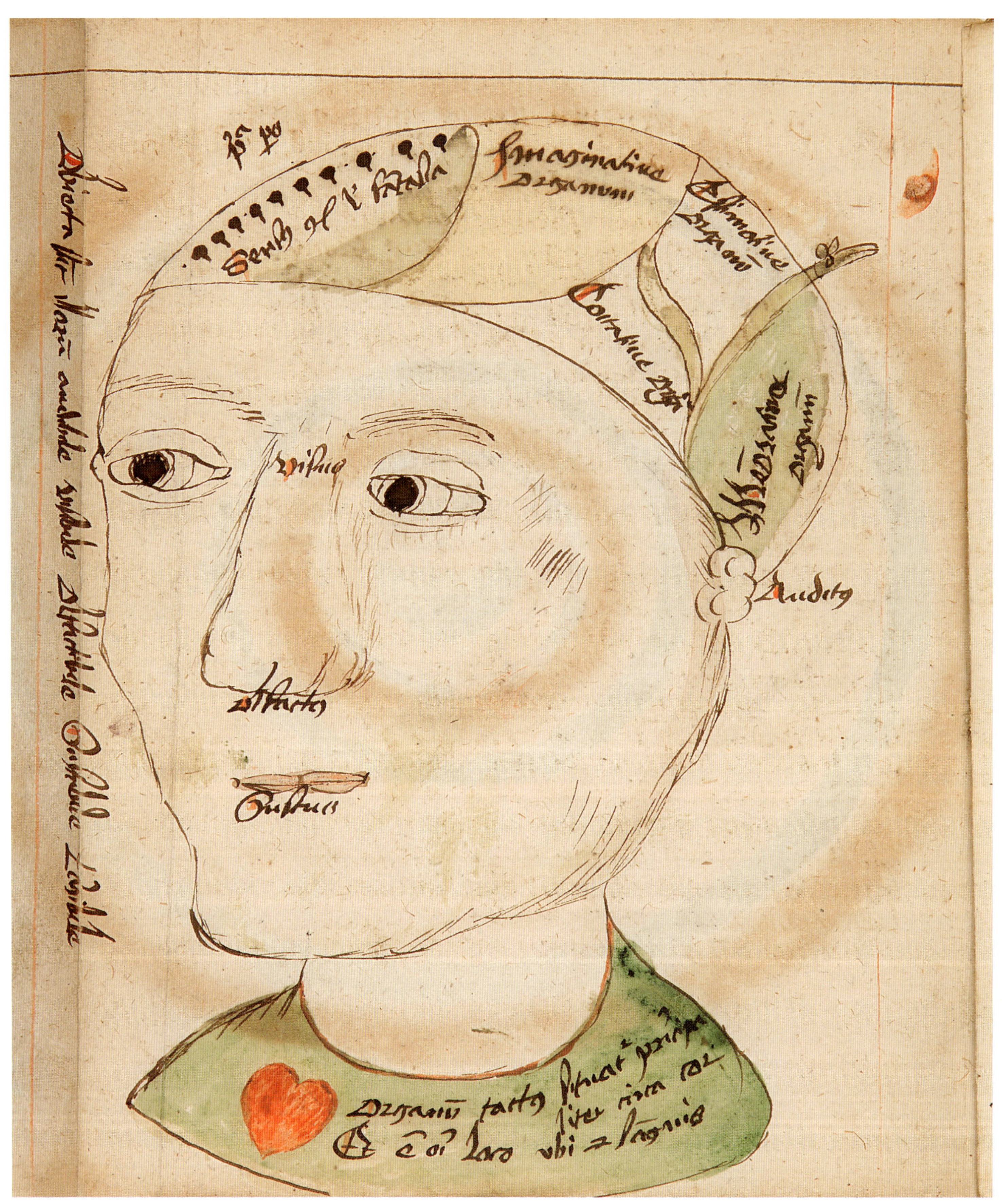

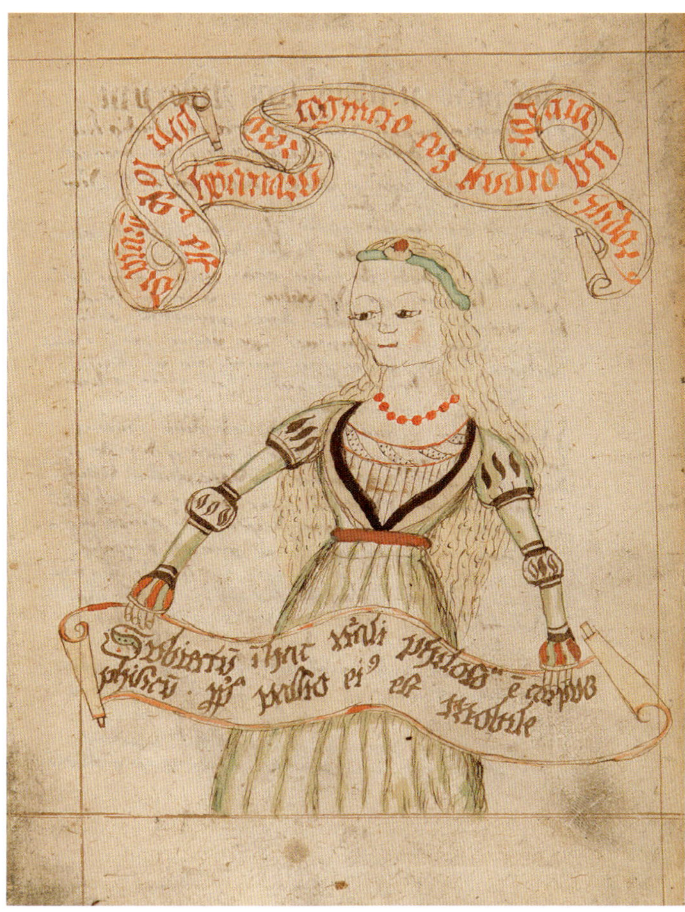

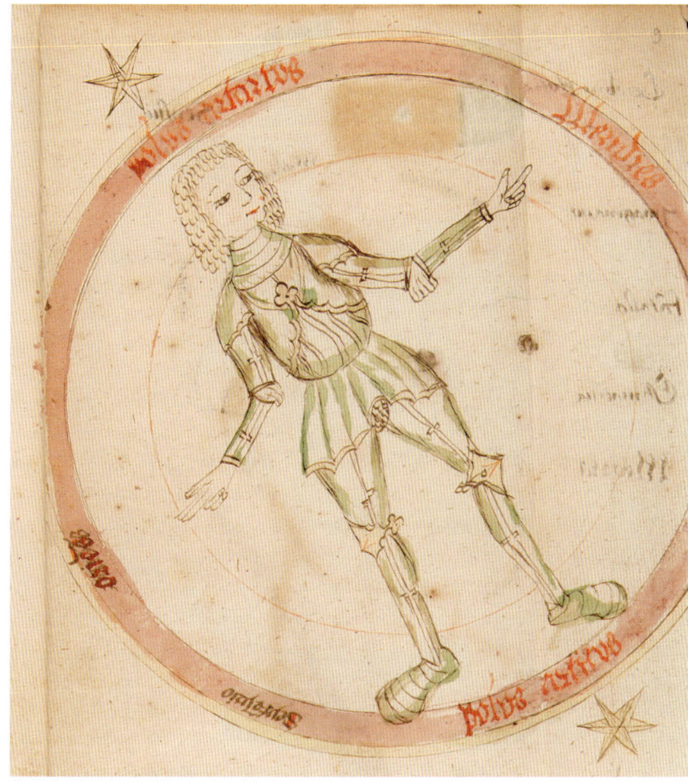

Pseudo-Isidore of Seville, *De philosophia naturali*
Possibly Mainz, Germany, 15th century

This brief summary of natural philosophy stems from the ambience of university disputation in the late fifteenth century. It contains specific criticism of two contemporary figures, Nicholas of Orbelles (here called "Dorbellus") and Etienne Brulêfer ("Brulifer"), both of whom are described as originators of theological error. A number of the illustrations are devoted to the structure of the human being. A tree of human nature derives man from the categories of animal, body and substance. A diagram of the head (f. 11) shows the positions of the faculties in the brain, including fantasy, imagination, cognition, estimation and reason. It also provides locations for the organs of sense. Further diagrams show the connections between the four temperaments (phlegmatic, sanguine, choleric and melancholic) and the elements and the universe (structured in typical Aristotelian manner, with the earth surrounded by the elements and the celestial orbs). The overall tenor of the text is supportive of the Thomist tradition, referring particularly to Thomas Aquinas's five proofs for the existence of God derived from observation of the natural world. From the early fourteenth century this method of proof had been challenged by adherents of John Duns Scotus (*c.* 1265–1308), who argued that metaphysicians could not use created beings as analogies for divine being. This Scotist argument is attacked in the present text.

The work is erroneously attributed to Isidore of Seville (*c.* 560–636), best known in the Middle Ages for his encyclopaedia, the *Etymologiae* (see LJS 184 [IX, no. 2]).

DESCRIPTION Paper, 14 folios, 200 x 135 mm, in Latin, sloping semi-cursive script, black ink, top lines and some headings in broken-character calligraphy; 8 full-page, 1 half-page watercolour illustrations. Unbound.
PROVENANCE Reiss und Sohn, 2002, no. 123
BIBLIOGRAPHY DSB IV 255

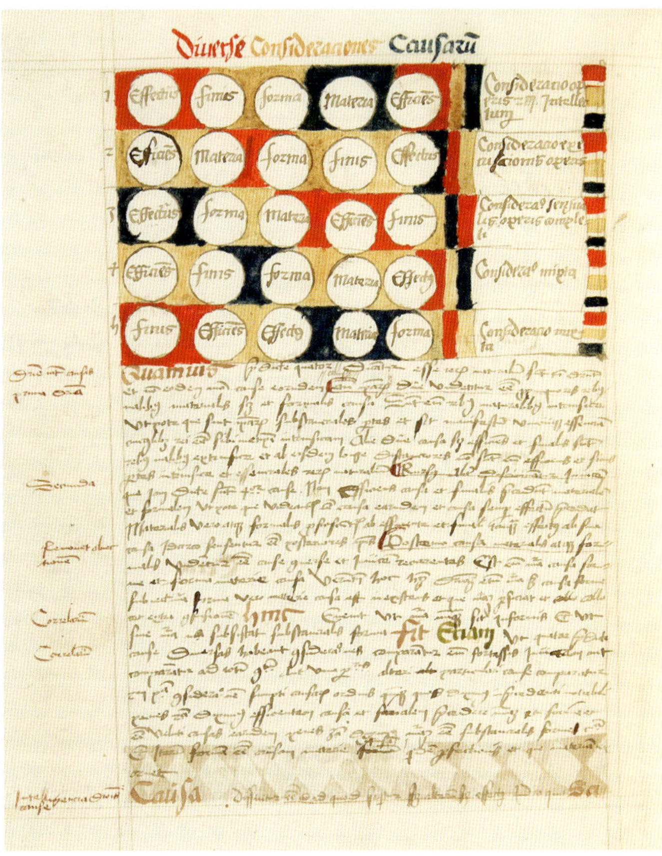

LJS 223
f. 159v

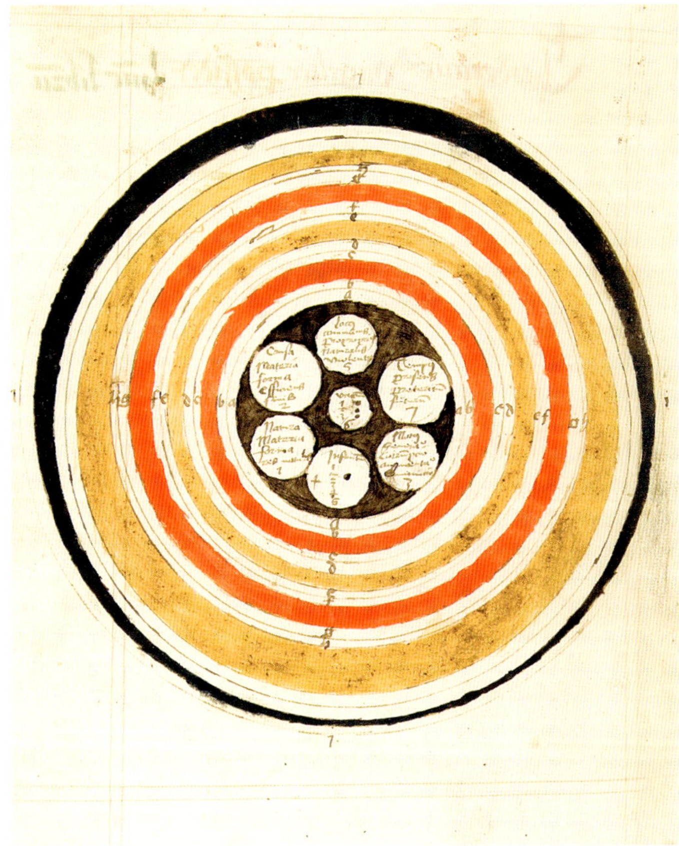

LJS 223
f. 153v

20 LJS 223

Quaestiones logicales and other texts
Bavaria, *c.* 1510

The beginning of the sixteenth century saw a new wave of
humanist translations and commentaries on Aristotle. The
present manuscript gives evidence of this trend. Most of it
consists of a number of works on logic, in the form of
quaestiones and short tracts (some incomplete) on the
Categories, *De interpretatione* and the *Posterior Analytics*, among
others. The last quarter of it contains several works on the
Physics. These include commentaries by Antonius Carpentier
not only on the *Physics* itself, but also on the introduction to
the *Physics* by Jacques Lefèvre d'Etaples.

Lefèvre d'Etaples (*c.* 1460–1536) composed translations and
commentaries on Aristotle's works between the end of the
fifteenth century and the second decade of the sixteenth. His
introduction to the *Physics* was published in 1492. Less is
known about Carpentier and only one other copy of his two
works contained here has come to light.

According to an inscription, the manuscript was a gift
from Johannes Wesbach of Ulm to the library of the
Carthusians at Buxheim (near Memmingen, in Bavaria).
Wesbach, a judge in Ulm from 1499 to 1507, donated a number
of manuscripts to this library. This manuscript can be dated
to *c.* 1510 by the watermark in the paper.

DESCRIPTION Paper, 205 folios, 270 x 200 mm, in Latin, hurried
bâtarde script, brown ink, rubrics in red; tables and diagrams
throughout, some coloured. Blind-stamped calf binding.
PROVENANCE J. Halle; J. Rosenthal, 1928; Les Enluminures, 1997
BIBLIOGRAPHY Lohr II 79-80

21 LJS 203

Porphyry's *Isagoge* and other texts on logic
France (?), 1666

As this manuscript shows, Aristotle's logical texts remained a
subject of commentary in the seventeenth century. This
compilation of philosophical texts begins with a translation
of Porphyry's *Isagoge* (see also LJS 229 [no. 13] and 56 [no. 15]):
composed in the third century, the *Isagoge* remained the

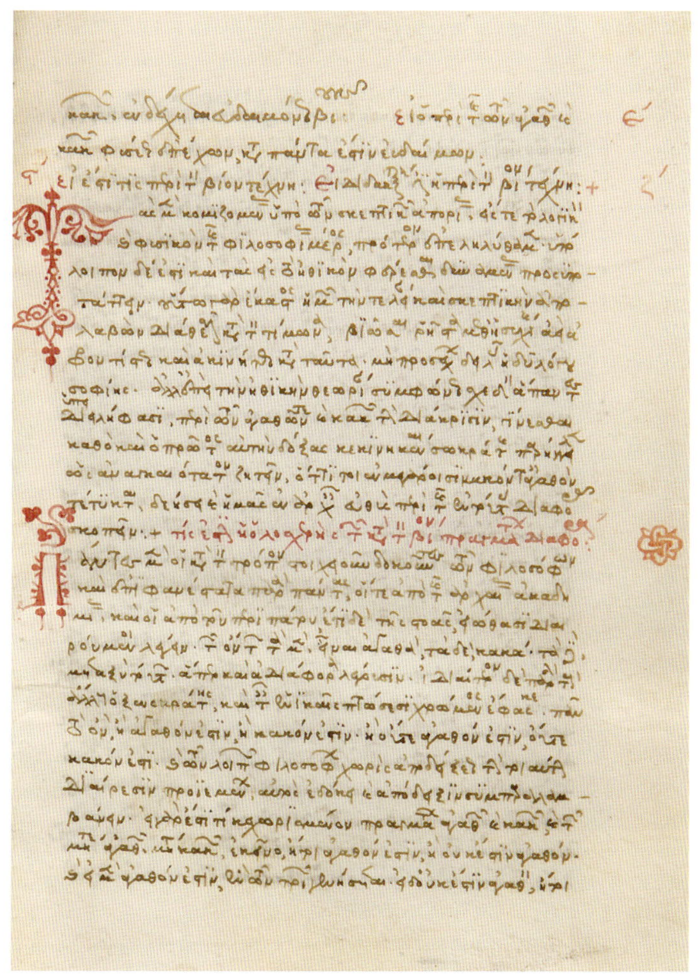

380
294r

Sextus Empiricus, *Pros mathēmatikous*
Italy, *c.* 1430–40

Sextus Empiricus (*c.* 160–*c.* 210) was a physician and philosopher known chiefly for his profession of radical philosophical scepticism in the tradition of Pyrrho of Elis (*c.* 360–*c.* 270 BC). His major work is a critique of learning in eleven books, generally grouped under the title *Pros mathēmatikous* (Against the professors). The text is divided into attacks on every branch of the standard curriculum – grammar, rhetoric, geometry, arithmetic, astrology, music, logic, physics and ethics. According to Sextus, none of these disciplines could arrive at truth, since knowledge was tied to sense impressions, and objects themselves were unknowable.

Sextus's philosophy, and the epistemological argument which underpinned it, became popular in the sixteenth century. Prior to this, a few copies of his works circulated in Italy in the fifteenth century, and were read by humanists chiefly for their value as a literary and historical source. The present manuscript is in the hand of Isidore of Kiev, Greek Orthodox Patriarch of Russia, and probably dates from the period of his attendance at the Council of Florence (1438–45). Following his death in Rome in 1463 it entered the Vatican Library, and it is recognizable in the detailed inventory of Greek manuscripts carried out under Pope Leo X in 1518. It apparently disappeared from the library during the sack of Rome in 1527.

DESCRIPTION Parchment, 276 folios, 162 x 100 mm, in Greek, regular round minuscule, headings, rubric and initials in pale red, some marginal glosses by the scribe. Mid-16th-century brown morocco binding, gilt with floral design.
PROVENANCE Vatican Library, Vat. Lat. 3951; Nicholai von Bodeck of Danzig (1652 or 1657); acquired through Sam Fogg, May 2000
BIBLIOGRAPHY Cao; DSB XII 340–41; Annas and Barnes XI–XXXI; Schmitt

fundamental introduction to logic well into the Renaissance. There follow three otherwise unknown commentaries by Christopher Labbeltrie of the Augustinian order, on the *Categories, De interpretatione* and the *Posterior Analytics*. Also included is another unknown work by a certain Larois, on dialectic, and an unattributed work on the philosophy of Seneca.

DESCRIPTION Paper, 229 folios, 205 x 172 mm, in Latin, cursive script, four or more scribes, black ink. Vellum binding with ties.
PROVENANCE Early notations in French on front flyleaf: *Pour adresser a mons*[ieur] *delaberdure de gaverelle pour envoier a son frere a tournay. La logique de m*[onsieu]*r son pere*, with signature in a different hand, *De Laverdure/ D Besquelles*; Ernest Noyes; Heritage Book Shop; John Stanitz ms. 34

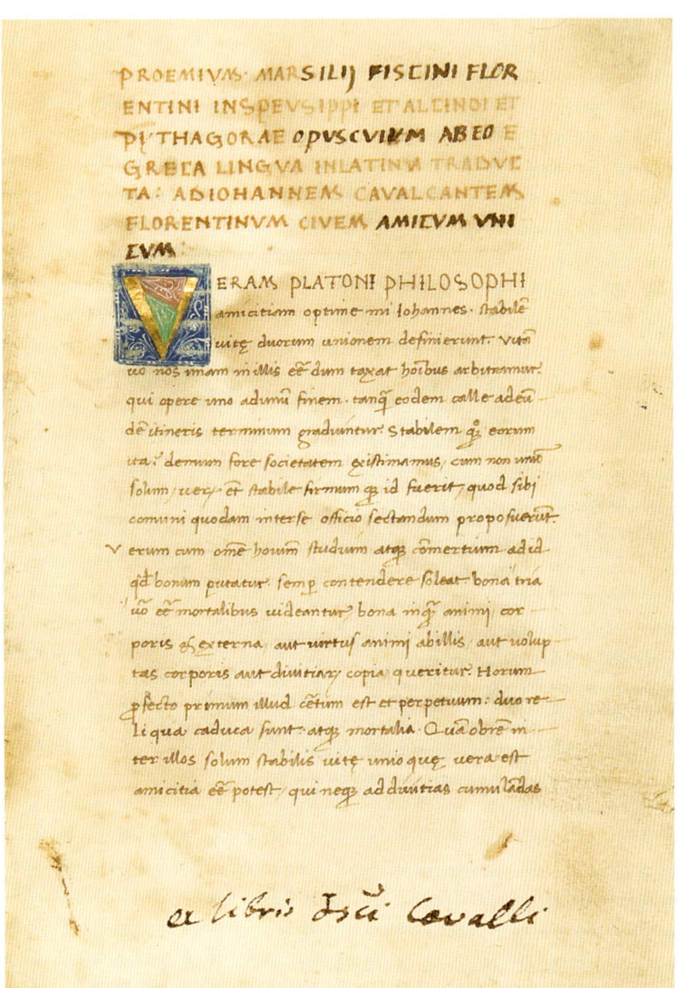

LJS 438
f. 2r

23   LJS 438

Ficino, Translations of Platonist texts
Florence, late 15th century

The Florentine Marsilio Ficino (1433–1499) undertook the project of translating and commentating on the corpus of Platonic and Neoplatonic works. He hoped that his contribution to the diffusion of these works would strengthen support for Plato's replacing Aristotle as the philosopher of choice among Christians. The present manuscript contains a number of texts relating to this project. There are translations into Latin of a short work by Speusippus (who succeeded Plato as head of the Academy), of Alcinous's *De doctrina Platonis*, and of the *Aurea precepta* (Golden verses) attributed to Pythagoras. These translations are dedicated to Ficino's friend Giovanni Cavalcanti, to whom he also addresses a short letter on the subject of friendship and how best to use the teachings of Plato. Other miscellaneous texts follow, several of which are addressed to other contemporary Florentine figures.

DESCRIPTION Paper, 97 folios, 210 x 137 mm, in Latin, elegant uniform humanistic script in brown ink, titles in red majuscules; three illuminated initials, gold on coloured ground with white scrollwork. Contemporary binding, oak boards, leather back.
PROVENANCE Umberto Pregliasco, July 2002
BIBLIOGRAPHY Hankins

24   LJS 179

Lucretius, *De rerum natura*, translated into Italian by Alessandro Marchetti
Italy, 9 January 1746

Little studied in the Middle Ages, the *De rerum natura* (On the nature of things) of Lucretius (*c.* 95–*c.* 55 BC) became better known in the Renaissance after it was rediscovered by Poggio Bracciolini in 1417. Although there were several Italian printed editions in the early sixteenth century the work remained tainted by heterodoxy on account of its materialist philosophy and no edition appeared after 1515. It continued to circulate in manuscript, however.

Alessandro Marchetti (1633–1714) taught philosophy and mathematics at Pisa from 1660 until his death. He was influenced by Galileo and was generally anti-Aristotelian, hence his interest in Lucretius and the theory of atoms. His translation was completed in 1669, but its publication in Italy was forbidden; as this manuscript shows, it was still being copied by hand in Italy in the mid-eighteenth century (although it had been published in England in 1717). Marchetti dedicated the translation to Cosimo III de' Medici.

DESCRIPTION Paper, 147 folios, 162 x 110 mm, in Italian, small cursive script, brown ink, rubrics in epigraphic capitals, penwork cartouche on title.
PROVENANCE Sylvester Douglas (1747-1823), Baron Glenbervie; sold at Messrs. R.H. Evans, 1823; Thomas Thorpe; Sir Thomas Phillipps, ms. 2571; Sotheby's, 5 June 1899, lot 835, unsold; Robinson Bros., 1945; H.P. Kraus, List 203 (1983), no. 206; John Stanitz, ms. 10
BIBLIOGRAPHY Sarton I 205; DSB VIII 536-39; Saccenti; Gambino Longo 19-35; Jones

II Music

Study of the trivium was followed by study of the quadrivium. The quadrivium featured mathematics – divided into arithmetic and geometry – and astronomy; prior to these, however, a student would study music, which ancient theorists, following the lead of the Pythagoreans, considered to be a branch of mathematics. The manuscripts selected here represent not only the reception of Greek and Latin works in the Middle Ages and Renaissance but also Arab and later Persian music theory.

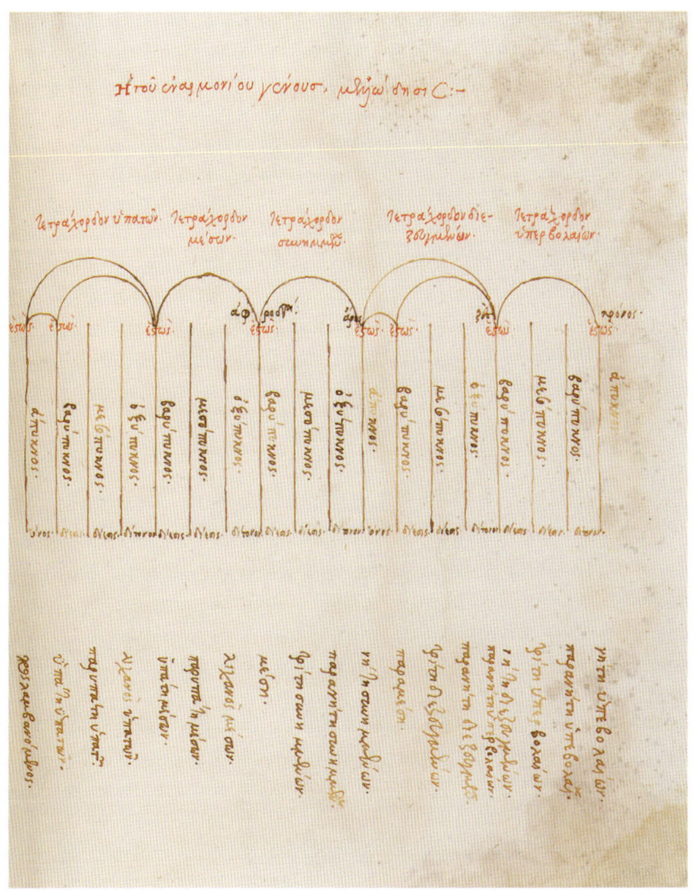

1   LJS 97

Porphyry, Commentary on Ptolemy's *Harmonics* (*Eis ta harmonika Ptolemaiou hypomnēma*)
Spain or Italy, *c.* 1560–80

Ptolemy's *Harmonika* (Harmonics), written in the second century, is a systematic treatise on music theory in three books, including sections on harmonics, acoustics, interval theory, modes and the relationship between notes, parts of the human soul and the heavenly bodies. In the third century a commentary on this text was composed by the eminent Neoplatonic philosopher Porphyry, who became head of the school originally founded by Plotinus. Porphyry's commentary covers roughly half of Ptolemy's text, concentrating on harmonics and acoustics: it is of particular value for the use it makes of previous and otherwise unknown sources, such as Ptolemais of Cyrene, who is one of the few known female scholars of the ancient world.

This manuscript bears the name of the celebrated scribe and manuscript dealer Andreas Darmarios. Darmarios had established a manuscript-copying workshop in Trent in 1562. The continuing Council of Trent enabled him to meet a number of patrons, and as a result he was able to expand his business to Spain; his visits there continued into the late 1580s. Darmarios obviously noted a certain demand for Porphyry's commentary: he was involved in the production of at least two other copies, one of which is now in the Escorial and the other in the Beinecke Library of Yale University.

DESCRIPTION Paper, 242 folios, 290 x 200 mm, in Greek, cursive script, headings and decorative initials in red, many marginal notes; 8 pages with diagrams. Contemporary stamped and tooled binding.
PROVENANCE Andreas Darmarios; J.H. de Speyr Passavant, of Basle; Sir Thomas Phillipps (1792-1872), ms. 3877; Phillipps sale, Sotheby's, 8 July 1975, lot 3404; The Garden Ltd; sold Sotheby's, New York, 9 November 1989, lot 65; Sotheby's, London, 17 June 1997, lot 47
BIBLIOGRAPHY Barker II 229-44; Düring; Grove XV 123

2 LJS 47

Boethius, *De institutione musica*
France, *c.* 1490

Aside from his considerable body of work on logic and the trivium, Boethius also produced treatises on two of the elements of the quadrivium, arithmetic and music. Taking his cue from the Pythagorean tradition, he viewed music as being based on number; the two treatises were therefore intimately linked. As well as its purely mathematical content, however, *De institutione musica* includes an ethical stance, as is visible from the title of the first chapter: "Music forms a part of us through nature, and can ennoble or debase character". There

are, he continues, three kinds of music: the cosmic music of the spheres (*musica mundana*), the music uniting the human body and soul (*musica humana*), and the music produced by instruments. Only the last of these is considered audible. The work then concentrates on ratios and pitches, illustrated with tables and diagrams.

The earliest manuscripts of *De institutione musica* date from the ninth century; copies were made throughout the Middle Ages and interest was evidently still strong in the fifteenth century. This manuscript, which can be dated to the end of the fifteenth century by its paper, appears to be a combination of the earlier textual tradition of the tenth century with the diagrammatic tradition of later copies. The

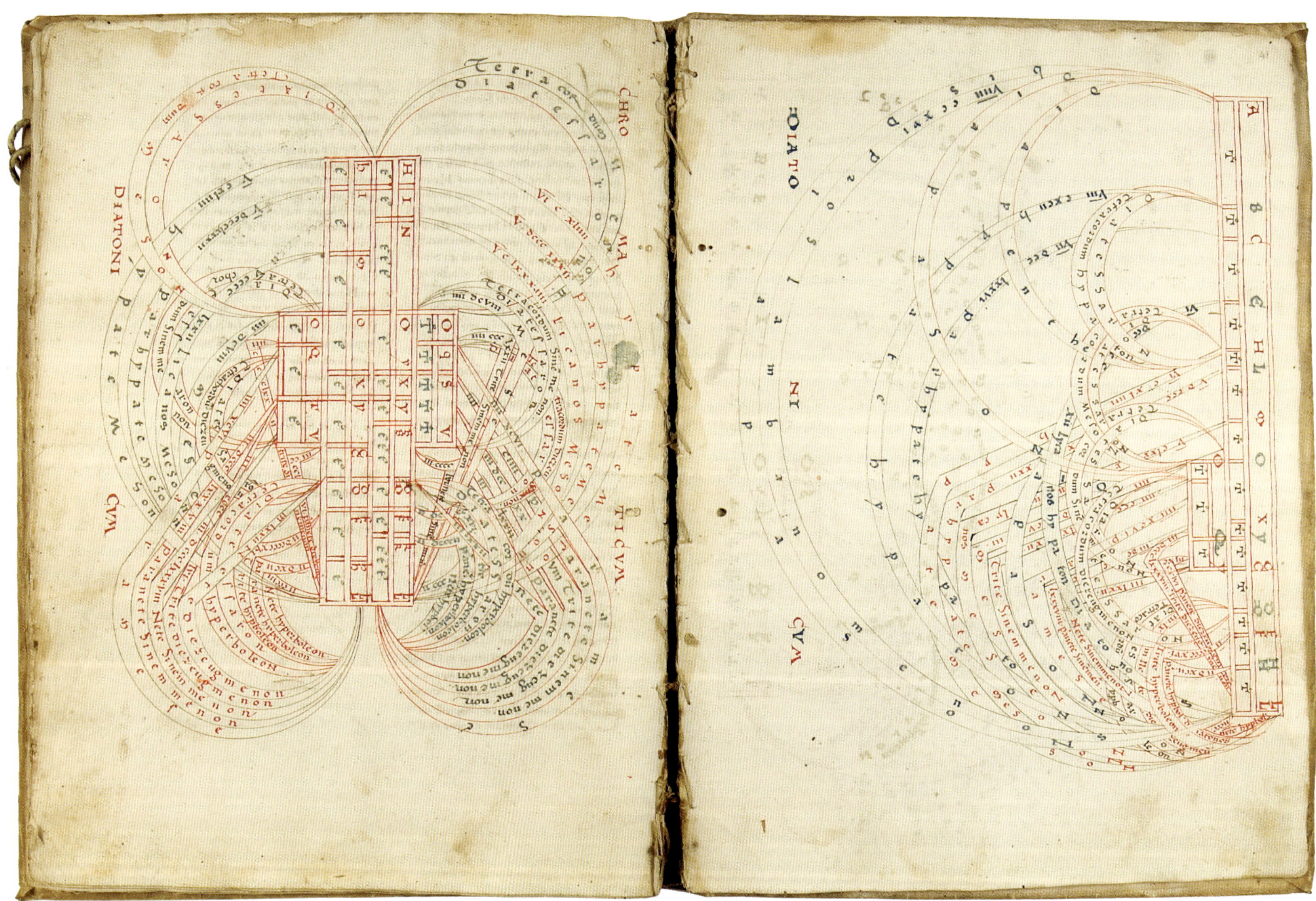

LJS 47, ff. 40v-41r

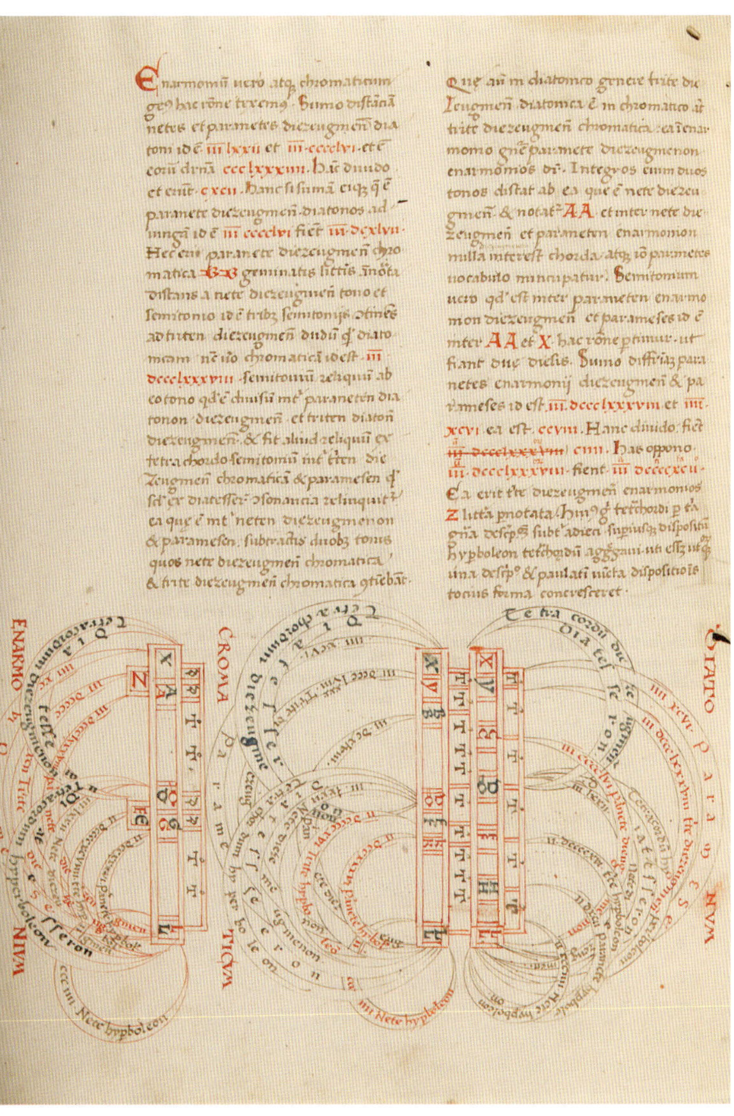

47, f. 37r

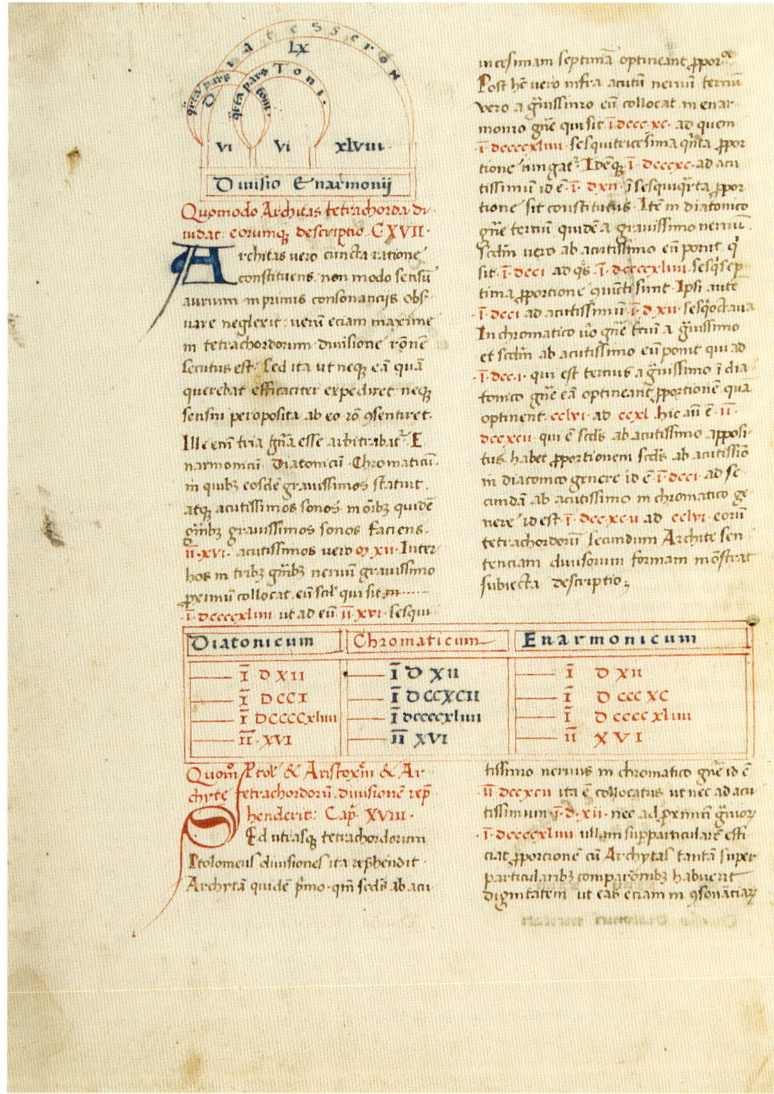

LJS 47, f. 51v

diagrams were an important feature of the work, and in this
manuscript have been drawn with considerable care.

DESCRIPTION Watermarked paper, 52 folios, 281 x 204 mm, in
Latin, rounded semi-humanistic script, brown ink, rubrics, headings
and initials in red and blue; many tables and diagrams. Parchment
binding, probably early 18th century.
PROVENANCE J. and J. Lubrano 1997
BIBLIOGRAPHY Bower (1988 and 1989); C. Meyer; DSB II 228-36

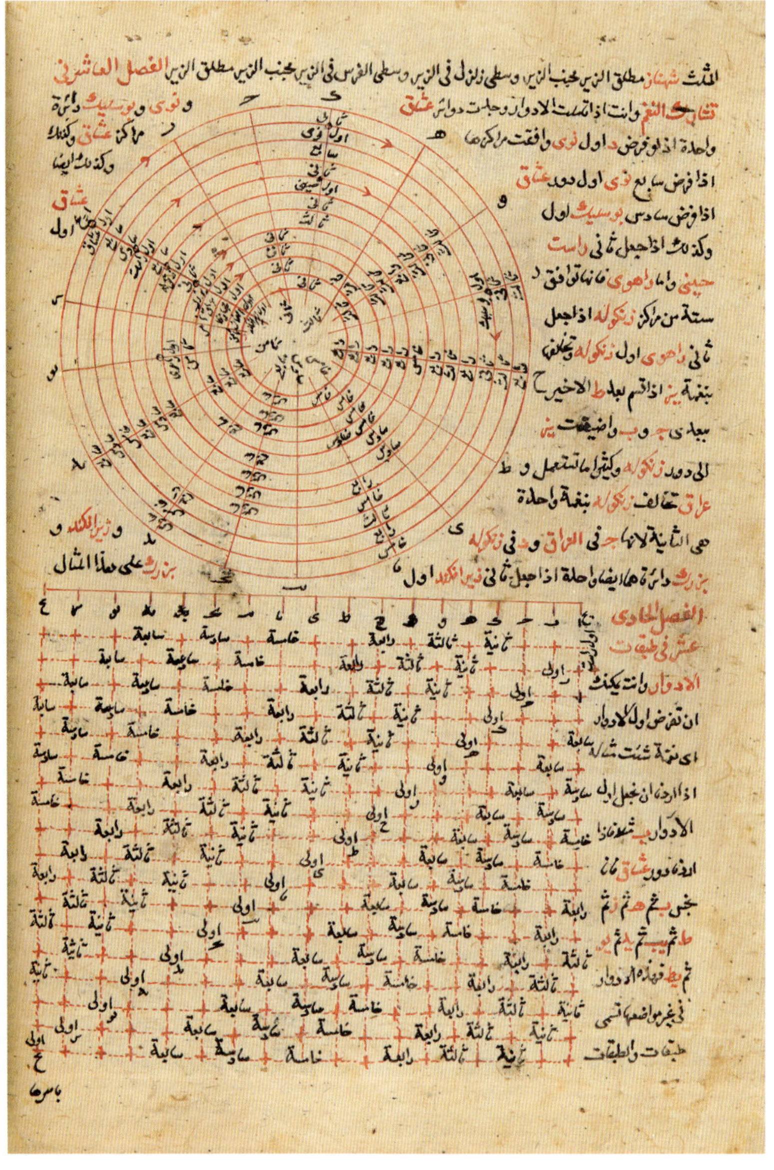

LJS 235, p. 16

LJS 235, p. 21

3　LJS 235

Al-Urmawi, *Kitab al-adwar*
Ottoman empire, 16th century

Safi al-Din al-Urmawi (*c.* 1216–1294) was a renowned musician whose *Kitab al-adwar* (Book of cycles) became the most widely circulated music treatise in the Muslim world. He composed it at the age of about twenty, during a period of employment as a copyist in the library of the caliph al-Musta'sim. Among other matters, it deals with the division of frets, ratios of intervals, consonance and dissonance, cycles, and rhythmic and melodic modes. It also contains a discussion of the five-string lute, or 'ud, which was at that time a fairly innovative instrument. The work was translated several times into Persian and Turkish, and a number of commentaries were written on it. From the beginning of the eighteenth century it attracted the interest of French scholars; al-Urmawi's description of the octave was to prove influential in Europe as a result.

This copy is especially notable for the exceptional precision and clarity of its diagrams.

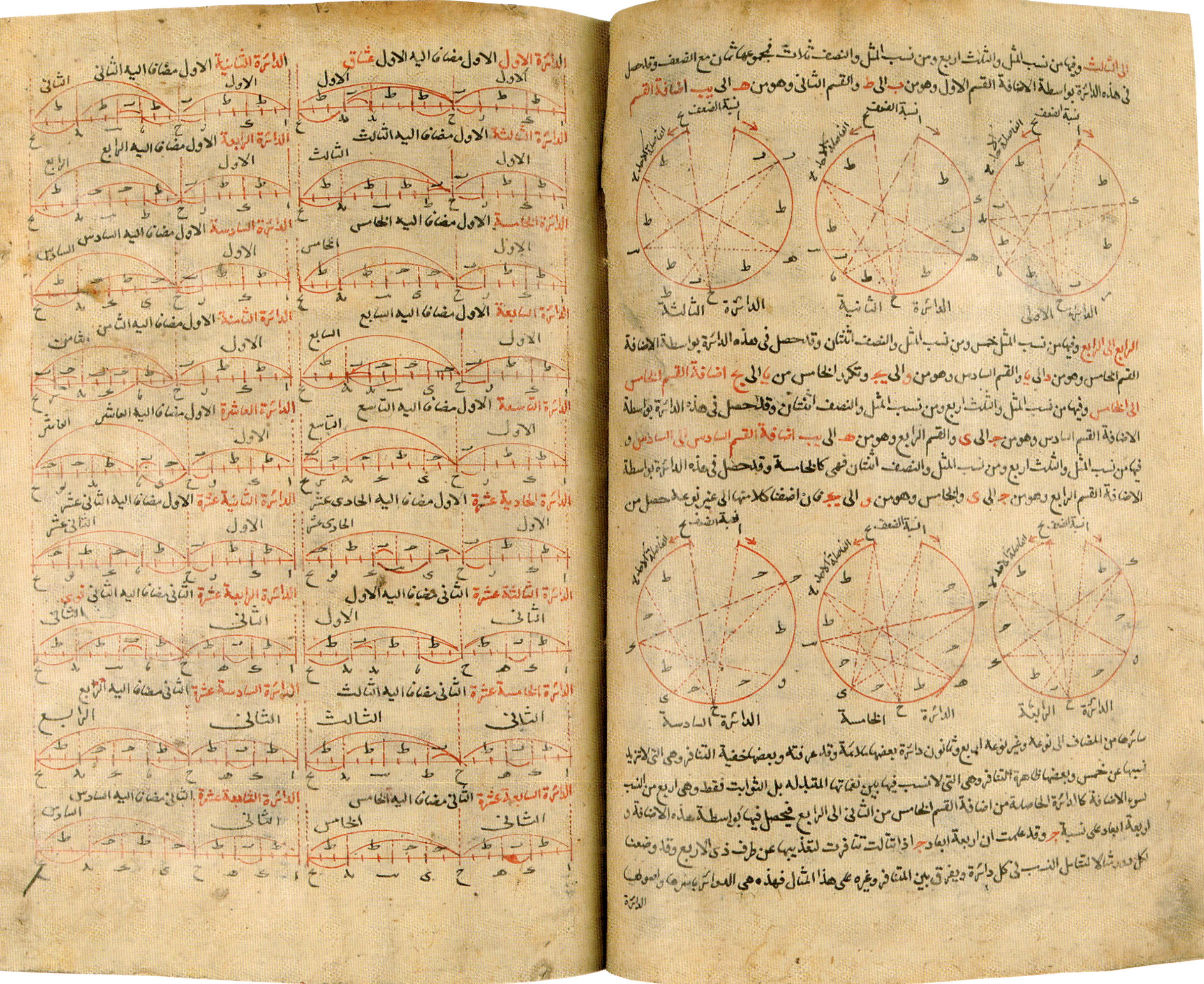

235
8-9

DESCRIPTION Paper, 24 pages, 235 x 165 mm, in Arabic, naskh
script, black and red ink; numerous diagrams in red. Red leather over
board binding, blind-stamped, tooled panels.
PROVENANCE Sam Fogg, 1998
BIBLIOGRAPHY EI VIII 805-07; Wright; Shiloah 308-12; Farmer

4 LJS 294

Al-Urmawi, *Kitab al-adwar*
Mosul, Iraq, 7 Dhu'l Qa'da 1103 AH / 22 July 1692

This is another copy of the previous text, signed by the scribe
Mas'ud ibn Husayn al-Musiqi al-Musali.

DESCRIPTION Paper, 26 folios, 300 x 206 mm, in Arabic, naskh
script, black ink, rubrics red; many words and small diagrams in red.
Original maroon morocco binding, blind-tooled.
PROVENANCE Christie's, London, 20 April 1999, lot 327

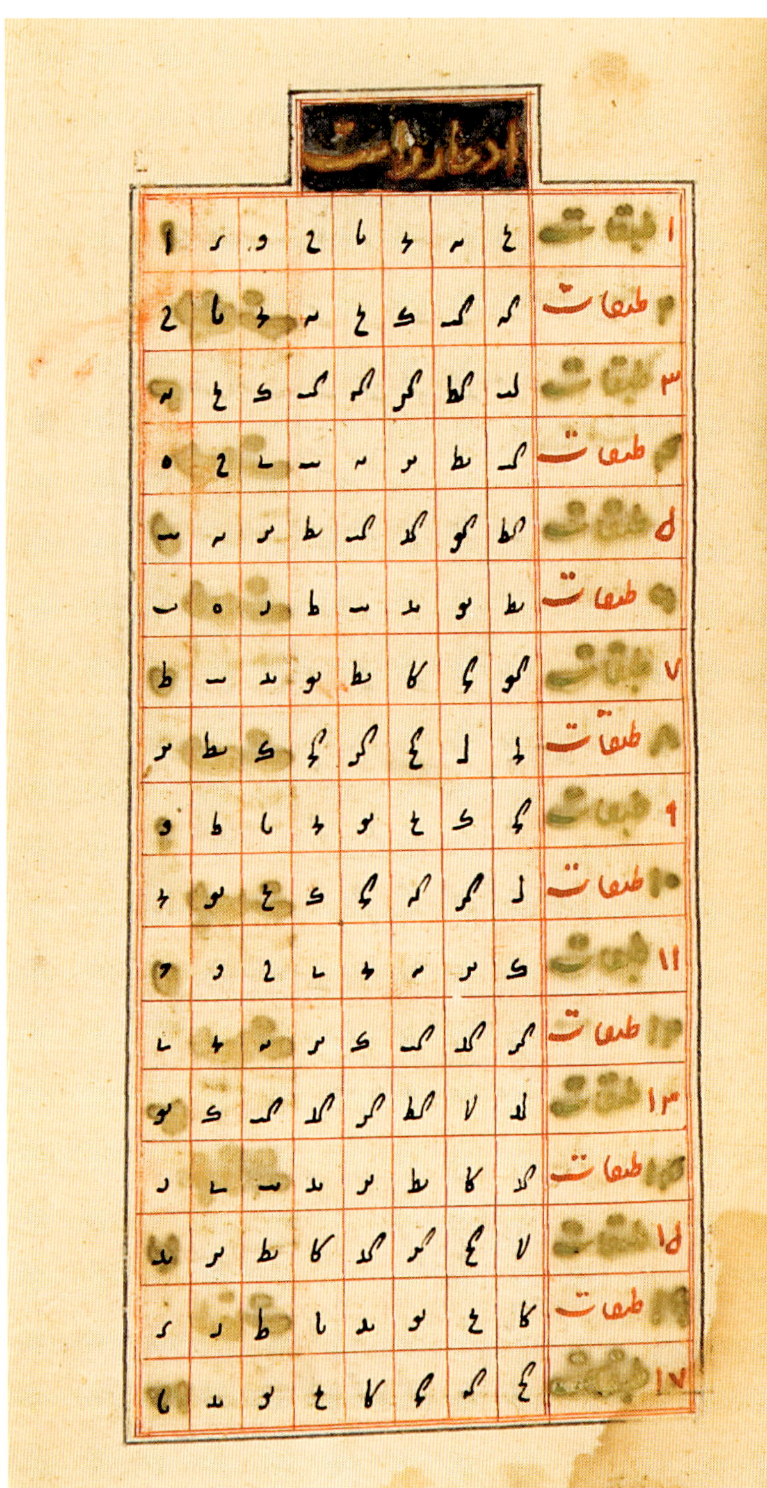

LJS 295, p. 74

5 LJS 295

Al-Urmawi, *Risala al-sharafiyya fi'l nisab al-ta'lifiyya* Persia, AH 815 / 1412 AD

Musta'sim, for whom the *Kitab al-adwar* (see LJS 235 [no. 3] and 294 [no. 4]) was written, was the last 'Abbasid caliph. After the fall of Baghdad in 1252 al-Urmawi was adopted as a musician by the family of Shams al-Din al-Juwayni, vizir of the Mongol conquerer Hülegü. His second work, 'The Sharafian Treatise on Musical Proportions', was composed *c.* 1267 for Shams al-Din's son, Sharaf al-Din Harun. It comprises five discourses, which consider, among other things, acoustics and sound; intervals, consonance and dissonance; the divisions of fourth, fifth and octave; the Arabic transcription of the fifteen Greek names for notes; rhythm and performance.

DESCRIPTION Paper, 59 folios, 148 x 88 mm, in Persian, nasta'liq script, black ink, significant words in red, headings in gold thuluth; numerous tables and diagrams in red, green, blue and black; opening illuminated headpiece, dated AH 1054 / 1644 AD. Red morocco binding.

PROVENANCE Sotheby's, London, 22 April 1999, lot 25

BIBLIOGRAPHY Shiloah 312-15

6 LJS 425

Kitab tawdih al-alhan, Persia, 17th century

This is a Persian adapatation of a Deccani work on music, copied and adapted by a certain Ruhhani (or Ruhbani).

DESCRIPTION Paper, 67 folios, 320 x 198 mm, in Persian with final pages in Hindi, neat nasta'liq script, black ink, headings and significant words in red; numerous diagrams and charts in red, later illuminated headpiece. Contemporary figured silk satin covers.

PROVENANCE Sotheby's, London, 18 October 2001, lot 42

7   LJS 418

Life of St Blaise and Mass
Italy, 13th century

As well as a short text on the life of St Blaise, this manuscript
contains a Mass with musical notation in neumes on one red
line. This is followed by two representations of the Guidonian
hand, a pictorial device for teaching solmization by
associating notes with parts of the hand.

DESCRIPTION Parchment, 8 folios, 334 x 210 mm, in Latin, rounded
gothic script, headings in red, capitals touched in red, initials in red
or greenish brown; one historiated initial in the form of a bird;
sketch of St Blaise (f. 1r). Full red morocco binding by Rivière.
PROVENANCE 17th-century inscription; Maggs Bros., *The Art of
Writing*, cat. 542 (1930), no. 53; Albert Elkus, of the San Francisco
Conservatory of Music, bought in September 1933 from Dawson's
Book Shop, Los Angeles; Sotheby's, London, 19 June 2001, lot 32

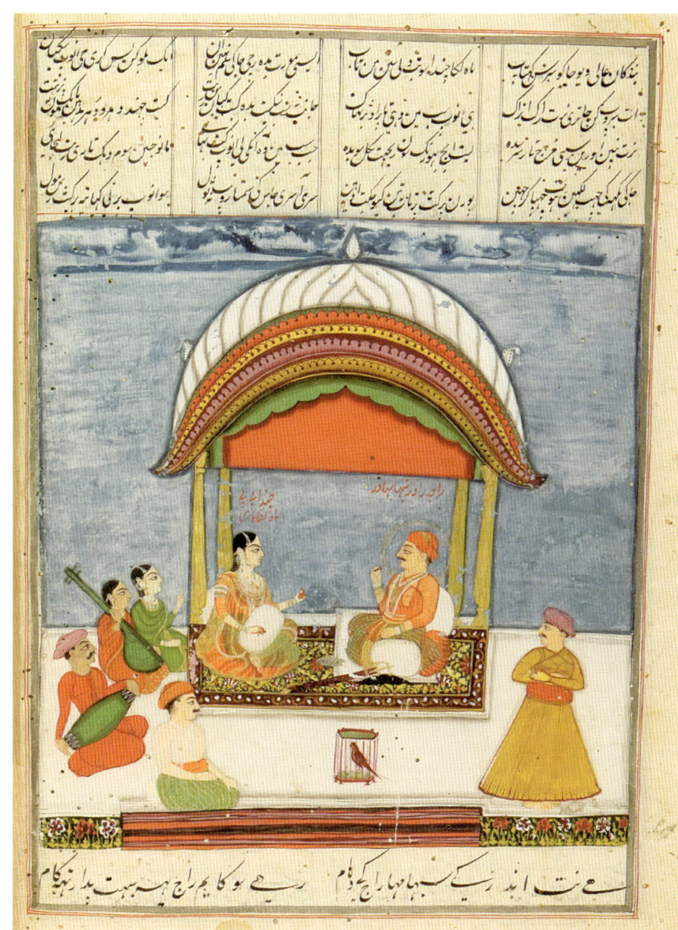

LJS 63
f. 2v

8   LJS 63

Ragamala
Deccan, colophon dated AH 1214 / 1799 AD

The 52 paintings in this manuscript are visual interpretations
of Indian musical modes, divided into 'families' of one male
Raga with four, five or six female Raginis. The family
structure used here corresponds to the uncommon Hanuman
system, in the iconographic tradition associated originally
with Amber in Rajasthan. The colophon gives the date 1799
and a signed miniature on f. 24 gives the date 1804. It is likely
that the manuscript was produced in one of the feudatory
states of the Nizam of Hyderabad, who is pictured in the first
painting.

DESCRIPTION Vellum, 40 folios, 360 x 250 mm, in Sanskrit,
nasta'liq script, black and red ink; 52 minatures. 19th-century gilt
green morocco binding.
PROVENANCE Bikaner royal collection; Sam Fogg, 1996

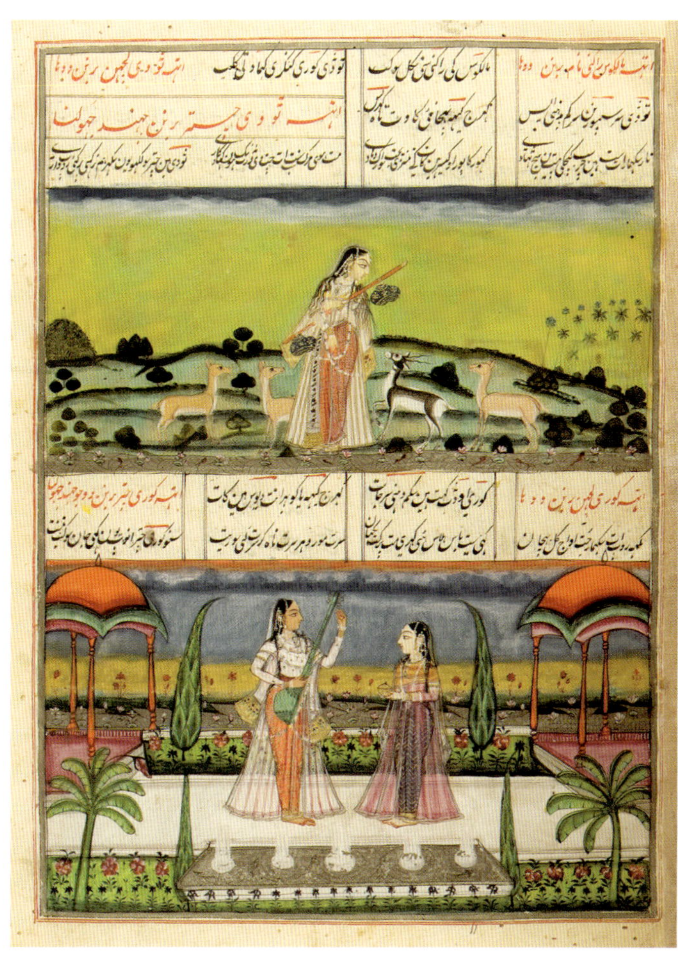

LJS 63
f. 9v

III Mathematics

The origins of mathematical notation are visible in the
cuneiform inscriptions of Babylonian tablets, dating from two
millennia BC. In the Middle Ages, mathematics – divided into
arithmetic and geometry – constituted the second and third
parts of the quadrivium. The basis for the study of geometry
remained Euclid's *Elements*. The reception of this text in the
Muslim world is traced by several of the following
manuscripts (see LJS 37 and 460 [no. 6], LJS 286 [no. 9]). Also
included here are early Arabic works on arithmetic and
algebra. In the transmission of ideas from the Arabs to the
Latins, the single most important event was the western
adoption of Hindu/Arabic numerals. Their growing
acceptance throughout the thirteenth and fourteenth
centuries is reflected in several of the following manuscripts.

Didactic handbooks sometimes used verse to explain
arithmetical operations (LJS 462 [no. 17]). Such handbooks
were also developed with the specific intention of teaching
arithmetic for mercantile purposes: Muscarello's *Algorismus*
(LJS 27 [no. 18]) is a fine example. But the application of
mathematics was not always purely for commercial reasons:
in the following selection we see its use in covert
communication (LJS 51 [no. 20], 225 [no. 21], 423 [no. 24]),
intellectual diversion (LJS 232 [no. 22]) and fortune telling
(LJS 251 [no. 23]).

In terms of mathematical theory, a watershed was reached
at the end of the seventeenth century, exemplified here by the
work of Isaac Newton (see LJS 199 [no. 25]). A selection of
manuscripts originating from the educational context of
eighteenth- and nineteenth-century universities concludes the
section.

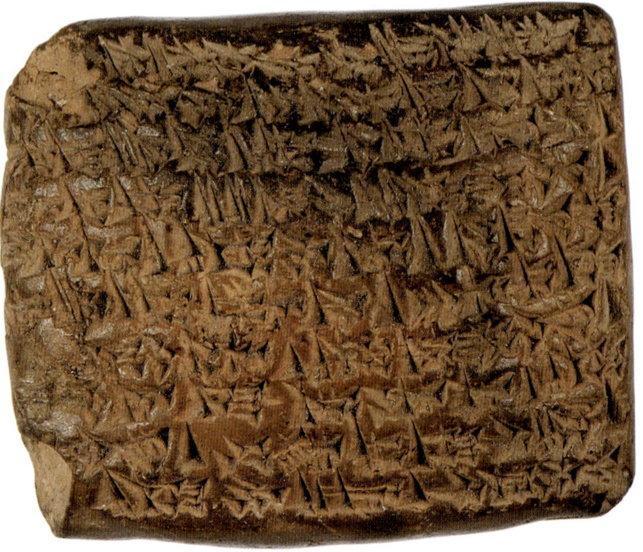

LJS

1   LJS 99

Mathematical tablet
Southern Mesopotamia, *c.* 21st–19th century BC

More than a million tablets have been excavated from
Mesopotamia but only a few hundred have any mathematical
content. This is a rare example of a table offering an
approximation to square roots.

DESCRIPTION A light brown, partially baked clay tablet,
65 x 51 mm; 24 lines of Sumerian cuneiform in a fine script.
PROVENANCE Sam Fogg, March 1997

2   LJS 301

Mathematical tablet
Babylonia, *c.* 20th–18th century BC
The tablet contains fourteen mathematical tables.
DESCRIPTION Very large clay tablet; tables separated by double ruling.
PROVENANCE Sam Fogg, May 1999

3   LJS 302

Surveying tablet
Babylonia, 18th century BC

This shows field plans detailing their lengths and areas.

DESCRIPTION A complete round bun-shaped clay tablet, 95 x 97 x
36 mm, diagrams, cuneiform text annotations.
PROVENANCE Sam Fogg, May 1999

4   LJS 269 and LJS 270

Mathematical tablets
Babylonia, *c.* 20th–18th century BC

The tablets contain multiplication tables for the Old
Babylonian mixed sexagesimal and decimal system.

DESCRIPTION Brown unbaked clay tablets, 61 x 38 mm and 60 x
41 mm, inscribed with 23 lines of Babylonian script, mainly numbers.
PROVENANCE Sam Fogg, June 1998

5   LJS 228

School writing tablet
Egypt, probably Faiyum, 6th–7th century

This tablet contains decimal multiplication tables.

DESCRIPTION Single sheet of prepared wood, coated with gesso
but unpolished, up to 92 x 390 mm and about 4-5 mm thick, pierced
with pairs of holes to form a folio of a simple wooden codex,
inscribed in black ink with four columns; verso stained dark brown.
PROVENANCE Charles Ede, *Writing and Lettering in Antiquity*, cat. IX
(1983), no. 29; Sotheby's, London, 2 December 1997, lot 93

6   LJS 37 and 460

Epitome of Euclid's *Elements*
Near East, AH 502 / 1108-09

Euclid's *Stoicheia* (Elements), in thirteen books, was written in
Alexandria at the beginning of the third century BC. It
consists of proofs of geometrical and arithmetical
propositions, rigorously and logically structured, and its
method dominated mathematics until the nineteenth century.
Over two millennia it was constantly edited, translated,
commented upon and abridged. This manuscript bears
witness to such activity in the Arab world, where several

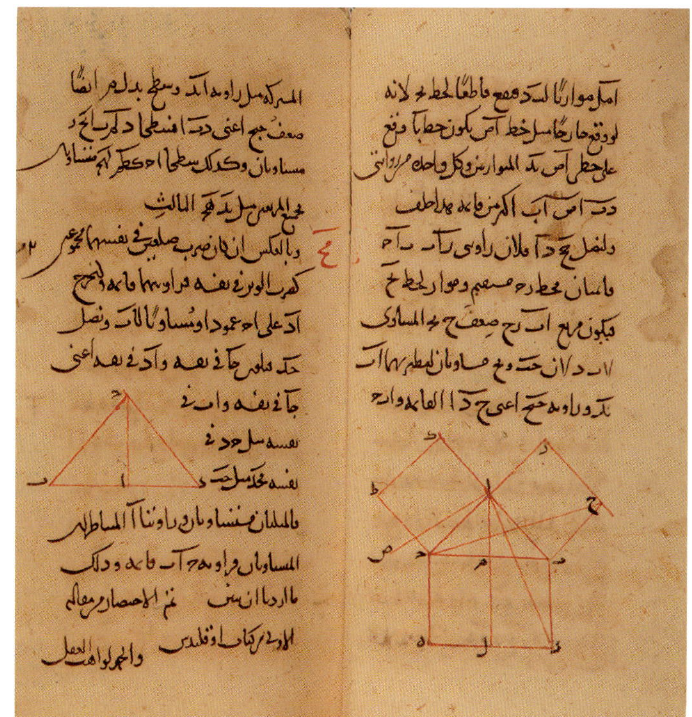

LJS 37
ff. 16v-17r

translations of the *Elements* were made between the eighth and
tenth centuries. Epitomes, or *ikhtisar,* of these translations
were made by, among others, Avicenna (see LJS 440 [I, no. 6]
and 446 [V, no. 1] *et sqq.*) and Omar Khayam's colleague
Muzaffar al-Asfuzari (d. before 1122).

   This copy is dated twice, to the month of Jumada I 502
(December 1108–January 1109) and to the month of Ramadan
502 (April 1109). No indication is given of its origin, but the
line measurements used by the scribe are commonly
associated with Egypt.

DESCRIPTION Paper, 92 folios (LJS 37) and 80 folios (LJS 460), 188 x
95 mm, in Arabic, naskh script in brown ink; 251 charts and
diagrams in red (LJS 37); copious diagrams (LJS 460). Contemporary
brown morocco binding (LJS 37).
PROVENANCE Ownership marks in Persian, LJS 37 f. 1r; Sir Thomas
Phillipps; LJS 37: Christie's, London, 11 April 1994, lot 61; Sam Fogg, June
1995; LJS 460: Christie's, South Kensington, 17 October 2003, lot 407
BIBLIOGRAPHY DSB IV 438-43

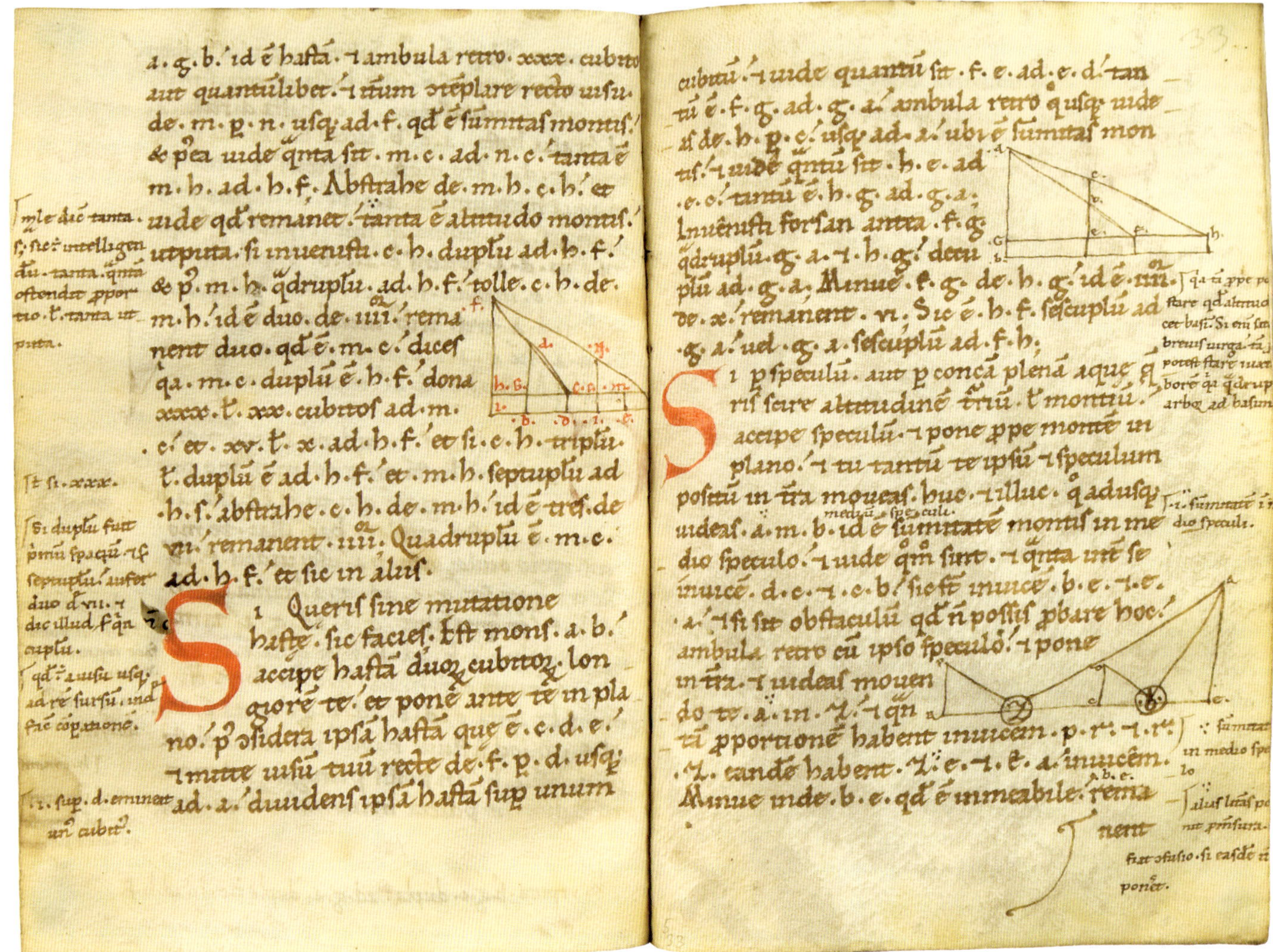

7 LJS 194

Gerbert of Auvergne, *Isagoge geometriae*
Northern Austria, mid-12th century

Gerbert of Auvergne (*c.* 945–1003; from 999 to his death Pope
Sylvester II) was a noted mathematician and educator. This
manuscript contains a number of texts by him on geometry.
It includes substantial sections from four chapters of his
Isagoge geometriae and his 'Letter to Adebaldus' (*i.e.* Adelbold
of Utrecht, *c.* 970–1026) on the isosceles triangle, with
Adelbold's reply, and a short treatise on the construction of
the astrolabe.

DESCRIPTION Parchment, 56 folios, 155 x 106 mm, in Latin,
romanesque script in two hands, dark brown ink, rubrics in red,
some capitals touched in red, numerous 1-line initials in red; about
100 painted initials, mostly 3-line or 4-line, in red, and six initials (3-
line to 10-line) in red, infilling in brown, with twisting scrolls and
vine-stems and one winged dragon; over 120 diagrams in margins
and inset in text; annotations in two hands. 18th-century blind-
stamped calf binding.

PROVENANCE Collation in the hand of a Renaissance humanist;
Hieronymus Wilhelm Ebner (1673-1752), von Eschenbach; John
Henry Bohn (1757–1843); Sir Thomas Phillipps, ms. 4437; Harrison D.
Horblit; H.P. Kraus, cat. 155 (1979), no. 18; Bruce Ferrini; Sam Fogg,
cat. 14 (1991), no. 1; John Stanitz, ms. 25

BIBLIOGRAPHY DSB V 364-6; Sarton I 669-71

8 LJS 465

Abu 'Uthman al-Tajibi, *On Geometry*
Spain, 13th century

The text is an otherwise unattested treatise on geometry,
describing the creation and mathematical properties of
regular geometrical shapes.

DESCRIPTION Paper, 7 folios, 203 x 144 mm, in Arabic, andalusi
script, sepia ink, annotations in red; numerous diagrams of triangles,
quadrilaterals, circles and composite shapes. Later brown tooled
morocco binding.
PROVENANCE Sam Fogg, June 2004

9 LJS 286

Al-Tusi, *Tadhkira usul handasa al hisab li Uqlidis*
Persia, Rabi I AH 890 / April 1485

The accomplishments of Nasir al-Din al-Tusi (1201–1274)
extended over many disciplines: he was a scientist,
mathematician, philosopher and theologian (see further LJS
392 [IV, no. 4], 407 [IV, no. 5] and 279 [IV, no. 10]). One subject
to which al-Tusi returned in a series of works was Euclid's
Elements, of which he produced two different redactions and a
number of commentaries. One of these commentaries is
contained in this manuscript.

DESCRIPTION Paper, 213 folios, 180 x 111 mm, in Arabic, fine naskh
script, black ink, diacritics in red, marginal annotations, additional
commentary on last folios; over 600 drawings and diagrams in red.
Red morocco binding, blind-stamped with gilt-stamped spine.
PROVENANCE Ownership notes and seals, 15th–19th centuries;
Sam Fogg, December 1998
BIBLIOGRAPHY EI X 746-52; Sarton II 1001-03; Al-Daffa and Stroyles

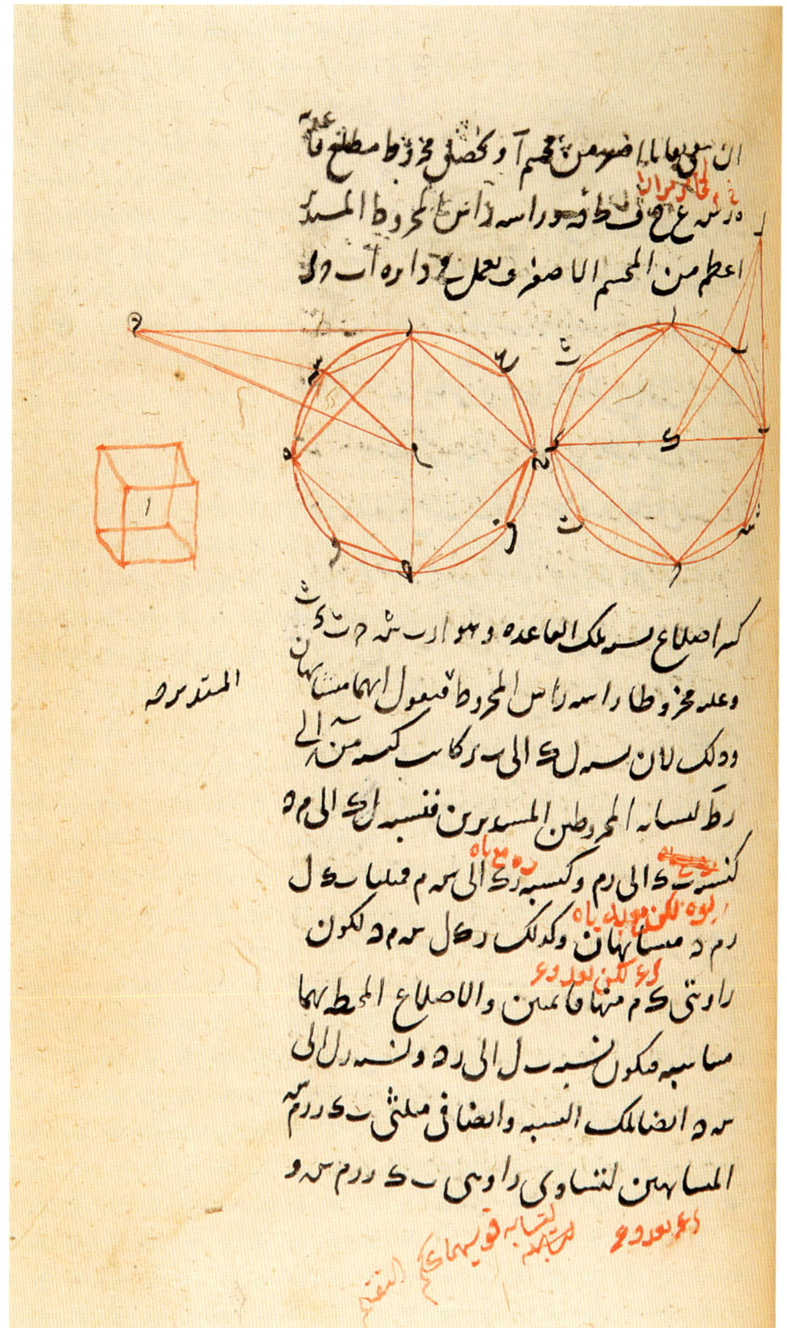

LJS 286, f. 180r

10 LJS 293

Al-Hassar, *Kitab al-bayan wa al-tadhkira fi san'at 'amal al-'iyar*, Part 1
Baghdad, Safar 590 / January–February 1194

Abu Bakr al-Hassar was a noted mathematician active in the
western Islamic world in the twelfth century; this is a near
contemporary copy of his treatise on arithmetic and algebra.
According to the colophon, the scribe, 'Ali ibn Muhammad
ibn 'Abdullah al-Baghdadi, copied it in the *madrasa* of al-
Nizamiyah in Baghdad – a famous institution of learning
founded by Nizam al-Mulk in 1064. In the century after it was
copied, this manuscript was to be found in the library of the
celebrated Persian mathematician Nasir al-Din al-Tusi (for
whom see LJS 286 [no. 9]), who was in the service of Hülegü
Khan when he conquered Baghdad in 1258. In 1271 the present
treatise was translated into Hebrew by Moses ibn Tibbon of
Granada.

DESCRIPTION Paper, 87 folios, 232 x 165 mm, in Arabic, naskh
script, black ink. Early binding, maroon calf over paper boards.
PROVENANCE Nasir al-Din al-Tusi; Christie's, 20 April 1999, lot 320
BIBLIOGRAPHY Sarton II 400

11 LJS 464

Commentary and epitome of works by Ibn al-Banna
Granada, AH 749 / 1348

Ibn al-Banna al-Marrakushi (1256–1321) was active in a
number of fields; more than eighty works are attributed to
him, covering grammar, rhetoric and logic, magic, divination
and astronomy. The present manuscript shows his special
interest in mathematics, particularly in calculations involving
fractions and square roots; the final chapter is on algebra. It is
entitled *Sharh al-talkhis*, or Commentary on the 'Abridgement',
referring to the *Talkhis amal al-hisab* (Summary of arithmetical
operations), one of Ibn al-Banna's best-known works.

DESCRIPTION Paper, 97 folios, 140 x 210 mm, in Arabic, maghrebi
script, sepia ink, rubrication and calculations in red, five pages of
computational tables (27r, 34v, 35r, 46v, 49v). Later red tooled leather
binding with flap.

LJS 464
f. 39v

LJS 481
p. 309

PROVENANCE Sam Fogg, July 2004
BIBLIOGRAPHY EI III 731; Brockelmann G II 531, S II 363-64

12 LJS 481

Abu ʻUthman Saad bin Ahmad bin Ibrahim bin Leon al-Tajibi al-Andalusi, *Talkhis*
Spain, 13th century

Another commentary on Ibn al-Banna's *Talkhis*.
DESCRIPTION Paper, 156 folios, 190 x 270 mm, in Arabic, sinuous maghrebi script, black ink, calculations in red, bold script marking divisions; five pages of computational tables. Later red-tooled leather binding.
PROVENANCE Sam Fogg, July 2004

13 LJS 296

Al-Kashani, *Idah al-maqasid li fara'id al-fawa'id*
Isfahan, Shaʻban 720 AH / September 1320

Imad al-Din al-Kashani, also known as Kashi, was a Persian mathematician active in the first half of the fourteenth century. According to its colophon, the present manuscript is "the work of the hand of the author".

DESCRIPTION Paper, 163 folios, 246 x 109 mm, in Arabic, naskh script, black ink, overlining and marginal annotations in red, some small diagrams. Original calf binding, gilt-stamped and rebacked.
PROVENANCE Christie's, London, 19 April 1999, lot 323

14 LJS 312

Joseph ben Moses Sarfati, *Ir Sichon* (On arithmetic)
Spain, 15th century

This considers basic calculations and commercial arithmetic.
DESCRIPTION Paper, 59 folios, 137 x 105 mm, in Hebrew, semi-cursive script, brown ink. 17th-century Italian gold-tooled brown mottled calf covers.
PROVENANCE Solomon Hirschell (1761–1842), first Chief Rabbi of England; Jew's College, London, no. 137; Beth Din congregation, London, no. 133; Christie's New York, 23 June 1999, lot 100

15 LJS 436

Mahmud ibn Abi Bakr al-Kalabadi al-Bukhari, *Dau' al-siraj*
Near East, AH 747 / 1346-47

Islamic tradition provided complex rules for dividing inheritances among family members. This gave rise to the need for textbooks explaining the necessary calculations. The standard work in the field was the *Kitab al-fara'id al-sirajiyya* by the eleventh-century jurist al-Sajawandi. The present manuscript is a copy of a commentary on al-Sajawandi's work probably written in the later thirteenth century.

DESCRIPTION Paper, 123 folios, 180 x 127 mm, in Arabic, naskh script in two hands, black ink, occasional words in red, marginal annotations in several hands; opening in large muhaqqaq script; numerous diagrams and tables in red and black. Brown morocco binding with flap.
PROVENANCE Sam Fogg, June 2002
BIBLIOGRAPHY EI VIII 739

16 LJS 216

Johannes de Sacrobosco, *Algorismus*, *De sphaera*, and *Computus lunaris*
Paris (?), *c.* 1256–70

The life of Johannes de Sacrobosco (otherwise known as John of Holywood) is clouded in obscurity but his works were among the most widely diffused of medieval teaching books. His manual of arithmetic, the *Algorismus,* focuses on practical rather than theoretical issues. It includes rules for addition, subtraction, multiplication, division and square and cubic roots. His methods of calculation remained commonly in use for over two centuries.

The *Algorismus* was often copied, as here, alongside his cosmological and astronomical work *De sphaera* (see further LJS 26 [IV, no. 11]) and his *Computus lunaris* (otherwise known as *De computo ecclesiastico*). The *Computus* discusses the division of time according to movements of the sun and moon: Sacrobosco criticized the Julian calendar and suggested altering it in terms very similar to the revision eventually carried out in 1582 under Pope Gregory XIII.

Sacrobosco worked in Paris, producing these texts between

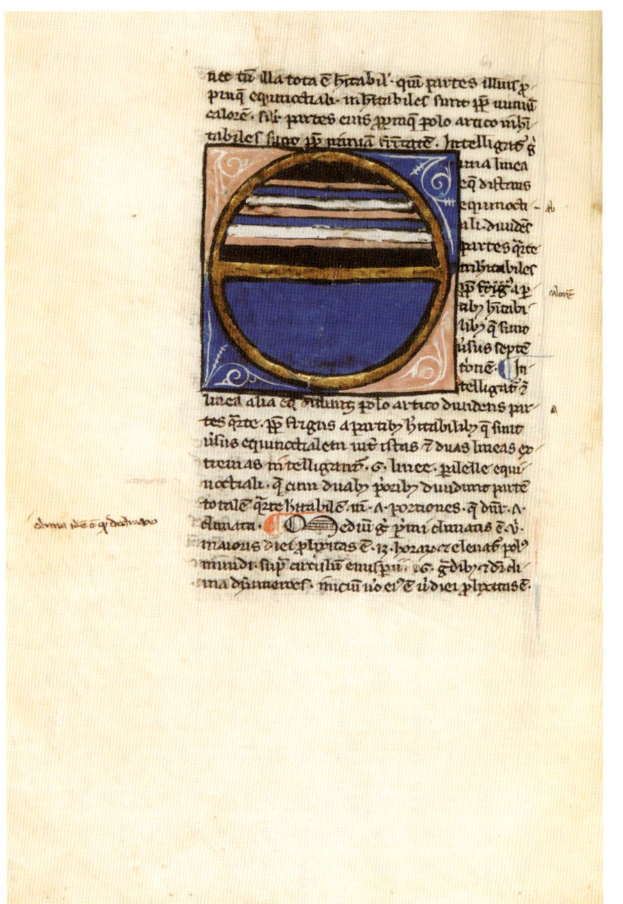

1220 and 1232. The date of his death is uncertain, and has been given as either 1244 or 1256. By this time, *De sphaera* was already a standard teaching tool and was in wide use all over Europe. Stylistically, the three historiated initials in this manuscript appear to be related to the 'Bari workshop', a Paris workshop active between 1250 and 1270. This is therefore a near-contemporary copy of his seminal work.

DESCRIPTION Parchment, 58 folios, 171 x 120 mm, in Latin, gothic bookhand, black ink, rubrics and small initials in red, black and blue, three gold and polychrome historiated initials; 7 large painted figures. Modern red velvet binding.

PROVENANCE Honeyman, ms. astron. 11 (ms. 56), sold Sotheby's, 2 May 1979, lot 1089; Maggs Bros.; Sam Fogg, 1995; John Stanitz, ms. 47

BIBLIOGRAPHY DSB XII 60-63; Thorndike

17   LJS 462

Alexander of Villa Dei, *Carmen de algorismo*
Spain, 1st half 14th century

The *Carmen de algorismo*, a didactic poem by the French Franciscan mathematician Alexander of Villa Dei (d. *c.* 1240), was widely read, rivalling in popularity Johannes de Sacrobosco's *Algorismus* (see LJS 216 [no. 16]). It consists of 284 lines of hexameter verse, dealing with integers and their operations. It was the first Latin text in which zero (*cifra*) was treated as a numeral, and played a major role in the diffusion of Hindu/Arabic numerals.

The second text contained in the present manuscript, entitled *Compotus manualis*, is a treatise, also in verse, on the calendar. Its central purpose is to establish fast and feast days; it also discusses the movements of the sun and moon. When published in Strasbourg in 1488, the *Compotus manualis* was attributed to one Anianus, although the identity of this person is unknown.

This manuscript was originally part of a compendium of medieval scientific works, including Johannes de Sacrobosco's *De sphaera*, the almanac of Profacius Judaeus (Jacob ibn Tibbon), and several works concerning the use of the *quadrans vetus* or 'old quadrant'. The compendium was acquired by

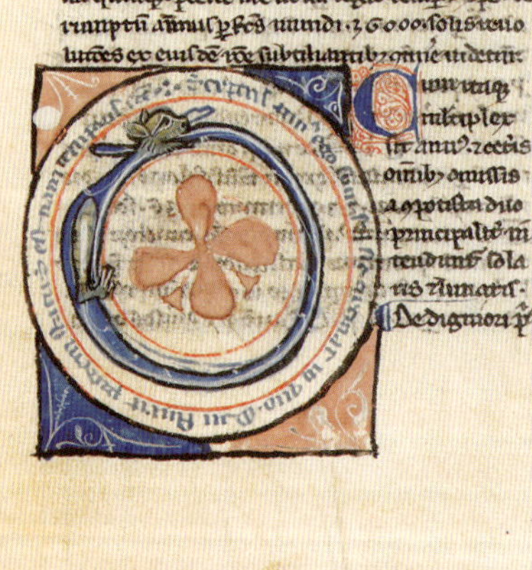

LJS 462
f. 1r

William Jones (*c.* 1675-1749), mathematician, Fellow of the Royal Society and an early disseminator of Isaac Newton's work (see LJS 199 [no. 25]). Jones rebound its constituent parts separately and later passed them on to his pupil, George Parker, 2nd Earl of Macclesfield (1697–1764). They were housed in the library of Shirburn Castle, where this manuscript had the shelfmark I.3.

DESCRIPTION Parchment, 14 folios, 227 x 149 mm, in Latin, large rounded Iberian gothic script, dark brown ink, headings in red, capitals touched in red, paragraph marks alternately in red and blue; notes *c.* 1500, English hand, on final page; 16 2-line initials in red or blue with purple or red penwork. Bound in 18th-century English marbled paper boards.

PROVENANCE Erased medieval inscription (f. 14r); William Jones; George Parker, 2nd Earl of Macclesfield; Sotheby's, 22 June 2004, lot 586

BIBLIOGRAPHY Sarton II 616-17; Halliwell 73-83; ODNB xxx 661-62; Smith

18   LJS 27

Pietro Paolo Muscarello, *Algorismus*
Nola, 1478

The manuscripts of Johannes de Sacrobosco and Alexander of Villa Dei mentioned above (see LJS 216 [no. 16] and 462 [no. 17]) exemplify the trend for manuals of practical arithmetic which began in the twelfth century. Over the following centuries such manuals continued to be produced, with a particular emphasis on commercial transactions. While mathematical instruction, as enshrined in the quadrivium, remained highly theoretical and based on classical authors such as Euclid (see LJS 37 and 460 [no. 6]) and Boethius (see LJS 101 [I, no. 1] and 47 [II, no. 2]), an alternative curriculum of practical and commercial arithmetic developed, largely as a result of the expansion in Italian trade during the Middle Ages and Renaissance. The earliest 'textbook' of this trend was the *Liber abaci* (1202) of Leonardo of Pisa (otherwise known as Fibonacci). Over the next two centuries, such instruction became formalized in schools for merchants' children, attending generally between the ages of eleven and sixteen. By the mid-fifteenth century, Italy was known all over Europe for its dominance in the field of commercial arithmetic.

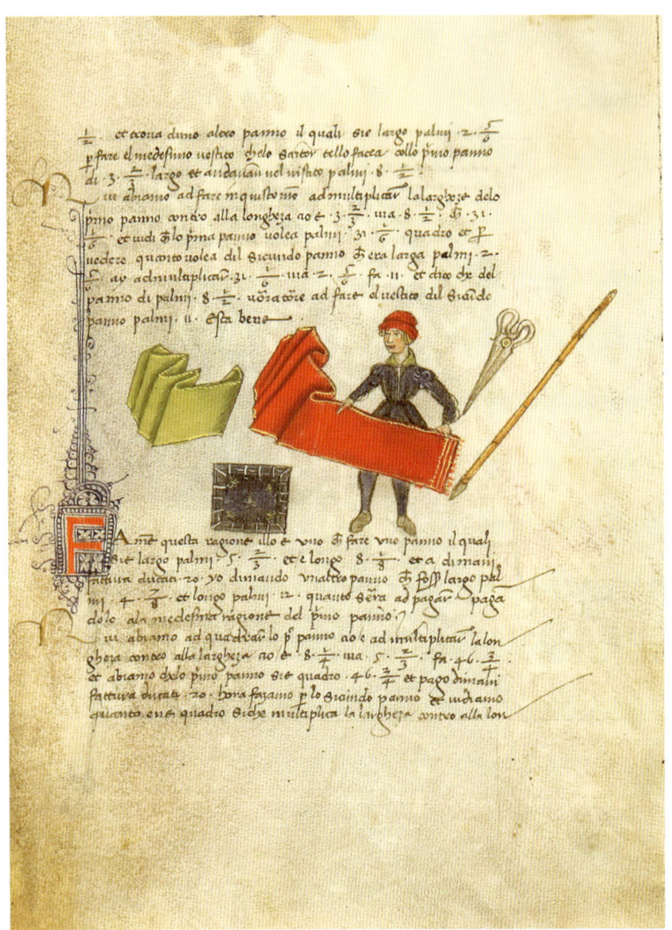

LJS 27
f. 100r

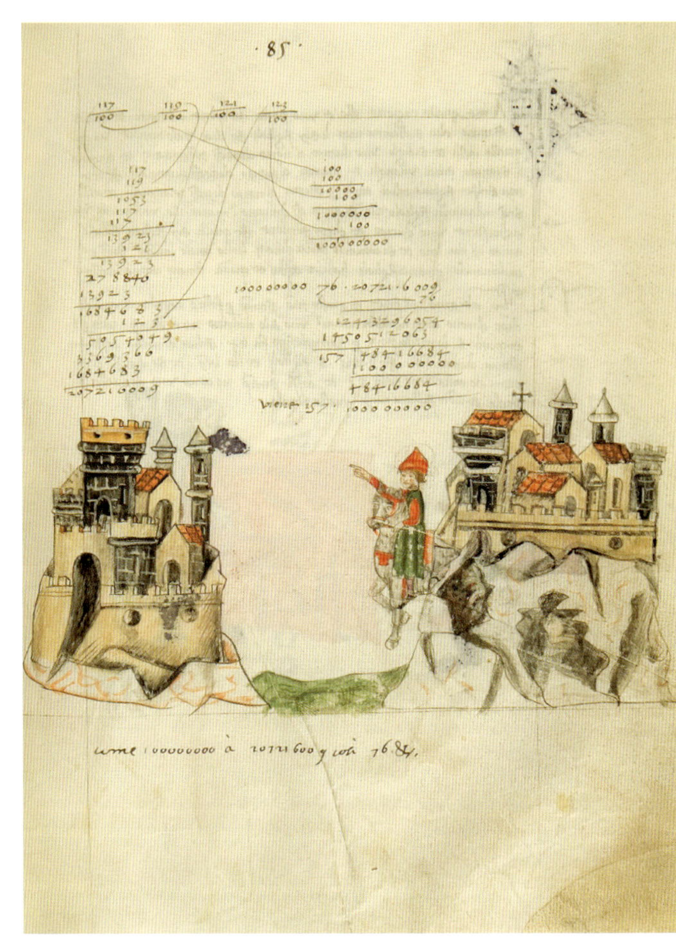

LJS 27
f. 85r

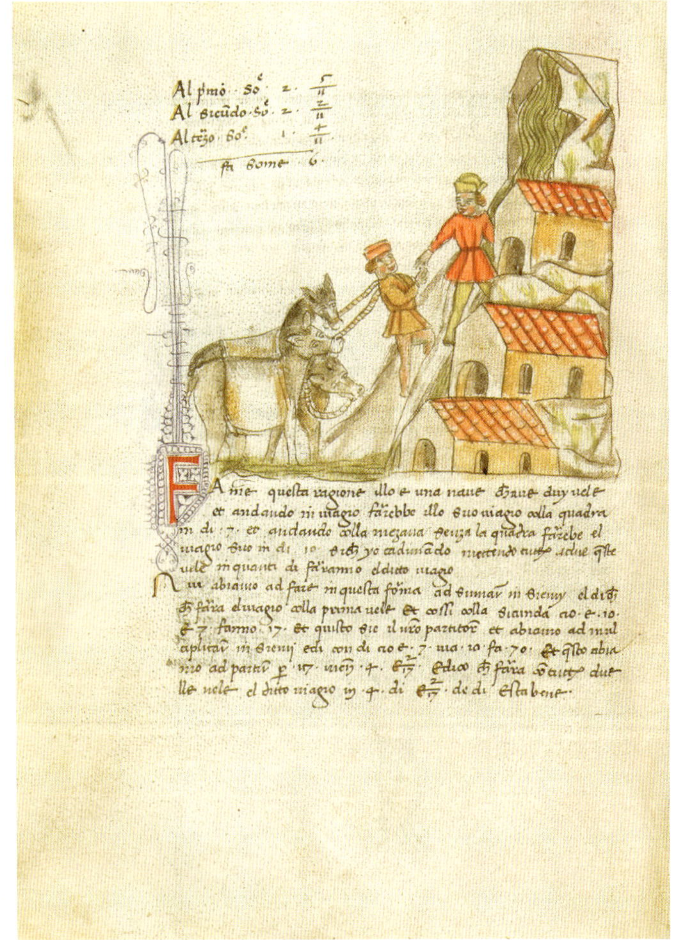

LJS 27
f. 77v

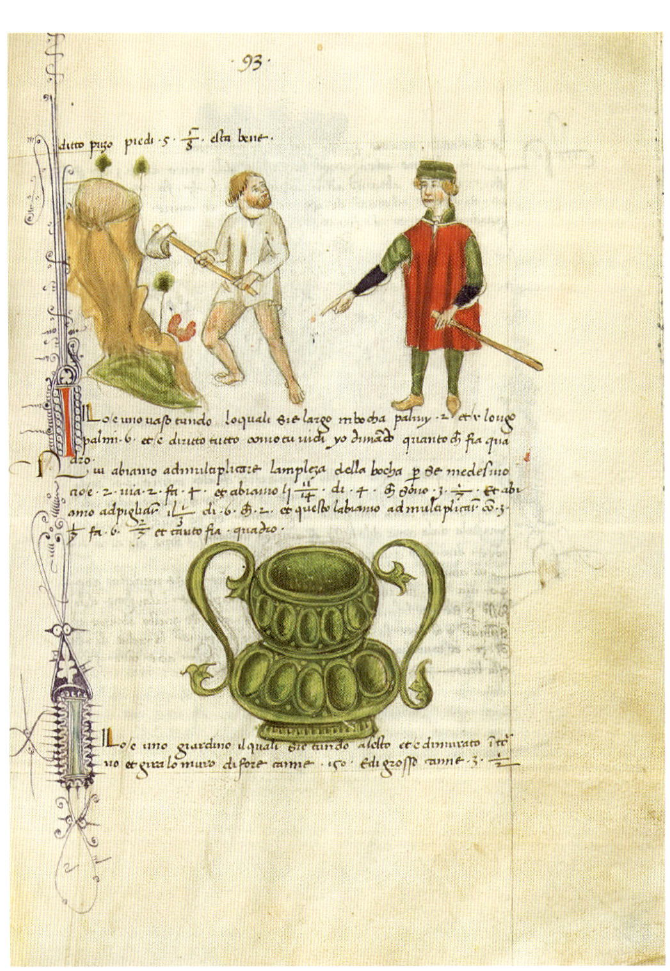

LJS 27
f. 93r

The present manuscript stems from this tradition of teaching commercial arithmetic. It begins with a series of multiplication tables, followed by a group of arithmetical problems, stated and then solved, with their workings shown. According to its colophon, it was completed by Petrus Paulus Muscharellus in 1478, in the town of Nola, near Naples. Muscarello may well have been the author, as well as the scribe, of this otherwise unknown text.

The manuscript is copiously illustrated with scenes of everyday life, in which there figure merchants, tailors, sailors, hunters and woodcutters as well as various architectural features, measuring instruments and other objects such as barrels and ovens.

DESCRIPTION Parchment, 115 folios, 211 x 154 mm, in Italian, semi-cursive sloping bookhand, dark brown ink, elaborate decorated initials, historiated initial and fully illuminated border (f. 1); 54 coloured drawings (some with gold), several tables and mathematical diagrams. 18th-century mottled calf binding.
PROVENANCE Illuminated for a member of the Albertini family of Nola (arms on f. 1r); Stefano Scarella di San Remo (17th century); Sotheby's, London, 23 June 1992, lot 73
BIBLIOGRAPHY *Algorismus*

19 LJS 289

Algorismus
Italy, probably *c.* 1450-75

The present manuscript, like the previous, is devoted to the application of arithmetic to commercial transactions. As well as describing operations such as multiplication and division it gives particular attention to the working-out of proportions using the 'rule of three'. This was a common feature of such texts at this time, designed to enable merchants to answer such questions as, "If one pound of saffron is worth seven pounds of *pizoli*, what will 25 pounds of saffron be worth?" It also contains problems on money-changing and alloys. It differs from other such works, however, in its inclusion of a set of problems relating to the geometric mean of two integers (known as *convignievole*).

DESCRIPTION Parchment, 98 folios, 120 x 105 mm, in Latin, Italian cursive commercial script, brown ink. Contemporary blind-tooled binding, possibly Neapolitan.
PROVENANCE Fiammetta Soave, *One Hundred Fine & Rare Books and Manuscripts* (1994), no. 3
BIBLIOGRAPHY Swetz 1-33

20 LJS 51

Alphabets and encoded letters
Possibly Syria, 15th century

This anonymous text is a compilation of encoded communications, in roughly a hundred and fifty alphabets, many invented; some of these have been transcribed back into Arabic by another hand. The author mentions a number of authorities for his alphabets, among whom are Shihab al-Din al-Jundi al-Ala'i, Burhan al-Din al-Qudsi and Taqi al-Din Muhammad ibn Ja'far al-Husayni; the author also appears to have been influenced by an early treatise on arcane alphabets attributed to Ibn Wahshiyah.

DESCRIPTION Paper, 106 folios, 178 x 133 mm, in Arabic, naskh script, black ink, and a variety of other scripts, some with transcriptions into Arabic in red, occasional marginal notes. Half-leather binding, stamped.
PROVENANCE Sam Fogg, June 1996

21 LJS 225

Michele Zopello, *Liber litterarum simulationis*
Rome, 1455–58

This is the dedication copy of an otherwise unknown work on codes and ciphers written by Michele Zopello for Pope Calixtus III. The author describes the use of codes, which he characterizes especially in terms of getting messages to and from besieged towns, and outlines a method of word substitution for the encoding of documents: following the order of the alphabet, words beginning with A are turned into words beginning with C, and so on successively; and, "If the substitution for one word does not sound right, it can be harmonized with another which is better" (f. 5r). To this end

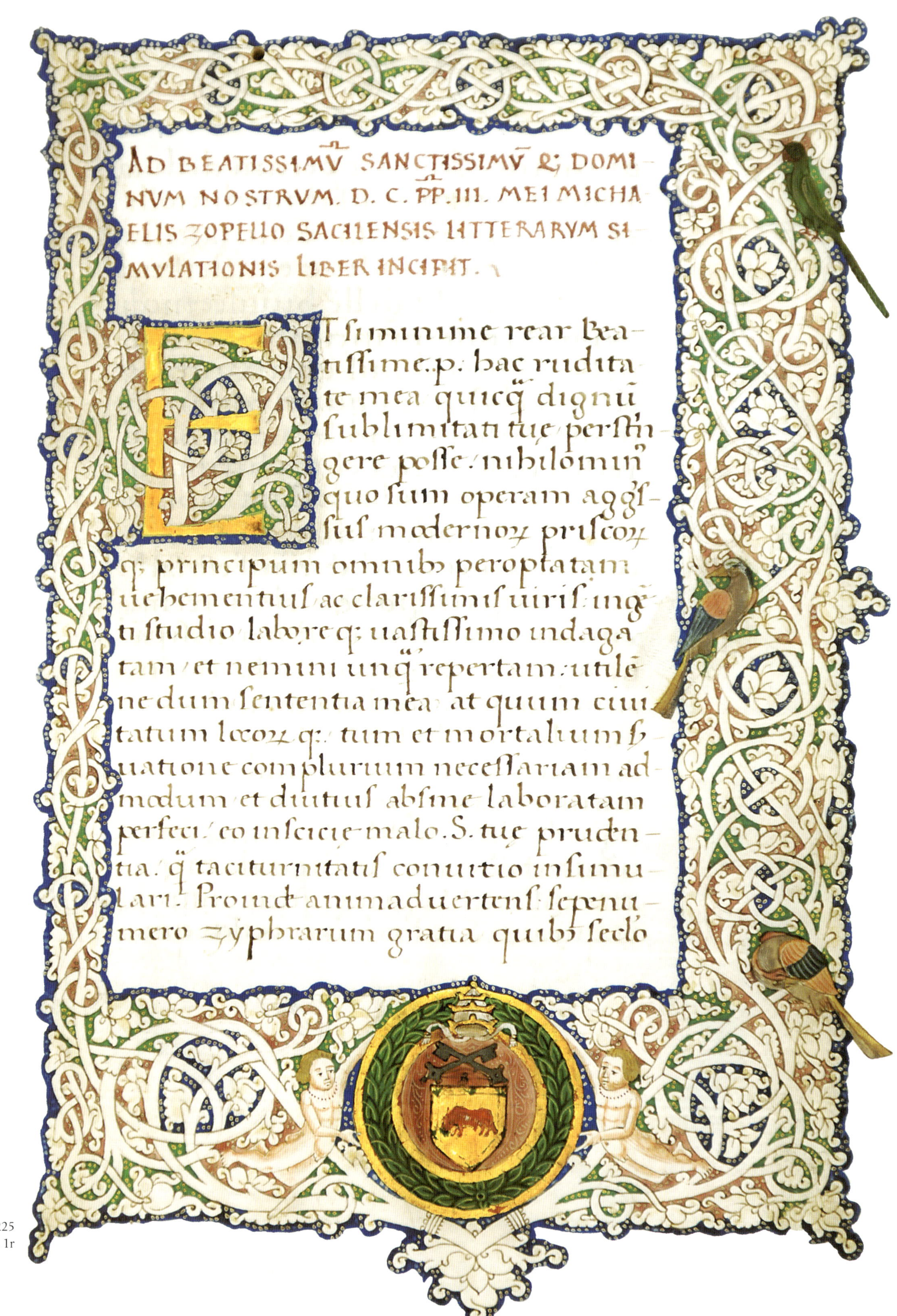

AD BEATISSIMŪ SANCTISSIMŪ Q; DOMI-
NUM NOSTRUM. D. C. PP. III. MEI MICHA-
ELIS ZOPELLO SACILENSIS LITTERARUM SI-
MULATIONIS LIBER INCIPIT.

Et si minime rear bea-
tissime.p. hac rudita-
te mea quicq̄ dignū
sublimitati tuę persti-
gere posse. nihilominū
quo sum operam aggs-
sus modernoꝝ priscoꝝ
q: principum omnibꝫ peroptatam
uehementius ac clarissimis uiris. ingī-
ti studio labore q: uastissimo indaga-
tam et nemini unq̄ repertam. utilē
nedum sententia mea. at quum ciui-
tatum locoꝝ q: tum et mortalium ħ
uatione complurium necessariam ad-
modum et diutius absme laboratam
perfeci. eo inscicie malo. S. tuę prudn-
tia. q̄ taciturnitatis conuitio insimu-
lari. Proinde animaduertens sepenu-
mero zyphrarum gratia quibꝫ seclo

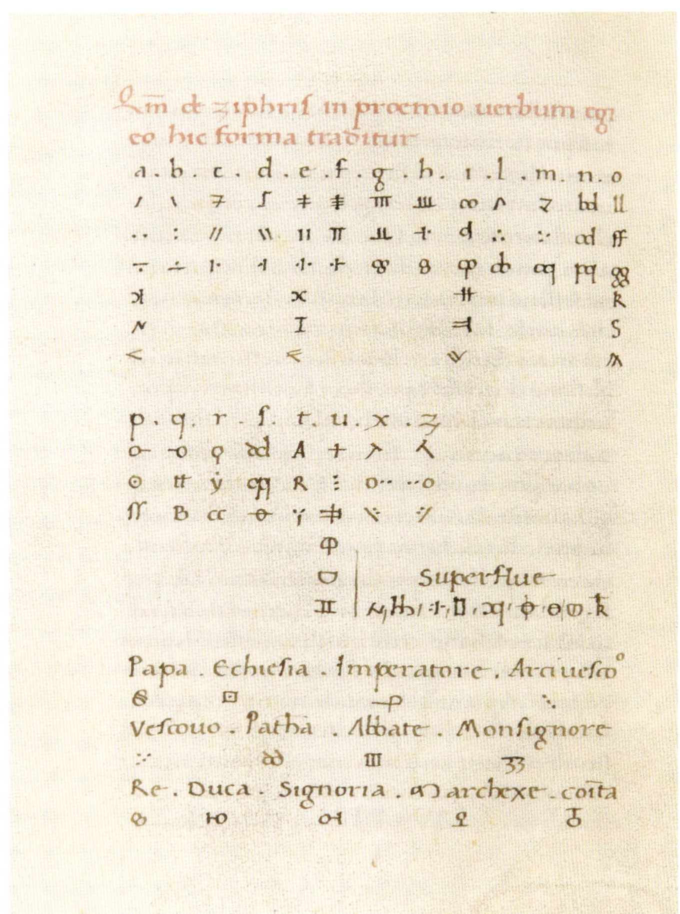

Alfonso da Borgia (1378–1458) was Pope Calixtus III for the last three years of his life. His arms figure on the titlepage of this manuscript, illuminated by Gioacchino di Giovanni de Gigantibus, who fulfilled a series of commissions for the papacy and Italian nobles between the 1440s and 1470s.

DESCRIPTION Parchment, 20 folios, 223 x 150 mm, in Latin and Italian, rounded Gothic script, brown ink; 2-line initials throughout, gold with blue border, 7-line initial (f. 1r) with full-page border and arms of Calixtus III. Contemporary blind-stamped calf binding.
PROVENANCE Sotheby's, London, 20 June 1989, lot 49; Martin Breslauer; Christie's, London, 26 June 1996, lot 19

22 LJS 232

Benedetto Varchi, Treatise and notes on rithmomachia Italy, mid-16th century

The sixteenth century saw a flourishing of interest in rithmomachia ('battle of numbers'), a game first cited in the 11th century and typically attributed to Pythagoras. It was played on a board like chess and was based on the theory of numeric proportions expounded in Boethius's *Arithmetic*. This interest was stimulated by a brief description in the 1496 edition of Boethius by Jacques Lefèvre d'Etaples. By 1539 the game had made its way to Florence, as this manuscript relates.

The rules of the game, and the arithmetical theory on which it was based, are expounded in this compilation of works by Benedetto Varchi (1503–1565; a leading member of the Florentine Academy) and Carlo Strozzi. Varchi, it is said, was sent the game by Cosimo Rucellai, who had received it from his father; Varchi had learnt the game and begun to play it with certain of his friends, at which point an explanation of its rules was requested by Luca Martini, whose attempts to learn the game himself had been hindered by a lack of knowledge of Boethian number theory. Subsequently, Varchi composed a summary of this theory, the *Trattato delle proportioni et proportionalità* (here ff. 3r–26r), while his friend Strozzi wrote a dialogue in which he learns the rules from Cosimo Rucellai (ff. 26v–46r). Several pages of further matter concerning the game follow.

Interest in the game remained throughout the sixteenth

the central section of the work gives a list of words, in Italian, each followed by two alternative substitutions. As A is turned to C, "amici" can be rendered by either "chiari" or "cavagli"; B changes to D, hence "biancha" becomes "divina" or "dolphina". The author advises that, after being written, the encoded letters should be delivered by "a suitable young woman, accustomed to this job".

Following the list of substitutions the author gives two sample letters, first plain, then in code. For example, the phrase "havendo fata questa pace" is rendered "*Haver fata questa mercantia*"; reference to the guide shows that "*pace*" can be substituted by "*mandata*" or "*mercantia*' according to the writer's choice.

The final two pages give an alternative cipher system, by which letters are substituted with symbols (a choice of six symbols per vowel and three per consonant); other symbols render common titles such as *papa* (pope), *imperatore* (emperor) and *vescovo* (bishop), as well as town names.

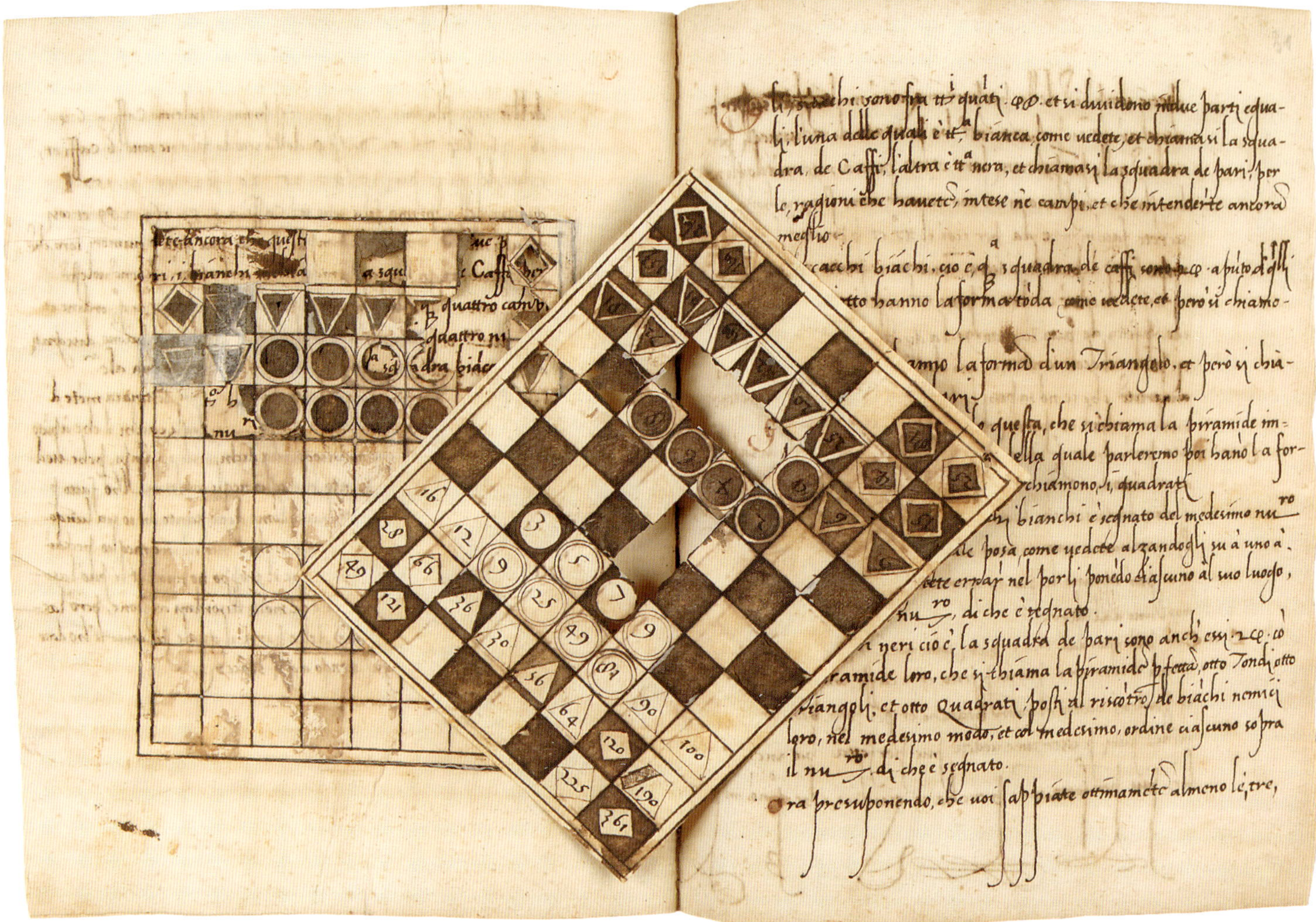

LJS 232
ff. 30v–30r

century, as publications by Claude de Boissière (Paris, 1556) and Francisco Barozzi (Venice, 1572) attest; this compilation of works circulated only in manuscript, however.

DESCRIPTION Paper, 60 folios, 220 x 166 mm, in Italian and Latin, humanistic script, brown ink, red rubrics, some with blue initials; six diagrams and drawings. Parchment wrapper.

PROVENANCE Ownership inscription of Marco Antonio; bookplates of Bibliotheca Bardi-Serzelli and Giannalisa Feltrinelli; Christie's, London, 3 December 1997, lot 220

BIBLIOGRAPHY Smith (1923) I 198–200; Smith (1970) 12, 62–65, 271, 340; Moyer 109–22

23 LJS 251

Hartmann Schopper, *Ars artium sive ars magna cabalistica* Germany, 2nd half 17th century

The Jewish tradition of kabbalah became known to European Christians from the end of the fifteenth century onwards. Originally comprising a variety of schools, and concerned in particular with cosmogony and biblical exegesis, in its Latin reception it was to become particularly aligned with numerology. In the late sixteenth and seventeenth centuries a number of manuscripts circulated which used so-called 'kabbalistic' techniques of deriving numerical sums from letters, for the purpose of fortune-telling, answering questions and solving problems. An early work of this nature was *The Art of Arts, or Great Kabbalistic Art* of Hartmann Schopper, written *c.* 1564. His list of sources is a combination

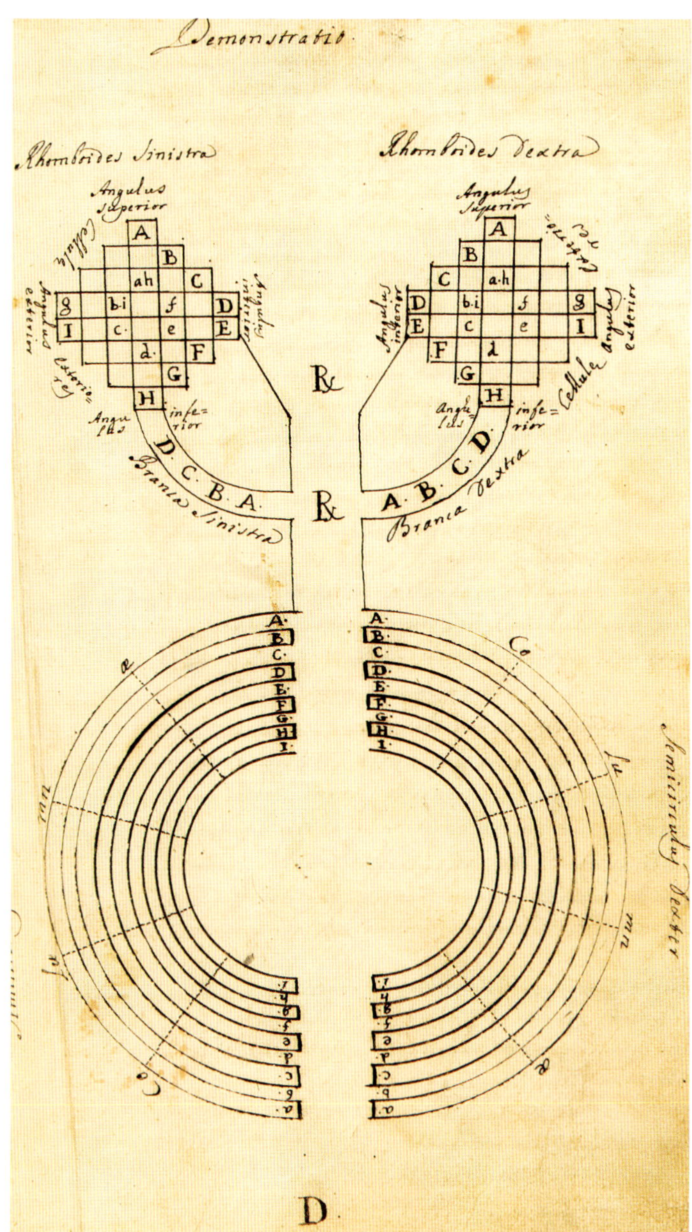

251
p. 62

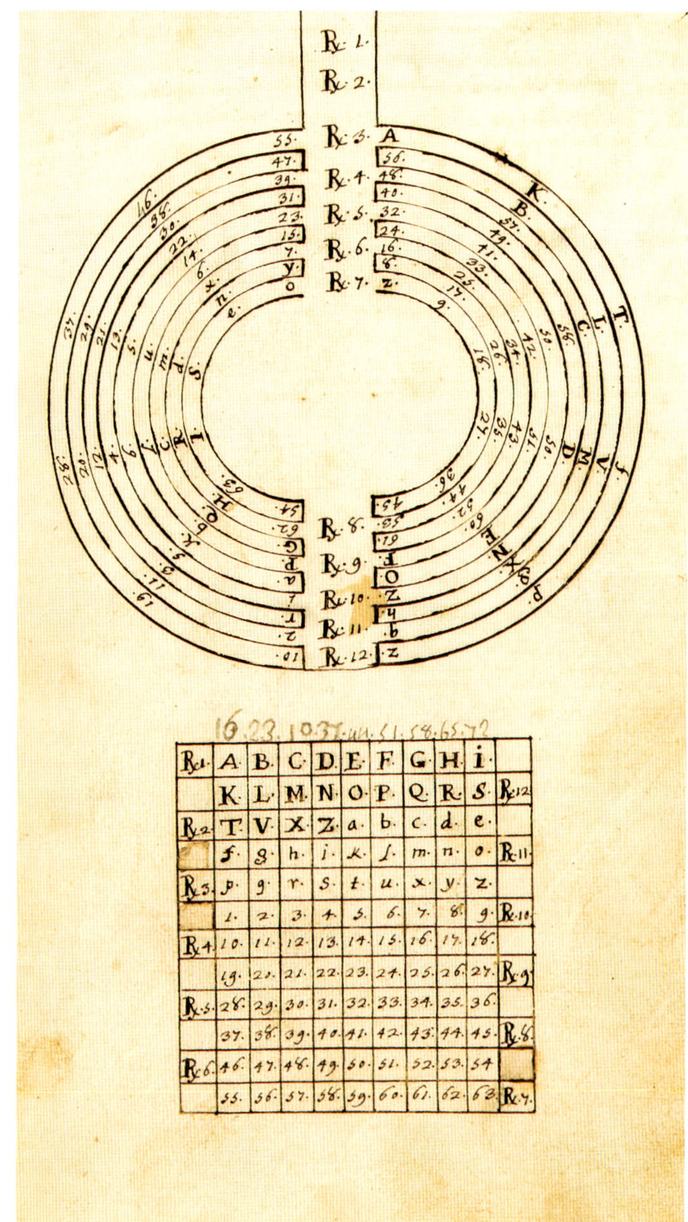

LJS 251
p. 75

of ancients such as Pythagoras, medieval kabbalistic works such as the *Sefer yetsirah*, the *Zohar* and Nahmanides, and later scholars such as Giovanni Pico della Mirandola (who was his major source), Johannes Reuchlin and Paulus Ricius. Evidence from the mathematical notation used in this manuscript suggests that this is an updated copy of the work, made between 1655 and 1700.

DESCRIPTION Paper, 139 folios, 282 x 202 mm, in Latin, humanistic cursive script, black ink; numerous tables and diagrams. Parchment binding.

PROVENANCE Albert Woodcock, 1886; Sam Fogg, August 1998

24 LJS 423

De zifras
Spain, *c.* 1600

The author of this work identifies himself as a cryptographer working for the viceroy of Navarre; his responsibilities encompassed decoding correspondence from Oran (Algeria) and Rome. He dedicates the work to Juan Fernandez de Velasco, a high-ranking Spanish official. It begins with a general discourse on the theory of signs, including not only ciphers but also such disciplines as astrology, music, geography, logic and rhetoric; mention is made of alternative writing systems – hieroglyphs and Chinese characters – as

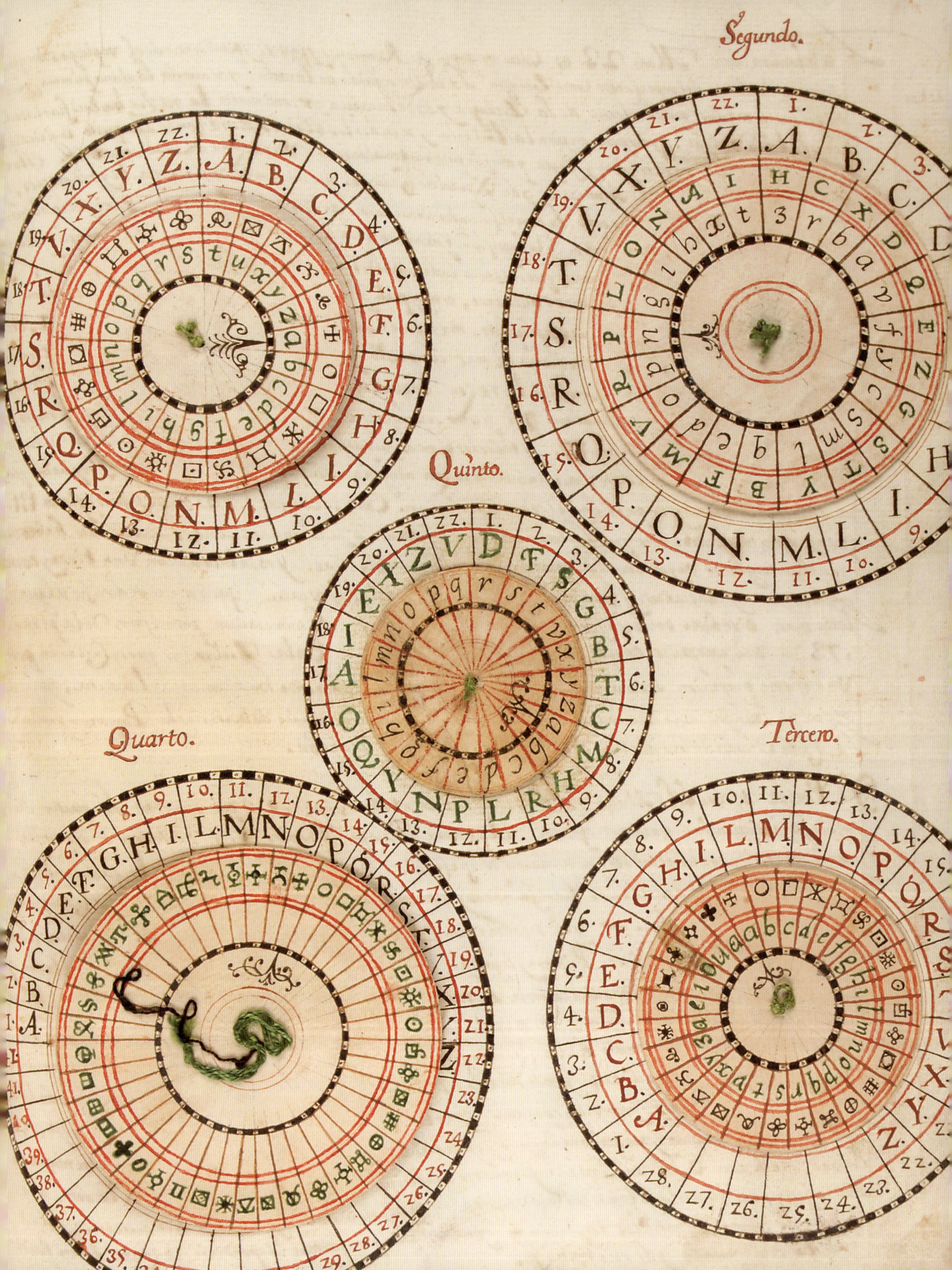

Segundo.
Quinto.
Quarto.
Tercero.

well as emblems and other types of symbol. This is followed by twenty-four methods of encoding and decoding, which include moving volvelles (revolving paper discs attached to the pages with pins and thread) and grilles for placing over texts. Dating from *c.* 1600, the manuscript precedes the first printed work on ciphers by a Spaniard, the *Steganographia* of Juan Caramuel y Lobkowitz (published in Latin, 1635).

DESCRIPTION Paper, 364 pages, 372 x 280 mm, in Spanish, neat script in brown ink; 31 full-page illustrations, some with moving parts. Contemporary Spanish calf binding.

PROVENANCE Martayan Lan, cat. 28 (September 2001), no. 189

25 LJS 199

Isaac Newton, *Artis analyticae specimina vel geometria analytica* Cambridge, *c.* 1710

This manuscript contains early work by Isaac Newton (1642–1727) on calculus, specifically on "fluxions" or rates of change with respect to time. Newton began his work on this subject around 1664; in 1669 he became aware of similar work being done by Nicolaus Mercator (1619–1687) and wrote up the results of his research in a tract entitled *De analysi per aequationes infinitas.* He expanded this a year later in the work contained in this manuscript, under the title *Methodus fluxionum et serierum infinitarum.* This treatise circulated in manuscript but was not published in Newton's lifetime.

Around 1710, the present copy of the *Methodus fluxionum* was made by William Jones (see LJS 462 [no. 17]), who gave it the title it bears here. Jones used the manuscript as source material for his work of 1711, *Analysis per quantitatum series, fluxiones ac differentias,* in which he argued for the primacy of Newton's research into calculus over that of Leibniz; rivalry between the two mathematicians had been a matter of public debate since 1699.

Jones's copy of Newton's text was later used in the preparation of Samuel Horsley's 1779 edition of Newton's *Opera omnia,* in which Jones's later title is maintained; Newton's autograph copy, which Horsley also used for his edition, was by this time lacking its first folio. Jones deposited his manuscript in the library of Thomas Parker, 1st Earl of Macclesfield, at Shirburn Castle.

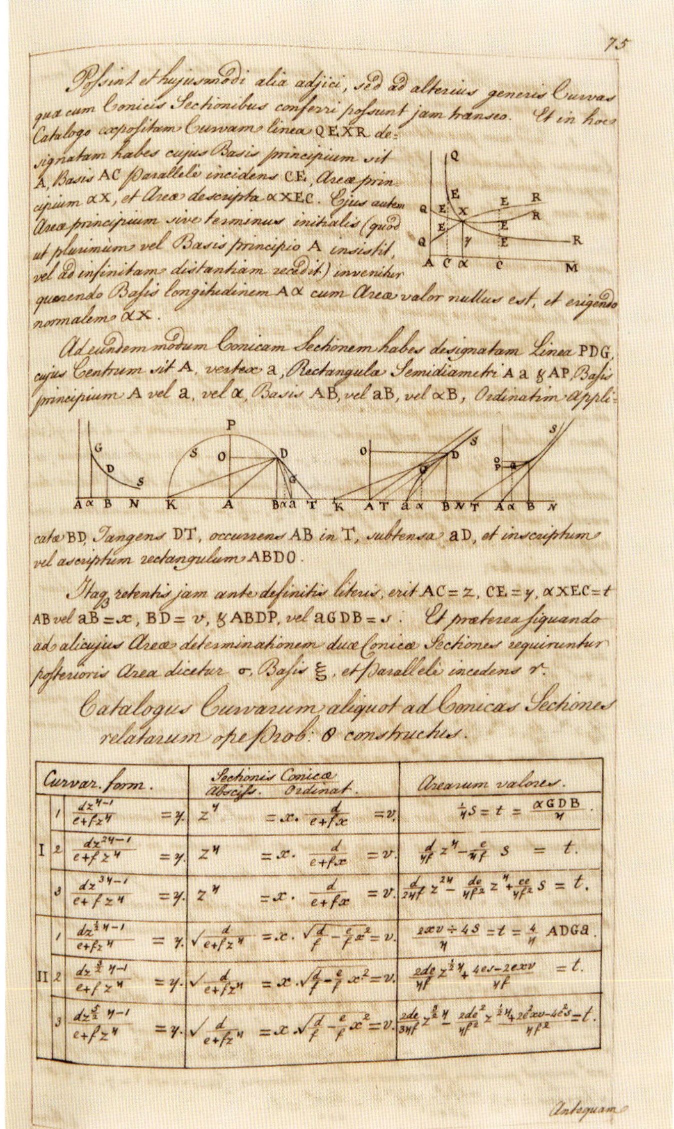

LJS 199
f. 75r

DESCRIPTION Paper, 72 folios, 310 x 200 mm, in Latin, cursive script, brown ink, margins outlined in red, catchwords. Contemporary reversed calf binding.
PROVENANCE William Jones; Thomas Parker, 1st Earl of Macclesfield; Nigel Phillips; Bernard Quaritch, cat. 1135 (1991), no. 64, and cat. 1175 (1994), no. 78; John Stanitz, ms. 30
BIBLIOGRAPHY DSB X, 45-50, 87 n. 41; ODNB XXX 661; Whiteside 32-353; Horsley I

26 LJS 173

Enchiridion mathematicum and *Prohemium astrologiae*
Wittenberg, 1629–32

The *Enchiridion mathematicum* is an introduction to
mathematics, as taught at the University of Wittenberg in the
first half of the seventeenth century. It deals with a variety of
topics, from basic arithmetic to complex Euclidean geometry,
and was apparently written by a student of Ambrosius
Rhodius (1577–1633), professor of mathematics at Wittenberg
from 1608 and author of a commentary on Euclid's *Elements*
(Wittenberg, 1634). The second text is a comprehensive
introduction to astrology, written in the house of Paul Roeber
(1587–1651), professor of theology at Wittenberg from 1627
and author of a work on astrology published in 1627.

DESCRIPTION Paper, 168 folios, 219 x 178 mm, in Latin, humanistic
cursive script, brown and red ink, at least four scribes. Modern
mottled calf over paper board binding.
PROVENANCE Robert Honeyman; Sotheby's, 2 May 1979, lot 1214;
H.P. Kraus, cat. 155 (1980), no. 10; John Stanitz, ms. 4

27 LJS 183

Student's notebook on arithmetic and algebra
Possibly Cambridge, *c.* 1675–85

This notebook gives an idea of the typical course of studies in
mathematics at Cambridge University in the later seventeenth
century.

DESCRIPTION Paper, 141 folios, c. 149 x 99 mm, in English and
Latin, cursive script, brown ink. Original parchment binding.
PROVENANCE Sir Thomas Phillipps (according to H.P. Kraus; no
label or stamp); Robinson Brothers, 1945; H.P. Kraus; John Stanitz, ms. 14

28 LJS 208 and 209

Giovanni Battista Nigroni, *Opusculum mathematicum,*
with *In libros magnorum moralium questiones selecte*
Possibly Genoa, 1675

These manuscripts, a two-volume thesis, contain a tract on
geometry, notably that of the regular polygon.

DESCRIPTION Paper; 94 pages, 209 x 158 mm (vol. 1) and 76 pages,
207 x 154 mm (vol. 2); in Latin, cursive script, brown ink; title within

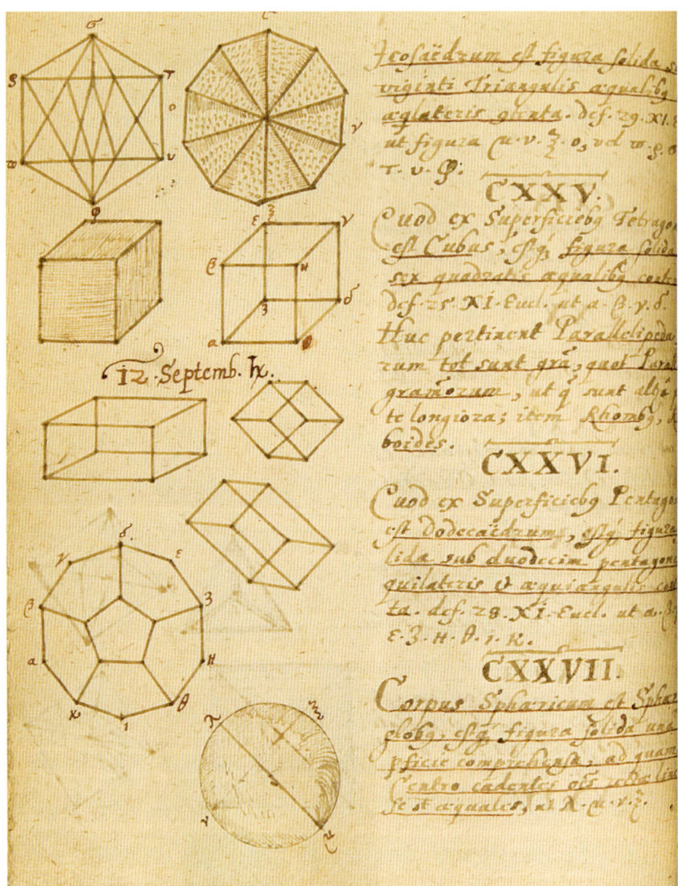

cartouche of ink and wash, diagrams throughout (vol. 1).
Contemporary parchment binding with author's initials G B N.
PROVENANCE Apparently submitted by Nigroni as a thesis under
the direction of the Italian Jesuit Giovanni Salvaterra (1632–1680);
John Stanitz, ms. 39

29 LJS 320

Geometria
Germany, 18th century

A discussion of planar geometry, trigonometry, logarithms,
stereometry and perspective, with a substantial number of
practical problems, and horological exercises at the end.

DESCRIPTION Paper, 159 pages, 162 x 110 mm, in German and Latin,
cursive script, black ink, rubrics and headings in red; highly finished
geometrical and surveying diagrams and drawings on almost every
page, in coloured inks and sometimes wash. Marbled paper over
board binding.
PROVENANCE Martayan Lan, August 1999

30 LJS 181

Textbook notes on plane and spherical geometry
France, after 1789

These notes cover some of the elementary procedures of
constructing figures, aspects of spherical geometry such as
the spherical triangle and its properties, and some basic
points in the theory of proportion. Four of the pages bear
calculations in advanced algebra, employing cubic and
quadratic equations.

DESCRIPTION Paper, 12 folios, 210 x 125 mm, in French, cursive
script, brown ink; 14 small geometric diagrams in margins.
Disbound.
PROVENANCE Sir Thomas Phillipps (according to Kraus; no plate or
stamp); Robinson Brothers, 1945; H.P. Kraus, ms. 842; John Stanitz, ms. 12

31 LJS 213

Joseph Nicolas Nicollet, *Traité élémentaire
et synthétique des sections coniques*
Chambéry, France, 1809

An illustrated treatise on conic sections.

DESCRIPTION Paper, 63 folios, 281 x 206 mm, in French, cursive
script, brown ink. Contemporary blue and green paper board binding.
PROVENANCE Thomas Heller, Inc., 1995; John Stanitz, ms. 44

32 LJS 221

Augustin Louis Cauchy, *Mémoire sur les rapports qui existent
entre le calcul des résidus et le calcul des limites*
Paris, 27 November 1831

The title, in full, translates as 'Memoir on the relations
between the calculus of residuals and the calculus of limits,
and on the advantages offered by these two new calculi in the
solution of algebraic equations or transcendental equations'.

DESCRIPTION Paper, 80 pages, 214 x 176 mm, in French, cursive
script, black ink. Original marbled paper board binding.
PROVENANCE Written by Augustin Cauchy for the Académie des
Sciences in Paris, dated 27 November 1831; two early ownership
stamps on title; bookplate inside front cover: *Bib. Dom. Laval. S.J.*;
Rodolphe Chamonal, no. 51, May 1997; John Stanitz, ms. 52

33 LJS 206

Karl Theodor Wilhelm Weierstrass, *Theorie der
analytischen Functionen*, lecture notes by A.L. Daniels
Berlin, 1879–81

K.T.W. Weierstrauss (1815–1897) was a leading German
mathematician.

DESCRIPTION Paper, 328 pages, 252 x 209 mm, in German, cursive
script, brown ink. Original half cloth and marbled board binding.
PROVENANCE A.L. Daniels (front flyleaf: *A.L. Daniels/Berlin-Göttingen
1879-1903/49 Mansfield Ave./Burlington VT/1910*); Sydney Ross,
Rensselaer Polytechnic Institute, Troy, NY (bookplate); 19th Century
Shop, cat. 39, p. 23; John Stanitz, ms. 37

34 LJS 207

Karl Theodor Wilhelm Weierstrass, *Theorie der
Variationsrechnung*, lecture notes by A.L. Daniels
Berlin, 1879–81

DESCRIPTION Paper, 405 pages, 269 x 225 mm, in German and
Latin, cursive script, brown ink. Original half cloth and marbled
board binding.
PROVENANCE A.L. Daniels; Sydney Ross, Rensselaer Polytechnic
Institute, Troy, NY (bookplate); 19th Century Shop, cat. 39, p. 23;
John Stanitz, ms. 38

35 LJS 218

Student's notes, corrected by Jules Henri Poincaré
Sorbonne, Paris, *c.* 1881–83

These notes were taken from the lecture course in
mathematics given by Henri Poincaré (1854–1912) at the
Sorbonne in the early 1880s soon after he started teaching in
1879. The attribution of the marginal corrections to Poincaré
himself is based on an early manuscript note.

DESCRIPTION Paper, *c.* 450 pages in total: four notebooks, 13
assignments and three letters, varying dimensions; in French, cursive
script, black ink. Disbound.
PROVENANCE Written for his use by E. Pomey at the Sorbonne,
c. 1881–83; Rodolphe Chamonal, *Livres anciens* (April 1997), no. 37;
John Stanitz, ms. 49

IV Astronomy, Astrology and the Calendar

The medieval conception of the cosmos was essentially that of Aristotle, as modified by Ptolemy: the earth was fixed at the centre of the universe, surrounded by solid spheres which held the planets – the Moon, Mercury, Venus, the Sun, Mars, Jupiter, Saturn – and, beyond these, the sphere of the fixed stars. Increasing accuracy of measurement and calculation rendered the shortcomings of this model gradually more apparent and a number of attempts were made to refine it. Nonetheless, the geocentric system remained in broad acceptance into the seventeenth century, and alternative hypotheses, such as that of Copernicus, proposing that the earth travelled around the sun, were greeted with scepticism.

Aside from its task of determining the structure of the universe, astronomical observation was necessary for calculating the calendar and for navigation. The influence of the heavenly bodies on earthly life was commonly accepted; their positions therefore served as a basis for setting auspicious or inauspicious days for many branches of human activity.

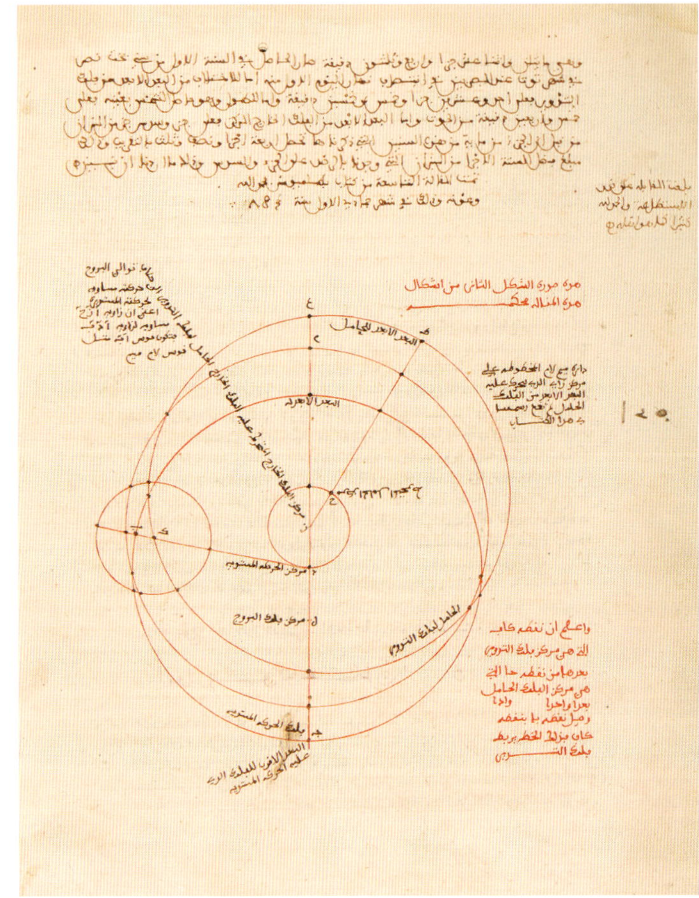

1 LJS 268

Ptolemy, *Almagest*
Andalusia, AH 783 / 1381

The cornerstone of ancient and medieval astronomy was Ptolemy's *Almagest*. Written in Greek in the second century, it constituted a complete exposition of ancient astronomy, organized in thirteen books. It was translated into Arabic several times during the ninth century; the title *Almagest* derives from the Arabic *al-majisti,* a calque on the Greek *megistē,* meaning 'greatest'. The Arabic version was translated into Latin in 1175 by Gerard of Cremona, and it was this, rather than a little-known Latin translation of the Greek text made *c.* 1160, which dominated western astronomy until the seventeenth century. Few manuscript copies of the Arabic text survive, however.

This manuscript provides intriguing testimony of the mingling of cultures and intellectual traditions in fourteenth-

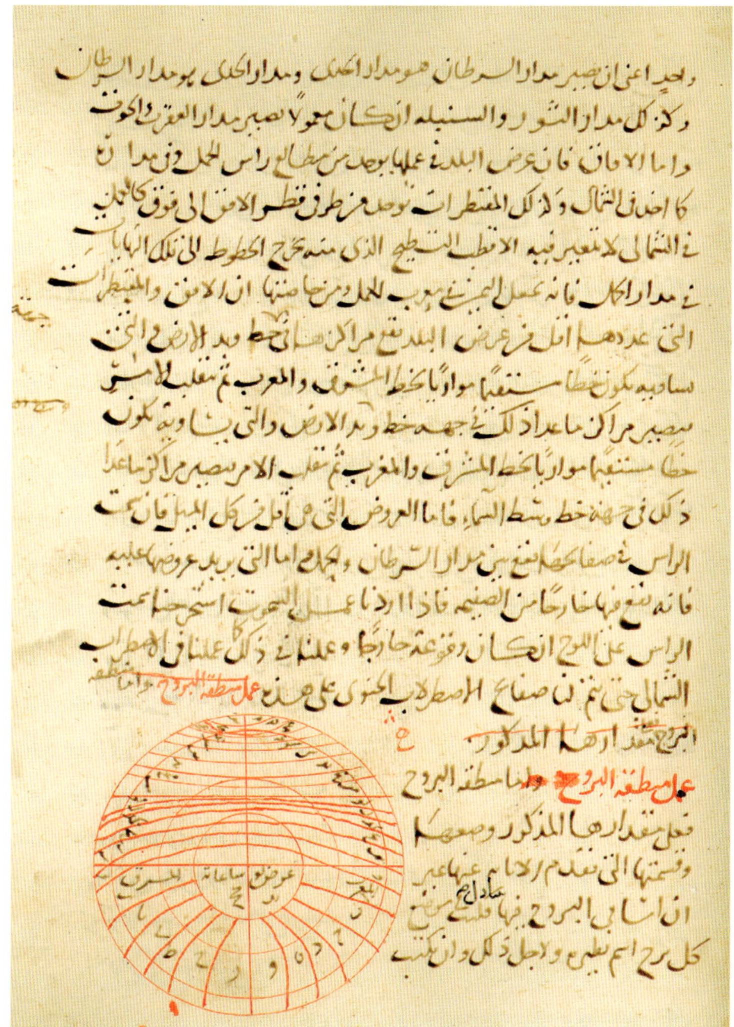

LJS 478, f. 16v

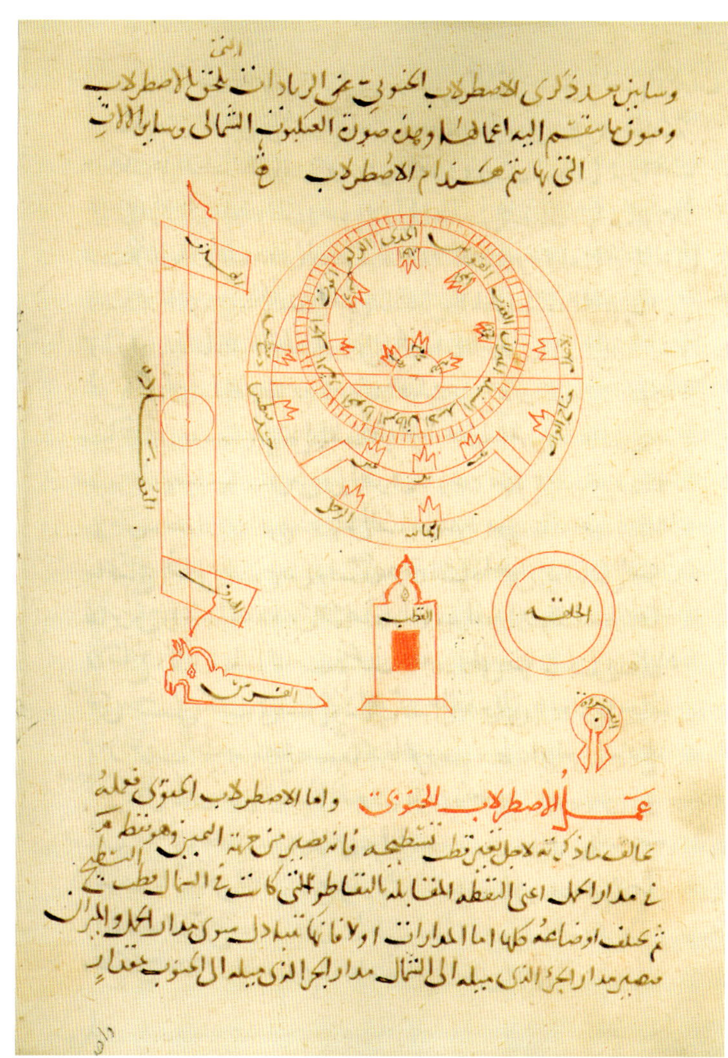

LJS 478, f. 17r

century Spain. It was written by a Muslim scribe, Ahmad ibn Salamah Sanhaja, for his teacher, a Jewish astronomer known as Qursunna al-Isra'ili. Qursunna was employed by Peter IV, King of Aragon. The manuscript is dated according to the Muslim, Jewish and Christian calendars, to 783, 5141 and 1381 respectively.

DESCRIPTION Paper, 185 folios, 280 x 215 mm, in Arabic, maghrebi / andalusi script, titles and headings in red; numerous small diagrams and tables. Stamped morocco binding with flap.
PROVENANCE Qursunna al-Isra'ili; Imam Ahmad Lutfullah, Muhammad al Ra'is and Imam Muhammad Abd al-Kathir al-Kinani; Misjo Rinijo (Monsieur Rinillot?), French ambassador, 1922; Sam Fogg, June 1998
BIBLIOGRAPHY DSB XI 186-206; Toomer

2 LJS 478

Al-Biruni, *Kitab fi isti'ab al-wujuh al-mumkina fi sana'at al-asturlab* (On the construction of the astrolabe); two treatises attributed to Nastulus; other astronomical works
Persia or Anatolia, 23 and 26 Jumadi II 625 / 28 and 31 May 1228

Abu'l-Rayhan al-Biruni (973–c. 1050) was a contemporary and correspondent of Ibn Sina (Avicenna; see LJS 446 [V, no. 1] *et sqq.*). He ranks among the foremost mathematicians and astronomers of the medieval Muslim world, and also wrote on a diverse variety of other subjects, including geography and natural sciences. His treatise at the beginning of this compilation, 'On the construction of the astrolabe', discusses different sorts of astrolabe in which the standard discs representing projections of the northern sky are replaced with various combinations of northern and southern projections.

These variant astrolabes, known as 'crab' and 'drum' astrolabes, had, according to al-Biruni, been invented by the tenth-century astronomer and maker of astrolabes Nastulus, along with a *huqq al-qamar* ('box for the moon'), which was a mechanism added to an astrolabe to model the changes of the phases of the moon. In the present manuscript al-Biruni's work is followed by two works on these inventions. These previously unknown treatises have now also been attributed to Nastulus.

A treatise on an instrument for finding the *qibla* (direction of Mecca) and two further treatises on the ecliptic and the compass complete the manuscript.

DESCRIPTION Paper, 87 folios, 254 x 170 mm, in Arabic, naskh script, brown and black ink, title words in red; 115 diagrams, 7 tables. 13th-century binding with replacement flap.

PROVENANCE Sam Fogg, 2006

3 LJS 412

Qusta ibn Luqa, *Risala fi'l-'amal bil-kura* (Treatise on working with the globe) and other texts
Cairo, Safar 950 AH / May–June 1543

Qusta ibn Luqa (*c.* 820–*c.* 912), a Christian by birth, was a renowned translator, physician and astronomer active in Baghdad. His 'Treatise on working with the globe', contained in the first twenty pages of this manuscript, is the earliest known comprehensive treatise on the spherical astrolabe, an instrument which, in Qusta's words, takes the form of "a globe, fashioned after the picture of the firmament"; it can be used to show "the discrepancy and difference in the journey of the sun and moon, and the other stars, according to the countries; and the cause of length and shortness of day", among other applications. This work was translated into Latin, Hebrew, Spanish and Italian. A revised version of the Spanish translation was included in *Los libros de saber del astronomia*, a compilation of astronomical works made under the aegis of King Alfonso X in 1276–77. Also included in the present manuscript are two short anonymous treatises, *Risalat*

LJS 4
f. 18r

kaifiyat al-arsad (Treatise on the manner of astronomy) and *Al-'amal bi'l-usturlab* (On the use of the astrolabe).

DESCRIPTION Paper, 18 folios, 230 x 152 mm, fine Ottoman naskh script, significant words and phrases in red and green, titles in larger green naskh; 9 diagrams in red and black. Marbled paper wrappers.
PROVENANCE Sotheby's, London, 1 June 1987, lot 138
BIBLIOGRAPHY EI I 727, V 529-30; Worrell; Sarton I 602; HUM 552-54; LDS I 153-208

4 LJS 392

Al-Tusi, *Tahrir al-mijisti*, with commentary of al-Nisaburi
Persia?, AH 13 Dhu'l Qa'da 813 / 9 March 1411

A focal point for the continued promulgation of the

DESCRIPTION Paper, 223 folios, 262 x 167 mm, in Arabic, small naskh script, black ink, overlining in red, some rubrication in gold. 17th-century brown morocco binding with flap.
PROVENANCE Seal impressions, erased; Sam Fogg, November 2000
BIBLIOGRAPHY EI I 1100; X 750-01; DSB XI 202; Sarton II 1008

5 LJS 407

Anthology of the work of al-Tusi
Persia, early 14th century

The manuscript is in an elegant personal hand, possibly that of a scholar writing for his own use.

DESCRIPTION Paper, 76 folios, 166 x 110 mm, in Arabic, elegant personal naskh script, black ink, chapter headings and other significant words in red, occasional later marginal commentary in sepia; 15 diagrams in red and black. Later red morocco gilt-stamped binding.
PROVENANCE Sam Fogg, March 2001

6 LJS 388

Al-Jaghmini, *Al-mulakhkhas fi'l hay'a*
Persia, AH 29 Rabi' I, 786 / 21 May 1384

This very popular astronomical textbook, entitled 'The Epitome of Astronomy', was written in Arabic by an Iranian astronomer, Mahmud al-Jaghmini, and also translated into Persian. Little is known of its author; according to some accounts, he died in 1221, according to others, in 1344–45. It has been argued that he used al-Tusi's *Tadhkira fi 'ilm al-hay'a* as a source, and that the first date is therefore incorrect. The hand suggests that this manuscript originates from Persia and was copied by a practitioner or student of astronomy for his own use.

The wide circulation of this work is further attested by the number of commentaries which were written on it, as the following examples show (LJS 410, 408, 474 [nos. 7, 8, 9]).

DESCRIPTION Paper, 20 folios, 168 x 98 mm, in Arabic, neat nasta'liq script in black ink, copious marginal notes, some words highlighted in red; five astronomical diagrams in red. Red morocco binding.

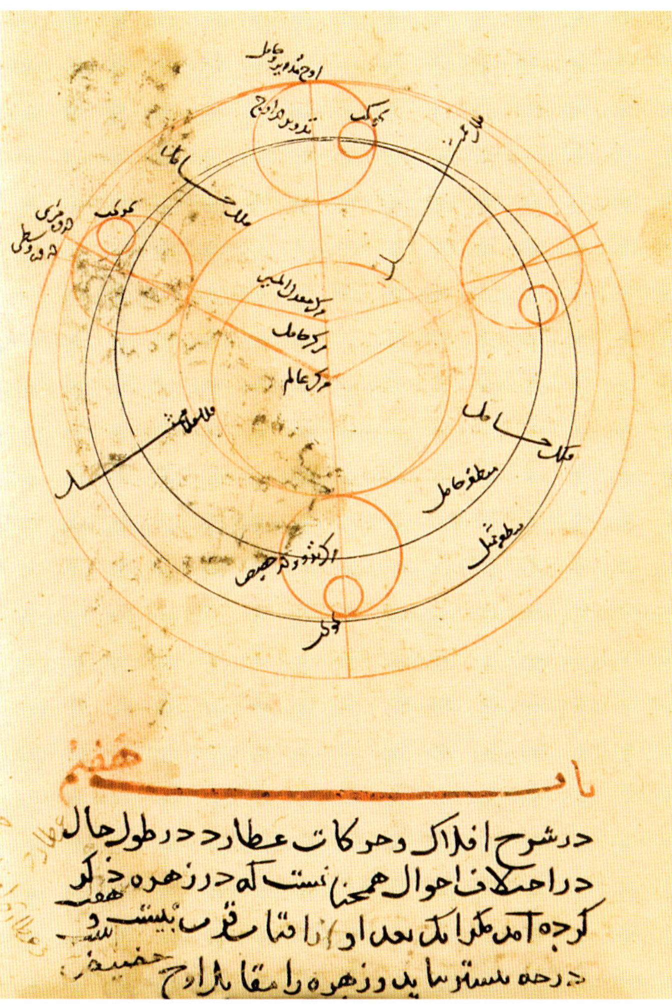

LJS 412
f. 54v

Ptolemaic system in the Islamic world was the work of Nasir al-Din al-Tusi (1201–1274). Ptolemy's *Almagest* had been translated into Arabic several times in the ninth century AD; over the next centuries inconsistencies in Ptolemy's system became apparent, and al-Tusi proposed revisions of the Ptolemaic system in his *Tadhkira fi 'ilm al-hay'a* (Memorandum of astronomy), a synthesis of the *Almagest*, condensed and put into narrative form for the general reader. It was a popular work which became the subject of numerous commentaries (see LJS 279 [no. 10]). He also provided his contemporaries with a new recension of Ptolemy's text, the *Tahrir al-mijisti* (1247). In 1304-05 this recension was itself commented on by Hasan ibn Muhammad Nizam al-Din al-Nisaburi. Both the recension and its later commentary are contained in this manuscript. They were copied by Muhammad ibn al-Husayn al-Hasan in 1411 AD.

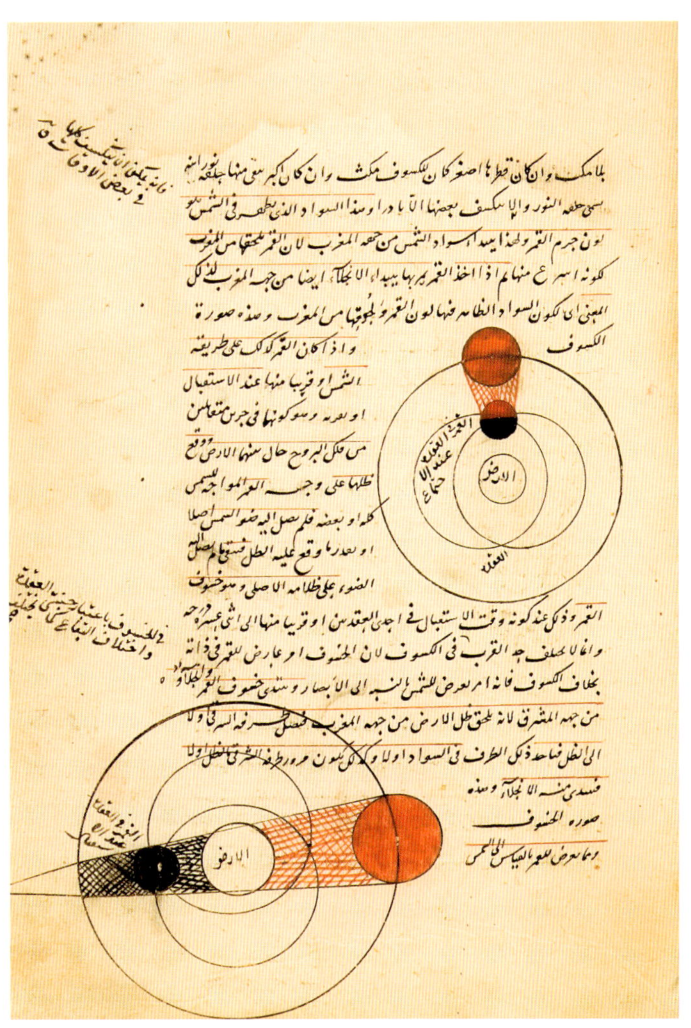

PROVENANCE Seal impressions of Muhammad al-Dawla,
AH 1246 (?) / 1830-31; Sam Fogg, cat. 22, no. 60
BIBLIOGRAPHY Sarton III 699-700; EI II 378

7 LJS 410

Commentary on al-Jaghmini's *Al-mulakhkhas fi'l hay'a*
Persia, possibly 15th century

This manuscript, filled with diagrams and notes made by
many different readers, demonstrates the use of al-Jaghmini's
'Epitome of Astronomy' in a pedagogic context.

DESCRIPTION Paper, 62 folios, 220 x 140 mm, in Arabic, nasta'liq
script, significant sentences underlined in red, extensive marginal
commentary; numerous diagrams in red. Modern binding.
PROVENANCE Sam Fogg, March 2001

8 LJS 408

Qadi-Zade al-Rumi, commentary on al-Jaghmini's *Al-mulakhkhas fi'l hay'a*
Samarqand, end of Ramadan 830 AH/ 25 July 1427

Qadi-Zade al-Rumi (*c.* 1359–*c.* 1432) was one of three
astronomers to be intimately involved in the famous
Samarqand observatory (*marsad*) established under the
patronage of Ulugh Beg, governor of Transoxiana, in 1420 (see
LJS 400 [no. 38]). Aside from the detailed observations which
he carried out there, he is best known for this work, a
commentary on Mahmud al-Jaghmini's *Al-mulakhkhas fi'l hay'a*
(see LJS 388 [no. 6]), completed, according to a pun in the
colophon, in AH 813. The present copy was made in AH 830,
during Qadi-Zade's own lifetime; indeed, in noting one

marginal comment the copyist claims that he heard it from the author himself (f. 59). The work begins with a dedication to Ulugh Beg, grandson of Timur and a skilled astronomer in his own right.

DESCRIPTION Paper, 65 folios, 168 x 117 mm, in Arabic with some Persian, compact nasta'liq script, black ink, red overlinings, copious marginal notes; 23 astronomical diagrams in red and black. Brown morocco binding, tooled and gilded.

PROVENANCE Persian seal impressions at beginning and end; undated owner's signature, "The guilty servant of God, Haydar ibn Shahi Hamdani"; Sam Fogg, March 2001

BIBLIOGRAPHY EI VI 601; XII 502

9 LJS 474

Qadi-Zade al-Rumi, commentary on al-Jaghmini's *Al-mulakhkhas fi'l hay'a*
Timurid Empire, north-east Persia, 15th or 16th century

Another copy of the previous work (LJS 408 [no. 8]).

DESCRIPTION Paper, 92 folios, 235 x 160 mm, in Arabic, 15 lines to a page, over 20 representations and explanatory images of the solar system. Leather binding.

PROVENANCE Bouman Oriental Books, 28 March 2005

10 LJS 279

Al-Khidri, *Al-Takmila fi sharh al-tadhkira*
Persia, 17th century or later

The role of al-Tusi's *Tadhkira fi 'ilm al-hay'a* (Memorandum of astronomy) in the promulgation of the Ptolemaic system has already been mentioned (see LJS 392 [no. 4]). The considerable influence of this work is attested by the large number of commentaries and supercommentaries which developed around it.

In 1507, 'Abd al-'Ali ibn Muhammad ibn Husayn al-Birjandi composed a commentary on al-Tusi's work, *Sharh al-tadhkira*. A supercommentary on this work was then written by Shams al-Din Muhammad al-Khidri (otherwise known as al-Khafri), which is contained in this manuscript. Al-Khidri completed this 'Complement to the Commentary on the Memorandum' on 4 Muharram 932 / 23 October 1525.

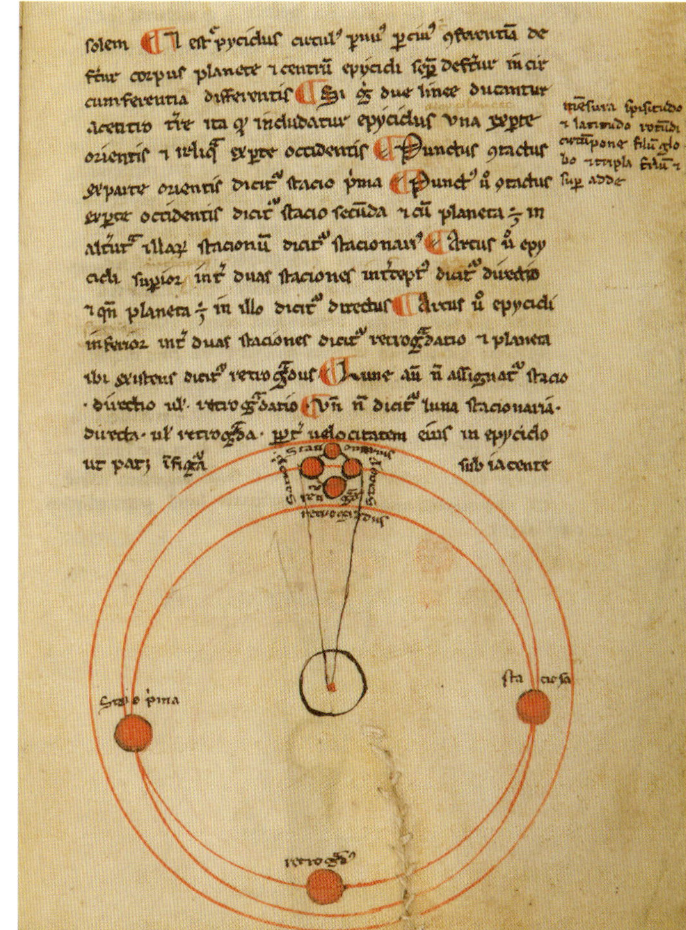

LJS 26
f. 28r

DESCRIPTION Paper, 292 folios, 296 x 177 mm, in Persian, neat nasta'liq script, significant phrases underlined in red, marginal annotations and commentary in red and black, margins ruled in colours and gold; opening illuminated headpiece, numerous diagrams in black, red and gold. Red morocco binding, gilt.

PROVENANCE Sotheby's, London, 15 October 1998, lot 42

BIBLIOGRAPHY Ragep 63-64

11 LJS 26

Johannes de Sacrobosco, *Algorismus* and *Tractatus de sphaera*
Italy, mid-13th century

The single most important vehicle for the reception of the Ptolemaic model in the Latin medieval world was Johannes de Sacrobosco's *De sphaera*, probably written in the first quarter of the thirteenth century (for another example, again together

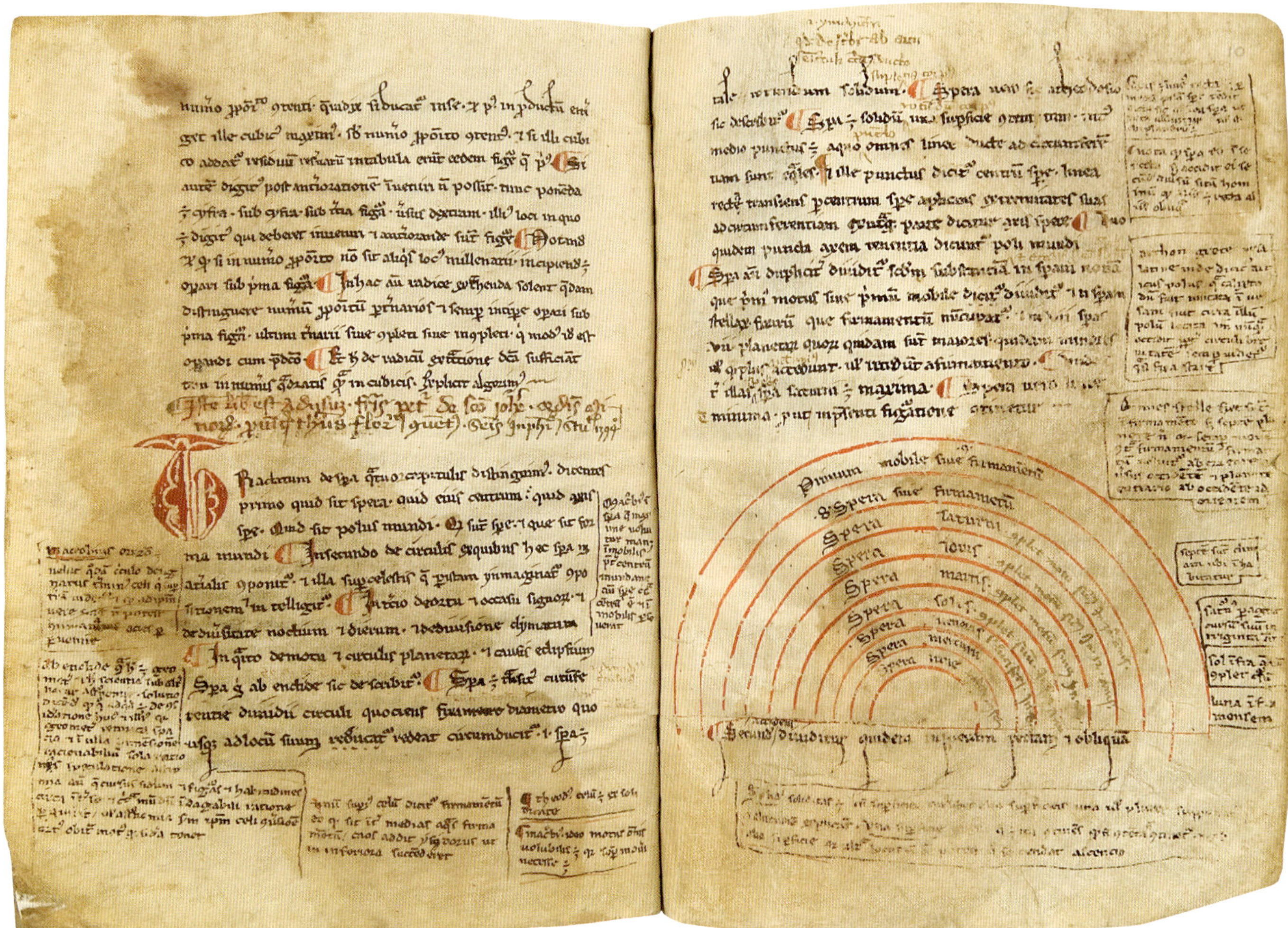

LJS 26
ff. 9v-10r

with Sacrobosco's *Algorismus*, see LJS 216 [III, no. 16]).
Sacrobosco used not only the *Almagest*, which had been
translated into Latin in 1175, but also Arabic commentators on
Ptolemy as well as earlier Latin sources such as Macrobius's
'Commentary on the Dream of Scipio'. He described a
spherical earth, divided into five climatic zones, sitting at the
centre of the universe; it was surrounded by nine concentric
revolving spheres containing the planets and stars. The seven
diagrams in this manuscript include the five zones; the
movements of the sun and moon around the earth;
explanations of lunar and solar eclipses; and a serpent
encircling a flower and biting its own tail.

Sacrobosco died *c.* 1256; this is therefore a near-
contemporary copy of his works. According to an annotation
on f. 9v, the present manuscript was used by a Florentine
physics student, Pietro di Santo Giovanni, in 1399.
Sacrobosco's works remained a core element of the university
curriculum as late as the seventeenth century.

DESCRIPTION Parchment, 31 folios, 180 x 134 mm, in Latin, early
Gothic script, black ink; 17 painted initials, 10 astronomical
diagrams. Modern binding.
PROVENANCE Brother Pietro di Santo Giovanni; Sotheby's, London,
2 December 1986, lot 35
BIBLIOGRAPHY Sarton II 618

12 LJS 64

Illustrations to Georg von Peuerbach's *Novae theoricae planetarum*
Northern Italy, mid-16th century

In the Renaissance, while Sacrobosco's work (see LJS 26 [no. 11]) continued to be used, mathematicians and astronomers began to provide updated and more accurate techniques and data. Of importance among these was Georg von Peuerbach (1423–1461), whose teaching book on planetary theory, *Novae theoricae planetarum*, appeared in 1454. It had a long-lasting influence: first published in 1474, it continued to circulate widely, both in print and in manuscript, into the seventeenth century. It was translated into French, Italian and Hebrew and was the subject of numerous commentaries. Peuerbach's view that the planetary spheres were solid, crystalline structures remained widely accepted until it was disproved by Tycho Brahe in the later sixteenth century.

The present manuscript contains 78 diagrams designed to explicate Peuerbach's text, many of which have been ingeniously constructed to include volvelles (revolving paper discs; see also LJS 423 [III, no. 24]). These diagrams provide information about the orbits of the sun, moon, planets and signs of the zodiac. Peuerbach himself wrote a treatise on the making of such moving diagrams, entitled *Speculum planetarum*. He was well known as a teacher, both in northern Italy and in Vienna, and it is likely that he used such constructions during his teaching. The present manuscript was presumably used for the same purpose, since in 1655 it was owned by Francesco Rolandi, a teacher of mathematics from Turin.

DESCRIPTION Paper, 39 folios, 288 x 214 mm, 78 diagrams (25 with moving parts), in black, red and brown ink with yellow washes; captions in Latin, fine humanistic script. Tooled contemporary dark brown morocco binding.

PROVENANCE Francesco Rolandi, 1650 and 1655; Pietro Guiseppe Mattei Cattochii, 1708-09; Libreria Antiquaria Hoepli, *Livres, manuscrits et imprimés* (1954), no. 2; Honeyman, Ms. Astron. 4 (Ms. 9); Sotheby's, New York, 2 May 1979, lot 1112; Laurence Witten, cat. 10 (1979), no. 65; Christie's, London, 26 June 1991, lot 43; Sam Fogg, cat. 15 (1992), no. 48; William Patrick Watson, cat. 7 (1996), no. 79

BIBLIOGRAPHY DSB XV 473-79; Aiton

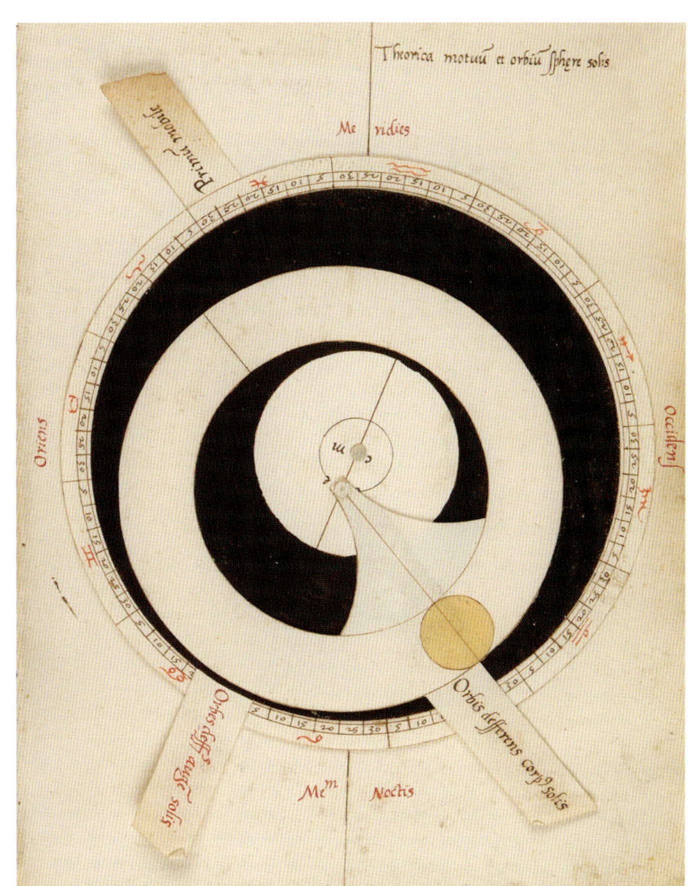

LJS 64
f. 8r

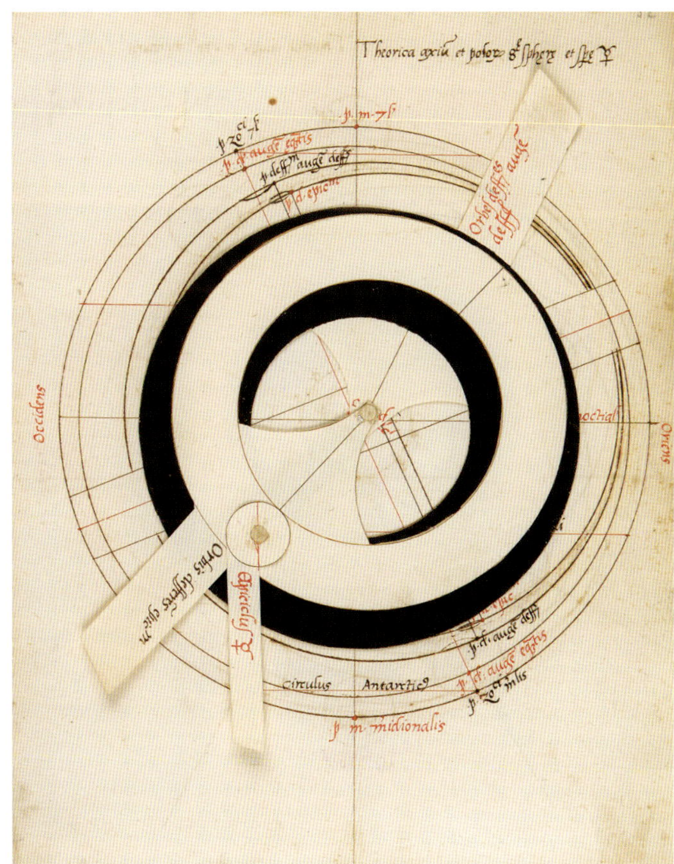

LJS 64
f. 52r

13 LJS 472

Abraham bar Hiyya, *Heshbon mahalekhot ha-kokhavim*
Possibly Spain, 15th century

Abraham bar Hiyya (d. *c.* 1136) was a philosopher,
mathematician and astronomer living in Barcelona. He is
generally considered to have been the first author to expound
the Ptolemaic system in Hebrew. The work in question,
Hokhmat ha-hizzayon (Calculation of the course of the stars),
was a two-part treatise on geography and astronomy of
which the second part is contained in this manuscript.
Abraham was regarded in later centuries as an authority on
intercalation, which is one of the matters discussed in this
text. As such, he also compiled astronomical tables, which
were influential for several centuries (see LJS 57 [no. 24]).

DESCRIPTION Paper, 98 folios, 198 x 140 mm, in Hebrew, Sephardic
semi-cursive script, brown ink, several glosses on marginal tabs.
Paper covered boards.

PROVENANCE Samuel David Luzzatto; Solomon Halberstam,
ms. 110; Montefiore Endowment, no. 422; Sotheby's, New York,
27 October 2004, lot 307

BIBLIOGRAPHY EJ II 130-33

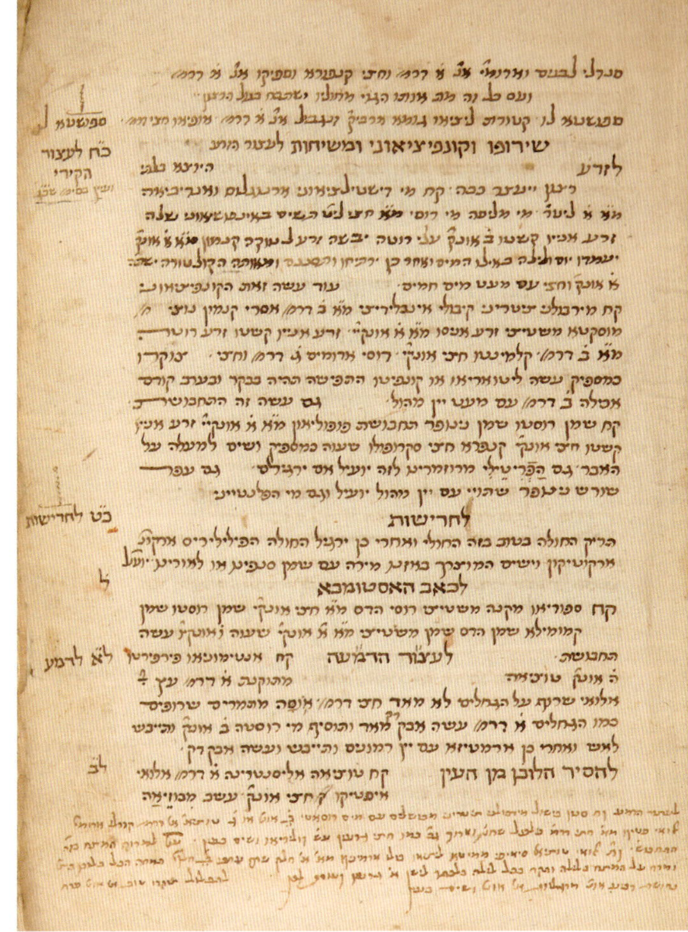

LJS 4
f. 5r

14 LJS 42

Moses Almosnino, Two Scientific Commentaries
Salonika, 1551

As described above (LJS 26 [no. 11]) the fundamental
university textbook on astronomy in the Middle Ages and
Renaissance was Johannes de Sacrobosco's *De sphaera*, which
work was updated in the fifteenth century by Georg von
Peuerbach's *Novae theoricae planetarum* (see LJS 64 [no. 12]). In
the mid-sixteenth century, despite the new theories proposed
by Copernicus (see LJS 397, 175 [nos. 16, 19]), these works
continued to be read and commentated – not only in Latin
but also in Hebrew, as this manuscript shows. The two
commentaries included here are the work of Moses
Almosnino (*c.* 1515–*c.* 1585), a rabbi and scholar in the Jewish
community in Salonika, then part of the Ottoman empire.

Almosnino based his commentary on the Hebrew
translation of *De sphaera* by Solomon Abigdor (completed

1399). For Peuerbach's work he used the version of his
colleague Ahron Afia. Almosnino composed his two works in
1546, as stated in the colophon on f. 168r of the present
manuscript; they generally circulated together under the title
Beit elohim ve-sha'ar ha-shamayim (The House of the Lord and
the Gate of Heaven, a quotation from Genesis 28: 17). As was
common among sixteenth-century commentators of
Sacrobosco, Almosnino included a great deal of extra
information, much of which related to new geographical
discoveries: he mentions America (f. 23v), the Caribbean
islands and the Portuguese discoveries in 1499 of San Antonio
and San Luzio.

According to its colophons (ff. 76 and 168) this manuscript
was written by the scribe Chaim Luzio for Perez ben Yehuda
Mintz Ashkenazi in 1551, a mere five years after the text was
composed.

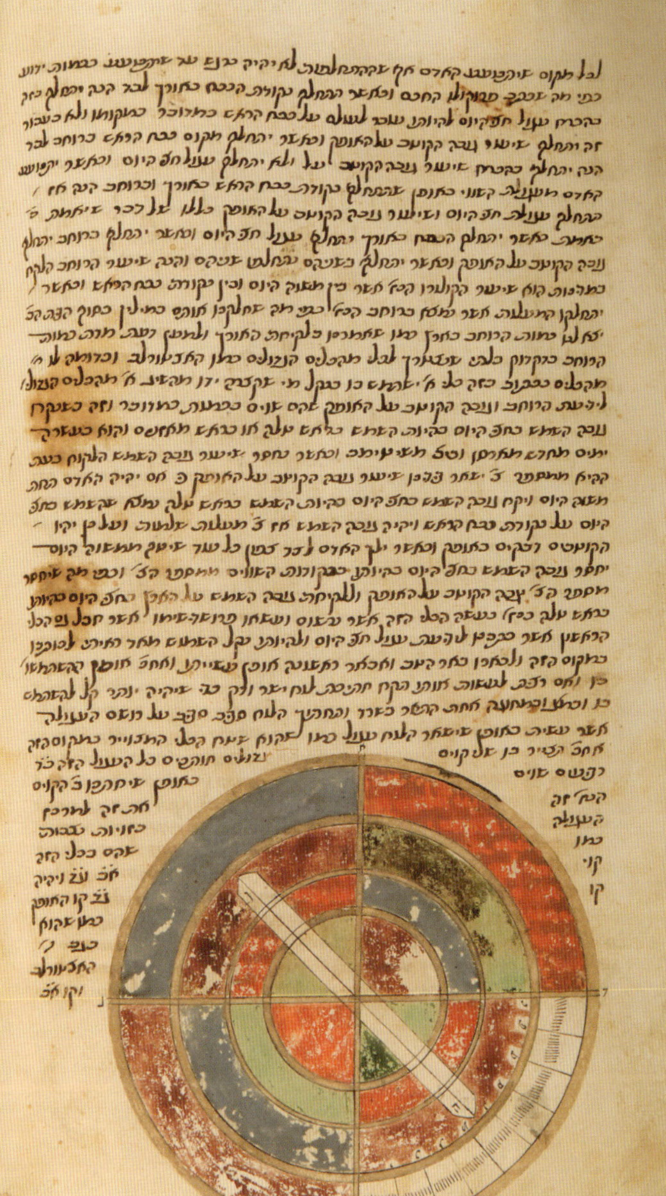

DESCRIPTION Paper, 169 folios, 268 x 187 mm, in Hebrew, Near-Eastern Spanish rabbinic cursive script, dark brown ink, headings in larger script; approximately 144 diagrams, 8 in colour. Greek blind-stamped goatskin binding.
PROVENANCE Peretz ben Yehuda Mintz Ashkenazi, Salonika; Yitzhak Nahum Kuzi, Damascus, 1902; Sotheby's, Tel Aviv, 24 May 1987, lot 52; Sotheby's, London, 17 December 1991, lot 47
BIBLIOGRAPHY EJ II 670-71; Sarton III 1382; HUM §409; Thorndike 40-42; Tzvi Langermann

15 LJS 414

Compendium of astrological works
Persia, *c.* 1636-70

This is probably a student's copy of a series of scientific works, several dated 1670 at the madrasa of 'Ali Jah Mahmud Beg Nazir.

DESCRIPTION Paper, 168 folios, 193 x 125 mm, nasta'liq script, 59 tables in red and black, seven illustrations, annotations and calculations throughout. Black morocco binding bearing the name Ibrahim ibn Mohammed Baqir.
PROVENANCE Sam Fogg, March 2001

16 LJS 397

Student's notes on astronomy
Wittenberg, *c.* 1550

This manuscript sheds light on astronomical teaching at the University of Wittenberg in the middle of the sixteenth century. At the time astronomy students at Wittenberg were under the tutelage of the Protestant reformer and educationalist Philipp Melanchthon (1497–1560). The period is notable for the early reception of Copernicus's *De revolutionibus,* which had been published in 1543. Melanchthon's circle regarded Copernicus's theory of a moving earth with suspicion, and Melanchthon himself refuted it as contrary to Scripture. Nonetheless, the studies undertaken by this group of scholars at Wittenberg show the acceptance of some aspects of Copernicus's work; Copernicus is cited on f. 30r of the present manuscript. Also discussed are the use of geometry to calculate distances, atmospheric refraction and the use of astronomical tables.

DESCRIPTION Paper, 40 folios, 200 x 194 mm, in Latin, loose italic script, dark brown ink, section headings in red; numerous pen and ink diagrams and calculations. Marbled wrappers.
PROVENANCE Reiss, 4 November 1998, lot 4; H.P. Kraus, cat. 215, no. 254
BIBLIOGRAPHY Westman

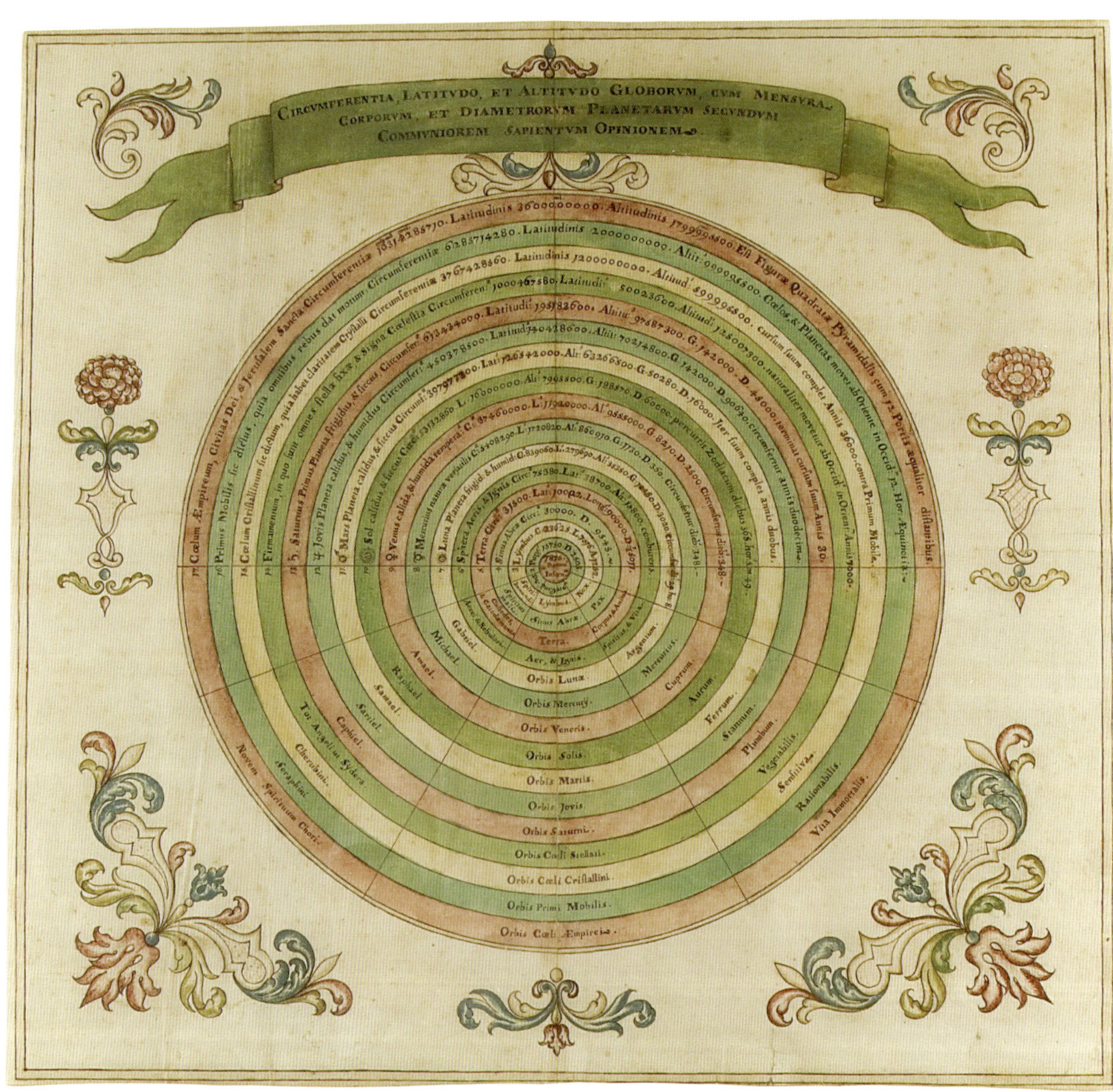

LJS 323

17 LJS 323

Watercolour showing the planetary system
Italy, 16th–17th century

This watercolour is entitled *Circumferentia, latitudo, et altitudo globorum cum mensura corporum et diametrorum planetarum secundum communiorem sapientum opinionem* (Circumference, latitude and altitude of the spheres, with the measurement of bodies and diameter of the planets, according to the common opinion of the wise). It is divided into sections relating to astronomy, religion, astrology and alchemy.

DESCRIPTION Paper, 493 x 504 mm, watercolour, text in Latin.

PROVENANCE Dr Sam Schaefler, September 1999

18 LJS 200

Giovanni Alfonso Borelli, 26 signed letters to Dionigi Guerrini, Quartermaster-General of Ferdinando II de' Medici
Pisa, Poggio Adorno, Livorno and Naples, 17 November 1664–21 June 1667

Borelli (1608–1679) was a pupil of Galileo, active in a number of scientific fields including mathematics, physiology, mechanics and astronomy. This group of letters contains a number of references to his observations of comets in 1664 and 1665, as well as to his book on the satellites of Jupiter (*Theoricae Mediceorum planetarum*, 1666).

DESCRIPTION Paper, 47 folios, 280 x 200 mm, 1 column,

approximately 20 lines, in Italian, brown ink, cursive script. Disbound, in quarter leather clamshell case.

PROVENANCE Sir Thomas Phillipps; W.H. Robinson, 1945; H.P. Kraus, cat. 155 (1991), no 18; John Stanitz, ms. 31

19 LJS 175

Donato Rossetti, *Figure de' sistemi del mondo d'Aristotile, Copernico, e Ticone*
Italy, c. 1680

In the seventeenth century the Aristotelian world-view continued to be promulgated in university textbooks. The Aristotelian (more strictly, Ptolemaic) system of the cosmos, with the earth at the centre of a series of solid concentric orbs, was maintained in such works. Over the course of the century, however, textbooks began to place in opposition to this traditional model the alternative theories of Copernicus (1473–1543) and Tycho Brahe (1546–1601). Copernicus, who argued that the earth revolved around the sun, was typically dismissed on Scriptural grounds even when the usefulness of his hypothesis was admitted. Tycho, on the other hand, did not countenance the idea of a heliocentric universe. Yet his compromise position, which maintained the central role of the earth but demolished the solid orbs, was influential in the eventual dissolution of the Aristotelian system.

This manuscript gives an example of how the systems were compared at this time. Its author, Donato Rossetti, was taught at the University of Pisa in the second half of the seventeenth century. He was linked to the Florentine Accademia del Cimento, the first European organization founded exclusively for the purpose of scientific experiment.

DESCRIPTION Paper, 24 folios, 298 x 205 mm, in Latin, humanistic cursive script, brown ink, title in gold with grey wash cartouche; 46 drawings in pen and brown wash. Original limp parchment binding.

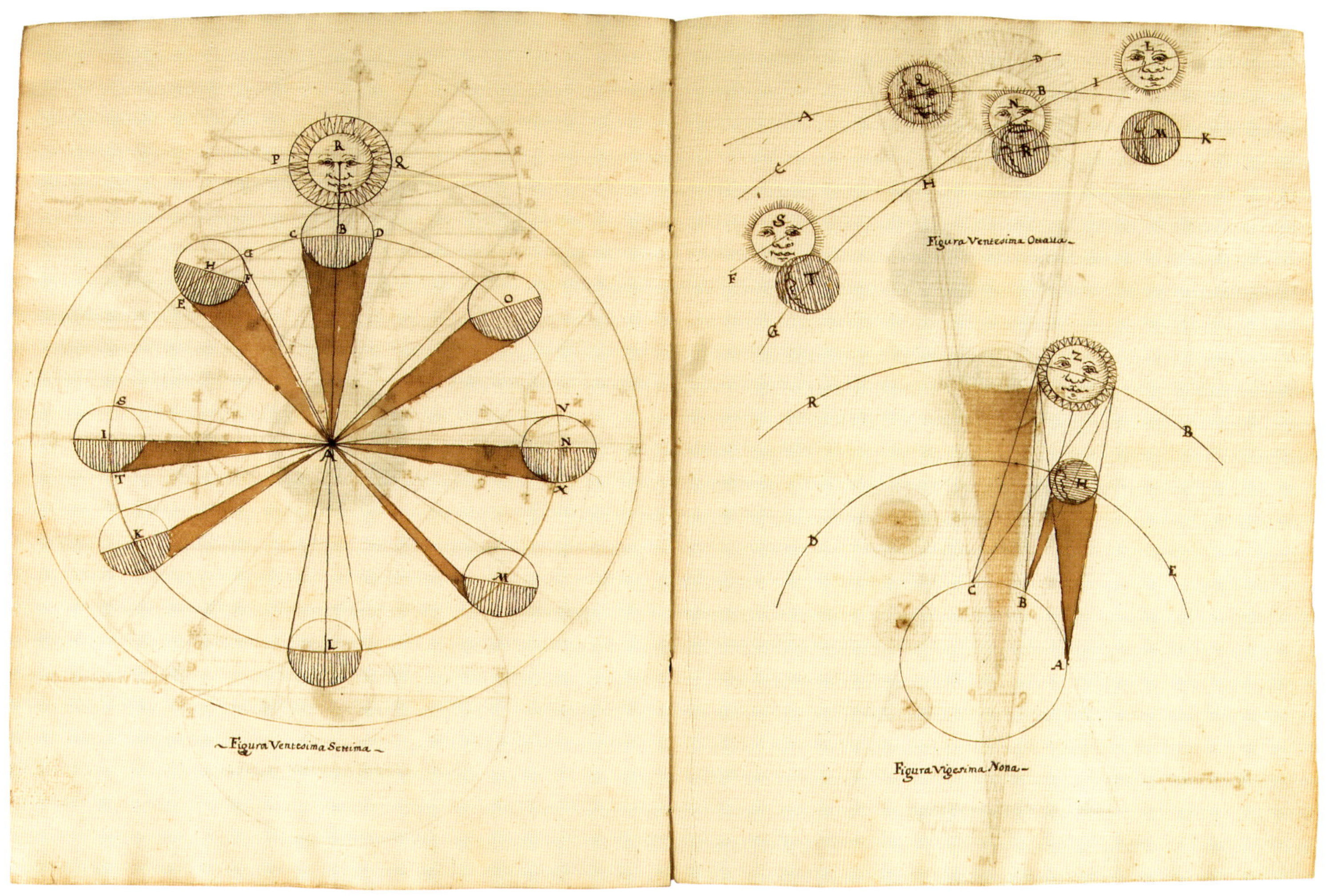

LJS 175
ff. 9v-10r

PROVENANCE Pietro Ginori Conti; Robert Honeyman; Sotheby's, New York, 2 May 1979, lot 1129; Laurence Witten, ms. 12108; John Stanitz, ms. 6
BIBLIOGRAPHY DSB II 401-16, III 401-11; Randles 150-218; Lopez 17-20; Reif

20 LJS 182

Giovanni Domenico Cassini, *Les observations de l'équinoxe du printemps de cette année 1703, comparées avec les plus anciennes* Paris, March 21–May 1703

Cassini (1625–1712) was one of the founders of the Paris Observatory. This manuscript contains a report on his observation of the vernal equinox, 21 March 1703 at 8 am. These observations, and their bearing on year length, contributed to his ongoing project of calendar reform.

DESCRIPTION Paper, 10 folios, in French, black ink, cursive script. Disbound.
PROVENANCE Sir Thomas Phillipps (according to H.P. Kraus, ex ms. 21129; no ex-libris in the present folios); Robinson Brothers, 1945; H.P. Kraus; John Stanitz, ms. 13

21 LJS 205

Gaius Marcucci, Dissertation on the Copernican system Recanati, Italy, *c.* 1810

This manuscript was probably written for an examination at the Jesuit Seminary in Recanati, Italy. Like LJS 175 (no. 19), it juxtaposes the systems of Copernicus, Tycho Brahe and Aristotle. In this case, however, the author argues that, contrary to earlier belief, the acceptance of a heliocentric system is not incompatible with the Catholic faith.

DESCRIPTION Paper, 46 folios, 267 x 197 mm, in Latin, brown ink, cursive script; elaborate titlepage with border in pen and wash; also includes 11 folding plates with 12 figures, nine signed. Decorative printed paper board binding.
PROVENANCE Pickering & Chatto, cat. 717 (1994), no. 12; John Stanitz, ms. 36

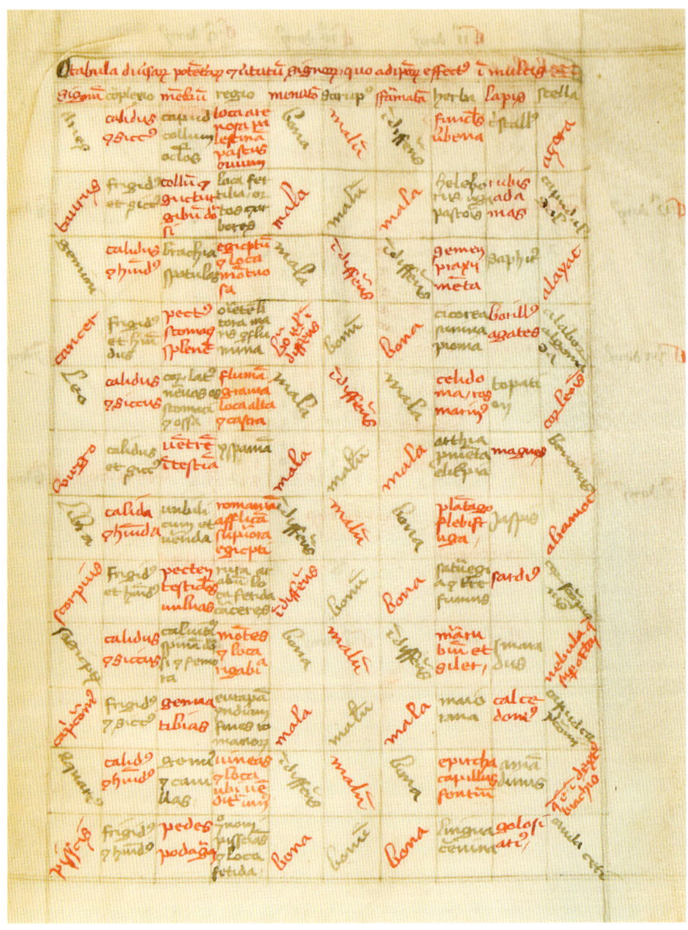

LJS
f. 4v

TABLES

22 LJS 361

Collection of astronomical and astrological tables Naples, 1327

This collection of astrological tables was compiled by a Dominican friar in 1327, while he was a student in Naples; later that century it was lent to another Dominican, Umilis of Gubbio, for a surety of one florin. The manuscript contains a number of tables, drawing on "ancient and modern astrologers". Some of these are for the calculation of feast days and days of the week (from 1204 to 1512), time variations according to latitude and longitude, and hours in the day and night. The remainder of the manuscript is largely devoted to the relationships between the planets and signs of the zodiac and sublunar entites, compiled in a variety of lists. These lists encompass the effects of planetary movements on luck; on body parts, plants and stones; and on human activities. Among these activities are having a haircut, marrying or going to prison (assessed as good, bad or medium according to the position of the moon in the houses of the zodiac) as well as selling animals of different colours, writing, shaving, bathing and planting trees.

DESCRIPTION Parchment, 48 folios, 218 x 150 mm, in Latin, two columns, neat scholarly hand, dark brown and red ink, some marginal drawings and notes; 25 full-page tables and diagrams. Original binding, reversed leather over thick bevelled boards.
PROVENANCE Dominican convent in Naples; Sotheby's, London, 8 December 1975, lot 60; Comites-Latentes collection, Geneva, ms. 174; Sotheby's, London, 1 December 1998, lot 76; Sam Fogg, February 2000
BIBLIOGRAPHY *Iter* V 638 (item 174)

23 LJS 204

Immanuel Bonfils, *Shesh kenafayim*
Italy, 3 Av [20 July] 1509

Immanuel Bonfils was among the pre-eminent mathematicians of fourteenth-century Provence. This work, 'Six Wings' (also known as *Kanfe nesharim*, 'Wings of Eagles'), is a compilation of astronomical tables used for calculating the Jewish calendar. It proved very successful. Numerous manuscript copies exist; it was the subject of a Greek commentary (by a contemporary of Bonfils, Georgios Chrysococces) and was later translated into Latin (in 1406). As this manuscript shows, it continued to be used in the sixteenth century.

The 'Six Wings' takes its name from the six divisions of the work, each of which contains tables concerning the movements of the sun and moon, solar and lunar eclipses, and the day of the new moon. Bonfils made use of the tables devised by the ninth-century Arab astronomer al-Battani, which had a considerable influence in both the Arabic and the Latin traditions; he recalculated them for the Jewish calendar and adjusted them to the longitude and latitude of Tarascon, where he lived.

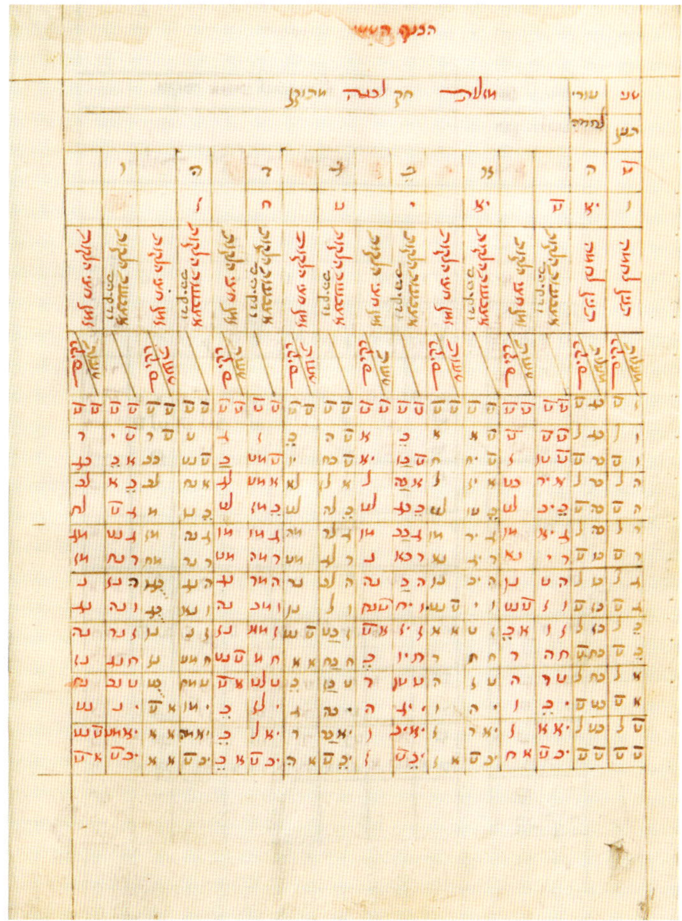

LJS 204
f. 25v

According to the colophon, the scribe, Joseph ben Isaac Gallico, compiled this version of the tables by comparing two differing copies and correcting their mistakes.

DESCRIPTION Parchment, 27 folios, 174 x 126 mm, in Hebrew, Italian square and cursive script by two (?) scribes, brown ink, table headings in red; 42 pages of astronomical tables in red and brown. Modern half calf binding over marbled boards.
PROVENANCE Shmuel Benjamin; Abraham Halevy; J.J. Isach; Yitzhak ben Shabtah Me Hazkeinim; Shlomo Raphael ben Abraham of Fano (cleared by the censors 'Mezukak'); David Solomon Sassoon, ms. 476; Sotheby's, New York, 12 May 1981, lot 2; Swann Galleries, 19 December 1991, lot 161; Martayan Lan, cat. 11 (1994), no. 60; John Stanitz, ms. 35
BIBLIOGRAPHY EJ IV 1207-08; Sarton III 1116; Gandz; EI I 1104-05

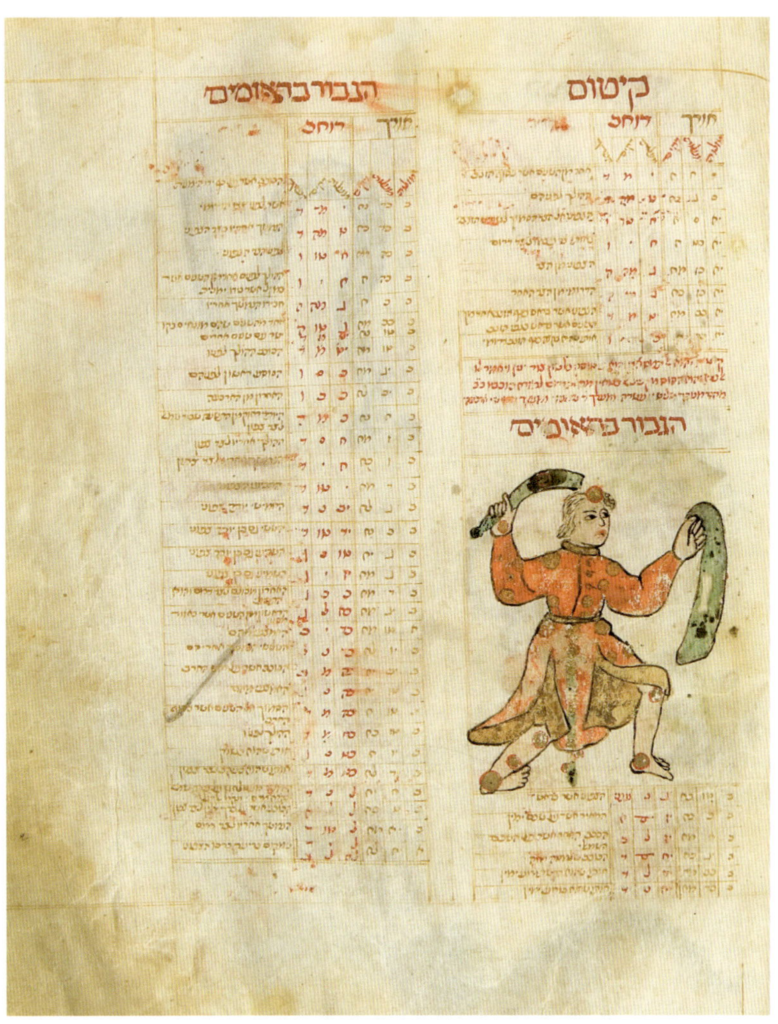

LJS 57, p. 133

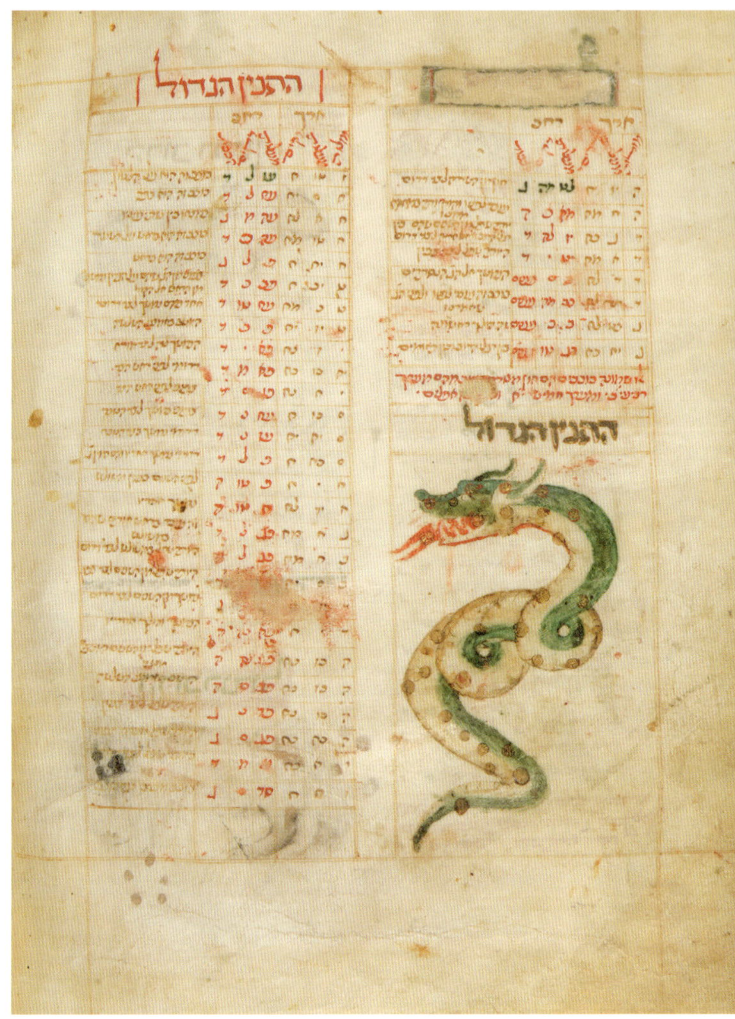

LJS 57, p. 118

24 LJS 57

Astronomical anthology
Catalonia, *c.* 1361

Jewish astronomers of the thirteenth and fourteenth centuries
played a central role in transmitting Greek and Arabic
astronomical texts to the Latin west. They also produced
astronomical tables which they derived from Arabic and
Persian sources. Both facets of this activity are visible in this
sumptuously illustrated manuscript, which is associated with
the court of Peter IV, King of Aragon from 1336 to 1387. It
opens with a treatise on the calendar compiled for the king in
1361 by Jacob ben David ben Yom Tov. This builds on the
calendars devised by Abraham bar Hiyya (d. 1136) and Levi
ben Gershom (d. 1344), among others. It was subsequently
translated from Hebrew into Catalan for the king's use. Also
included here are a miscellany of four short astronomical
texts and a Hebrew translation of Ptolemy's *Almagest* (see LJS
268 [no. 1]). The 48 gold and polychrome miniatures are
remarkable for their mixture of traditional astronomical
iconography with depictions of fourteenth-century life.

DESCRIPTION Parchment, 114 folios, 275 x 204 mm, in Hebrew,
very fine Sephardic cursive script (several scribes); decorated
headings, 110 tables and diagrams, 48 miniatures. Modern binding.
PROVENANCE David Solomon Sassoon, ms. 823; Carl Alexander
Floersheim Trust for Art and Judaica; Sotheby's, London,
10 December 1996, lot 48

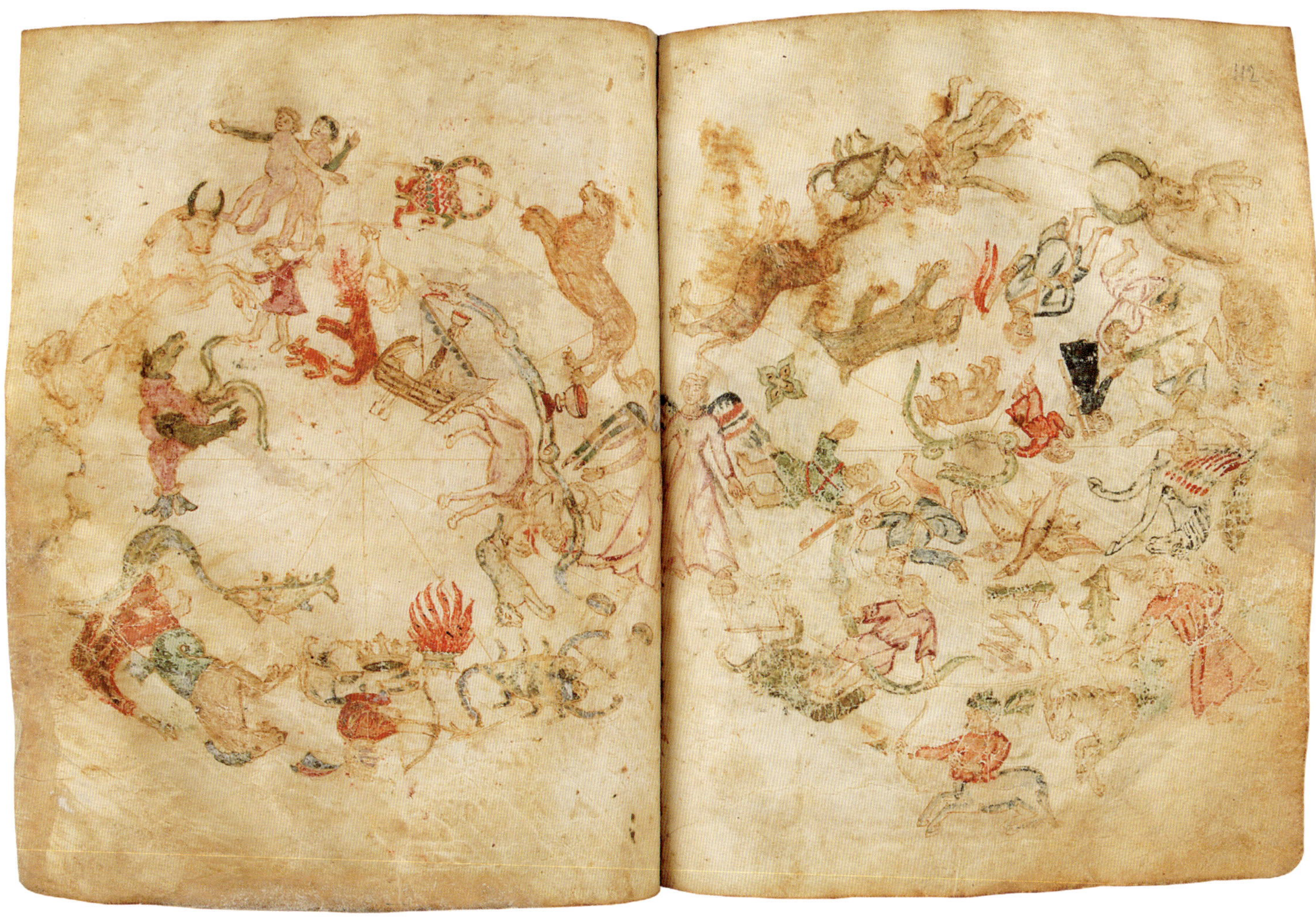

LJS 57, pp. 112-13

Tabula proportionis minutorum

Each degree column (46–60) gives the value as *minuta;secunda* (m;s) for the argument in the left-hand column (1–30).

arg	46	47	48	49	50	51	52	53	54	55	56	57	58	59	60
1	0;46	0;47	0;48	0;49	0;50	0;51	0;52	0;53	0;54	0;55	0;56	0;57	0;58	0;59	1;0
2	1;32	1;34	1;36	1;38	1;40	1;42	1;44	1;46	1;48	1;50	1;52	1;54	1;56	1;58	2;0
3	2;18	2;21	2;24	2;27	2;30	2;33	2;36	2;39	2;42	2;45	2;48	2;51	2;54	2;57	3;0
4	3;4	3;8	3;12	3;16	3;20	3;24	3;28	3;32	3;36	3;40	3;44	3;48	3;52	3;56	4;0
5	3;50	3;55	4;0	4;5	4;10	4;15	4;20	4;25	4;30	4;35	4;40	4;45	4;50	4;55	5;0
6	4;36	4;42	4;48	4;54	5;0	5;6	5;12	5;18	5;24	5;30	5;36	5;42	5;48	5;54	6;0
7	5;22	5;29	5;36	5;43	5;50	5;57	6;4	6;11	6;18	6;25	6;32	6;39	6;46	6;53	7;0
8	6;8	6;16	6;24	6;32	6;40	6;48	6;56	7;4	7;12	7;20	7;28	7;36	7;44	7;52	8;0
9	6;54	7;3	7;12	7;21	7;30	7;39	7;48	7;57	8;6	8;15	8;24	8;33	8;42	8;51	9;0
10	7;40	7;50	8;0	8;10	8;20	8;30	8;40	8;50	9;0	9;10	9;20	9;30	9;40	9;50	10;0
11	8;26	8;37	8;48	8;59	9;10	9;21	9;32	9;43	9;54	10;5	10;16	10;27	10;38	10;49	11;0
12	9;12	9;24	9;36	9;48	10;0	10;12	10;24	10;36	10;48	11;0	11;12	11;24	11;36	11;48	12;0
13	9;58	10;11	10;24	10;37	10;50	11;3	11;16	11;29	11;42	11;55	12;8	12;21	12;34	12;47	13;0
14	10;44	10;58	11;12	11;26	11;40	11;54	12;8	12;22	12;36	12;50	13;4	13;18	13;32	13;46	14;0
15	11;30	11;45	12;0	12;15	12;30	12;45	13;0	13;15	13;30	13;45	14;0	14;15	14;30	14;45	15;0
16	12;16	12;32	12;48	13;4	13;20	13;36	13;52	14;8	14;24	14;40	14;56	15;12	15;28	15;44	16;0
17	13;2	13;19	13;36	13;53	14;10	14;27	14;44	15;1	15;18	15;35	15;52	16;9	16;26	16;43	17;0
18	13;48	14;6	14;24	14;42	15;0	15;18	15;36	15;54	16;12	16;30	16;48	17;6	17;24	17;42	18;0
19	14;34	14;53	15;12	15;31	15;50	16;9	16;28	16;47	17;6	17;25	17;44	18;3	18;22	18;41	19;0
20	15;20	15;40	16;0	16;20	16;40	17;0	17;20	17;40	18;0	18;20	18;40	19;0	19;20	19;40	20;0
21	16;6	16;27	16;48	17;9	17;30	17;51	18;12	18;33	18;54	19;15	19;36	19;57	20;18	20;39	21;0
22	16;52	17;14	17;36	17;58	18;20	18;42	19;4	19;26	19;48	20;10	20;32	20;54	21;16	21;38	22;0
23	17;38	18;1	18;24	18;47	19;10	19;33	19;56	20;19	20;42	21;5	21;28	21;51	22;14	22;37	23;0
24	18;24	18;48	19;12	19;36	20;0	20;24	20;48	21;12	21;36	22;0	22;24	22;48	23;12	23;36	24;0
25	19;10	19;35	20;0	20;25	20;50	21;15	21;40	22;5	22;30	22;55	23;20	23;45	24;10	24;35	25;0
26	19;56	20;22	20;48	21;14	21;40	22;6	22;32	22;58	23;24	23;50	24;16	24;42	25;8	25;34	26;0
27	20;42	21;9	21;36	22;3	22;30	22;57	23;24	23;51	24;18	24;45	25;12	25;39	26;6	26;33	27;0
28	21;28	21;56	22;24	22;52	23;20	23;48	24;16	24;44	25;12	25;40	26;8	26;36	27;4	27;32	28;0
29	22;14	22;43	23;12	23;41	24;10	24;39	25;8	25;37	26;6	26;35	27;4	27;33	28;2	28;31	29;0
30	23;0	23;30	24;0	24;30	25;0	25;30	26;0	26;30	27;0	27;30	28;0	28;30	29;0	29;30	30;0

Nota inueni plus in [illegible] minus [illegible]
Anno domini 1410 mense [illegible] pro [illegible] diem
martii et [illegible] pro tot [illegible] que [illegible]
ipe in [illegible] anno z [illegible]
z in minuto [illegible] per predictum [illegible]
[illegible] si nouerio palpa 25
2 · 22 · 78 · 2a · 26 · 82 · 28 · 73
[illegible] diebus [illegible] vt [illegible] per [illegible]
[illegible] tot [illegible] in feruentis [illegible] inuat
[illegible] vero diebus equat [illegible] prope [illegible]
[illegible] in uenta [illegible] per [illegible]
[illegible] diez [illegible] 38 dies 76 · 28 · 73
si nouerio palpa [illegible] nimbi
[illegible] si deus voluit

25   LJS 174

Alfonsine Tables
Prague, 1401–04

Alfonso X of Leon and Castile ('el Sabio', the Learned;
1221–1284), a failure in his dynastic ambitions, was more
successful in his role as patron of scholarship. This success is
most clearly attested by the diffusion of the 'Alfonsine Tables'.
These astronomical tables were based on the 'Toledan Tables'
compiled by Abu Ishaq al-Zarqali of Cordoba (d. 1100);
Alfonso had al-Zarqali's tables updated with a series of new
observations made between 1262 and 1272, although he
retained the overall format of the earlier work. The tables used
calculations based on solar, lunar and planetary orbits,
declinations of stars, ascension, opposition and conjunction
of the sun and moon, as well as trigonometry of sines and
chords, for the purpose of predicting the motion of celestial
bodies.

Originally prepared in Spanish, the Alfonsine Tables
circulated widely in Latin. Their Latin reception was aided by
the 'Canons' of John of Saxony (1st half 14th century) and John
of Lignères (1322). These elaborations of the tables, together
with the Alfonsine Tables themselves, are included in this
manuscript, which was copied at Prague; a correction to the
calculations is provided for this locale.

DESCRIPTION Paper, 142 folios, 295 x 236 mm, in Latin, Gothic
cursive script in many hands, brown and red ink, rubrics in red,
initials and highlights in red, tables in red and brown. Contemporary
limp parchment binding.

PROVENANCE Counts of Ortenburg at Tambach castle, ms. E 355;
Sotheby's, London, 25 June 1985, lot 72; H.P. Kraus, 1987; John
Stanitz, ms. 5

BIBLIOGRAPHY Sarton II 834-40; DSB I 122, VII 139; EI XI 461-62

26   LJS 226

Astronomical diagrams
England and Spain, *c.* 1410

This miscellaneous collection of tables and diagrams for
astronomical and astrological calculation includes a template
for a horoscope and a circular calendar of the zodiac.

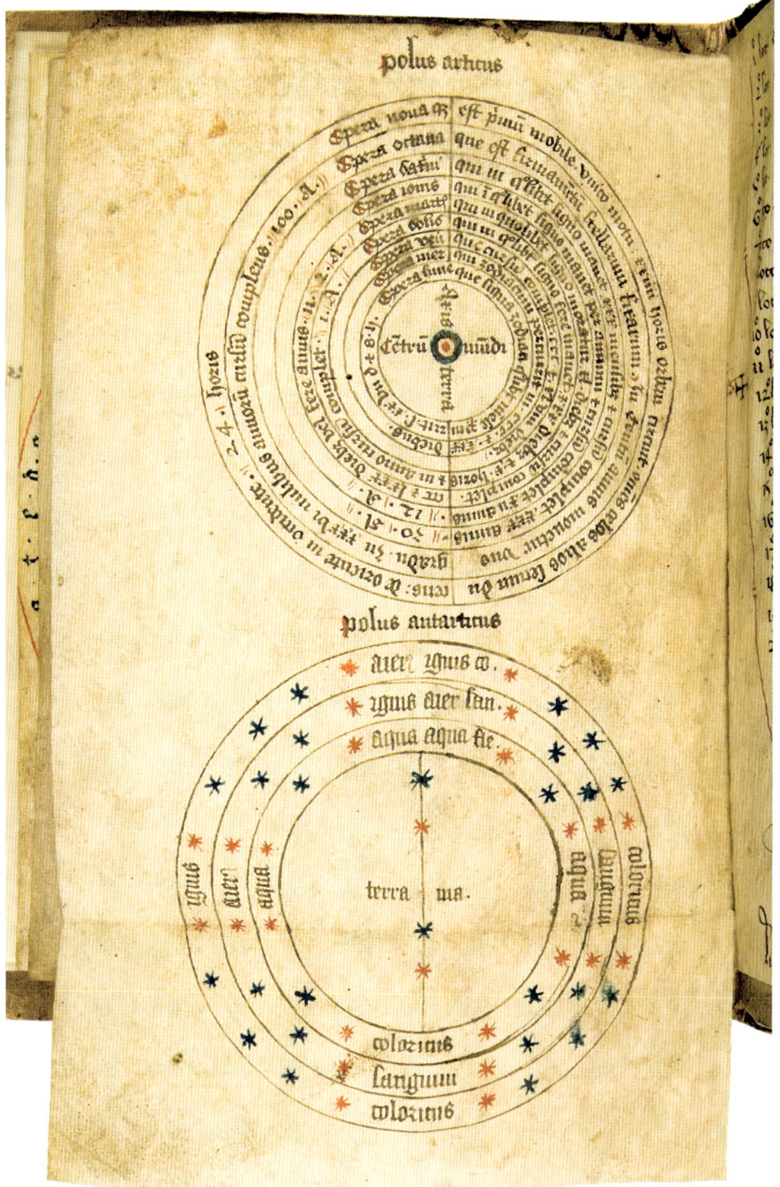

LJS 226, f. 4v

DESCRIPTION Parchment, 7 folios, 170 x 130 mm, diagrams in blue
and red or brown and red with gothic script and cursive rubrication
by several scribes. 19th-century quarter-marbled paper over
cardboard binding.

PROVENANCE Latin inscription on f. 3r: "bought from Master
Richard Chamberlain for 16 shillings and 8 pence"; Sir John
Chetwode, Oakley Hall, Staffordshire, 1861; Sam Fogg, July 1997

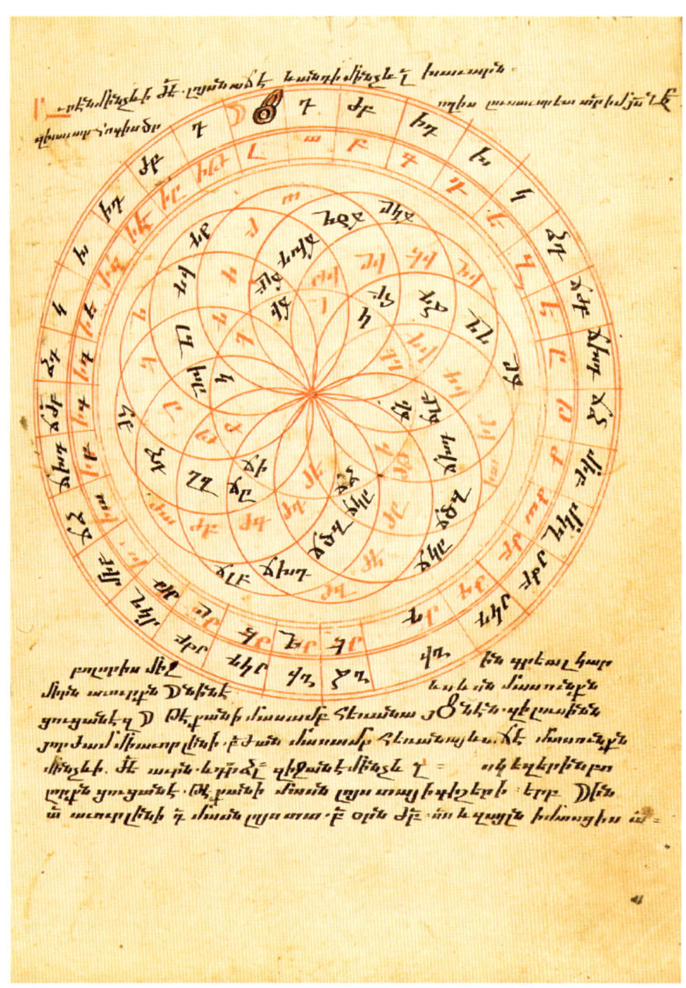

27 LJS 443

Collection of texts on the calendar
Armenia, 1416 and 1426

DESCRIPTION Paper, 258 folios, 185 x 140 mm, in Armenian, neat
bolorgir script, frontispiece in blue and red. Tooled calf binding.
PROVENANCE Written by order of T'ovma medsop'etsi and Hakob
vardapet Ghrimetsi; M. Ormanian (1841-1918), Armenian scholar and
Patriarch of Constantinople; Sam Fogg, November 2002

28 LJS 463

Calendar and texts on astro-medicine
Southern Germany, region of Lake Constance, 1443

This manuscript begins with a calendar of feast days for the

diocese of Constance in southern Germany; certain local
feasts, such as the consecration of the Cathedral of Constance
on 9 September, are given prominence. The calendar is
accompanied by two treatises on the zodiac and the planets
and by notes on a variety of related subjects – the four
complexions, blood-letting, bathing and eating and drinking.

Each month of the calendar is illustrated with the sign of
the zodiac and the labour of the month. Variant illustrations
of the signs of the zodiac are found in the treatise on the
zodiac, and the treatise on the planets contains
representations of the personification of each planet
alongside related signs. The sections on blood-letting and
bathing are also illustrated.

Such compilations were common in Germany in the
fifteenth century and were frequently printed from the 1480s
onwards (for another example, see LJS 449 [no. 29]). This
manuscript is consistent with the later printed editions, in
terms of both text and illustration.

DESCRIPTION Parchment, 72 folios, 230 x 163 mm, in German,
textura (in calendar and rubrics) and neat cursive, dark-brown ink,
red rubrics; 2-line initials alternately red and blue, sometimes with
penwork of contrasting colour; 53 coloured pen-and-ink drawings,
mostly in medallions. Pressed pigskin binding with metal clasps.
PROVENANCE Written by the scholar Heinrich Stegmüller of
Wiesensteig, who signed the manuscript in Buchau on the Federsee
(in the vicinity of Biberach) on 18 January 1443; Donaueschingen,
Fürstlich Fürstenbergische Hofbibliothek, ms. 494; Jörn Günther, A
Selection of Manuscripts and Miniatures (2003), no. 12; private collection,
USA; Sam Fogg, June 2004

29 LJS 449

Anthology of medical and astronomical texts
South-west Germany, c. 1446

This manuscript focuses on the perceived connection
between astrology and medical operations, in terms of
favourable and unfavourable days. To this end it includes a
number of astronomical tables indicating dates, eclipses and
duration of moonlight, as well as treatises on the planets and
the signs of the zodiac, with illustrations of the Labours of the
Months. These are juxtaposed with treatises on blood-letting,

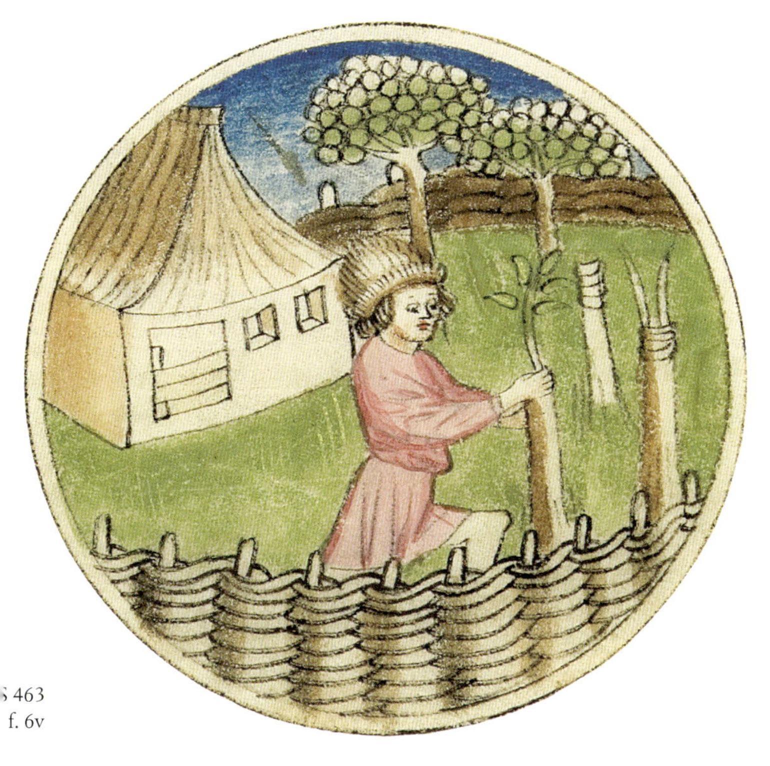

LJS 463
f. 6v

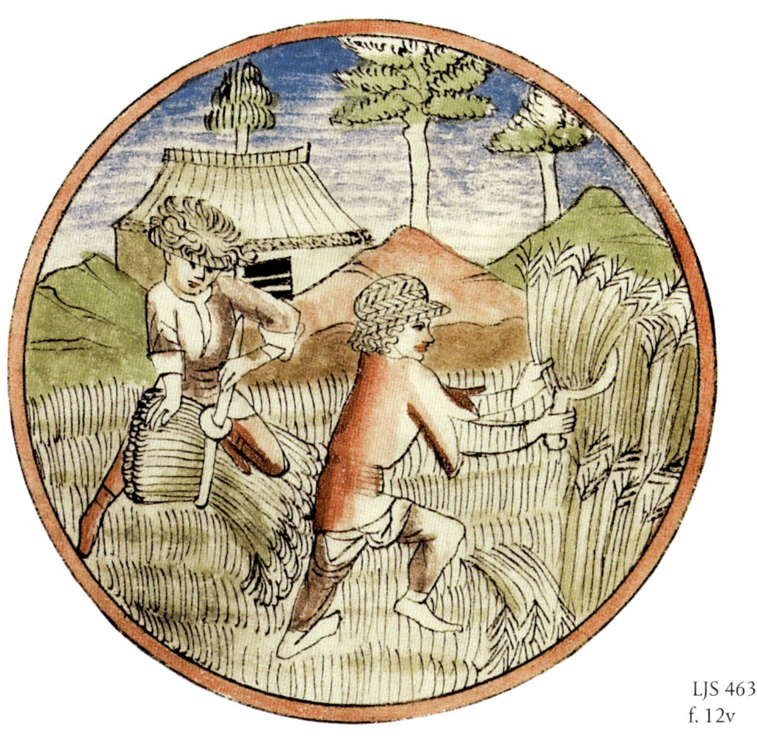

LJS 463
f. 12v

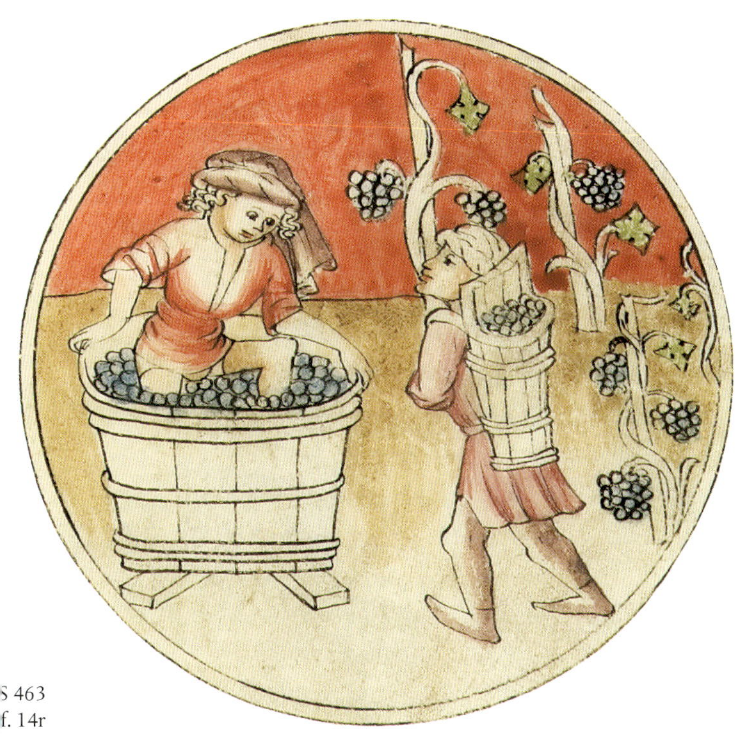

LJS 463
f. 14r

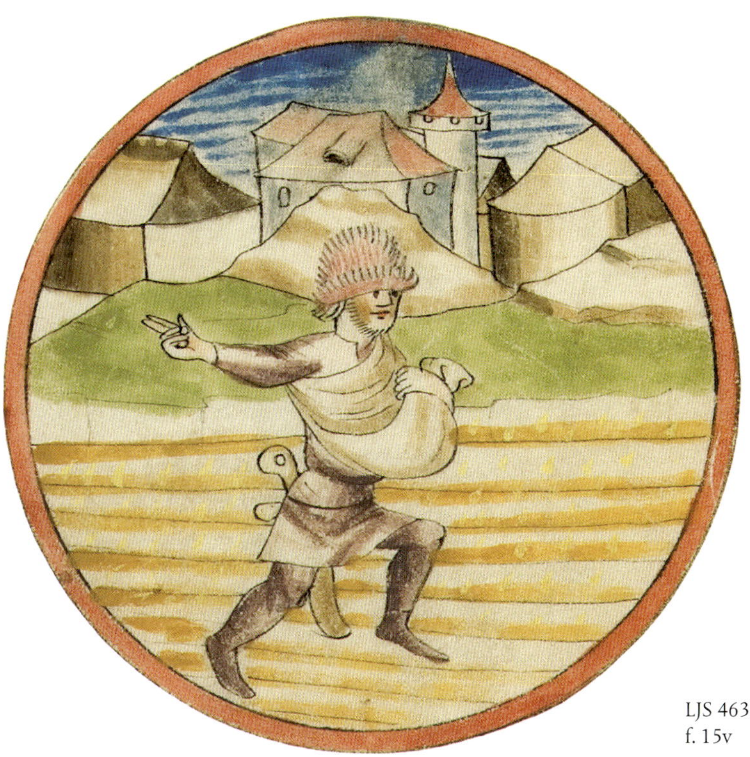

LJS 463
f. 15v

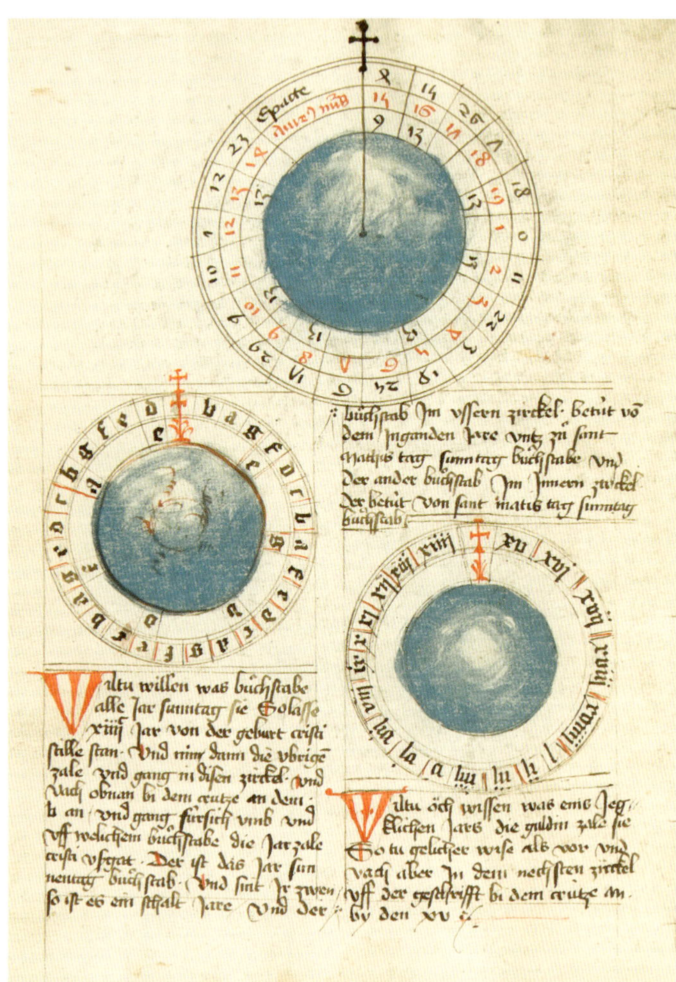

LJS 449
f. 11v

cupping and the examination of urine; a table on f. 8r
indicates days on which blood-letting should be carried out.
Such items are commonly combined in the *Volkskalender*
tradition which flourished in Germany in the fifteenth
century.

More unusual is the inclusion in this manuscript of a short
treatise on wine (attributed, in another copy, to Albertus
Magnus) and a work attributed to the Jewish astrologer Zaël
(8th–9th centuries), the *Liber sigillorum filiorum Israel quem
fecerunt in deserto*. This work is concerned with the occult
properties of seals or carved stones; a number of redactions
of it circulated from the twelfth century onwards, one of
which is contained in the *Liber de natura rerum* of Thomas de
Cantimpré (see LJS 23 [IX, no. 5]).

DESCRIPTION Paper, 36 folios, 294 x 210 mm, in German and Latin,
bâtarde script, brown ink, red rubrics, one red initial with green

penwork; 13 circular charts and 36 miniatures. Original vellum
binding, dated 1433.
PROVENANCE Labbey de Billy collection, sold 1 May 1826 in
Besançon; Sotheby's, London, 22 June 1982, lot 61;
Günther/Ferrini/Roth, *Illumination* (26 July 2002), no. 6
BIBLIOGRAPHY HMES II 388-90; Brévart

30   LJS 466

Tables of longitude and latitude, and other texts
Persia, *c.* 1450

DESCRIPTION Paper, 104 folios, 160 x 120 mm, in Persian and
Arabic, nasta'liq script, black ink, some words in red; tables and
diagrams in red and black. Brown leather binding.
PROVENANCE Sam Fogg, June 2004

31   LJS 476

Isaac ben Joseph Israeli the Younger, *Yesod 'olam*
Spain or Italy, *c.* 1460

Isaac ben Joseph Israeli 'the Younger', of Toledo, flourished in
the first decades of the fourteenth century. This text, *Yesod
'olam* (The foundation of the world), comprises a standard
introduction to astronomy in general – including an
explication of the Ptolemaic system and the movement of the
sun and moon – followed by specific information relating to
the Jewish calendar. The latter was intended not only for
practical purposes such as determining feast days but also for
exegetical chronology and interpretation of the Bible.

A number of commentaries on *Yesod 'olam*, in Hebrew,
circulated in the fifteenth and sixteenth centuries. In addition,
an epitome of the text in Arabic was begun by the author's
son, around 1330, but never completed.

DESCRIPTION Parchment and paper, 70 folios, 200 x 137 mm, in
Hebrew, rounded sephardic script in grey ink; 37 large illustrations,
one full-page, one unfinished, spaces left for six others. Modern
tooled red leather binding.
PROVENANCE Donation notice: *Geschenk des Dr. M. Dessauer in
Meiningen*
BIBLIOGRAPHY EJ IX 1062; Sarton III 691-92

LJS 172
p. 41

32   LJS 172

Johannes Regiomontanus, *Tabulae directionum et profectionum* and *Tabella sinus recti*
Hungary, *c.* 1470

Regiomontanus (Johann Müller of Königsberg, 1436–1476) was a colleague of Peuerbach (see LJS 64 [no. 12]), with whom he wrote a highly successful *Epitome* of Ptolemy's *Mathematical Syntaxis*, later used by Copernicus among others. Working in Hungary between 1467 and 1471 he computed his 'Tables of Directions', giving the longitude of celestial bodies in relation to the apparent daily rotation of the heavens. The present manuscript of the 'Tables of Directions' can be dated by its watermark to *c.* 1470, within Regiomontanus's lifetime and some twenty years before it was printed.

Regiomontanus was notable for his work on trigonometry. In his early treatise on triangles (*De triangulis omnimodis*) he had used a sexagesimal calculation of sines but he later suggested that they be calculated in a decimal manner. He incorporated decimal sines in his *Tabulae directionum*. This resulted in a significant gain in accuracy, which was of particular use to astronomers. His sexagesimal table of sines is also contained in this manuscript.

DESCRIPTION Paper, 95 folios, 220 x 152 mm, in Latin, gothic cursive script, black and red ink, spaces left for initials; folios 17r to the end contain elaborate tables in red and black. Modern mottled calf binding.
PROVENANCE French dealer's label inside front cover; Harrison Horblit, 1957; H.P. Kraus, cat. 155 (1980), no. 16; John Stanitz, ms. 3
BIBLIOGRAPHY DSB XI 348-52; Zinner; Bond; Struick 140

33 LJS 300

Johannes Regiomontanus, *Calendarium and Ephemerides*
Upper Austria (Lambach?), *c.* 1500

Regiomontanus (see LJS 172 [no. 32]) published his *Ephemerides*
and *Calendarium* in 1474. This edition, which gave the positions
of the heavenly bodies for every day from 1475 to 1506, earned
a certain fame after being used by Columbus to predict the
lunar eclipse of 29 February 1504 and thereby cement his
influence over the natives of Jamaica. The present manuscript
contains a complete copy of his tables, updated to begin in
1480, along with a table of time corrections centred around
100° east of Greenwich (giving zero corrections for
Brunswick, Nuremberg, Ulm and Milan). The paper and
provenance suggest that the manuscript originates in Austria.
In particular, the binding was made in the Benedictine Abbey
of Lambach; a few textual differences from the printed edition
pertain to specifically Benedictine feasts.

DESCRIPTION Paper, 377 folios, 162 x 120 mm, in Latin, gothic script,
dark brown ink, rubrics in red, tables and illustrations of eclipses in
brown and yellow. Original binding, blind-stamped with clasps.
PROVENANCE Benedictine Abbey of Lambach in Upper Austria;
bookplate of Duke Gabor von Festetics de Tolna of Hungary;
V. Heck, cat. IV (*c.* 1922); Harrison D. Horblit; H.P. Kraus; Irene and
Peter Ludwig, Aachen, 1965; J. Paul Getty Museum, 1983-97; Jörn
Günther, cat. 5 (1997), no. 29; Sam Fogg, April 1999
BIBLIOGRAPHY DSB XI 348-52; Morison 653-54

34 LJS 420

Perpetual calendar illustrating Metonic cycle
c. 1480

The Metonic cycle is the period of 19 Julian years, or 235 lunar
months, which is required for the solar and lunar year to
realign, so that the new moon and full moon recur on the
same date as at the start of the cycle. In the Christian Church
calculation of the Metonic cycle was necessary to determine
the date of Easter, the Sunday after the 14th day of the Paschal
moon.

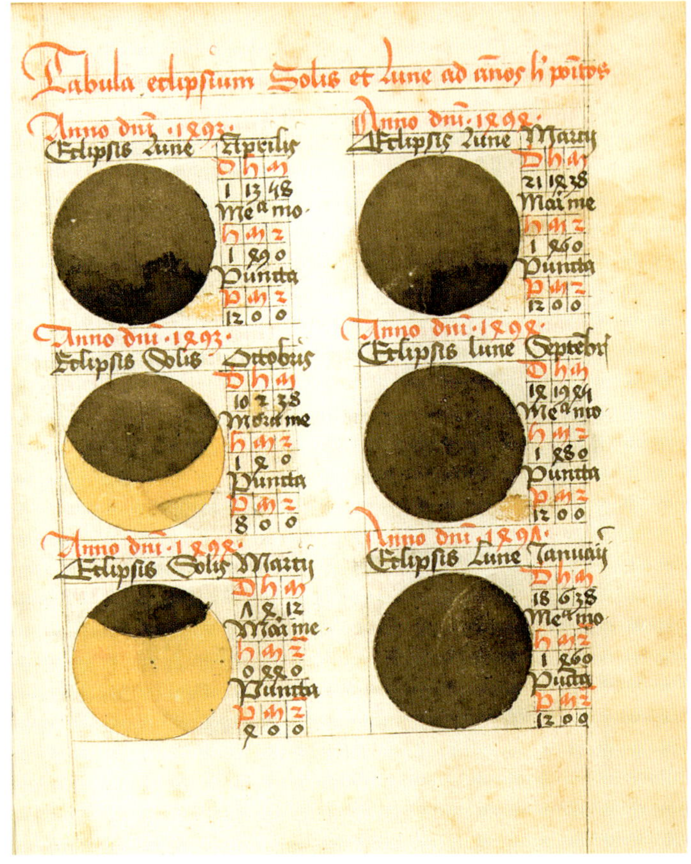

LJS
f. 14

DESCRIPTION Paper, 8 folios, 201 x 140 mm, in Latin, black ink,
several charts and diagrams in red and black. Parchment covers ruled
and stamped in gold.
PROVENANCE Sam Fogg, 2001

35 LJS 445

Johannes Lichtenberger, *Pronosticatio*, with
Regiomontanus's Calendar for 1475–1513
Nuremberg, *c.* 1500

Johannes Lichtenberger (*c.* 1440–*c.* 1503), an astrologer at the
court of the Emperor Frederick III in the 1470s, completed his
'Prophecy' on 1 April 1488, according to a note in the
incunable of the work published that year, from which the
present manuscript was evidently copied.

DESCRIPTION Paper, 227 folios, 230 x 160 mm, in German, bâtarde
script, dark brown ink; charts and diagrams in red, several drawings

of eclipses coloured with brown and yellow wash; pen-and-ink
drawings of signs of the zodiac, coloured wash. Original blind-
stamped pigskin binding.

PROVENANCE Veit Engelhardt, shoemaker of Nuremberg; Günther/
Ferrini, cat. (1999), no. 21; Günther/Burns, cat. (2001), no. 53; Sam
Fogg, December 2002

36 LJS 191

Introduction to astronomy, astrology, and weather prediction, with tables giving the positions of the heavenly bodies
England, c. 1490

DESCRIPTION Paper, 19 folios, 199 x 140 mm, in English (last folio
in Latin), Tudor secretary hand, brown ink.
PROVENANCE James Alleyn; Stuart, Marquess of Bute; Sotheby's,
London, 13 June 1983, lot 32, part 67; H.P. Kraus, cat. 180, no. 133; John
Stanitz, ms. 22

37 LJS 215

Scientific compilation
France, 1511

This compilation of scientific texts and tables is the work of
Imbert Fentryer, who signed it on 28 January 1511. It begins
with a number of astronomical and astrological tables. These
are followed by a miscellaneous collection of treatises, which
are concerned, among other things, with calculating the
solstice and equinox; astrolabes; weights and measures;
geometry; the making of dyes; and medical recipes.
Interspersed throughout are further astronomical tables,
calendars and tables of longitude and latitude. Among the
recipes is a cure for everything ("*Pour escandure de toute chose*").
DESCRIPTION Paper, 283 folios, 105 x 76 mm, in French and Latin,
bâtarde script, black ink, rubrics in red, coloured initials; numerous
tables. 18th-century morocco binding, gilt.
PROVENANCE Christian Friderich (dated 1633 and 1635); signed
"Demigieu 1760" on last folio; Rodolphe Chamonal, *Biennale des
Antiquaires* (1988), no. 19; John Stanitz, ms. 46

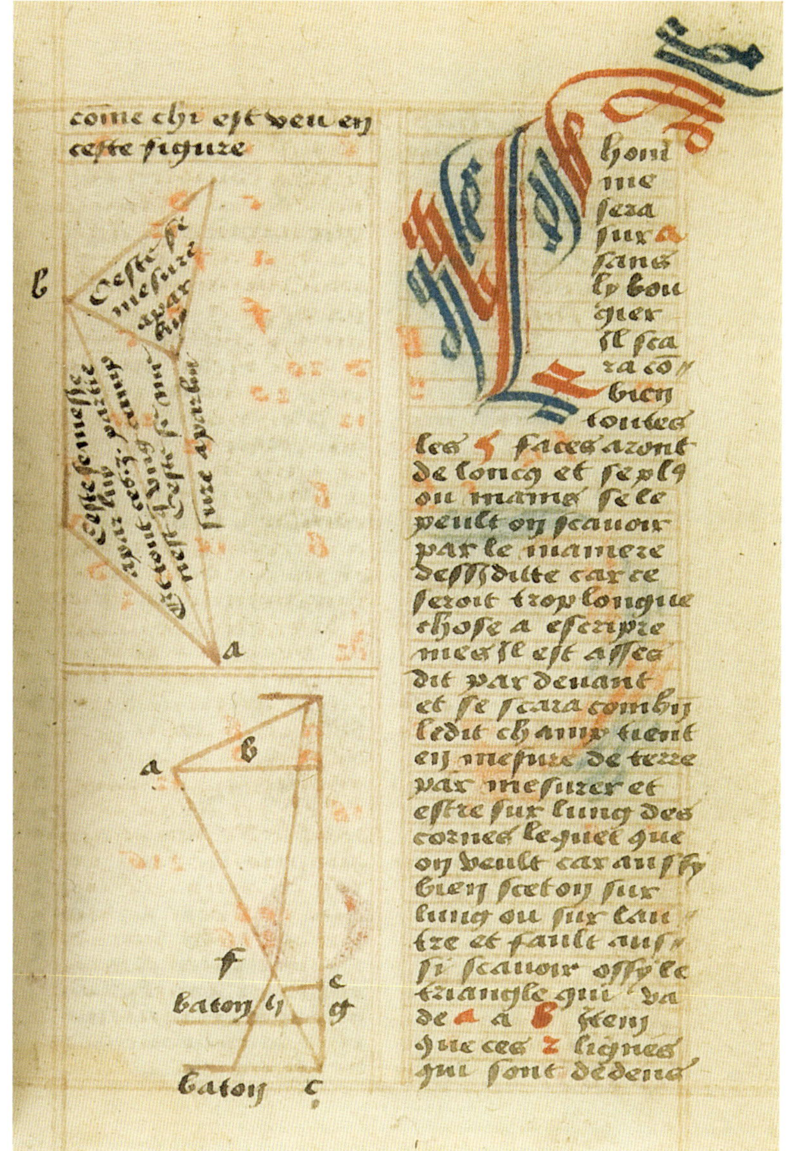

LJS 215, f. 126r

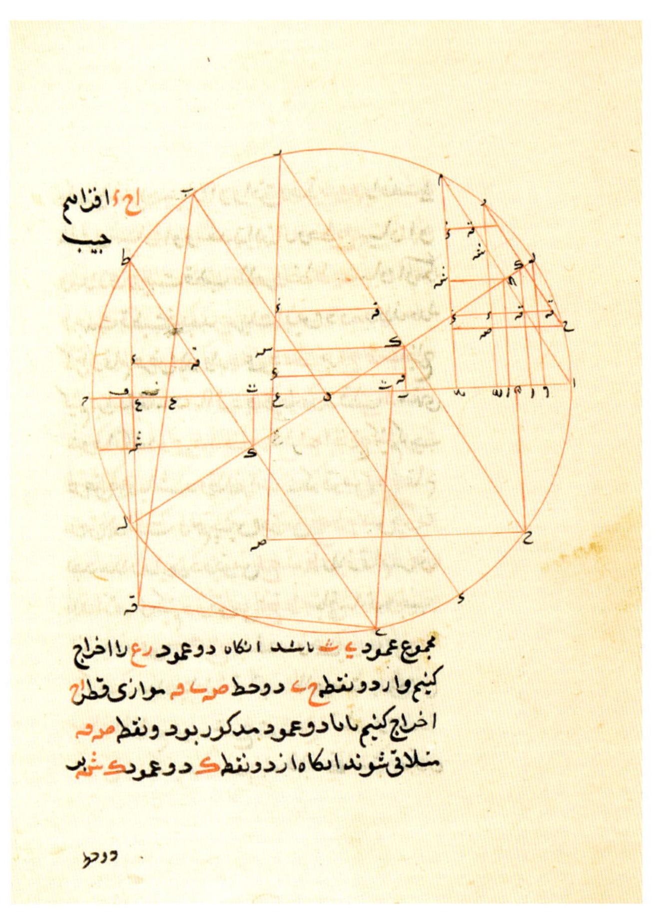

LJS 400
f. 204v

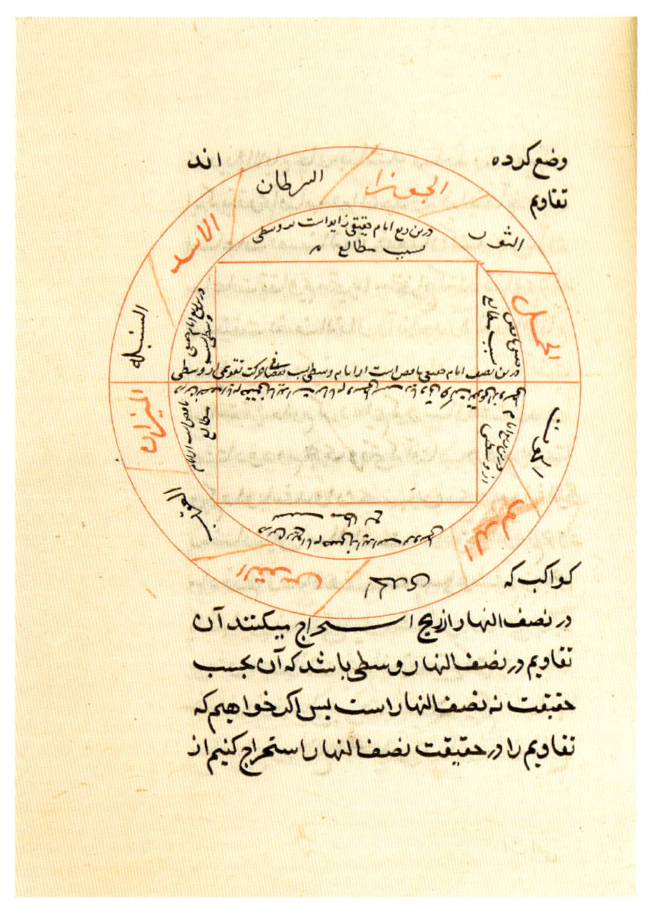

LJS 400
f. 233r

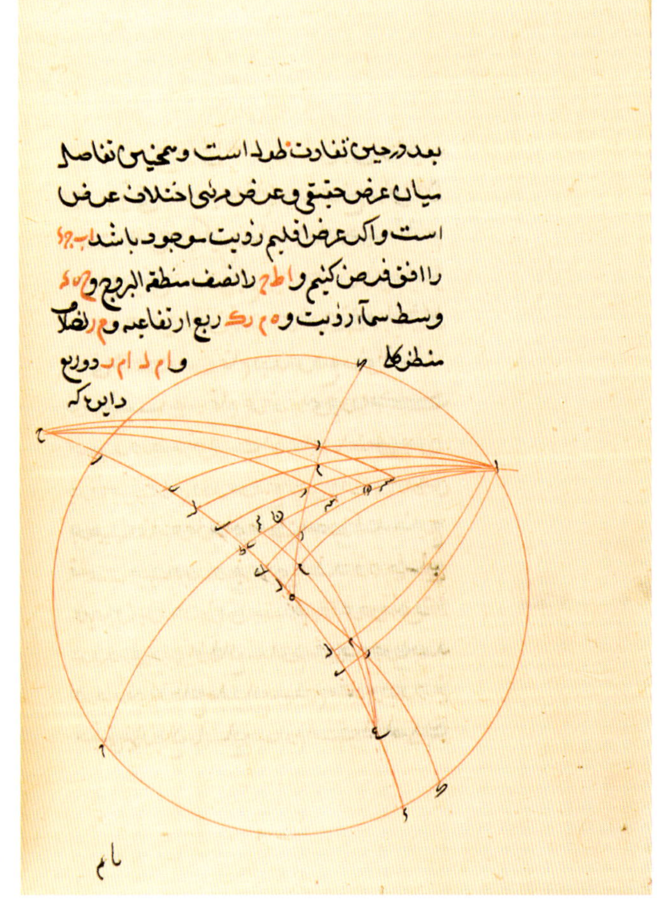

LJS 400
f. 374v

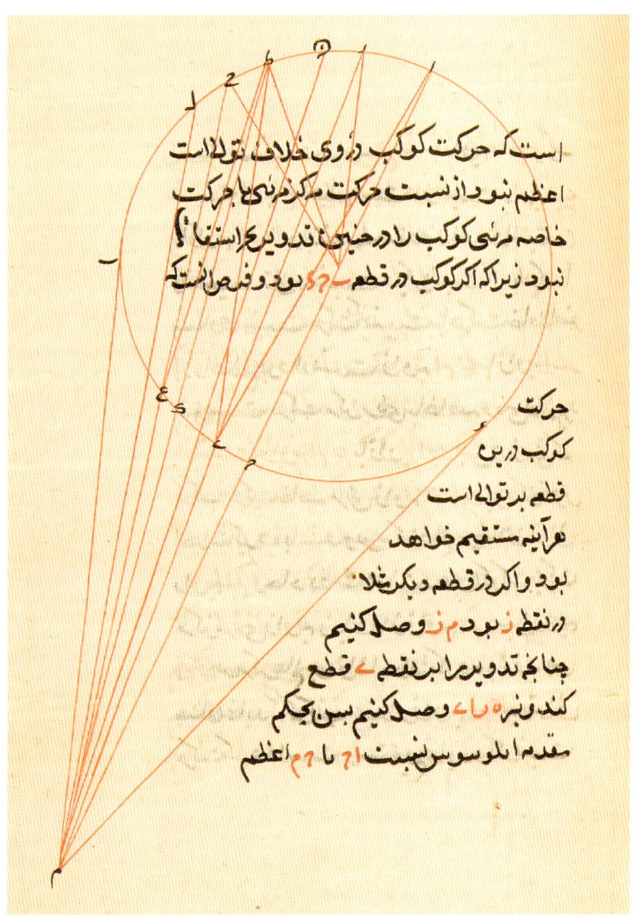

LJS 400
f. 326r

Al-Qushji, *Sharh-i Zij Gurgani*
Iran, AH 899 / 1493–94

In 1420 the astronomer-prince Ulugh Beg founded a *madrasa*
at Samarqand; attached to it was a three-story observatory.
Precise and systematic records were made at this observatory
for a period of some thirty years, aided by a 'Fakhri sextant'
designed for use in solar, lunar and planetary observations.
The result of this work was the famous astronomical tables
known as *Zij-i Gurgani*, completed in 1447: they include tables
of calendar calculations, of trigonometry and of planets, and a
catalogue of stars, many of which are remarkably accurate.
'Ali al-Qushji (d. 1474) was the third chief astronomer at the
observatory, having taken over after the death of Qadi-Zade
al-Rumi (see LJS 408 [no. 8]). This manuscript is a
commentary on the tables, composed by al-Qushji himself
and copied in the generation following al-Qushji's death.
Ulugh Beg himself had been assassinated in 1449. The
observatory remained standing into the sixteenth century but
was then destroyed; its ruins were discovered in 1908.

DESCRIPTION Paper, 409 folios, 177 x 126 mm, in Persian, naskh
script, black ink, some words and letters in red; 116 diagrams in red
with black lettering. Contemporary maroon morocco binding with
flap, stamped central medallions and Chinese cloudband motifs.

PROVENANCE Sam Fogg, December 2000

BIBLIOGRAPHY EI VI 601; DSB XIII 535-37

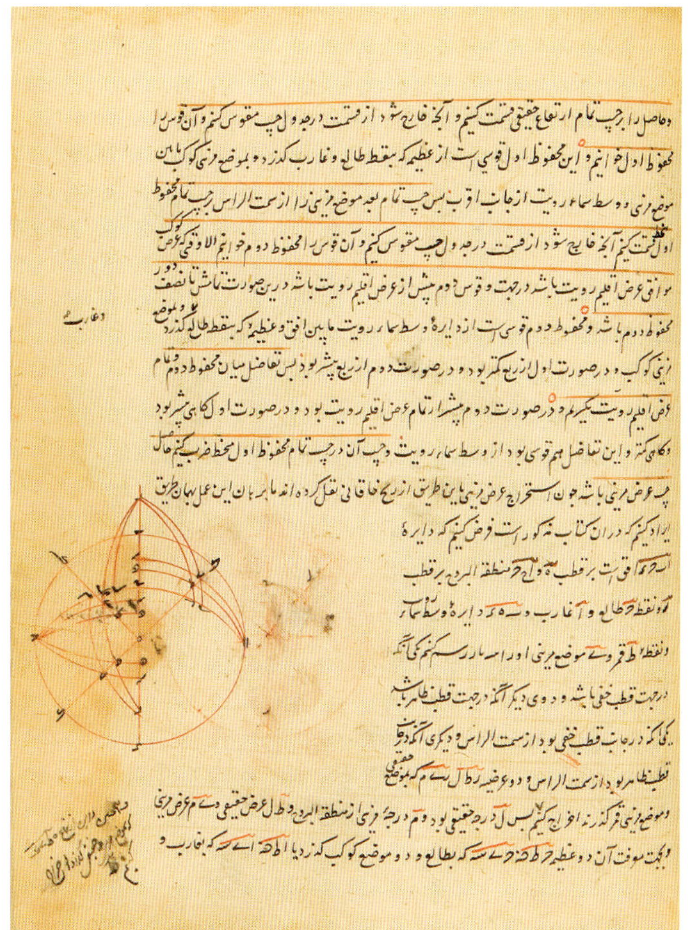

LJS 411
f. 204r

39   LJS 411

Abu 'Ali al-Birjandi, *Sharh-i zij-i jadid sultani*
Persia, *c.* 1523–28

This is a later commentary on the astronomical tables
developed at Samarqand (see LJS 400 [no. 38]).

DESCRIPTION Paper, 242 folios, 240 x 177 mm, in Persian, nasta'liq
script, significant sentences underlined in red, marginal
commentary; 133 diagrams, one in green, otherwise red, and 9
additional diagrams inserted, probably contemporary (two on blue
paper). Later brown morocco binding.

PROVENANCE Sam Fogg, March 2001

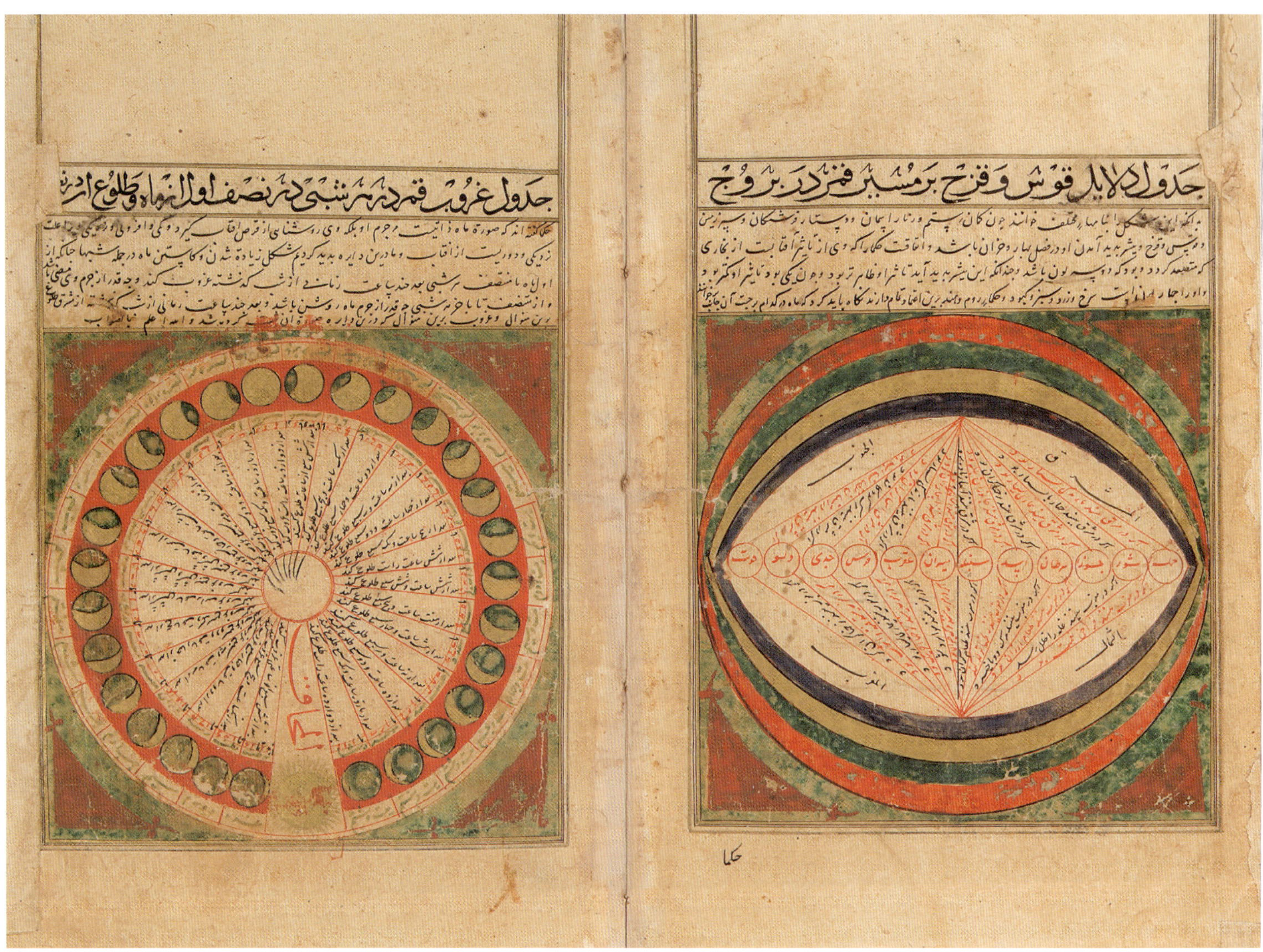

40 LJS 434

Taqwim

Timurid Empire, eastern Persia, *c.* 1507

This *taqwim*, or almanac, contains a number of tables of 'elections' (*ikhtiyarat*), an astrological technique for determining auspicious times for carrying out certain events. It also includes part of a horoscope diagram, dated Friday, 27 Shawwal 912 / 12 March 1507 and cast for the locality 92° 30' east and 26[?]° 21' north, in present northern Afghanistan.

DESCRIPTION Paper, 7 folios, 220 x 140 mm, in Persian, elegant nasta'liq script, black ink, significant words and numbers in red, headings in naskh script in black ink; 6 coloured diagrams and 8 tables. Loose 19th-century brown morocco binding.

PROVENANCE Sam Fogg, March 2002

BIBLIOGRAPHY EI III 1063-64, X 145-46

41 LJS 188

Ynstruction of the Ephimeredes

England, *c.* 1540

This is an example of the genre of 'canons for tables' or sets of instructions for the use of astronomical tables.

DESCRIPTION Paper, 20 folios, 190 x 140 mm, in English, cursive script, 16th-century hand, in brown ink, some initials and rubrication in red; six tables. Modern binding.

PROVENANCE Stuart, Marquess of Bute; Sotheby's, London, 13 June
1983, lot 32, part 6; H.P. Kraus, cat. 180 (1988), no. 134, and cat. 186
(1991), no. 35; John Stanitz, ms. 19

BIBLIOGRAPHY Eade 26-27

42 LJS 202

Placido Titi, *Primum Mobile with Theses*
England, late 17th or 18th century

Placido Titi (1603–1668), an Olivetan monk, composed several
astrological works. His *Tabulae primi mobilis cum thesibus ad
theoricen et canonibus ad praxim*, here translated into English,
was published in Padua in 1657. It consists of seventy "theses",
setting out Titi's theory of celestial influence, and forty-two
"canons", instructing in the use of astronomical tables.
Appended to this are nativities of thirty "illustrious men",
including kings, dukes, ecclesiastical figures, most of whom
were born in the second half of the sixteenth century. Titi
disliked the contemporary system of houses, which was
derived from Regiomontanus, and proposed an alternative
system based on temporal rather than spatial divisions. He
argued that stars operated as causes on human affairs
through the visibility of their light, and that their effects were
therefore dependent on their movement above the horizon.

Two printed editions of English translations exist, one by
Manoah Sibley (1789) and another by John Cooper (1814). The
present manuscript differs from both editions.

DESCRIPTION Paper, 83 folios, 379 x 250 mm, in English, cursive
script, brown ink, numerous neatly drawn astrological diagrams.
PROVENANCE Christopher Tower (b. 1775), of Weald Hall, Essex;
Frederick Hockley; George Winslow Plummer; E. & R. Kistner-
Nurnberg, 1988; H.P. Kraus, ms. R9477; John Stanitz, ms. 33
BIBLIOGRAPHY HMES VIII 302-04; Cooper and Baigent

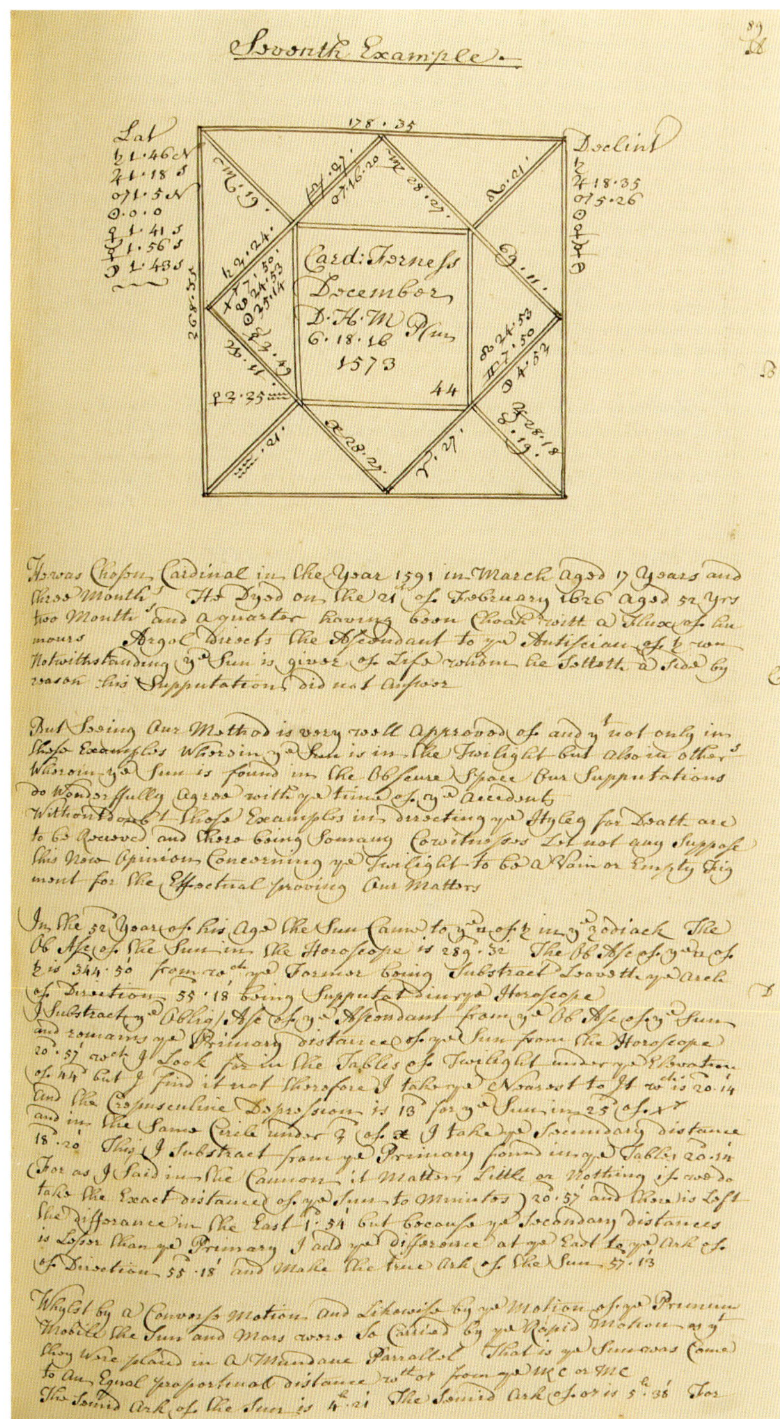

LJS 202, p. 89

V Medicine

The theoretical parameters of medicine in the Middle Ages
tended to follow the model of the four humours, associated
with the figure of Hippocrates (460–c. 370 BC) and refined by
the second-century AD physician Galen. Works by these
authors were translated into Arabic in the ninth century, and
later into Latin. To these two fundamental authorities may be
added Avicenna, author of the *Qanun* (LJS 446 [no. 1] *et sqq.*):
the translation and reception of this important text can be
traced in many of the manuscripts selected here.

Galen's anatomical writings were given visual form in the
Muslim world by illustrated texts such as the *Tashrih-i Mansuri*
(LJS 49 [no. 15]). At the same time, however, surgeons such as
al-Zahrawi (LJS 435 [no. 16]) were emphasizing more practical
aspects of medical procedure, with a particular emphasis on
the design and use of surgical instruments. Al-Zahrawi's
techniques proved influential in the Latin west, but these
difficult (and hazardous) operations were counterbalanced by
a large body of more popular works dealing with cures
derived from plants and other drugs. Several such books of
recipes – dealing with everything from headaches to death
(see notably LJS 220 [no. 28]) – are included here, making use
of ingredients ranging from everyday plants to more
recondite substances such as deer-horn and potable gold. The
botanical information included in these works originates in
the tradition of herbals, illustrated examples of which are
given at the end of this chapter (LJS 62 [no. 38] *et sqq.*).

Several of the following manuscripts trace attempts to
conquer particular diseases, such as syphilis and the plague
(notably LJS 195 [no. 27], 458 [no. 29] and 471 [no. 30]). Others
highlight methods of diagnosis, particularly through urine
samples (LJS 430 [no. 20]). The later abandonment of the
Galenic model is intimated in the works of Descartes (LJS 171
[no. 35]) and Leibniz (LJS 313 [no. 36]).

1   LJS 446

Ibn Sina, section from *Al-Qanun fi'l-tibb*
Spain (probably Cordoba or Toledo), 1st half 12th century

Abu 'Ali al-Husayn ibn Sina (980–1037), known to the Latin
west as Avicenna, was among the pre-eminent philosophers
and physicians writing in Arabic. One of his philosophical
treatises has already been mentioned (see LJS 440 [I, no. 6]),
but his greatest influence was exercised through the *Qanun fi'l-
tibb*. This 'Canon of Medicine' continued to define the
parameters of medical theory and practice for seven centuries
after it was written. It drew on classical sources, particularly
Hippocrates and Galen, the more contemporary *al-Hawi* of al-
Razi (for whom see LJS 391 [no. 17]) and Ibn Sina's own
experience as a physician.

The *Qanun* is divided into five books. Book I is a general
account of elements, humours, forces, causes of health and
sickness and forms of treatment. The remaining four books
cover drugs and their preparation (Books II and V) and
diseases, divided into those which are specific to certain
organs and those which are not (Books III and IV). The
section contained in the present manuscript is from Book III,
Al-amrad al-juz'iyya (head-to-toe diseases), which covers
diseases of the brain, nerves, eye, ear, joints and nails among
others.

Its calligraphy and paper date the present manuscript to
the first half of the twelfth century, within a hundred years of
Ibn Sina's death. It is an early representative of the circulation
of the *Qanun* in Spain. In the thirteenth century the
manuscript was annotated by a Jewish physician, who made
transliterations into Hebrew characters of terminology
relating to diseases of swelling and distension (f. 50r-v).

DESCRIPTION Paper, 92 folios, 240 x 160 mm, in Arabic, elegant
maghrebi script, brown ink, numerous marginal notes in Arabic,
annotations in Hebrew on one folio. No covers.
PROVENANCE Sam Fogg, December 2002
BIBLIOGRAPHY EI III 941-42; DSB XV 498-99

2 LJS 322

Ibn Sina, fragments of *Al-Qanun fi'l-tibb*,
Books III, IV and V
Persia or Turkey, possibly 13th century

DESCRIPTION Paper, 74 folios, 249 x 160 mm, in Arabic, naskh
script, non-vocalized and without diacritics, brown ink, rubrics and
headings in red. Disbound.
PROVENANCE Seal impressions ff. 22r, 26r; Sotheby's, London, 10
October 1991, lot 958; Sam Fogg, August 1999

3 LJS 426

Ibn Sina, *Al-Qanun fi'l-tibb*, Book I
Persia, late 14th century

DESCRIPTION Paper, 321 folios (some later replacements),
200 x 115 mm, in Arabic, naskh script in more than one hand,
headings and significant words picked out or underlined in red,
occasional marginal annotations. Brown morocco binding.
PROVENANCE Sam Fogg, October 2001

4 LJS 355

Ibn Sina, *Al-Qanun fi'l-tibb*, Books III, IV and V
Probably 15th century

DESCRIPTION Paper, 182 folios, 320 x 215 mm, in Arabic, clear
naskh script, black ink, significant words in red. Leather binding.
PROVENANCE Sam Fogg, November 1999

5 LJS 417

Ibn Sina, *Al-Qanun fi'l-tibb*, Books III, IV and V
AH 899-904 / 1494-98

DESCRIPTION Paper, 598 leaves, 316 x 173 mm, in Arabic, small,
neat naskhi script, two illuminated headpieces (the first rubbed),
copied by Farij al-Karab Yusuf ibn Husain ibn Fayyad al-'Arab. Later
composite brown and red morocco binding.
PROVENANCE Christie's, London, 3 May 2001, lot 32

6 LJS 427

Ibn Sina, *Al-Qanun fi'l-tibb*, Books II, III, IV and V
Persia, 16th–17th century

DESCRIPTION Paper, 367 folios, 320 x 220 mm, in Arabic, naskh
script (six folios in nasta'liq), black ink, significant words in red,
names of medicines and ailments noted in red in outer margins.
Possibly 19th-century Indian binding, stamped.
PROVENANCE Sam Fogg, October 2001

7 LJS 359

Ibn Sina, sections from *Al-Qanun fi'l-tibb* in Latin
England, 2nd half 13th century

Ibn Sina's *Qanun* was translated into Latin in its entirety by
Gerard of Cremona between 1150 and his death in 1187; it
formed the basis of university medical teaching from the
fourteenth to the sixteenth (and in some places the
seventeenth) centuries.

DESCRIPTION Paper, 18 folios, 280 x 210 mm, in Latin, brown ink
(Book I) and black ink (Book II), two scholastic scripts, red rubrics,
heading for Book I in red and blue, one 6-line initial in red and blue,
2-line initials in red and blue. Disbound, sewn into modern wrapper.
PROVENANCE William Clarke, 18th century; John Church, 19th
century; Bernard Quaritch, cat. 1270, no. 7
BIBLIOGRAPHY EI III 944-45; DSB XV 499

8 LJS 299

Ibn Sina, *Al-Qanun fi'l-tibb*, in Hebrew, with other
medical works
Yemen, 15th or early 16th century

The last four books of the *Qanun* were translated into Hebrew
in 1279 by Nathan ha-Me'ati. Subsequently the first book was
translated by Joseph ben Joshua Lorki in 1408. These two
versions were combined in the Hebrew incunable edition of
the *Qanun*, published in Naples in 1491–92. There also exists a
shorter recension of Ibn Sina's text, in Arabic, of which two
Hebrew translations were made, one by Moses ibn Tibbon
(1272) and the other anonymous.

The present manuscript contains four books of the *Qanun* in Hebrew, with additional sections on drugs, the liver and intestines and heart diseases. This is followed by a commentary on Galen, in Hebræo-Arabic. The copyist of this section – and of some other short miscellaneous Hebraeo-Arabic texts also contained in the manuscript – also made a large number of marginal annotations to the Hebrew text of the *Qanun*.

DESCRIPTION Paper, 147 folios, 208 x 153 mm, in Hebrew, Yemeni semi-cursive script, rubrics in square script; other works in Hebraeo-Arabic, a contemporary or slightly later Yemeni semi-cursive hand; many contemporary and later marginal annotations. Contemporary or near-contemporary blind-stamped red morocco binding.
PROVENANCE Sa'id Dannookh (who wrote many of the additional glosses); David Solomon Sassoon, ms. 428; Sassoon sale, Sotheby's, New York, 21 June 1994, lot 54; Sam Fogg, cat. 16 (1995), no. 83
BIBLIOGRAPHY EJ III 959; HUM §432

9   LJS 311

Ibn Sina, *Al-Qanun fi'l-tibb* in Hebrew, with Moses ben Maimon, *Ma'amar ha-nikbad*
Italy, 15th century

This copy of the *Qanun*, in Hebrew, is accompanied by an important work by the Jewish physician and philosopher Moses ben Maimon (1135–1204; known to the Latins as Maimonides). Maimonides holds a central place in medieval philosophy for his 'Guide of the Perplexed'. He is also notable for his medical works. The work included here is his treatise on poisons and antidotes. Maimonides wrote this, like his other works, in Arabic, under the title *Kitab al-summum wa'l-mutaharriz min al-adwiya al-qitala*. It was composed in 1199, and dedicated to his patron, the wazir al-Fadil. It was translated into Hebrew by Moses ibn Tibbon under the title *Ma'amar ha-nikbad*. A Latin translation, by Armengaud (*fl.* 1300), entitled *De venenis*, was popular in the fourteenth century.

The text is divided into two sections, one dealing with the treatment of stings and bites of insects, snakes and mad dogs, the other with poisons derived from plants and their antidotes.

DESCRIPTION Paper, 132 folios, 195 x 140 mm, in Hebrew, Italian semi-cursive script, brown ink. Modern maroon calf binding.
PROVENANCE Solomon Hirschell (1761-1842), first chief Rabbi of England; Jew's College, London, no. 118; Beth Din Congregation, London, no. 139; Christie's, New York, 23 June 1999, lot 15
BIBLIOGRAPHY Sarton II 372; EJ XI 779; Muntner

10   LJS 469

Sefer ha-seder ha-katan
Italy, *c.* 1490

This collection of letters relating to the Italian Finzi family also contains ten pages of a Hebrew translation of the *Qanun*. This is accompanied by a list of limbs, giving their qualities (hot, cold, etc.).

DESCRIPTION Paper, 21 leaves, 140 x 108 mm, in Hebrew, Italian Ashkenazi semi-cursive script. 19th-century marbled boards with cloth spine.
PROVENANCE Solomon Halberstam, no. 404; Montefiore Endowment; Sotheby's, New York, 27 October 2004, lot 350

11   LJS 444

Jamal al-Din Aqsarayi, *Hal al-mujiz*
22 Shawwal 884 AH/ 6 January 1480

As the *Qanun* circulated it was the subject of numerous commentaries and supercommentaries. One widely read such commentary was the *Mujiz al-qanun* by 'Ala' al-Din ibn al-Nafis (d. 1288), a native of Damascus who became personal physician to the Mamluk Egyptian Sultan Baybars I. The *Mujiz* is a summary of the *Qanun*, omitting the sections on anatomy and physiology.

The *Mujiz* was itself the subject of a number of commentaries, one of which is contained in the present manuscript. Its author, Jamal al-Din Aqsarayi (d. *c.* 1389) was a Turkish philosopher and theologian who taught at the Zinjirli madrasa at Aqsaray.

This copy was made in 1480 by the scribe Kamal al-Din Mahmud al-Astarabadi. On the evidence of the numerous

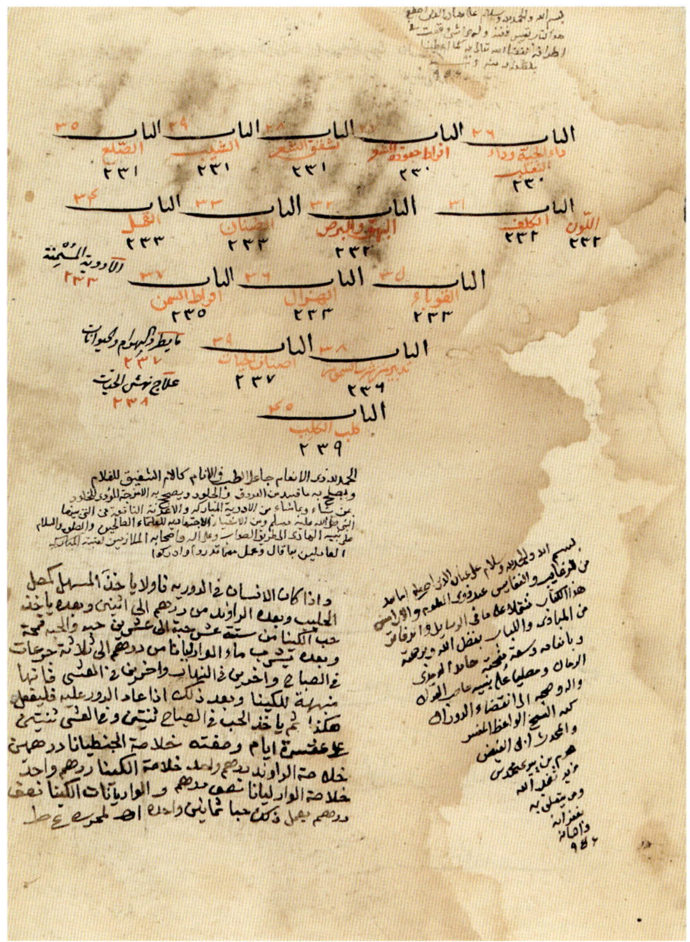

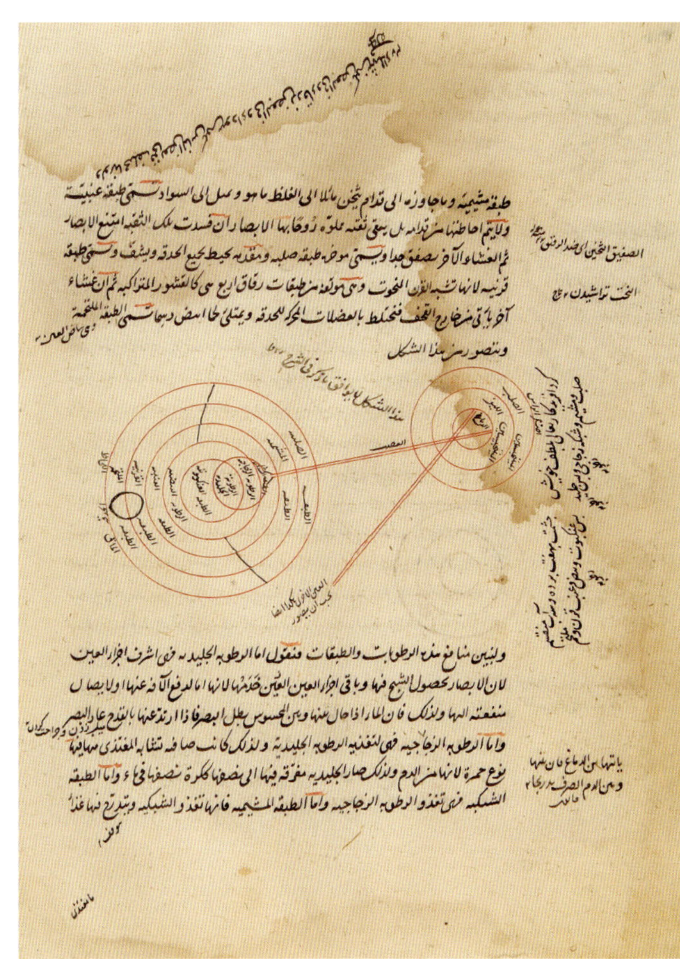

ownership marks and annotations, in Arabic and Turkish, it
remained in use into the nineteenth century. One owner
added some biographical information about Aqsarayi on the
title page; another, an invocation of the buttercup (*kabikaj*),
intended as a talisman to guard the manuscript against insects
and worms.

A diagram on f. 124v shows the human eye and the manner
in which it transmits representations to the brain.

DESCRIPTION Paper, 247 folios, 250 x 185 mm, in Arabic, naskh
script, black ink, headings and overlinings in red, catchwords;
one diagram. Contemporary pasteboard binding, remnants of 17th-
century cloth spine.

PROVENANCE 'Abd al-Fattah al-Qatin, Tabriz; Isma'il ibn al-Hajj 'Isa
Jurayji al-Muhanna, Rabi' II 1195 AH/ March–April 1781; Al-Hajj 'Abd
al-Qadir ibn al-Sayyid 'Abd Allah Efendi al-Astawani; Abd Allah

Efendi al-Astawani, 1239 AH / 1823-24; Butterfield's, 14 November
2002, lot 3001

BIBLIOGRAPHY EI II 419, III 897-98

12   LJS 393

Al-Nisaburi, Commentaries on Hippocrates and
Hunayn ibn Ishaq
Mamluk Egypt or Syria, mid-14th century

As well as serving as a source for later writers such as Ibn
Sina, Hippocrates was commentated by the eleventh-century
Persian physician Ibn Abi Sadiq al-Nisaburi; in fact, al-
Nisaburi became known after his death as 'the second
Hippocrates'. This manuscript includes one of his
commentaries on Hippocrates, entitled simply *Sharh kitab*

buqurat (Commentary on the book of Hippocrates) as well as a
Kitab ibn Ishaq, a commentary on a work of the renowned
ninth-century translator of Greek into Arabic, Hunayn ibn
Ishaq (known to the Latin west as Johannitus). Hunayn
translated works by Galen, Hippocrates, Plato, Aristotle,
Dioscorides and Ptolemy. He also produced a number of
original works, including an introduction to Galen's *Ars parva*.
In its Latin version this became one of the basic texts of the
medical curriculum (see LJS 24 [no. 18]).

DESCRIPTION Paper, 81 folios, 246 x 170 mm, in Arabic, neat naskh
script, black ink, titles in red ink. Later binding.
PROVENANCE Sam Fogg, November 2000
BIBLIOGRAPHY HMI 108-09; Ullmann 11; Sarton I 611

13 LJS 398

Sa'id ibn Hibat Allah, *Maqala fi khalq al-insan*
Mamluk Syria or Iraq, 15 Jumada II 689 AH / 25 June 1290

Sa'id ibn Hibat Allah (d. *c.* 1101) was physician to al-Muqtadi,
caliph of Baghdad from 1075 to 1094. He wrote two medical
treatises, a general synopsis of medicine and the present work,
'Discourse on the Creation of Man'. This text is of a twofold
nature. The first thirty-five chapters are concerned with the
practicalities of sexual intercourse and procreation: they deal
with such matters as sperm and the lack of it, the uterus,
impotence, pregnancy, abortion and contraception, the
development of the fetus, birth and childcare. The remaining
fifteen chapters are devoted to discussions of a more
philosophical nature, with particular reference to the soul and
the intellect. Particular attention is paid to the nature of the
reasoning faculty (*'aql*): subjects covered include the degrees of
human rationality, the views of ancient philosophers on the
intellect, and what happens to the reasoning faculty after the
death of the body. Also discussed are the difference between
the soul (*nafs*) and the spirit (*ruh*) and the views of the ancients
on the transmigration of souls.

DESCRIPTION Paper, 84 folios, 255 x 175 mm, in Arabic, non-
professional naskh script, black ink, chapter headings in red,
sporadic underlining in red and black, some marginal notes. Brown
morocco binding, central medallions and cornerpieces gilt-stamped.

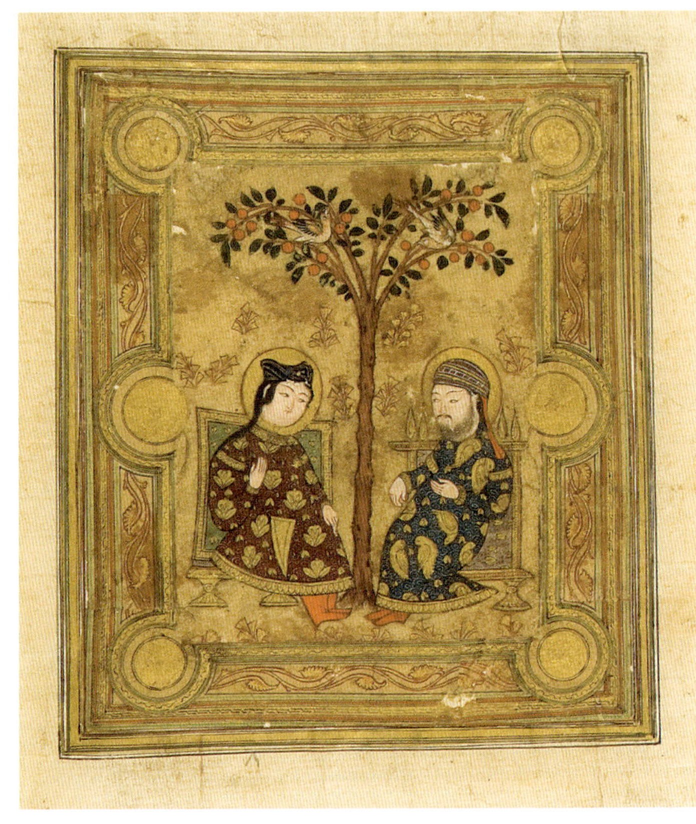

LJS 1
f. 21↔

PROVENANCE Copied by 'Abd al-Rahman ibn 'Abd al-Salam al-
Safuri; Persian records of 19th-century births; Sam Fogg, December
2000
BIBLIOGRAPHY Sarton I 772

14 LJS 189

Zayn al-Din al-Jurjani, *Dhakhira-i-Khwarazmshahi*
Persia, 14th century

The 'Thesaurus of the Shah of Khwarazm' of al-Jurjani
(d. *c.* 1136), so-called because it was dedicated to Shah Qutb al-
Din Muhammad (1097–1127), is a medical encyclopaedia in
nine books. Its contents cover physiology and anatomy;
general pathology; general remarks on treatment; the role of
diagnosis; fevers; specific diseases; surgery and fractures; and
poisons and their antidotes. It contains a considerable
amount of observation drawn from personal experience.
The work rapidly became extremely popular, and was ranked
alongside Galen and Avicenna as essential reading matter for

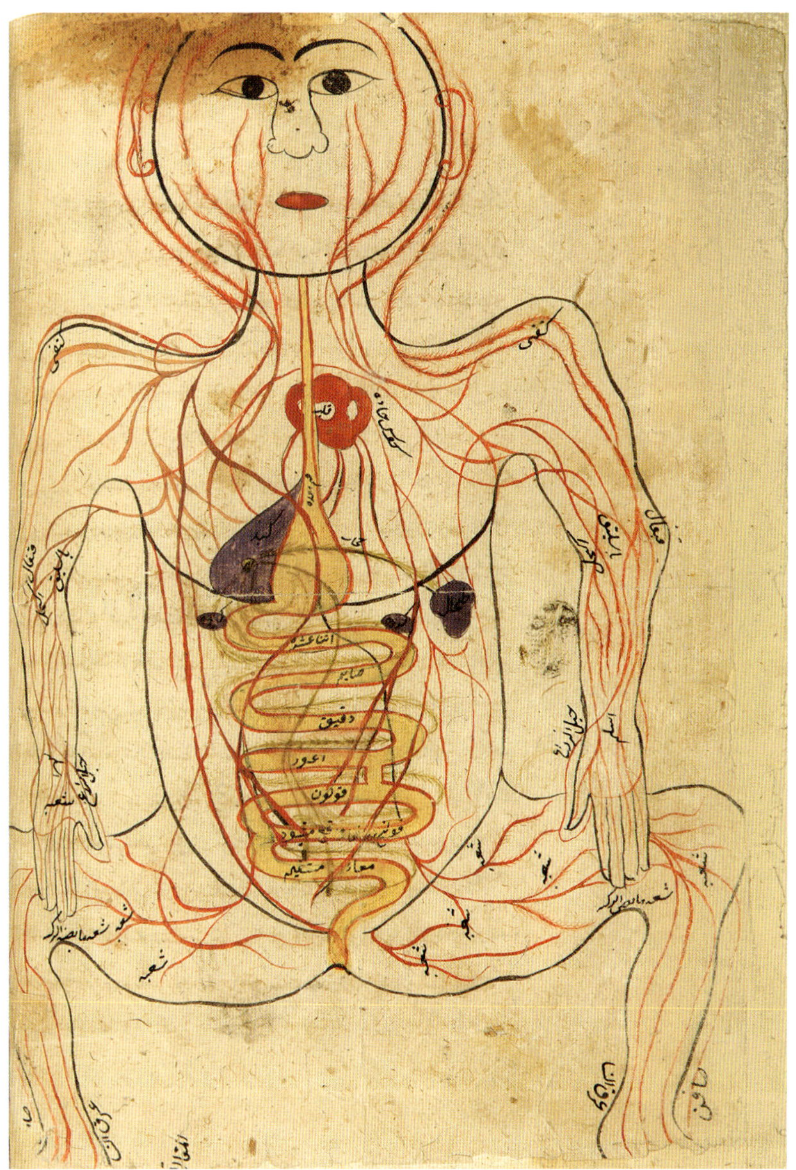

the medical student. Aside from this, however, it marks a
turning point in Persian medicine as the first major work
written in the vernacular rather than in Arabic: al-Jurjani's
terminology subsequently became standard.

Al-Jurjani produced several epitomes of this text. Various
translations, complete or partial, were made into Hebrew,
Urdu, Arabic and Turkish.

DESCRIPTION Pink paper, 352 folios, 395 x 317 mm, in Persian,
naskh script written by two scribes, black ink, rubrics in red;
one miniature, one shamsa in colours and gold, illuminated chapter
headings. Remnants of 18th-century blind-stamped leather binding,
laid down on red morocco.

PROVENANCE Hagop Kervorkian; Sotheby's, London, 27 April 1981,
lot 108; H.P. Kraus, cat. 186 (1991), no. 173; John Stanitz, ms. 20
BIBLIOGRAPHY EI II 603; Elgood 214-18

15 LJS 49

Tashrih-i Mansuri
Persia, 1411

The illustrations in this manuscript – featuring bones, nerves,
veins, arteries and a woman pregnant with a fetus – are some

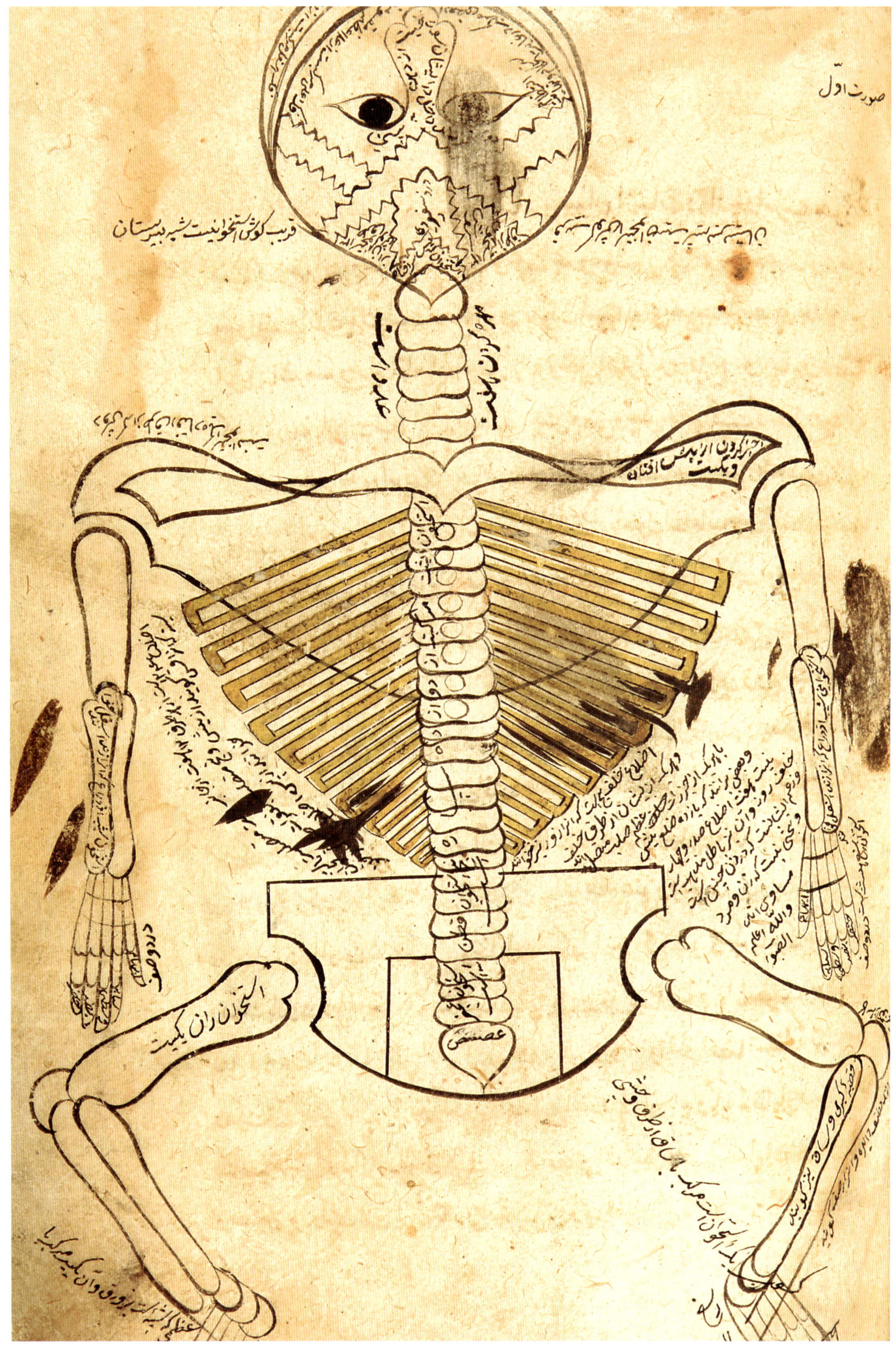

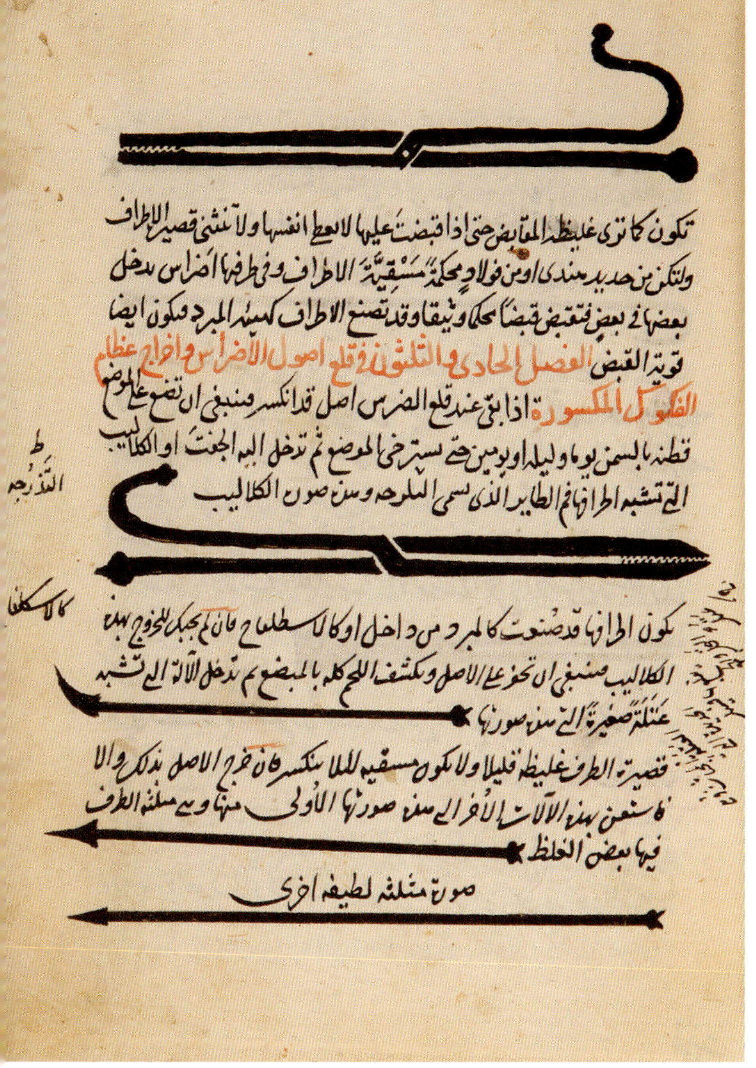

435, p. 17

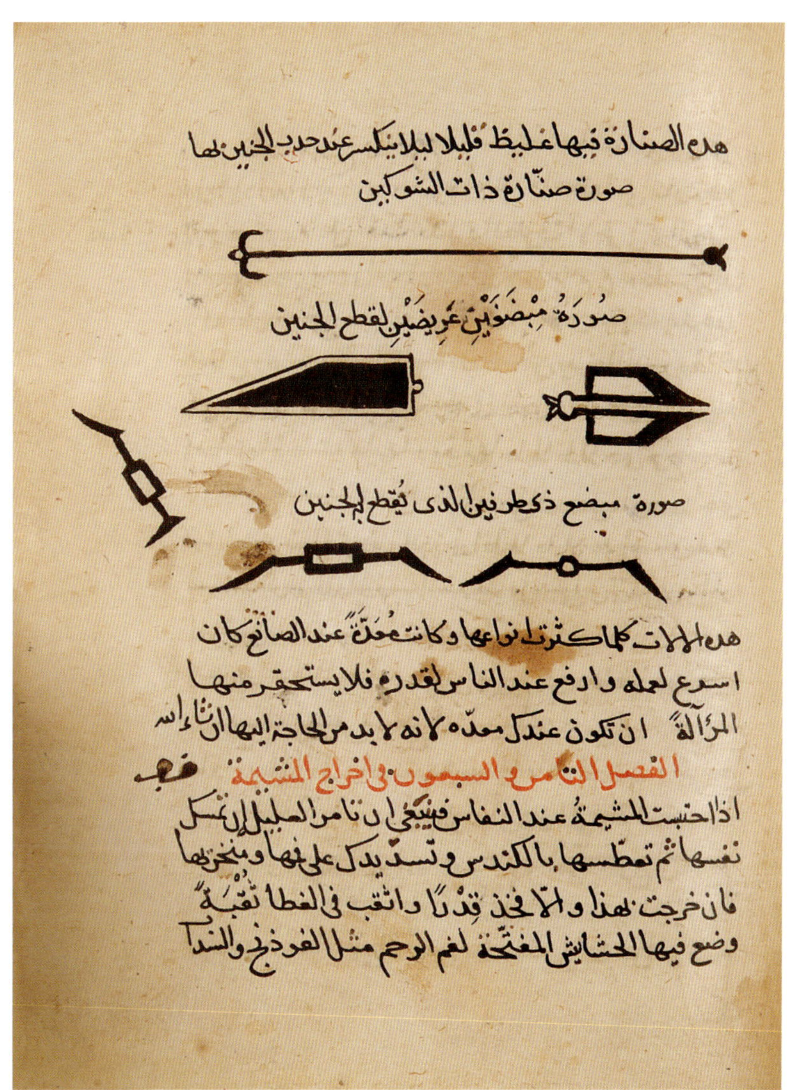

LJS 435, p. 36

of the oldest known representations of the body in the Islamic world. This is a very early copy of the *Tashrih-i Mansuri* (Mansur's anatomy), a popular anatomical work by the Persian physician Mansur ibn Muhammad ibn Ilyas. Mansur composed the treatise in 1396 AD. The colophon states that it was completed by the author himself in the month of Dhu'l-Hijja in the year 813 (1411). It is likely, therefore, that this is an autograph copy. Mansur's work was based on the anatomical writings of Galen. These had been introduced into the Muslim world by Hunayn ibn Ishaq in the ninth century, and remained in use until the seventeenth century.

DESCRIPTION Paper, 32 folios, 245 x 174 mm, in Persian and Arabic, naskh script; five full-page anatomical diagrams. Later red morocco binding.

PROVENANCE Muhammad Reza; Sultan's Hospital, Isfahan; Sotheby's, London, 18 October 1995, lot 51; Sam Fogg, June 1996

16   LJS 435

Abu'l-Qasim al-Zahrawi, *'Amal al-yad*
Mesopotamia, AH 869 / 1464

The Andalusian physician al-Zahrawi (d. after 1009), known to the Latins as Albucasis, is recognized as the most

influential surgeon of medieval Islam. This manuscript
contains Parts II (incomplete) and III of his work on surgery –
entitled literally 'Hand Work' – which constitutes the thirtieth
book of his medical encyclopaedia, *Al-Tasrif li-man 'ajiza 'an al-
ta'lif*. It was translated into Latin by Gerard of Cremona
(see also LJS 359 [no. 7]) and subsequently became well-
known in France through the work of Guy de Chauliac (d.
1370; cf. also LJS 424 [no. 22]). Included here are sections on
incision of arteries, removal of growths, tumours and
blockages, blood-letting and cupping; bone-setting from head
to foot, the treatment of dislocations, and the treatment of
sprains. The sections of Part II dealing with the sexual organs
are missing, however.

   Al-Zahrawi paid particular attention to surgical
instruments, devising and detailing the use of forceps, probes,
knives, scalpels, hooks, scrapers and lancets. His descriptions
of such instruments were accompanied by an innovative
tradition of illustration, as can be seen from this manuscript.
His focus was notably practical rather than theoretical, as can
be seen by his warning to the reader at the start of Part II: "In
the course of the work of which this book treats there often
occurs an effusion of the blood upon which life depends …
accompanied by uncertainty and fear; and in most cases
death will supervene". He advised surgeons to refrain from
operating when they were doubtful of the outcome, even if
they were offered great riches.

DESCRIPTION Paper, 108 folios, 172 x 125 mm, in Arabic, naskh
script, in two hands, black ink, headings in red, contemporary
corrections, marginal notes in a maghrebi hand; illustrations of
surgical instruments in black and red. Later brown morocco binding.
PROVENANCE Sotheby's, London, 2 April 2002, lot 23
BIBLIOGRAPHY EI XI 398-99; DSB XIV 584-85; Spink and Lewis

17   LJS 391

Al-Razi, Fragment from the *Liber almansurem*
c. 13th century

Abu Bakr Muhammad al-Razi (*c.* 854–925 or 935) was a
physician, philosopher and, by his own account, the author of
around 200 books. His medical works are in the tradition of
Galen, whom he nonetheless criticized on occasion (rejecting,

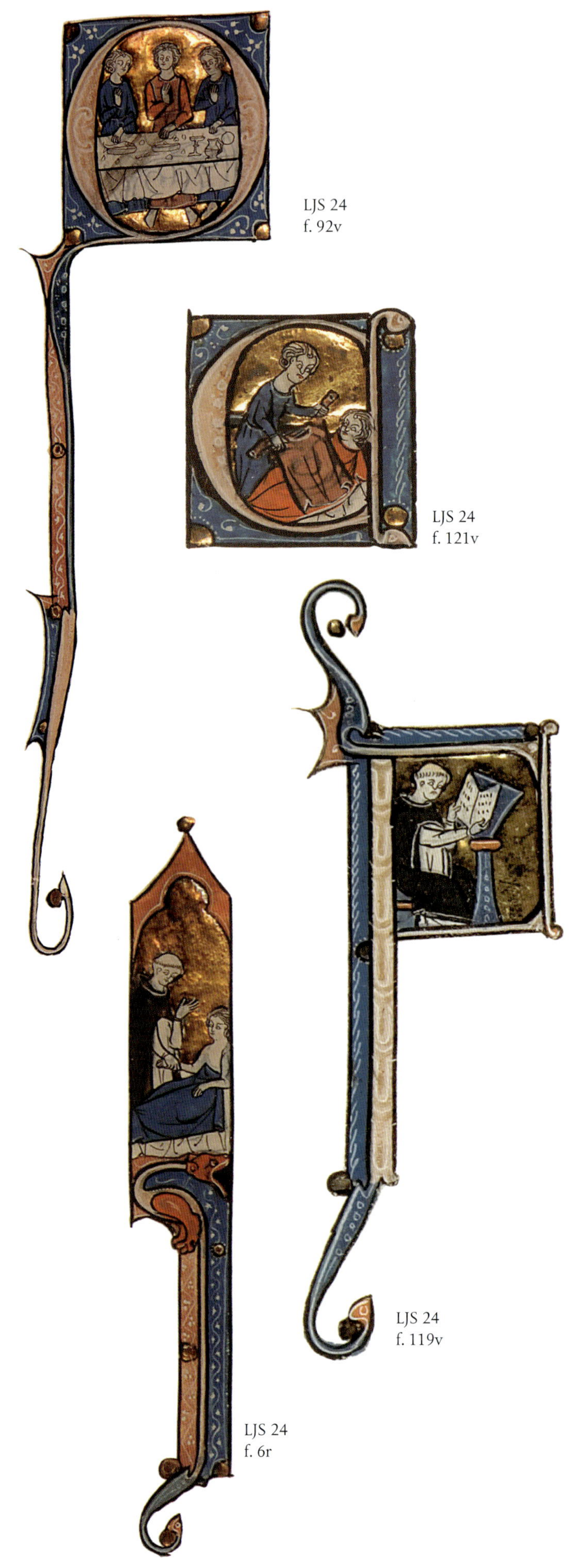

LJS 24
f. 92v

LJS 24
f. 121v

LJS 24
f. 119v

LJS 24
f. 6r

for example, the notion of the transmission of heat as derived from the theory of humours). He dedicated a medical handbook to his patron, Mansur ibn Ishaq, governor of Rayy; entitled *Kitab al-mansuri* in Arabic, it was translated in Latin in the twelfth century by Gerard of Cremona (see LJS 359 [no. 7] and 435 [no. 16]). The present folio is from a copy of this work.

DESCRIPTION Parchment, 1 folio, *c.* 152 x 355 mm, in Latin, proto-Gothic script.
PROVENANCE Phillip J. Pirages, cat. 45 (2000), no. 985
BIBLIOGRAPHY Sarton I 609; EI VIII 474-77; DSB XI 323-26

18 LJS 24

Medical miscellany
Paris, mid-13th century

This is an illustrated compendium of popular texts casting light on the practice of medicine and the lives of medical students in Paris in the thirteenth century. Twelve miniatures portray scenes involving doctors, patients and students; in four of these, the initial artist's guide sketch is still visible. The selection of texts represents standard works which were required reading at the time. It begins with the *Introductio ad artem parvam Galeni*, a brief introduction to Galenic medicine by the celebrated ninth-century translator of Greek into Arabic Hunayn ibn Ishaq (see also LJS 393 [no. 12]). This is followed by two more short works, both on the pulse, *Liber de pulsibus* by the Byzantine physician Philaretus and *De pulsu* by Giles of Corbeil. The bulk of the manuscript, however, is made up of four works by the physician and Neoplatonic philosopher Isaac Israeli (mid-9th–mid-10th century) on diet, urine, fevers and the elements. These were translated from Arabic into Latin by Constantine the African in 1087.

DESCRIPTION Parchment, 149 folios, 290 x 193 mm, in Latin, gothic script; decorated in red and blue with illuminated initials; 12 miniatures. Early 18th-century binding.
PROVENANCE Helmingham Hall, Suffolk, 18th century; arms of Sir Lionel Tollemache (1708–1770), 5th Baronet and 4th Earl of Dysart; Philip Robinson; Sotheby's, London, 6 December 1993, lot 53; Jörn Günther, *Mittelalterliche Handschriften und Miniaturen* (1995), no. 4; Sam Fogg, cat. 16 (1995), no. 46

19 LJS 479

Taddeo Alderotti, *Libellus de sanitate*, and other texts
Italy, 14th century (after 1323)

Taddeo Alderotti (*c.* 1223–1295), one of the pre-eminent physicians of the Latin Middle Ages, was largely responsible for founding the medical school at Bologna. The present manuscript contains a complete text of his 'Book of Health' in his own Italian translation, prepared for the Guelph leader Corso Donati in 1283. Organized according to the seasons of the year, it offers a practical guide to healthy conduct and the properties of herbs and plants.

Numerous other texts also have a place in the present manuscript, including a *Fiore di virtù*, an unidentified treatise on the Cardinal Virtues, an excerpt from the pseudo-Aristotelian *Secret of Secrets* (see LJS 459 [I, no. 7]) and a fragment of the 10th-century Suida Greek-Latin lexicon.

DESCRIPTION Parchment, 18 folios, 225 x 150 mm, in Italian (the Suida in Latin), gothic bookhand. Modern binding.
PROVENANCE Sam Fogg, cat. 15 (1992), no. 10, and cat. 16 (1995), no. 65; Sotheby's, London, 6 December 2001, lot 61; Robert Lenkiewicz; Sotheby's, London, 2 December 2003, lot 70

20 LJS 430

Bartholomaeus Montagnana, *Tractatus de urinis*
Possibly France, *c.* 1500

Bartolomaeus Montagnana's *Tractatus de urinarum indiciis perutilis* (Very useful treatise on the indications of urine) was first published in Padua in 1487. Urine, according to Montagnana, is the most useful of all signs for diagnosis of disease. He analyses it according to colour and contents, and outlines the distinctions between the urine of men and women and between that of humans and animals. This manuscript postdates the first edition of the text, and includes some textual variants from it which are found in a later edition of *c.* 1500.

DESCRIPTION Paper, 78 folios, 152 x 100 mm, in Latin, italicized flourished script, brown ink, chapter and paragraph titles in bold gothic script, a few 16th-century marginal annotations at beginning.

Modern limp parchment binding.

PROVENANCE Victor A. Schwarz; A. Sokol Books, cat. 40 (2002),
no. 88

21   LJS 395

Bartholomaeus Anglicus, Two fragments of *Liber de rerum proprietatibus*
Possibly France, 13th century

The pastedowns of this manuscript are made from the
fragments of an early copy of *De rerum proprietatibus* (On the
properties of things) by Batholomaeus Anglicus (*fl.* 1220–50),
concerning physiology.

DESCRIPTION Parchment, two part-folio fragment pastedowns,
215 x 185 mm, in Latin, regular gothic script in brown ink.
PROVENANCE A few contemporary annotations; George Dunn,
February 1907; Duncan Beresford-Jones; Christie's, London,
29 November 2000, lot 12

22   LJS 424

Compendium of medical texts
Bologna, 1500-01

This manuscript, compiled in 1500–01, offers a detailed
picture of the study of medicine at the University of Bologna
at that time. The compiler, a student by the name of Johannes
Mellarinus, put together a comprehensive selection of medical
writings from the tenth to the fifteenth centuries. The earliest
of these is al-Razi's *Liber almansurem* (see LJS 391 [no. 17]), in
Latin. There is also a long section from Ibn Sina's *Qanun* (LJS
446 [no. 1] *et sqq.*); a work by the French surgeon Guy de
Chauliac (see LJS 435 [no. 16]), entitled *De antidotis particularibus
et appropriatis membris,* and the *Tractatus de proportionibus
medicinarum et de modo investigandi complexiones earum* of Gentile
da Foligno (see further LJS 471 [no. 30]). The remainder of the
compilation is made up of fifteenth-century texts, including
the *Consilia de curatione febrium* (Advice for the cure of fevers) of
Niccolò Falcucci (d. 1412); *Recepte ordinate in variis egritudinibus*
(Treatments required in various diseases) by Johannes
Baverius de Baveriis (d. 1480); and *Libellus de egritudinibus
infantium* (Book about children's diseases) of Paulus
Bagellardus (d. 1492). One of these, *Practica curativa de variis
morbis* (Practical cure for various sicknesses), is by Ludovicus
de Leonibus (1465–1528), who taught medicine at the
University of Bologna during this period.

DESCRIPTION Parchment, 526 folios, 205 x 155 mm, in Latin, small
bastarda script, brown/black ink with pale red headlines.
Contemporary vellum binding.
PROVENANCE Martayan Lan, cat. 28 (2001), no. 157

23   LJS 198

Arnald of Villanova, *De simplicibus*
Spain, *c.* 1350–80

Arnald of Villanova (*c.* 1240–1311), a Catalan, was a prolific
writer on medical subjects as well as a renowned practitioner;
he was physician to Peter III of Aragon, his son Alfonso III
and Alfonso's brother James II. He also played a significant
role in the transmission of medical knowledge from Arabic
into Latin, translating works by Avicenna, Galen and Qusta
ibn Luqa among others. This effort was centred around the
University of Montpellier, where Arnald studied and taught,
and where he was partly responsible for forming the
curriculum.

This manuscript is a compilation of 'simples' (medicines
made from one component), divided into 85 chapters, giving
lists of plants for specified medical uses. Some of these uses
are broadly categorized as medicines for softening (*de medicinis
mollificativis*), opening (*aperientibus*), lessening (*attenuativis*) and
so on. Others are directed against specific disorders of parts
of the body, including the stomach, liver, spleen and kidneys.
The final two folios give an alphabetical list of plants, together
with tables of oils, flowers, roots, seeds and minerals. The text
was first published in a collected edition of Arnald's works in
Lyons in 1504; a more complete version was included in the
edition of his works published in Basle in 1585. Extra passages,
not included in the 1585 edition, are found in this manuscript.

DESCRIPTION Parchment, 21 folios, 178 x 130 mm, in Latin, early
Gothic script, brown ink, rubrics in red, red initials with (later) blue
or black penwork; tables and index. Disbound.

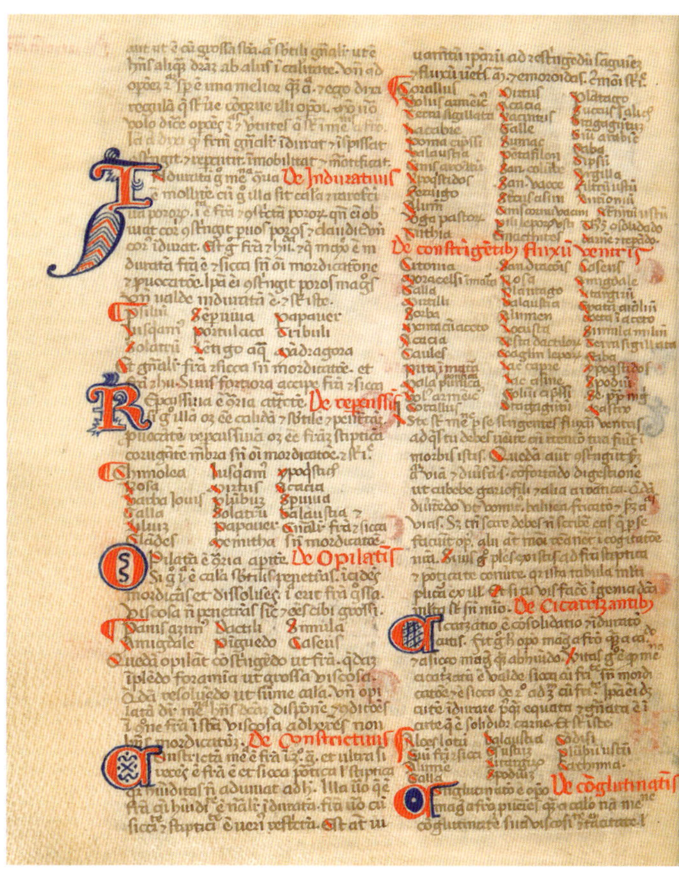

198
f. 5v

198
. 19r

PROVENANCE Les Enluminures, cat. 2 (1993), no. 23; John Stanitz, ms. 29

BIBLIOGRAPHY DSB I 289-91; Sarton II 893-95

24   LJS 437

Matthaeus Platearius, *De simplici medicina*
Southern Germany or Austria, *c.* 1400

De simplici medicina, written in the mid-twelfth century, is another compendium of simples (see LJS 198 [no. 23]). It lists drugs in alphabetical order, giving a description and detailing among other aspects their action, mode of application, and signs of purity or impurity. A large proportion of it is based on the medicinal properties of plants. In this respect it represented an updating of the herbals of Dioscorides and Pseudo-Apuleius (see LJS 62 [no. 38]). It was twice translated into Hebrew, by Solomon ben Moses of Melgueil (2nd half 13th century) and by Solomon ben Elia (1414).

Salerno, in southern Italy, where Platearius lived and taught, was famed for the skill of its doctors from the late tenth century onwards, and gradually became a renowned medical school. Its success in this area may be partly attributed to its geographical position, which facilitated its transmission of Greek and Arabic learning into Latin, although in its early stages it appears to have been more oriented towards practice than theory. Platearius was a central figure in developing the theoretical framework of medical teaching there. This is demonstrated by another work of his, a commentary on another compendium of drugs, the so-called *Antidotarium Nicolai*; it was the first commentary produced at Salerno.

DESCRIPTION Parchment, 74 folios, 195 x 128 mm, in Latin, gothic textura script, dark brown ink, marginal annotations; three 5- or 6-line initials, 16 2-line initials, in red and blue with penwork decoration; *c.* 250 2-line and *c.* 250 1-line undecorated initials, red and blue. 18th-century calf binding.

PROVENANCE Magister Pangacius, professor of medicine; Christoferus Chrewtznar; Jesuit College of Vienna, 1773; Reiss & Auvermann, 12 October 1993, lot 437; Sam Fogg, June 2002

BIBLIOGRAPHY Sarton II 241; Kristeller 138-59; Singer

25 LJS 421

'Letter from Hippocrates to Caesar'
France, *c.* 1350–75

Another example of the transmission of knowledge in
apocryphal letters (see LJS 459 [I, no. 7]), this manuscript
represents a tradition of letters allegedly addressed by the
celebrated physician Hippocrates of Cos (*c.* 460–*c.* 370 BC) to
Julius Caesar (*c.* 100–44 BC), advising on medical treatment.
The text originated in the thirteenth century and was
originally composed in Anglo-Norman, soon afterwards
being translated into French.

Around fifty surviving manuscripts attest that this was a
popular work; it accumulated material over time and there is
therefore considerable divergence between copies. This copy
includes recipes for treating headaches, sore eyes, toothache
and laryngitis ("*parole perdue*"). Use is made of such ingredients
as milk, rosemary, pork-bladder, egg shells and deer-horn.

DESCRIPTION Parchment, 24 folios, 180 x 118 mm, in Old French,
gothic bookhand, light brown ink, 2-line initials in red throughout,
2-line initial at opening with red infill and descender, a few marginal
annotations. 19th-century brown calf binding.

PROVENANCE Jean-Baptiste Barrois; from whom purchased in 1849
by Bertram, 4th Earl of Ashburnham, ms. 239; Ashburnham sale at
Sotheby's, London, 10 June 1901, lot 277; Les Enluminures, July 2001

BIBLIOGRAPHY DLF 926-27

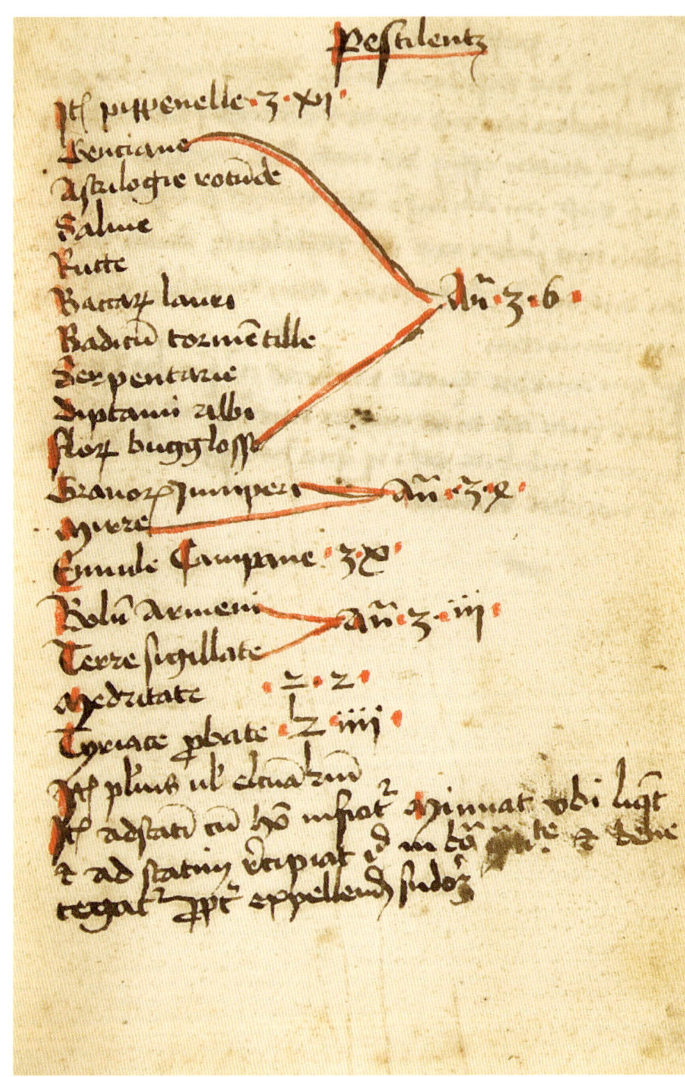

LJS
f. 24

26 LJS 236

Arnald of Villanova, *Thesaurus pauperum*, and other
medical texts
Northern Italy, 2nd half 15th century

This manuscript is a compilation of a diverse selection of
medical recipes. It contains two works by Arnald of Villanova
(for whom see LJS 198 [no. 23]), *Thesaurus pauperum* (Treasury
for the poor) and *Tractatus de proprietatibus aque vite* (On the
water of life). The *Thesaurus pauperum* contains remedies
against diseases of the hair, lethargy, mania, epilepsy and
many other conditions. These are accompanied by numerous
other groups of recipes. A *Liber computi de festis anni* discusses
the calendar and the effect of the passage of the moon
through the signs of the zodiac upon the bodily organs. There
is also the *Ars operativa medica*, attributed to the Catalan
philosopher Ramon Llull. The manuscript is notable for its
many annotations of names of northern Italian readers.

DESCRIPTION Paper, 233 folios, 147 x 108 mm, in Latin and Italian,
gothic cursive script by at least three scribes, brown ink, rubrics and
paragraph marks in red, initial spaces blank; one drawing of
chemical apparatus in brown ink (f. 260r). Original parchment
binding with metal bosses.

PROVENANCE Readers' signatures on ff. 165–167 and 265–66,
mentioning northern Italian placenames (Venice, Brescia, Ghedi);
Les Enluminures, December 1997

27 LJS 195

Medical miscellany
Germany, 2nd half 15th century

Much of this anthology of practical medicine is devoted to the
plague, described as "the six-day epidemic". It also includes
sections on urine, laxatives, water and wine, and various
diseases, as well as recipes for making coloured pigments.

DESCRIPTION Paper, 326 folios, 155 x 116 mm, in German (with
some Latin), Gothic cursive script by several scribes, brown ink,
rubrics in brown and/or red, capitals touched in red, some initials in
red; cut-out pointing hand with decorated coloured cuff, loosely
enclosed at ff. 65-66. Limp parchment binding.

PROVENANCE Library of the Fugger family, shelfmark SVIII K.9;
Sotheby's, London, 23 June 1992, lot 67; Les Enluminures, April 1993;
John Stanitz, ms. 26

28 LJS 220

Recueil de diverses recettes médicinales
Eastern France, *c.* 1475–90

The "diverse recipes" included in this manuscript are for gout,
headaches, loss of hair, running eyes, deafness, toothache,
coughing up of blood, scorpion bites, stillbirth, and "how to
know if a woman has conceived" or "if a man is dead". It also
discusses the four elements, the four humours, and the
relationship of the planets and signs of the zodiac to medical
operations.

DESCRIPTION Paper, 147 folios, 206 x 145 mm, in French with some
Latin, Gothic cursive script, brown ink. Original wood boards,
partially covered with original calf binding.

PROVENANCE Many early French notes and signatures, none dated;
Les Enluminures, 1997; John Stanitz, ms. 51

29 LJS 458

Marco Girolamo Vida, *Abscondita naturae*
Cremona, 1545

Vida (1485–1566) was a prominent poet and literary theorist,
and later bishop of Alba. As this manuscript shows, however,
he also took a keen interest in medicine. Its full title is
*Abscondita naturae collecta ab diversis philosophorum et medicorum
scriptum in inclita civitate Cremonensis* (The hidden things of
nature, collected from diverse volumes of philosophers and
doctors, written in the famous city of Cremona). It comprises
over 400 recipes, taken from published and manuscript
sources, some for treatment of ailments, others for cosmetic
or gastronomic purposes. These include hand creams,
colognes and lotions for preventing lines of aging in the face;
recipes against syphilis and the plague; and recipes for
potable gold. Besides this compendium of recipes the work
contains a series of near-contemporary case studies.

Soon after its compilation, the present manuscript passed
into the hands of the renowned physician Lodovico Settala
(1552–1633), who was particularly active in combatting the
plague, both in 1576 and in 1628; the second outbreak left him
partially paralysed for a time. Settala's coat of arms is added
to the titlepage and binding.

DESCRIPTION Paper, 187 folios, 206 x 157 mm, in Latin, neat cursive
script, brown ink, titlepage with decorative initial and strapwork and
arms of Ludovico Settala added. Contemporary calf binding, original
design of interlocking panels with grapes and flowers, arms of
Settala in the centre.

PROVENANCE Ludovico Settala; Sebastiano Calvi Physici (1685);
Martayan Lan, October 2003

BIBLIOGRAPHY OCIL 553, 626

30 LJS 471

Corpus of Latin medical texts translated into Hebrew
Italy, 14th–15th century

This corpus of texts represents the reception of Italian and
French medical writing by Jewish physicians in the fourteenth
century. The first text is a compilation of 292 cures for various
illnesses, entitled 'Experiments, syrups, electuaries and
mixtures' and attributed to Gentile da Foligno. Gentile, who
taught at Perugia and Padua, wrote (among many other
works) a pioneering treatise on the plague, from which he
himself died in 1348. This is followed by a translation of part
of a work by the Florentine physician Dino del Garbo (d. 1327)
on plasters and unguents, the Latin version of which was later

printed (Ferrara 1489); it is entitled, in Hebrew, *Sefer tsirugia* (Book of surgery). The third text is a translation, by Abraham Avigdor (b. 1351), of Bernard Alberti's *Introductorium in practica pro provectis*, a collection of prescriptions for fevers derived from Avicenna's *Qanun*, Book IV, I (see LJS 446 [no. 1] *et sqq.*).

Both Alberti and Avigdor were resident in Montpellier in the second half of the fourteenth century; Alberti's text was composed in 1358 and Avigdor's translation made soon afterwards, probably *c.* 1370. In the preface to his translation, Avigdor wrote that he had gone to Montpellier to study under Christian teachers and had found many useful books which he planned to translate into Hebrew: he subsequently translated works by the French physician Gerard de Solo (d. *c.* 1360) and the Catalan physician, also resident in Montpellier, Arnald of Villanova (see LJS 198 [no. 23] and 236 [no. 26]).

DESCRIPTION Paper and parchment, 85 folios, 220 x 150 mm, in Hebrew, Italian semi-cursive script. Parchment wrappers
PROVENANCE Samuel Halberstam, ms. 406; Montefiore Endowment, no. 441; Sotheby's, New York, 27 October 2004, lot 326
BIBLIOGRAPHY Steinschneider; Sarton III 837-38, 848-51, 1380-82, 1690; EJ III 962-63; DSB I 289-91

31 LJS 470

Collection of recipes, with John of Parma's *Practicella*
Siena, 1533

This collection of recipes in Hebrew includes a translation of the *Practicella*, a short treatise on medicine by John of Parma (*c.* 1250). It was copied in Siena by a well-known scribe, Abraham ben Mashullam of Sant'Angelo, who provided three colophons, giving different dates in 1533.

DESCRIPTION Paper, 115 folios, 227 x 165 mm, in Hebrew, Italian cursive script, brown ink. Contemporary morocco binding, gilt-tooled.
PROVENANCE Samuel David Luzzatto; Solomon Halberstam, no. 19; Montefiore Endowment; Sotheby's, New York, 27 October 2004, lot 430
BIBLIOGRAPHY Sarton II 1083

32 LJS 468

Meir Alguadez, *Sefer mekits nirdamim*
Italy, 16th century

Meir ben Solomon Alguadez was physician to King Henry III of Castille from 1390 to 1406. The list of medical recipes contained in this manuscript was originally written by him in Spanish (with additions by a disciple of his, named Joseph). In 1546 this compilation was translated into Hebrew by Joseph ha-Kohen (1496–*c.* 1578), a scholar, historian and physician active in Italy. Joseph entitled his translation 'The Awakener of Sleepers' and added some remedies for the "French disease", or syphilis, which had entered Italy in the late fifteenth century.

Two copies of this work were listed by Steinschneider in 1893. One is the present manuscript, then in the possession of Solomon Halberstam. The other, housed in the Biblioteca Nazionale in Turin, was damaged on 25–26 January 1904 by a massive fire, which destroyed some thirty thousand volumes.

DESCRIPTION Paper, 109 folios, 212 x 154 mm, in Hebrew, Sephardic semi-cursive script, brown ink, catchwords. Library buckram binding.
PROVENANCE Abraham Nizza; Judah Trabot of Nice; Israel Jeremiah (1608-09); R.N.N. Rabinowitz, sale Munich, March 1882, lot 36; Solomon Halberstam, no. 407; Montefiore Endowment, ms. 444; Sotheby's, New York, 27 October 2004, lot 329
BIBLIOGRAPHY Sarton III 1384; EJ II 623-24, X 241-42; HUM §484; Noja

33 LJS 389

Hua Shou, *Shisi Jing Fa Hui*
China, Ming dynasty (16th century)

This treatise, 'On Circulation', by Hua Shou (*fl.* 1341–70) was popular in both China and Japan. It describes 14 'mai' lines, or lines of circulation, inside the human body. Each of these lines is linked by a series of acupuncture points.

An edition of the text was prepared by Xue Kai, a physician at the royal hospital around 1500. This was published in a compilation of works under the title *Xueshi yian* (The clinical cases of the doctors Xue, *i.e.* Xue Kai and his son). The present manuscript, however, contains an additional preface, written

手少陽三焦經之圖

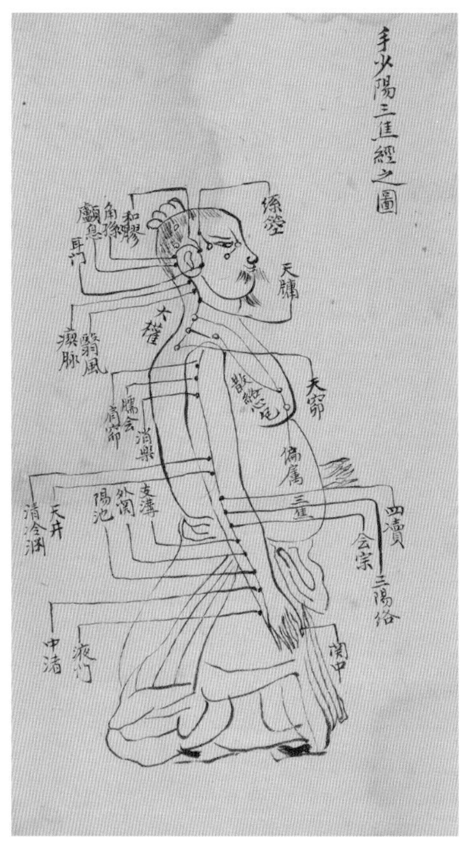

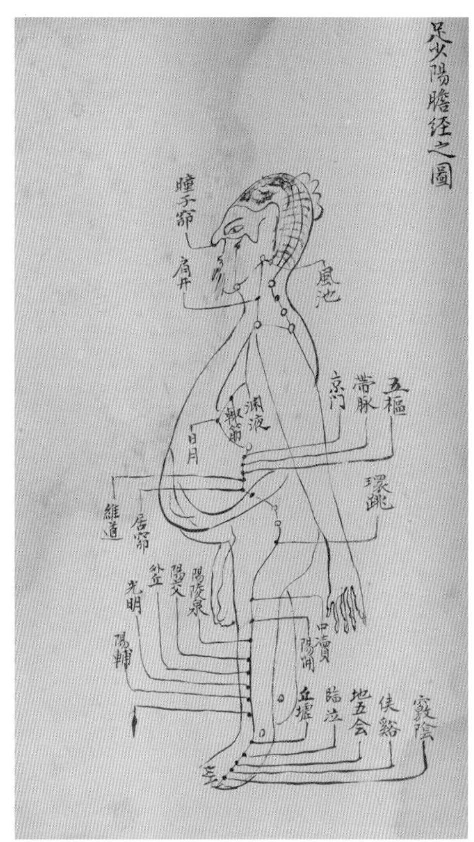

足少陽膽經之圖

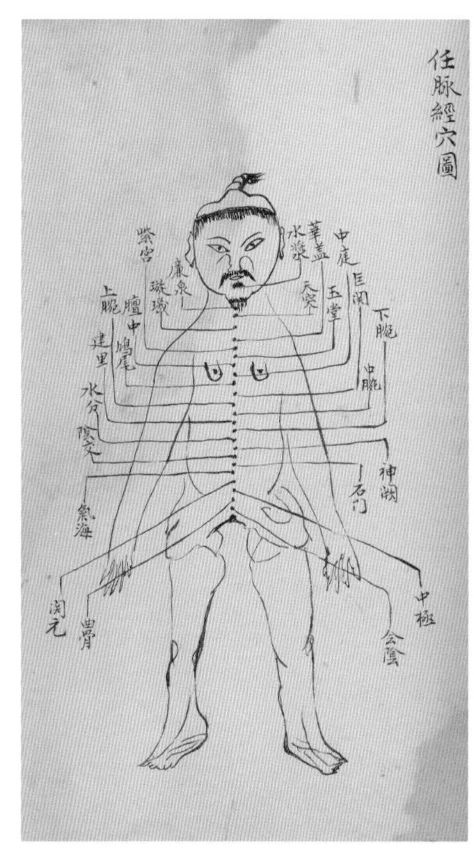

任脈經穴圖

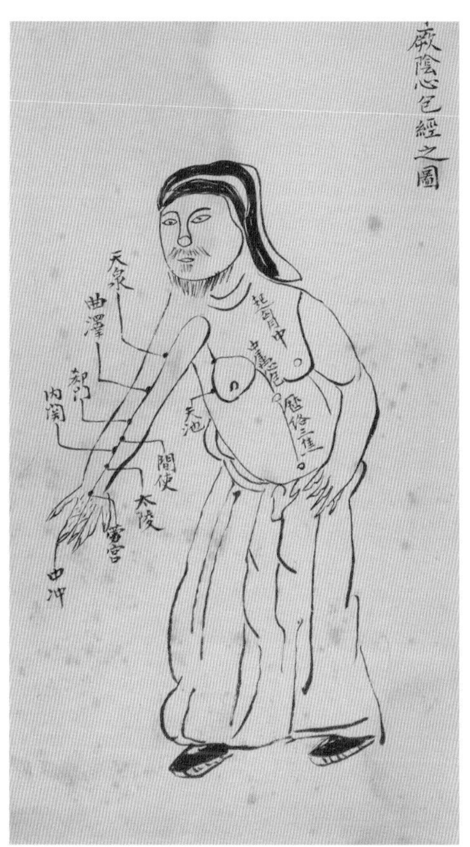

厥陰心包經之圖

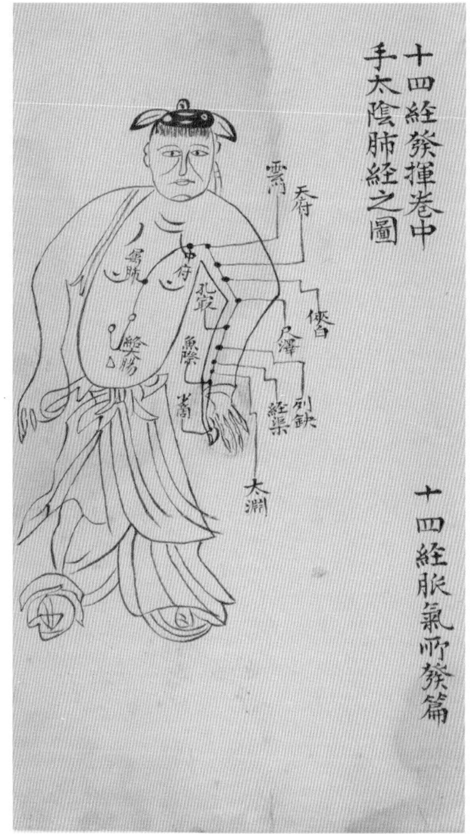

十四經發揮卷中
手太陰肺經之圖
十四經脈氣所發篇

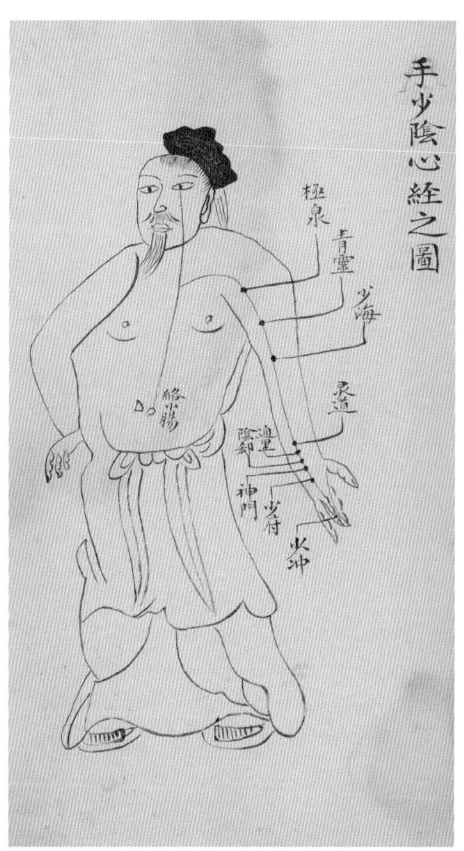

手少陰心經之圖

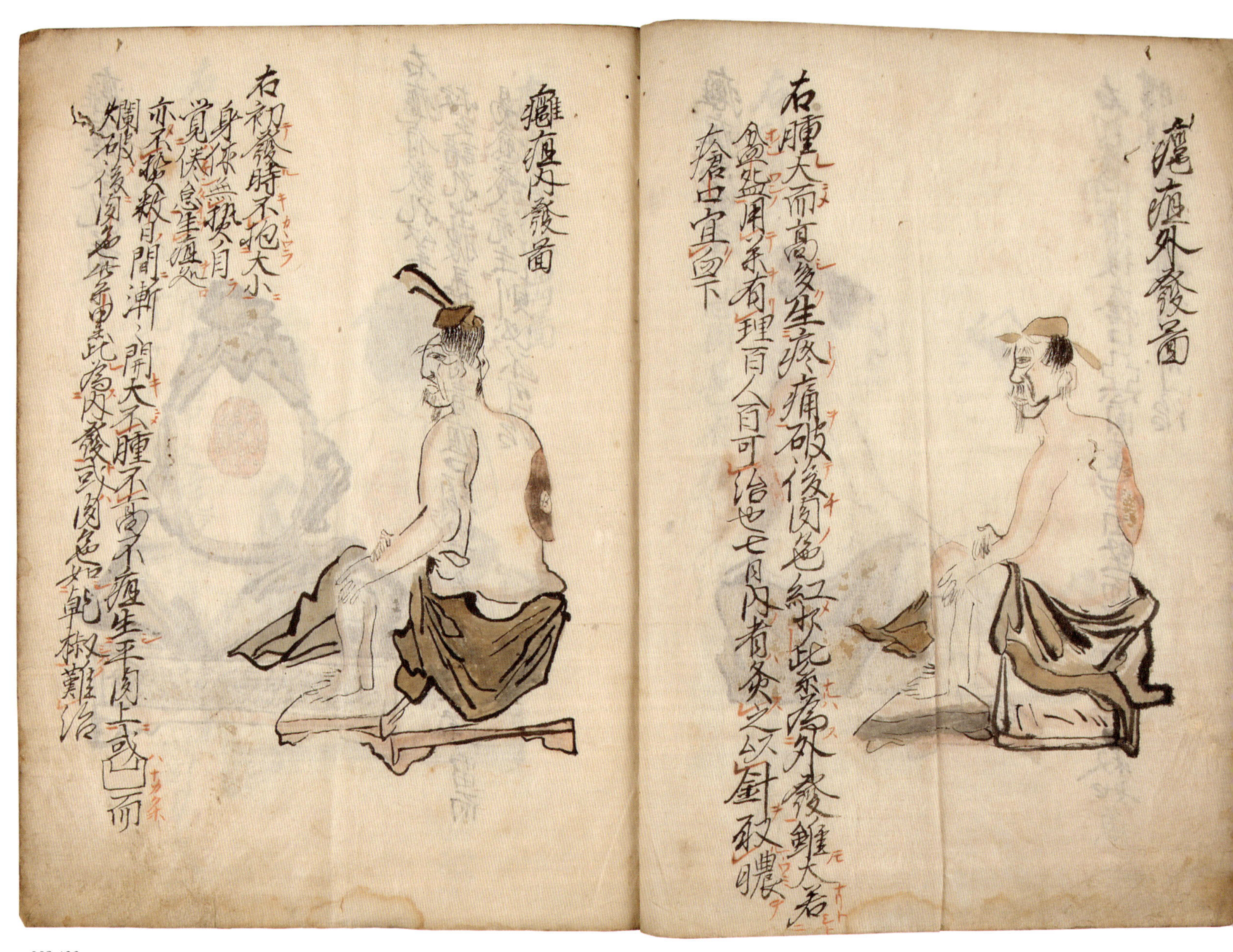

癰疽外發圖

右腫大而高、多生疼痛、破後復起、色紅次此紫、外發雖大者、盈盤用柴有理、百人百可治也、七月内者灸之、以針取膿、大倉口宜向下

癰疽内發圖

右初發時不抱大小、身体無熱八月、覚侯急生瘡処、亦不發救月間漸〻開大、不腫不當不痩、生平肉上、或□而爛破後、肉多通處内發、或肉色如乾椒難治

by Sheng Yingyang in 1528, which does not appear in the printed edition.

DESCRIPTION Bamboo paper, 54 folios, 310 x 180 mm, in Chinese, kaishu script; 14 illustrations. Mounted on modern paper, bound in three volumes in blue paper covers.

PROVENANCE Sam Fogg, cat. 23 (2000), no. 40

34 LJS 433

Yoso zusetsu
Japan, *c.* 1600

This treatise, 'On Abcesses and Tumours', on the diagnosis of abcesses and tumours and their treatment, largely through acupuncture and moxibustion (burning substances near the skin), is illustrated by depictions of patients – realistically portrayed in a variety of clothes, but with the affected area bare – and surgical tools.

No author's name is given, but we are informed that the text was copied by the scribe Hatano Baiko. Although written in Chinese, it was produced for use in Japan; the influence of Chinese medicine in Japan at this period was such that medical texts tended to be transmitted in the Chinese language.

DESCRIPTION Paper, 29 double sheet folios, 270 x 195 mm, in classical Chinese, black ink, vowels, punctuation and other guides in red; 51 large drawings in coloured ink and wash. Stitched binding, later wrappers.

PROVENANCE Martayan Lan, March 2002

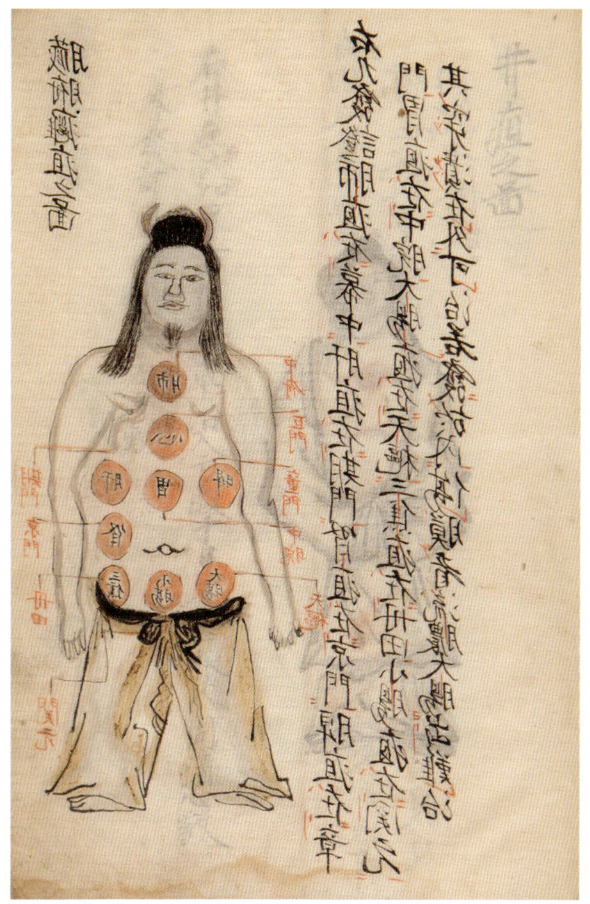

LJS 433
f. 13v

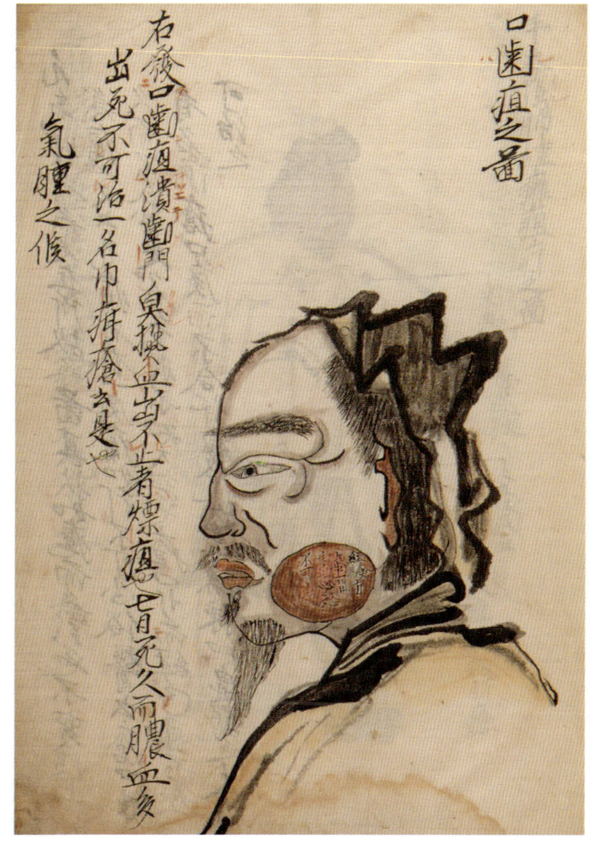

LJS 433
f. 21r

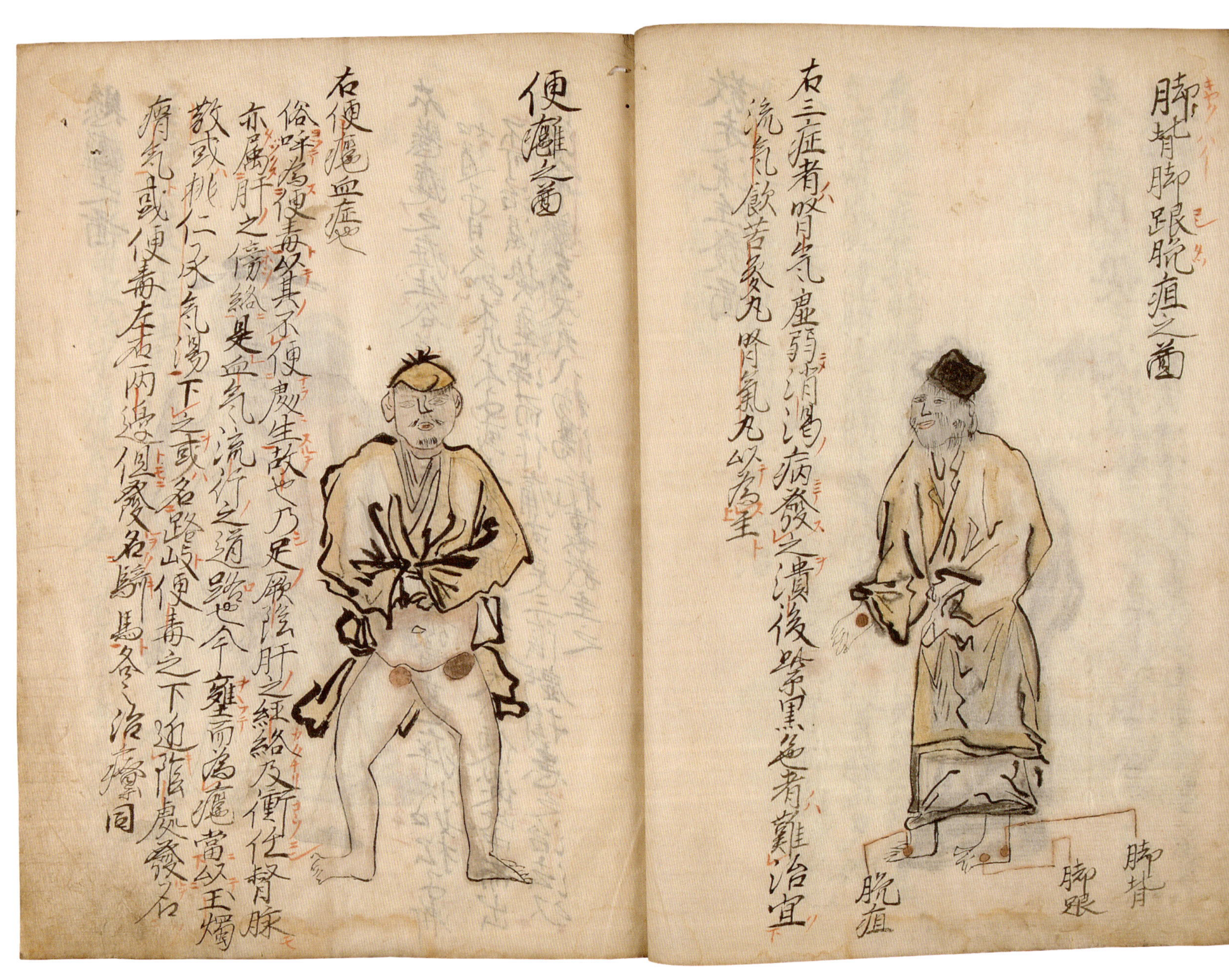
脚背 脚跟 脱疽之圖
便癰之圖
脱疽
脚跟
脚背

35 LJS 171

Tractatus simplex de cortice peruviano, with a commentary on Descartes's *Physica*, and other medical texts
Possibly Italy, after 1696

'Peruvian bark', otherwise known as 'Jesuits' bark', was commonly used in the seventeenth century as a cure for fevers. The means by which it acted was disputed, however. In this manuscript the anonymous author discusses and criticizes the theories of other medical authorities on the action of the bark. He follows this with his own hypothesis, based on the action of the bark on bodily fluids. His analysis of fluids rejects the traditional Galenic concept of humours, which was in decline by this period, although not entirely obsolete. He then discusses how to administer the bark, offering several recipes. His recommendation is that it should be used for intermittent fevers, but avoided for continuous ones.

The latest authority to which the author refers is Baglivi's *De praxi medica* of 1696, which this text must postdate. It is accompanied by three other treatises on fevers and two works on Cartesian *physica*, one simply titled *Physica*, the other *Regula pro recta methodo phylosophandi* (Rule for the correct method of philosophizing).

DESCRIPTION Paper, 212 folios, 183 x 127 mm, in Latin, humanistic cursive script, brown ink, large penwork initials at start of each text. Contemporary parchment binding.
PROVENANCE C.E. Rappaport, Rome, *Libri Rari* (1931); Harrison Horblit; H.P. Kraus, cat. 155 (1980), no. 13; Hellmut Schumann, cat. 542 (1984), no. 59; John Stanitz, ms. 2
BIBLIOGRAPHY Jarcho

36 LJS 313

Leibniz, Autograph working notes: *Causa secretionis liquarum a sanguine in corpore animali*
Possibly Germany, *c.* 1715

As mentioned above (LJS 171 [no. 35]) the traditional Galenic concept of the four humours came under increasing attack from the seventeenth century onwards. This necessitated new models of the nature and movement of fluids within the body.

Although not primarily known as a medical writer, the philosopher and mathematician Gottfried Wilhelm von Leibniz (1646–1716) had a particular interest in mechanics and forces. This interest led to his engagement with the Venetian mathematician and physician Pietro Angelo Michelotti (1673–1740) on the subject of separation of fluids. A letter from Leibniz to Michelotti on this subject, dated 17 September 1715, is to be found in Michelotti's *De separatione fluidorum in corpore animali dissertatio physico-mechanico-medica* (published 1721). It deals with the density of fluids and the size of the channels they pass through. This manuscript appears to constitute Leibniz's original working notes: several phrases reappear in the printed letter.

DESCRIPTION Paper, 1 folio, 332 x 217 mm, in Latin.
PROVENANCE Sotheby's, London, 17 June 1999, lot 53
BIBLIOGRAPHY DSB VIII 152

37 LJS 210

Paolo Naracci, Student's medical notes
North-east Italy, 1738

These notes, recorded by Paolo Naracci, are apparently from lectures by a Professor Buzzati of the Veneto, possibly at the medical school in Padua. The manuscript is arranged into chapters that deal systematically with different aspects of medicine, beginning with the definition of fever and disease.

DESCRIPTION Paper, 197 x 140 mm, 269 folios, in Italian, cursive script, in brown ink.
PROVENANCE Paolo Naracci (signature on titlepage); Phillip J. Pirages, cat. 34, no. 490; John Stanitz, ms. 41

Herbals

Herbal in the tradition of Dioscorides
Eastern Mediterranean, 15th century

The root of modern botany lies in the work of Dioscorides of
Anazarbus, who, around 50–70 AD, made a compilation of
over 600 plants "concerning medical matters" (*Peri hylēs
iatrikēs*, commonly known in Latin as *De materia medica*). This
became the standard source of information on plants, their
nomenclature and their medicinal properties. As such it was
frequently revised, expanded and contracted in the course of
its transmission through Greek, Latin, Arabic and vernacular
cultures. It was especially popular in the Renaissance.

The present manuscript is a part of this long Dioscorides
tradition, although it claims also to follow Galen and the
earlier Greek writer Isocrates. It opens with twenty pages of
illustrations, including 71 different plants, and two pictures of
Dioscorides; he is represented collecting plants and putting
them into bags and sitting on a bench next to the celebrated
physician Galen, who was an early reader of Dioscorides's
work. In the table of contents there are listed 697 chapters, of
which 679 are extant. The process of accretion and alteration
which accompanied the transmission of Dioscorides's text is
exemplified by the numerous notes which several readers
have added to this manuscript.

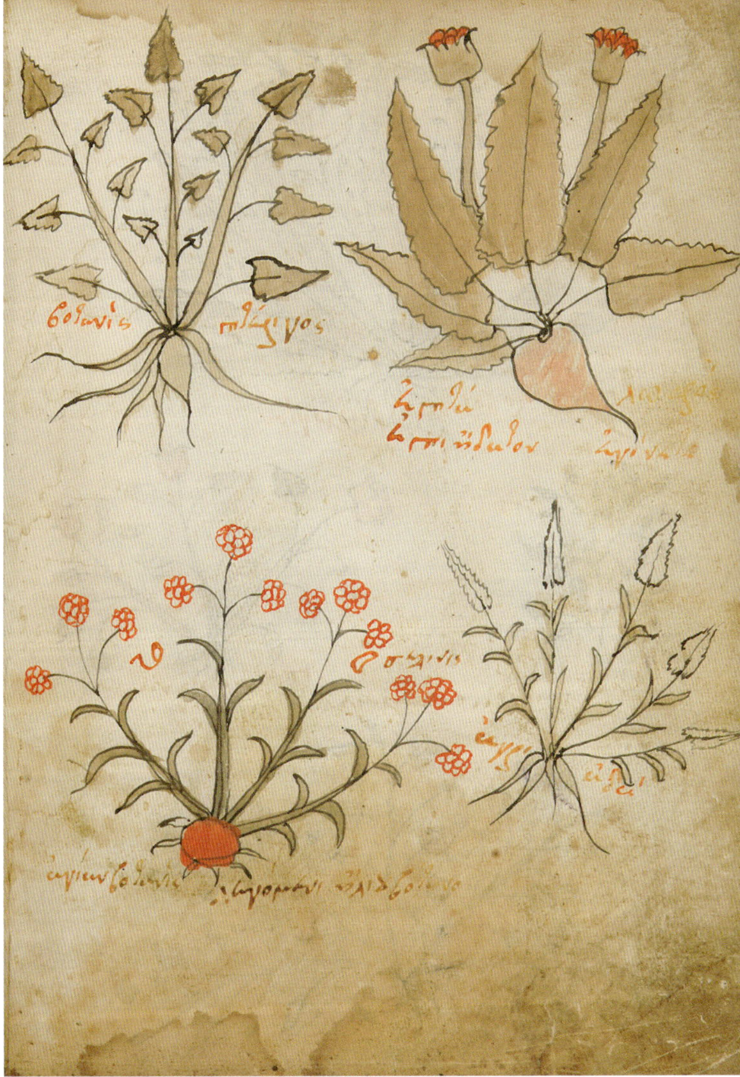

DESCRIPTION On paper, 119 folios, 261 x 190 mm, in Greek, cursive
minuscule in black ink, headings and initials in red, many additions
and notes in various hands; coloured drawings of 71 plants. Greek
blind-stamped binding, possibly 17th-century.
PROVENANCE Sotheby's, London, 10 December 1996, lot 61
BIBLIOGRAPHY DSB IV 119-23; Sarton I, 258-60

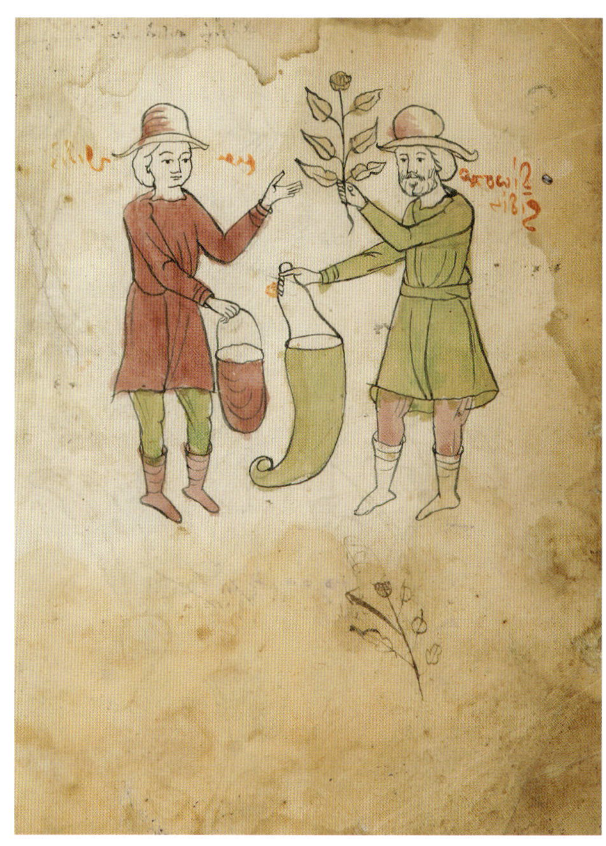

LJS 62
f. 1v

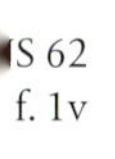

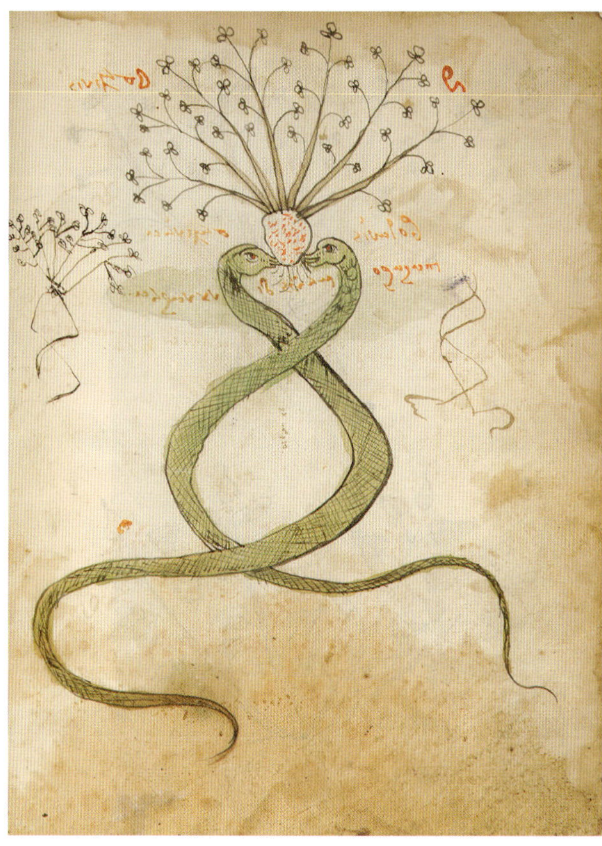

LJS 62
f. 8v

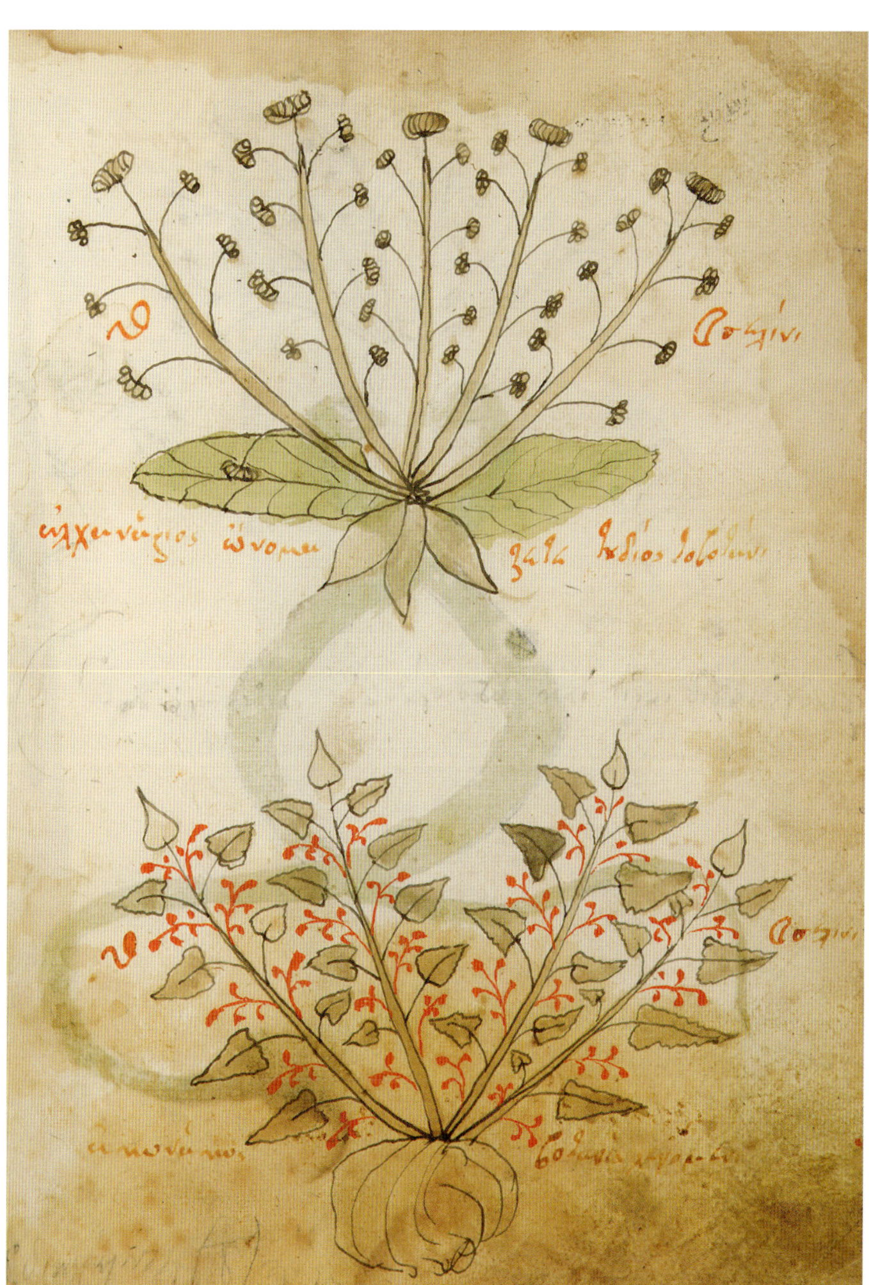

LJS 62, f. 8r

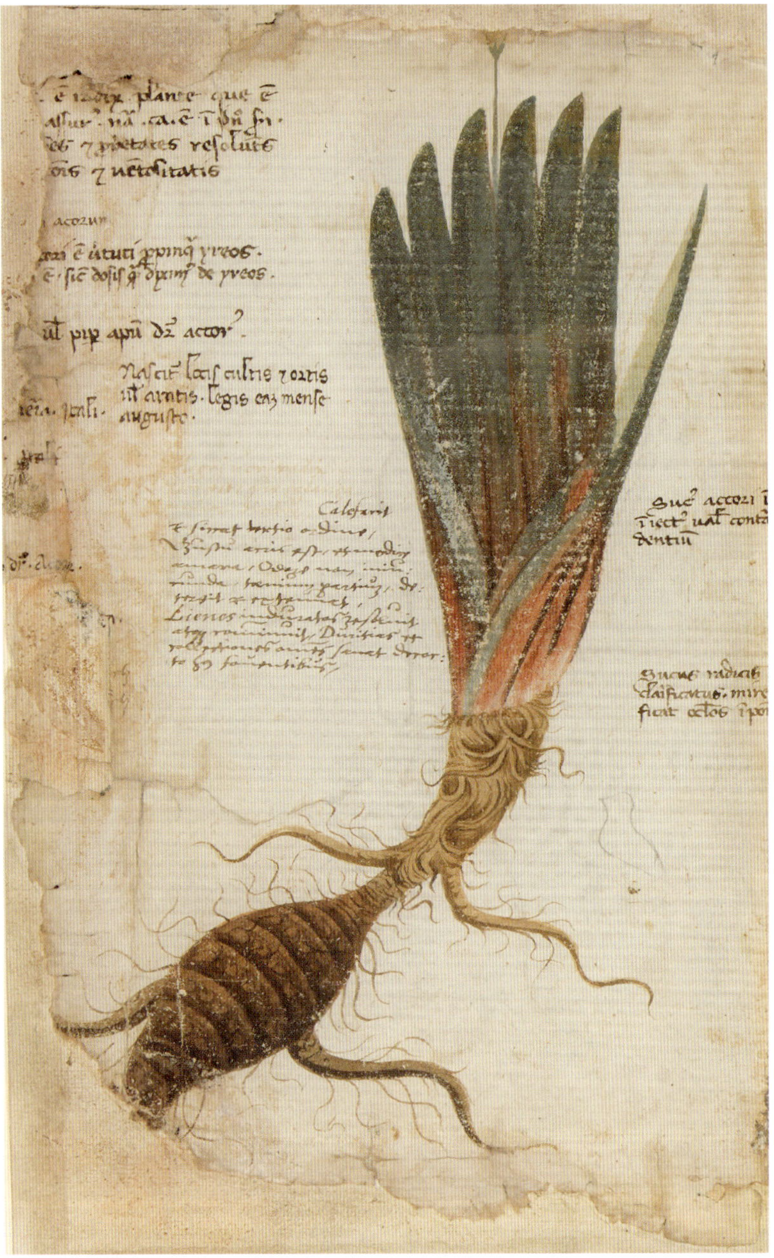

LJS 475, verso

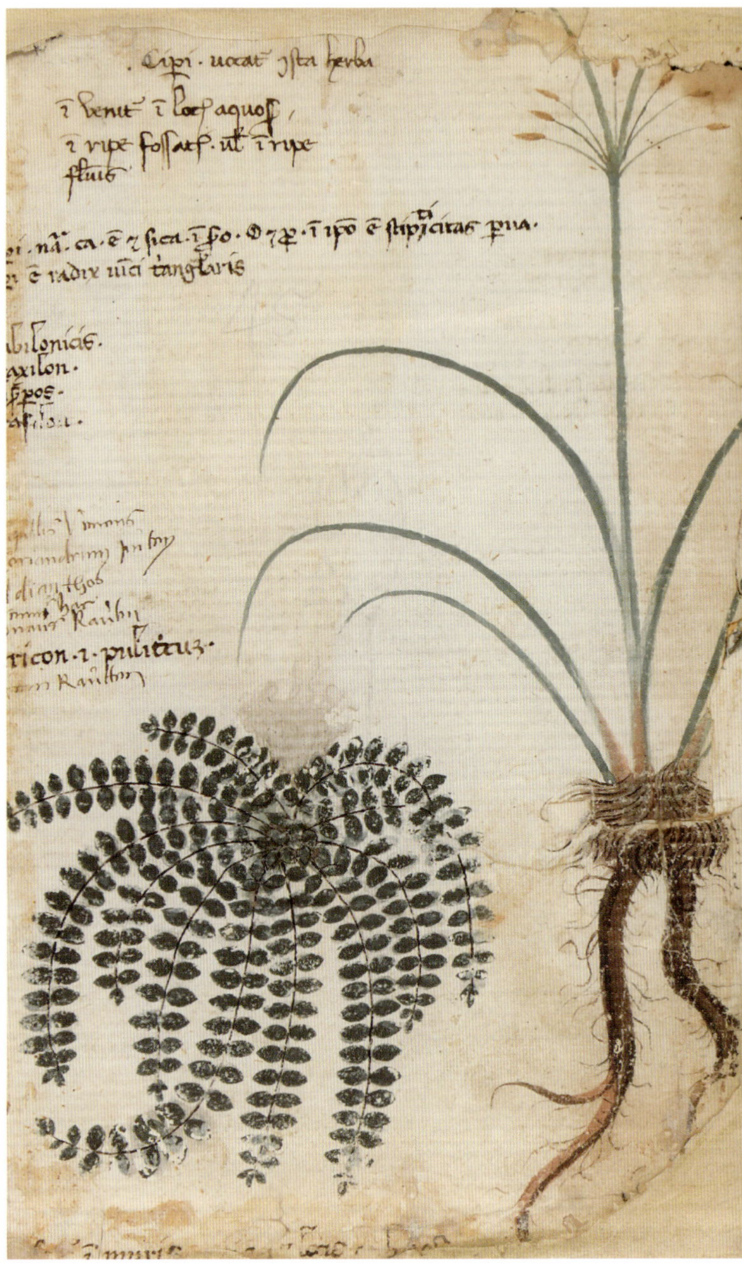

LJS 475, recto

39 LJS 475

Folio from a *Herbarium,* illuminated by Andrea Amadio
Belluno or Venice, *c.* 1415

The recto of this leaf from a herbal in the Dioscorides
tradition (see LJS 62 [no. 38]) has naturalistic representations
of a paypyrus and a fern. The verso has a clivia or iris. The
illustrations can be dated to about 1415 and ascribed to
Andrea Amadio on stylistic grounds.

In 1980 the Städelsche Kunstinstitut in Frankfurt exhibited
three leaves very similar to the present one. A further leaf
from the same *Herbarium,* in much worse condition, was lot 41
at Sotheby's, London, 22 June 1999.

DESCRIPTION Paper, 1 folio, 300 x 182 mm
PROVENANCE Jörn Günther, cat. 30, no. 16

Herbal
Northern Italy, 15th century

This herbal includes 192 illustrations executed in three distinct styles, drawing on long-established pictorial traditions. The manuscript begins with approximately 70 assured drawings that are captioned but are not accompanied by a descriptive text (*e.g.* "woad", f. 42). The second group is somewhat more workmanlike in style, and perhaps executed by the same person who wrote the adjacent texts. This campaign was responsible for an illustration of a female mandrake being uprooted by a snarling dog, with a discussion of the plant written (sometimes overwritten) in a hurried humanistic cursive. The third group comprises some 86 careful drawings which meticulously record the roots, leaves, fruits and flowers of each plant. This naturalistic style recalls that of the Carrara Herbal (British Library, Sloane ms. 2020; Padua, *c.* 1390–1404). The flavour of the manuscript's Italian suggests that it was produced in the Veneto.

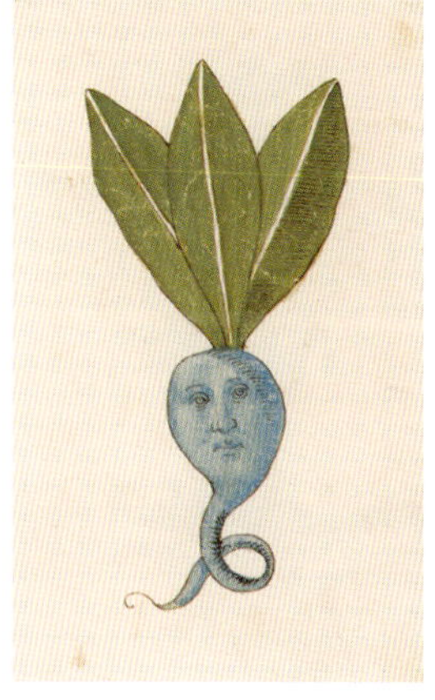

S 419
f. 42r

DESCRIPTION Paper, 100 folios, 245 x 176 mm, in Italian and Latin, humanistic cursive script; 192 illustrations, mostly coloured. Parchment binding.
PROVENANCE Signature of Rafael Gomez; Leo Olschki; W.S. Kundig, Geneva, sale 95, 23 June 1948, lot 42; Carlton R. Richmond; Sotheby's, New York, 30 October 1981, lot 68; Sam Fogg, June 2001

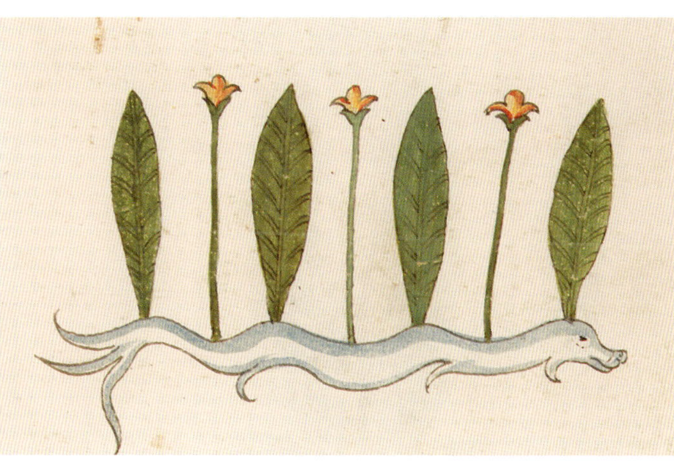

S 419
f. 35r

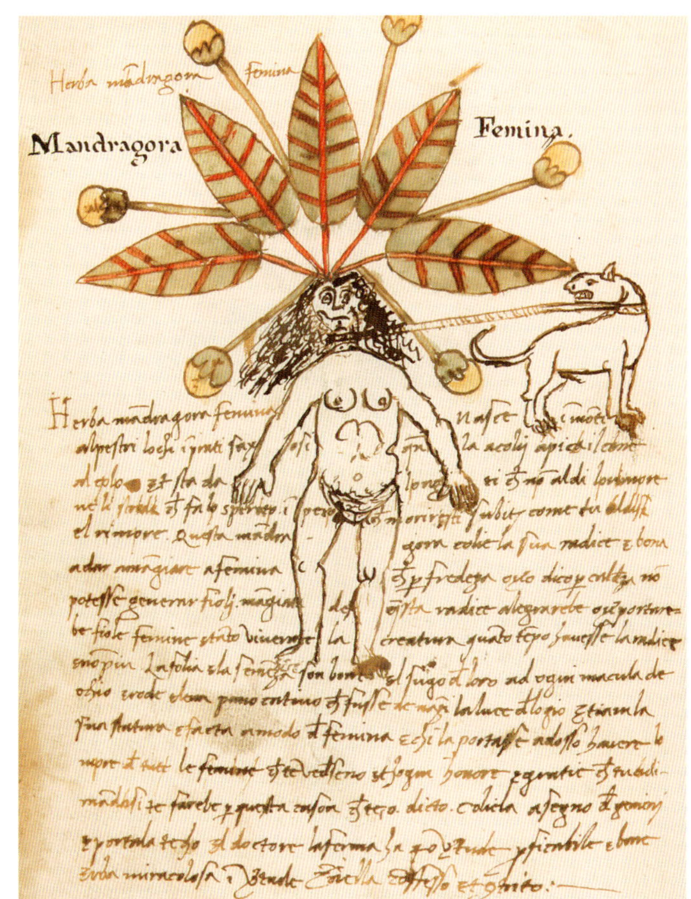

LJS 419
f. 38v

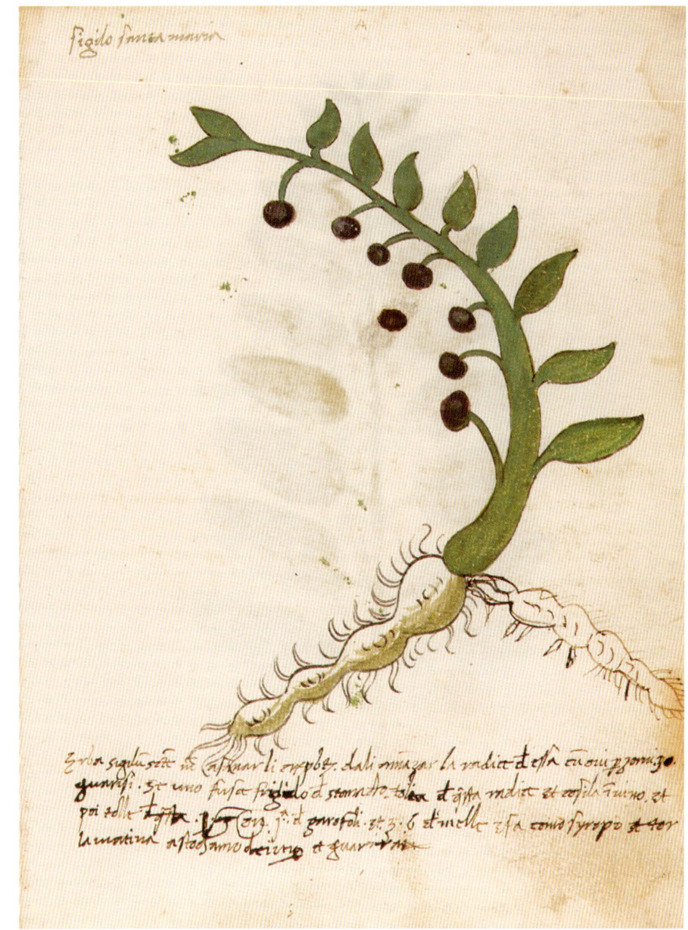

LJS 419
f. 28r

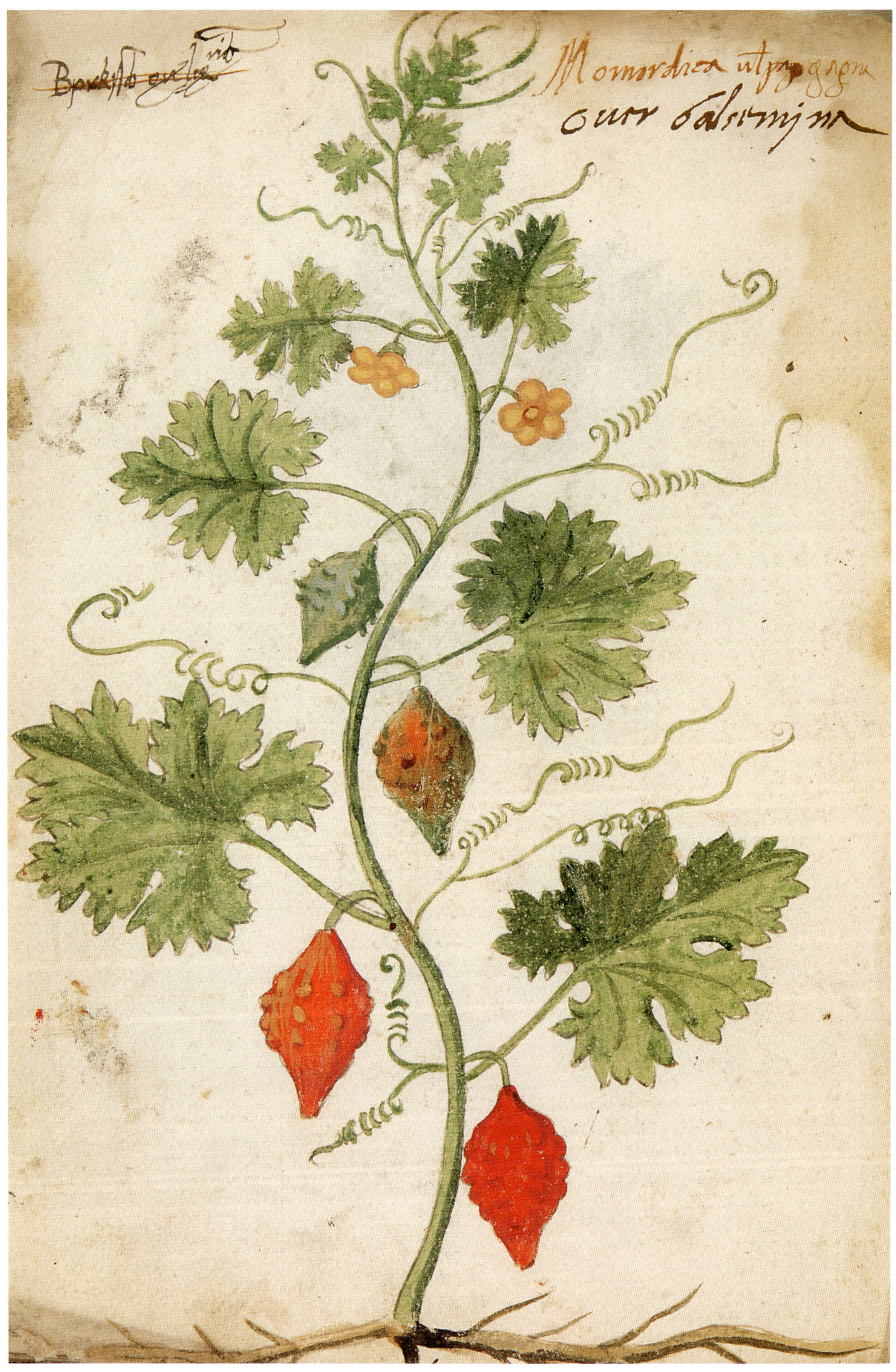
Momordica utpp gngn
ouer balsemjna
Momordica utpp gngn
ouer balsemjna

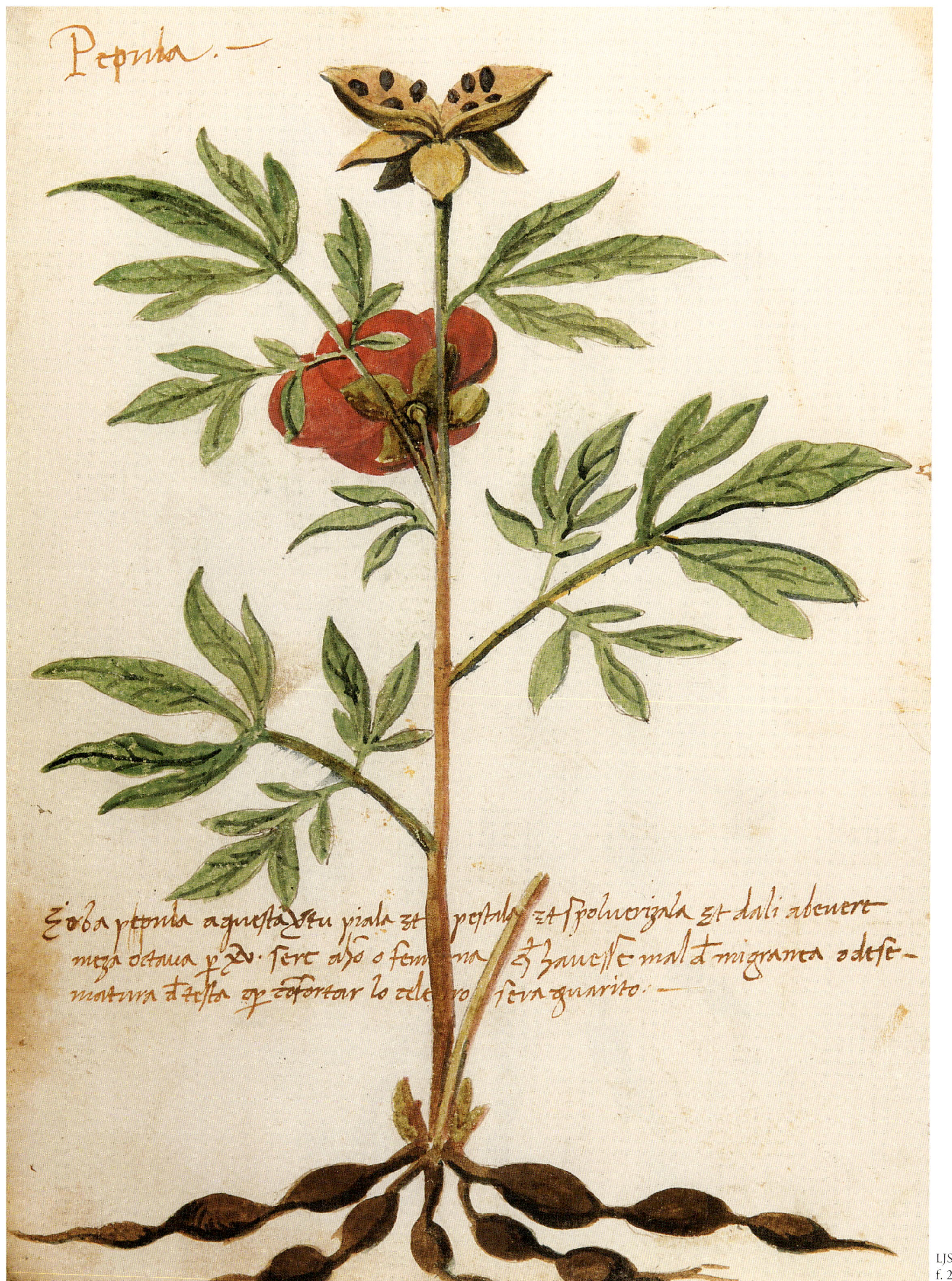

Erba pepula aguesta vtu piala et pestola et spoluerizala et dali abeuere
mega octaua p ɔ. sere aɔo o femena et hauesse mal d migranea o dese-
matura d testa op cofortar lo celeoro seva guarito : —

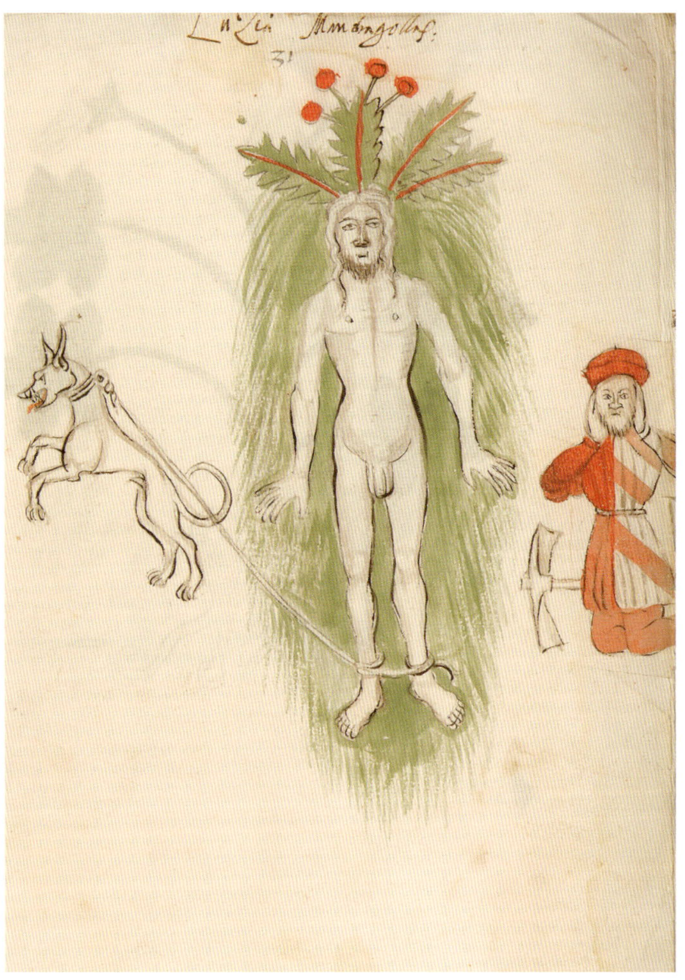

LJS 46
f. 31

41 LJS 46
Herbal
Northern Italy, *c.* 1520 (with *Description of Morocco*, England, *c.* 1600)

This manuscript consists of two distinct parts: the first is a herbal consisting of 110 tinted drawings with Italian captions made about 1520, to which English texts, including a description of the flora, topography and customs of the Kingdom of Morocco, were added between 1597 and 1603. The herbal's illustrations derive from the celebrated sixth-century Vienna Dioscorides (Österreichische Nationalbibliothek, ms. med. gr. 1, Constantinople, *c.* 512). The texts concerning Morocco are among the earliest accounts of Morocco in English, reflecting the expansion of English trade.

DESCRIPTION Paper, 101 folios, 305 x 205 mm (first part) and 290 x 205 mm (second part), in Italian, English, Spanish and Latin; 110 tinted drawings (first part). Parchment binding.
PROVENANCE Crest of the Lathams of Lancashire; "Thomas & Edward Syddell" inscribed on f. 1r, 16th century; Bonhams, December 1995; Sam Fogg, June 1996

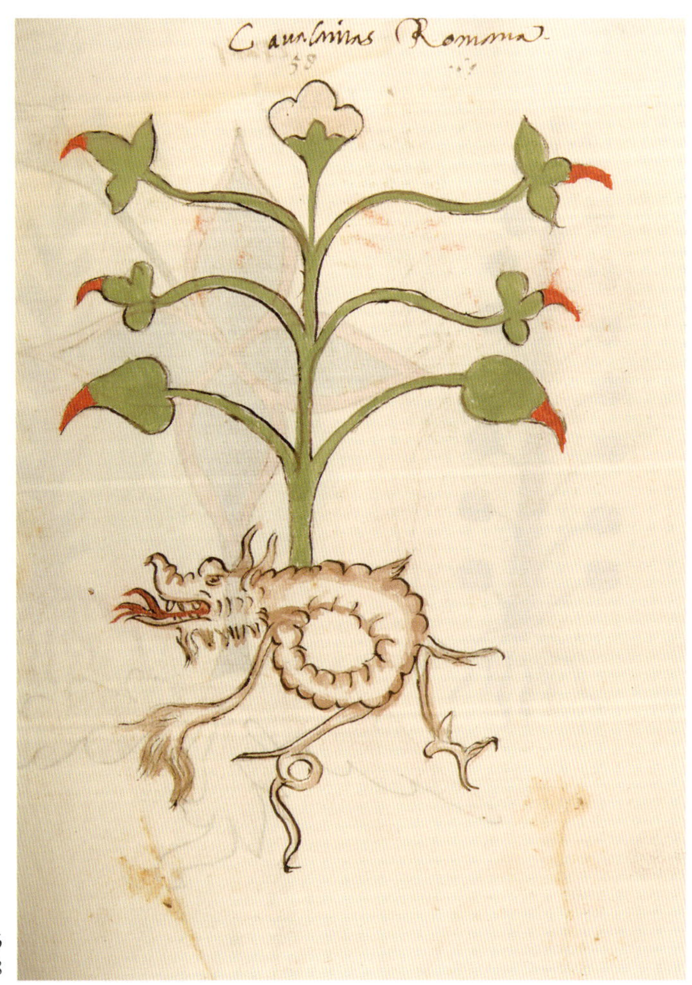

LJS 46
f. 58

42 LJS 278
Dioscorides, *Kitab-i hasha'ish*
Deccan, India, Muharram 1004 / September 1595

In the ninth century, Dioscorides's *De materia medica* (see LJS 62 [no. 38]) was translated into Arabic, and then into various other languages including Persian. The present copy of Dioscorides, in Persian, is fragmentary; other parts of the same manuscript are in the Freer Gallery of Art and the collection of Howard Hodgkin.

DESCRIPTION Paper, 169 folios, 400 x 280 mm, in Persian, nasta'liq script; 315 illustrations of 550 plants and several animals, in opaque watercolour and ink. Unbound.
PROVENANCE Sam Fogg, November 1998

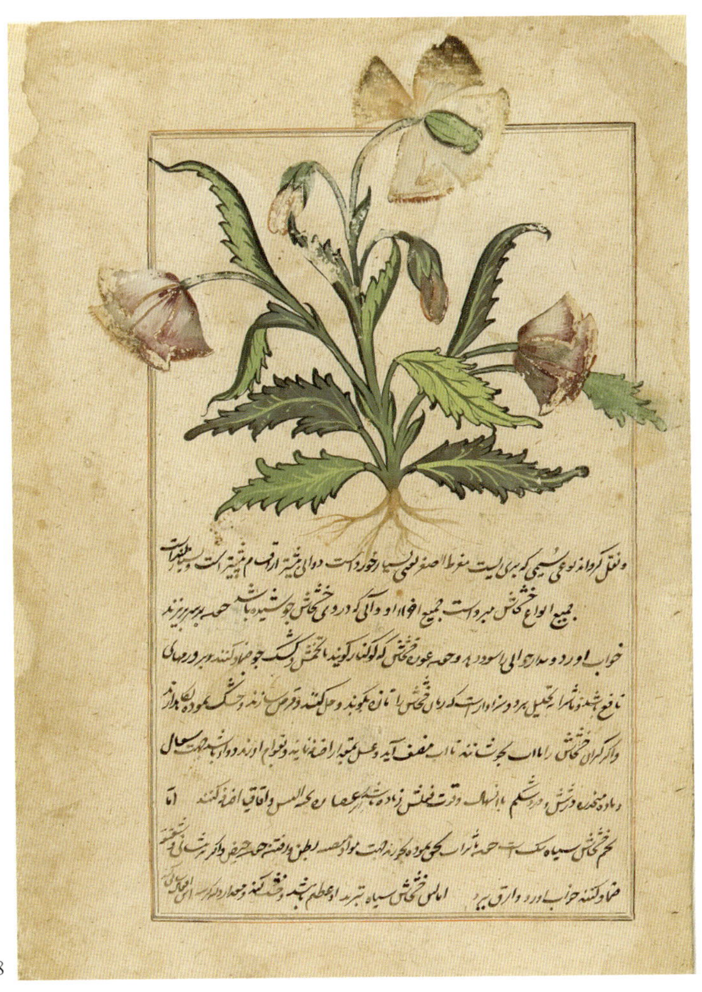

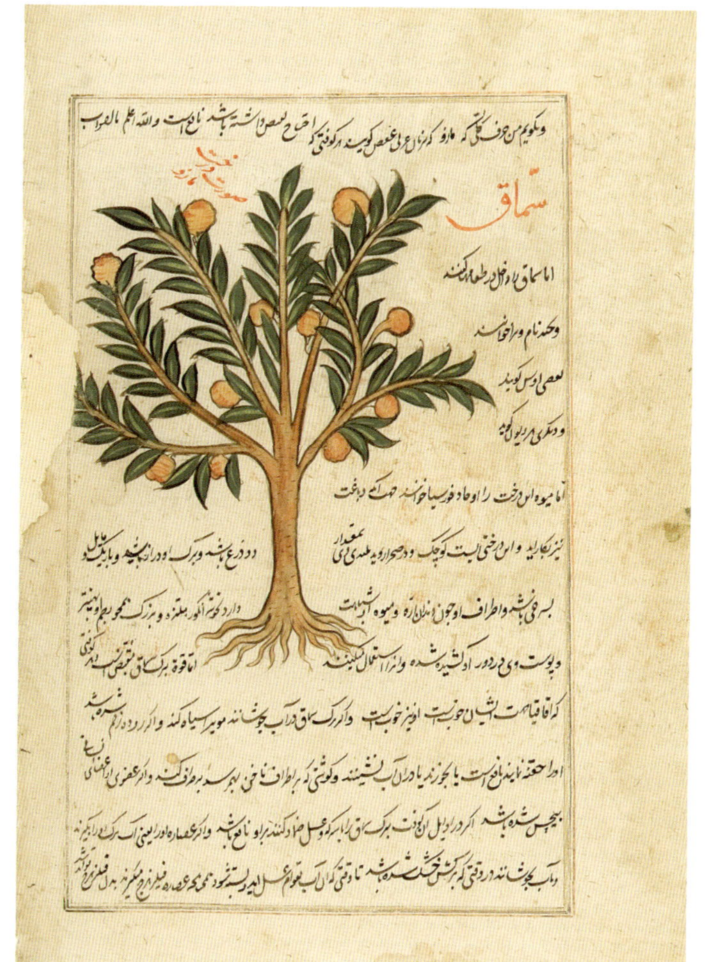

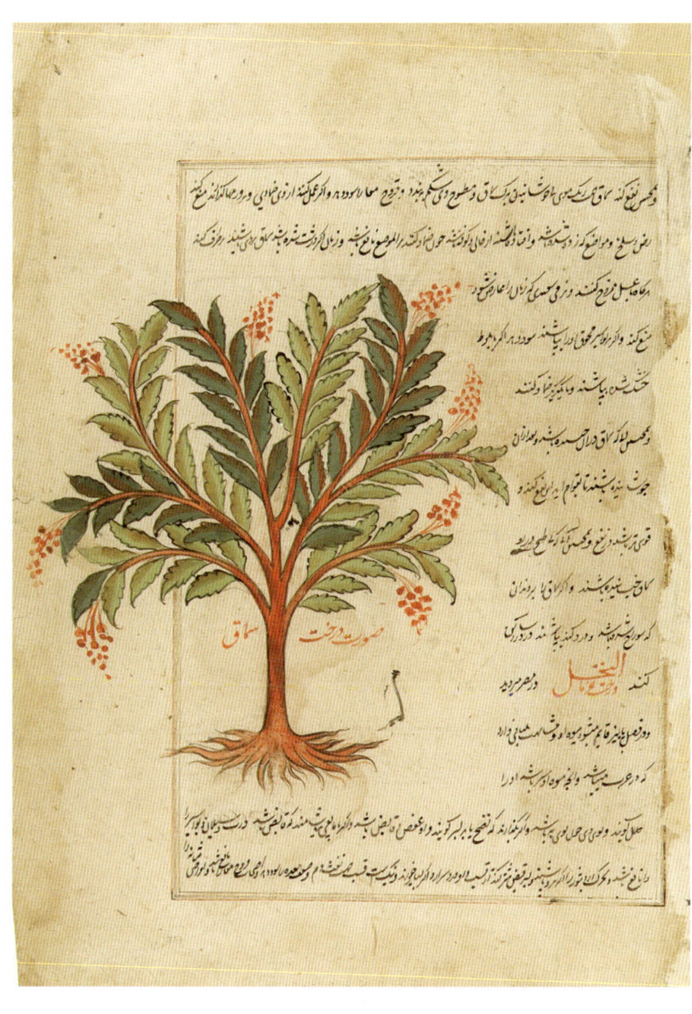

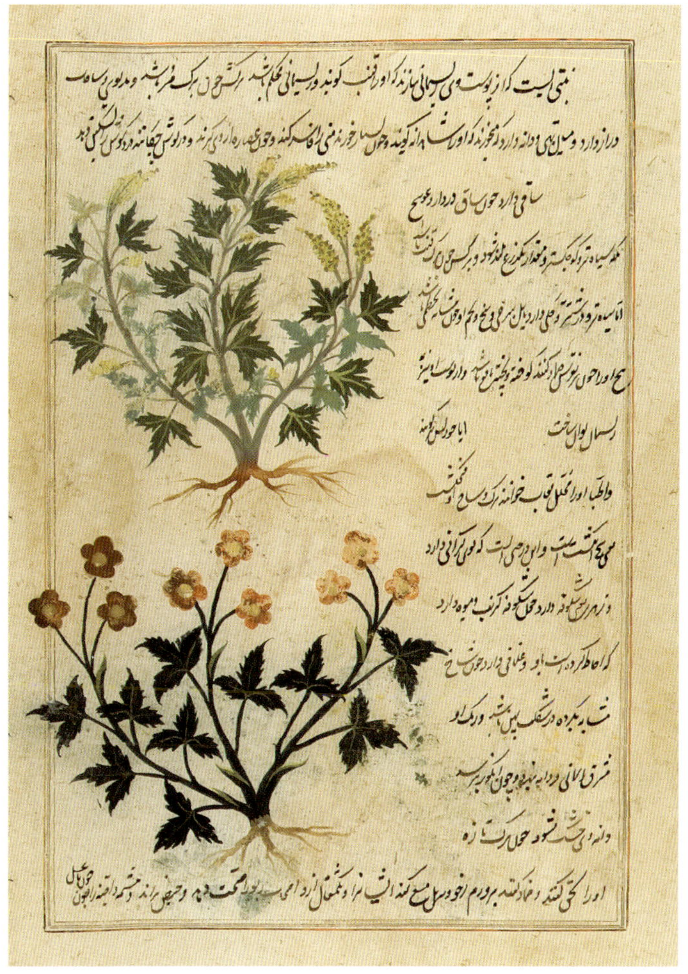

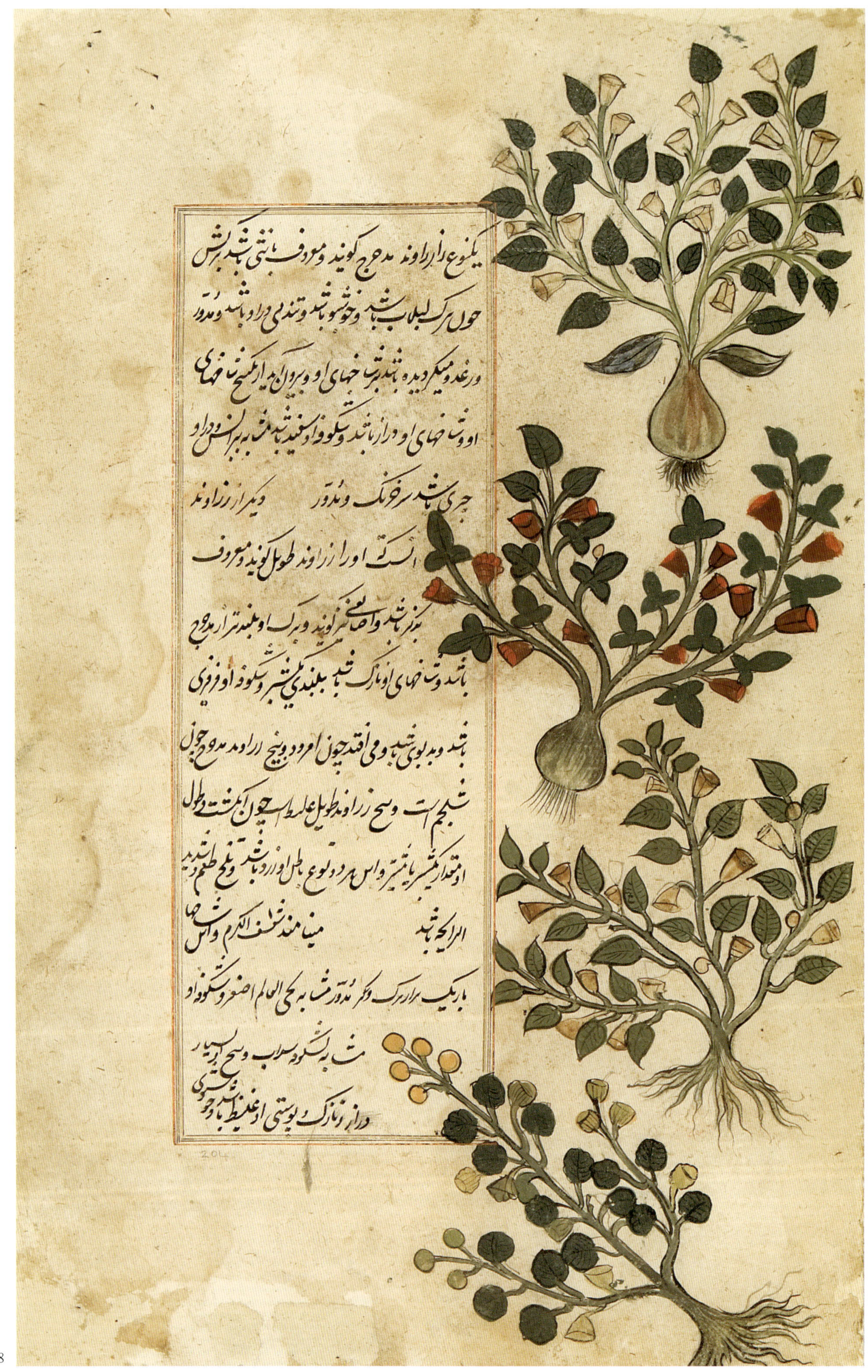

یک نوع را زراوند مدحرج گویند و مدور فربانتی شب برش
حوار که لبلاب شبه و خوشبو شده و تندی مراد باشد و مدور
ورغد و میکر دیده بتبر شبه خهای او و بیرون ایدار کسیخ نه خهای
او و نه خهای او در از باشد و سکوو او اسعید شبه غنه به بهر ش دراو
جهری شه سر خرنگ و مدور   دیگر از زراوند
انک اورا زراوند طهول گویند و معروف
بز شه و اصله مکر گویند و برک او بلند تر از مدحرج
باشد و نه خهای او مارک خنه بلندی متبر و سکوو او فردی
نه و بوی شه و می افندجون امرود و پیخ زراوند معروف چول
شنجم ست و سخ زراوند طهیل علم اسجوی اکرنشت طهال
اد مقدار مکثربا پخیبر واس مرد و توع پاطل او زار دناشتر و بلغ طعم پندید
المرا کیند   مبنامند نشن الکرم و اس حا
باریک سرار مرک دکر مدور مشا به کی المام اصغر و سکوو اد
مث به رسکوو سلاب و سخ پرسیار
زار رمارک و بوستی او غیط با بوسوری

VI Alchemy and Chemistry

Modern scholarship has not yet fully come to terms with the corpus of alchemical texts extant from the Middle Ages and Renaissance. In particular, the outline of Arabic alchemy, of which several examples occur here, has only been vaguely defined, and while several prominent alchemical authors are known by name (for example al-Jildaki [LJS 441 (no. 5)] and Jabir ibn Hayyan [LJS 403; no. 4]) their written contribution to the subject has yet to be assessed. Comprehension is further complicated by the common use of pseudonyms and encryptions (for example the symbolic alphabet of LJS 409 [no. 1]).

It is clear, however, that alchemy contains a variety of strands. In its best-known manifestation it deals with the transmuting of base metals into gold, and the search for the 'philosopher's stone'. These processes were also interpreted allegorically, however, as relating to the purification of the human soul, and alchemy therefore embraces mystical and philosophical writings as well as accounts of practical experiments. In sixteenth-century Europe the new wave of iatrochemistry, particularly associated with Paracelsus (see LJS 382 [no. 3]), introduced a more medical aspect to alchemical research. Subsequently alchemical ideas were received into the tradition of 'books of secrets', and combined with a heterogeneous body of lore drawn from a wide variety of disciplines (see LJS 448 [no. 6]).

Despite their obscurity, it is evident, if only from their illustrations, that these alchemical manuscripts prefigured modern techniques in chemistry. The manuscripts in the second half of this section highlight a variety of key moments in the development of modern chemistry.

1 LJS 409

Alchemical treatise
Persia, 15th century

This *Kitab al-kashf wa'l-bayan* and *Al-rumuz fi'l-burhan* (Book of illumination; Explanation and signs of proof) is an otherwise unrecorded alchemical treatise, apparently the testament of a practising alchemist to his son. There is no identification of the author or scribe, other than the remark that he is a "student of Ja'far al-Sadiq". This is probably a reference to the eighth-century alchemist Ja'far al-Sadiq, who is famed as the teacher of Jabir ibn Hayyan (see LJS 403 [no. 4] and 441 [no. 5]). The last folio has labelled illustrations of alchemical

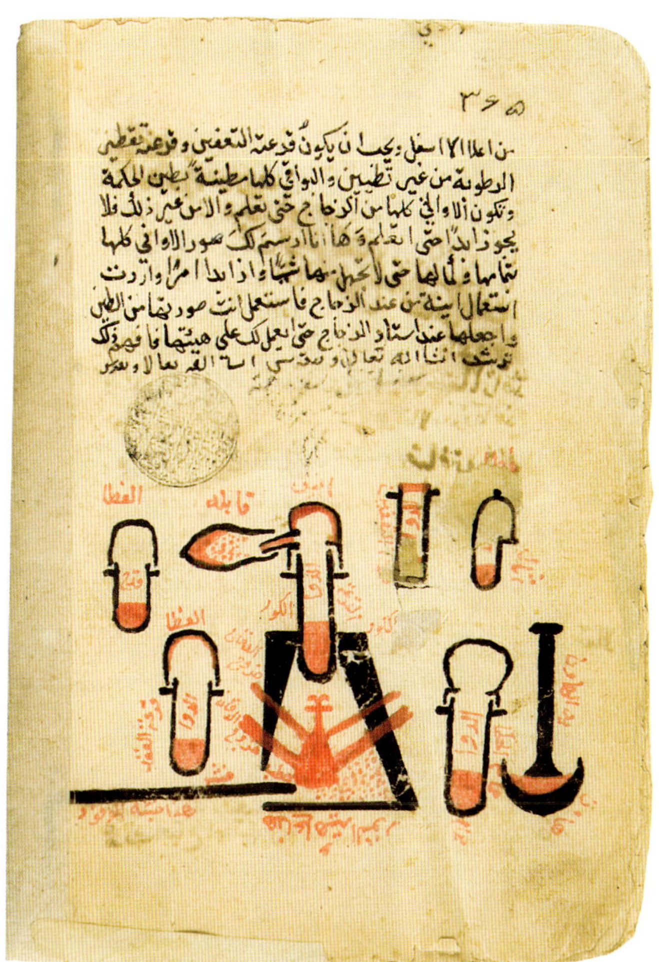

LJS 409
f. 4r

equipment – a pestle and mortar, a bunsen burner and various glass receptacles. The text also makes use of a symbolic alphabet, the key for which is given on f. 4r.

DESCRIPTION Paper, 9 folios, 152 x 105 mm, in Arabic, small cursive script, black ink, significant words and phrases in red; drawings of alchemical equipment in red and black (f. 9v). Brown morocco binding.
PROVENANCE Sam Fogg, March 2001

2 LJS 455

Two alchemical treatises: Ibn al-Baha, *Fawaid al-habib*; and *Zinjar al-hukama*, based on the work of al-'Abbas Ahmad ibn Sadrullah al-Hashimi
Probably Mamluk, Egypt, *c.* 1400

This manuscript appears to contain two works on alchemy, both of them otherwise unrecorded. The author of the first ('The Benefits of the Beloved') appears to be one 'Abdallah Muhammad known as Ibn al-Baha. The second work ('The Rust of the Physicians'), beginning on f. 196r, is based on the work of al-'Abbas Ahmad ibn Sadrullah al-Hashimi.

DESCRIPTION Paper, 235 folios, 247 x 160 mm, 25 lines of black naskh script by the scribe 'Ali ibn 'Abdallah al-Ansari. 19th-century red morocco binding with flap with tooled medallion.
PROVENANCE Mughal library inscriptions; two different seals of Faizi dated 992 AH / 1584; Abu'l Fayz al-Fayzi al-Fayyazi (954-1004 AH / 1547-1595); seal of Sharif dated 1003 AH / 1594-95; seal of 'Inayat dated 1016 AH / 1607-08; seal of Amanat Khan Jahani, dated 1042 AH / 1632-33; Christie's, London, 14 October 2003, lot 25

3 LJS 382

Georg Hayniger, Alchemical compendium
Vienna, *c.* 1476

This compendium of texts was compiled by a Viennese alchemist, Georg Hayniger von Dormpoch. It includes recipes provided for him by acquaintances as well as alchemical literature attributed to Ramon Llull and Albertus Magnus, among others. The recipes include one for the extraction of the quintessence of gold, provided by one Johannes Lewti and

tested by Hayniger, and several for potable gold and tincture of cinnabar. The compendium therefore anticipates the developments of the sixteenth century, associated principally with Paracelsus (1493–1541), by which the focus of alchemy shifted from transmuting metals to medical purposes.

Of particular interest are the drawings included in this manuscript, which not only illustrate abstract relationships such as that between elements and qualities (f. 89) but also show the tools of the alchemist's work, such as alembics, beakers and furnaces (ff. 15–20, 22–26). Hayniger evidently put the recipes he copied to the test in some cases, as he comments on their efficacy: "Nothing works better", he reports in one instance, or "made by George in this way". On the other hand, he sometimes comments merely that "the truth of this was reported to me by a trustworthy man". Various of the recipes are dated, the latest to 1476.

DESCRIPTION Parchment, 94 folios, 123 x 84 mm, in Latin, German and Czech, semi-gothic script, brown ink, subtitles and highlighting in red, orange and blue; six pen-and-ink drawings. Modern parchment binding.
PROVENANCE Engraved armorial bookplate of Johann David Baier; Sam Fogg, June 2000
BIBLIOGRAPHY Thorndike IV 332-56

4 LJS 403

Ibrahim al-Husayni, *Alchemical compendium*
Herat, AH 901–04 / 1496–99

Ibrahim al-Husayni was a practising alchemist who compiled this collection of texts in his workshop by the Bab al-Iraq in Herat, Afghanistan. This volume serves as commentary and guide to his research. Most of the texts do not have titles or any authorial attribution; they are the personal notes, fragments, commentaries and ideas of the writer, who describes himself at the end of penultimate text as "compiler and composer". Mention is made of the concept of balance (*mizan*) associated with the corpus of writings attributed to Jabir ibn Hayyan (see LJS 441 [no. 5]); balance, in this corpus, is a syncretistic concept, associated not only with specific gravity (in the tradition of Archimedes; see LJS 386 [VII, no. 1]) but also with speculations on letters, metaphysical

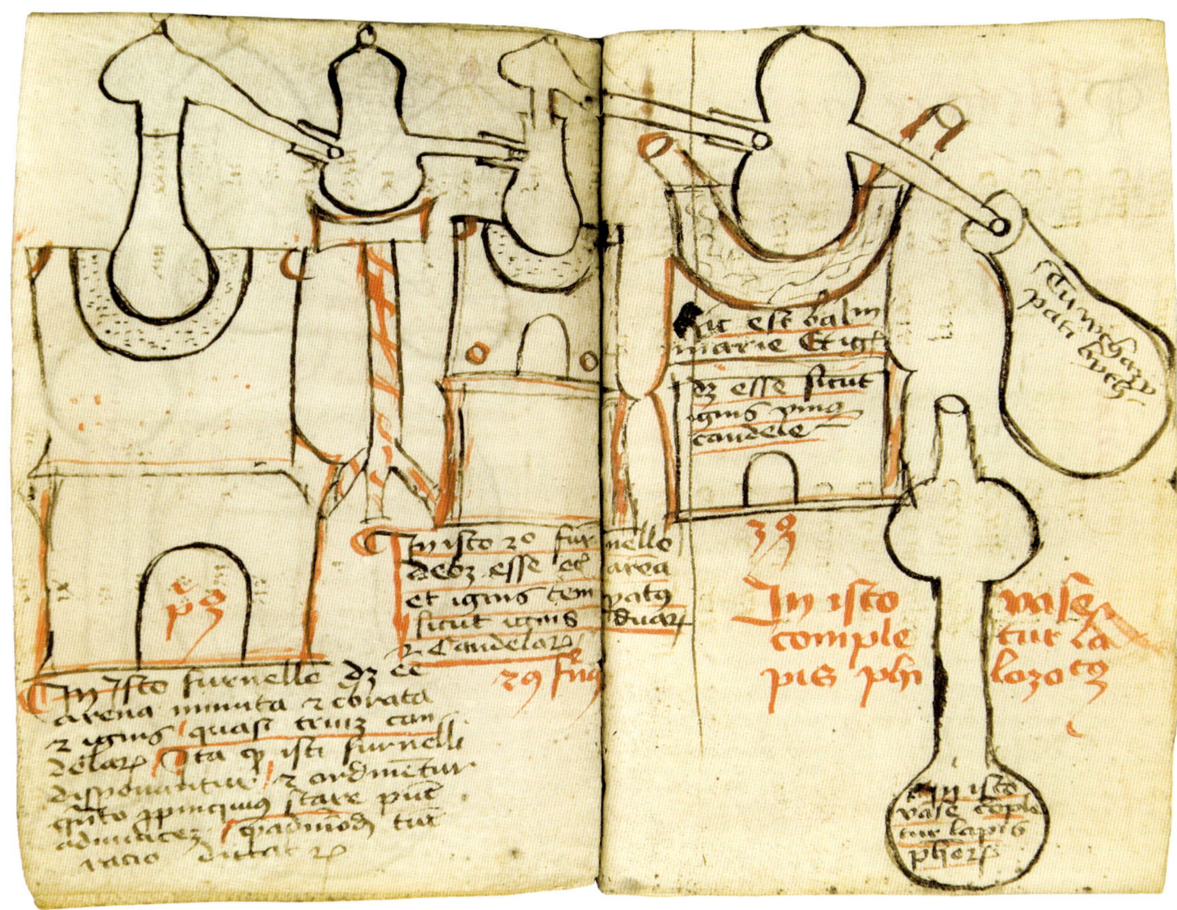

LJS 382
ff. 24v-25r

beings and the 'weighing' which will take place at the Last Judgement.

DESCRIPTION Paper, 173 folios, 160 x 115 mm, in Arabic, personal nasta'liq script in black ink, rubrics and overlining in red, copious marginalia. Brown morocco binding with flap.

PROVENANCE Seal impression of Abdul-Razak al-Musawi; Sam Fogg, February 2001

BIBLIOGRAPHY EI II 357-59

5 LJS 441

Two works on alchemy
Probably Aleppo, Syria, *c.* 1560

This volume illustrates the various currents of alchemy as practised and theorized in Islamic culture from the fourteenth to the sixteenth centuries. The first text is by 'Izz al-Din Aydamur al-Jildaki, an alchemist residing in Egypt in the first half of the fourteenth century. The second text, a pseudo-Platonic work, is accompanied by a *tafsir* (commentary) attributed to Jabir ibn Hayyan (*fl.* 8th century).

Jabir's writings united scientific investigation with metaphysical speculation, as in his concept of 'balance' (see LJS 403 [no. 4]). In particular, he predicted a new age in which Islamic revelation would be replaced by the doctrines of Greek science and philosophy. His knowledge of Greek thought was derived from the translations provided by Hunayn ibn Ishaq and his school (see LJS 393 [V, no. 12]). Using Greek philosophy as a basis for his experimental science, he avoided the hermetic and allegorical school of alchemy which characterized the Egyptian tradition and its foremost exponent, Zosimus. This tradition, however, underwent a revival in the Muslim world after the time of Jabir, and was received by, among others, 'Izz al-Din al-Jildaki, author of the first text in the present manuscript.

DESCRIPTION Paper, 128 folios, 212 x 160 mm, in Arabic, naskh script, black ink, significant words and sentences in red, occasional marginal annotations in second work; three drawings of plants in

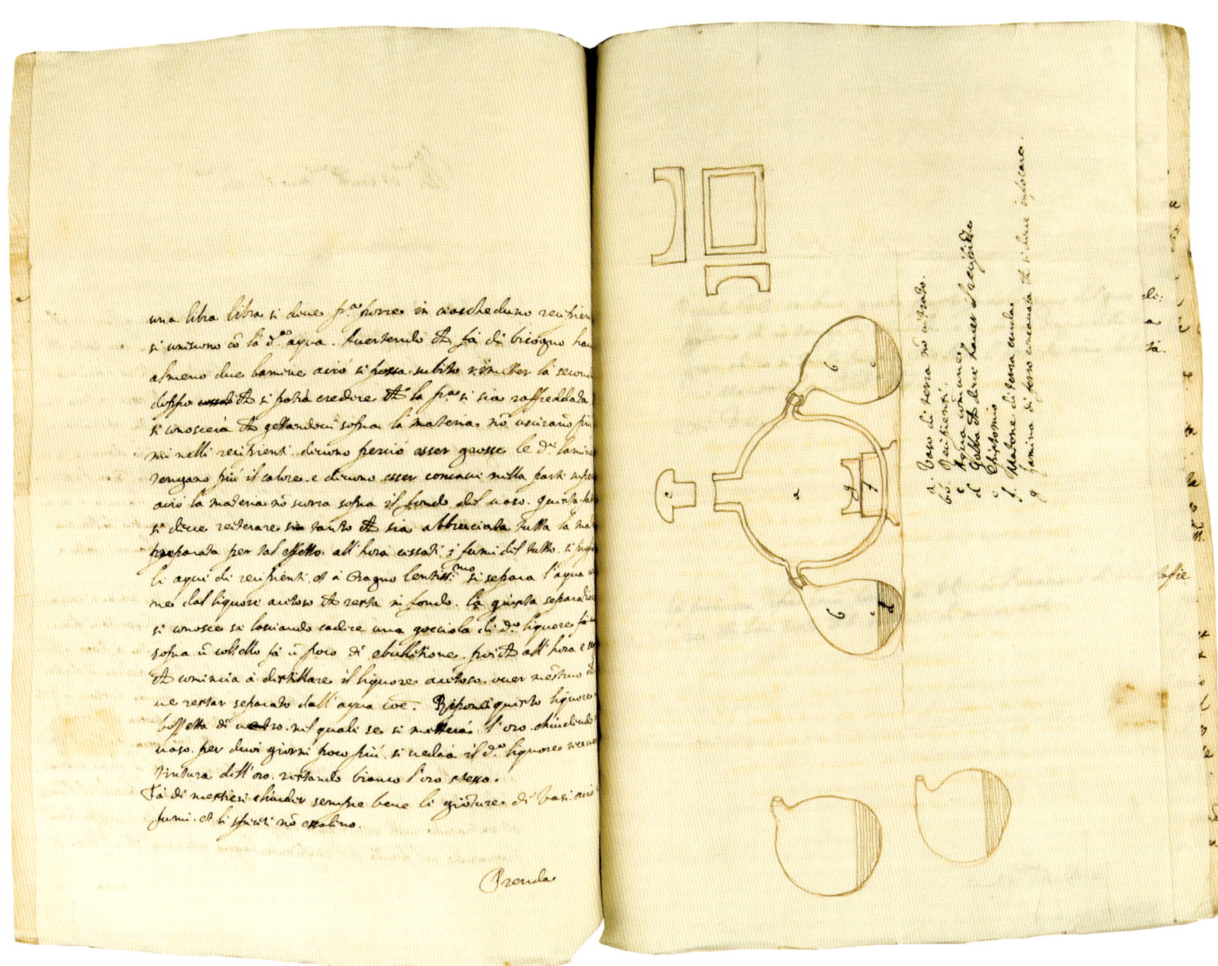

first work (ff. 91r-v), red ink, some green colouring. Later brown
morocco binding.

PROVENANCE Sam Fogg, November 2002

BIBLIOGRAPHY EI II 357-59; Brockelmann G II 138

6 LJS 448

Don Antonio de' Medici, *Book of Secrets*, with an autograph recipe by Giambattista della Porta
Florence, November 1614

'Books of secrets' were a common feature of medieval and
Renaissance science. Their tradition can be traced back to the
tenth-century Arabic *Secret of Secrets* attributed to Aristotle (see
LJS 459 [I, no. 7]). The present example of the genre, compiled
by Don Antonio de' Medici (1576–1621), attests the broad
range of interests that could be included in such a
compilation. Among these are alchemy, magic for
summoning angels, magnetism, clock-making, cures for
impotence and gout, and ceremonies for maintaining a
permanent supply of money. Don Antonio compiled this
miscellaneous collection both from recipes he himself had
written and from material sent to him by a variety of
contacts. Among these was the magician and natural
philosopher Giambattista della Porta (1535–1615), who
contributed a recipe for ensuring erections, sent to Don
Antonio from Naples on 12 July 1612. Of the many well-
known figures mentioned in this collection, the most famous
is certainly Galileo, with whom one of Don Antonio's
correspondents was evidently in close contact.

DESCRIPTION Paper, *c.* 400 folios, various sizes approximating 290
x 220 mm, in Italian and Latin. Contemporary heavy *cartonato*
binding

PROVENANCE Martayan Lan, May 2002

BIBLIOGRAPHY Eamon; Luti; DSB XI 95-98

CHEMISTRY

7 LJS 401

Modestin Fachs, *Probier Büchlein*
Germany, 2nd half 17th century

This is a manuscript copy of the *Probier Büchlein* (Little test book) of 1622 by Modestin Fachs (*fl. c.* 1567), containing the earliest suggestion that tin and lead gain weight upon heating during calcinations.

DESCRIPTION Paper, 265 folios, 152 x 203 mm, in German. Contemporary blue paper binding.
PROVENANCE Joseph A. Freilich; Sotheby's, New York, 10 January 2001, lot 181

8 LJS 402

Georg Ernst Multz von Walda, *Die eröffnete königliche oder hüngarische Kupffer-Handlung Schmölnitz and kürtzer Auszzug*
Germany, 1743

The text describes the mining of copper, including comprehensive information on smelting, with details on specific chemicals and processes.

DESCRIPTION Paper, two works, 409 and 214 pages, 168 x 213 mm. Contemporary calf binding.
PROVENANCE Joseph A Freilich; Sotheby's, New York, 10 January 2001, lot 405

9 LJS 170

Joseph Black, *Lectures on Chemistry*, vol. V, Lectures 61–76
Possibly Scotland, *c.* 1780

Joseph Black (1728–1799), the discoverer of latent and specific heats, is regarded as one of the founders of modern quantitative chemistry. These lectures convey his discoveries on air in alkaline substances; gypseous concretions; clays; flints; fusible earths; gems; the art of making porcelain; inflammable bodies; oils; balsams and resins; bitumen, etc.

DESCRIPTION Paper, 259 folios (versos blank), 192 x 121 mm, in English, smooth cursive script. Leather spine in six compartments.
PROVENANCE John Stanitz, ms. 1

10 LJS 214

Anton von Ruprecht, *Theoretisch-praktische Chemie*
Hungary, 1784

Anton Ruprecht (1748–1814), a noted figure in the development of modern chemistry, was known for his work in the discovery of the elements antimony and tungsten, for experiments with "molybdic silver" that helped to identify the element tellurium, and the discovery of element austrium in 1792.

DESCRIPTION Paper, *c.* 640 folios, 257 x 205 mm, in German, in brown ink, cursive script, autograph. Original green paper wrapper.
PROVENANCE Franklin Institute, Philadelphia; Thomas Heller (1995); John Stanitz, ms. 45
BIBLIOGRAPHY Próder

11 LJS 187

Pierre Louis Georges du Buat, *Thermomètre absolu*
Condé, 1801

Du Buat (1734–1809) is best known for his work in hydraulics. This manuscript represents one of his forays into the arena of meteorological instruments, the development of an 'absolute' thermometer.

DESCRIPTION Paper, 12 folios, 322 x 202 mm, in French, 1 column, 39 lines, in brown ink, autograph; one handwritten plate containing three figures pasted to inner back of paper wrapper. Sewn in a paper wrapper.
PROVENANCE John Stanitz, ms. 18

12 LJS 217

G.M. Raymond, *Rapport sur les poids et mesures, fait à la Societé Royale Académique de Savoie, dans sa séance du 22 décembre 1828, par une commission nominée à cette fin*
Savoy, 22 December 1828

This report urges the outright adoption of specific decimal liquid measures (*e.g.* litres), and more generally the pegging of older national measures that may be retained to specific percentages of international decimal measures.

DESCRIPTION Paper, 14 folios, 286 x 196 mm, in French, black ink, cursive script, single hand. Sewn with blue silk ribbon.
PROVENANCE Philadelphia Rare Books and Manuscripts Co.; John Stanitz, ms. 48

VII Technology

This chapter focuses on a variety of approaches to mechanical and physical problems, combined under the label 'technology'. It begins with two important Arabic works on water, the first (LJS 386 [no. 1]) on its use to determine density and the second (LJS 399 [no. 2]) on methods of finding and transporting it. These are followed by a collection of works on similar engineering and on other aspects of mechanics. Works on naval technology, including mapping (LJS 473 [no. 10] *et sqq.*), and on armaments (LJS 254 [no. 17] *et sqq.*), in two separate sections, conclude the chapter.

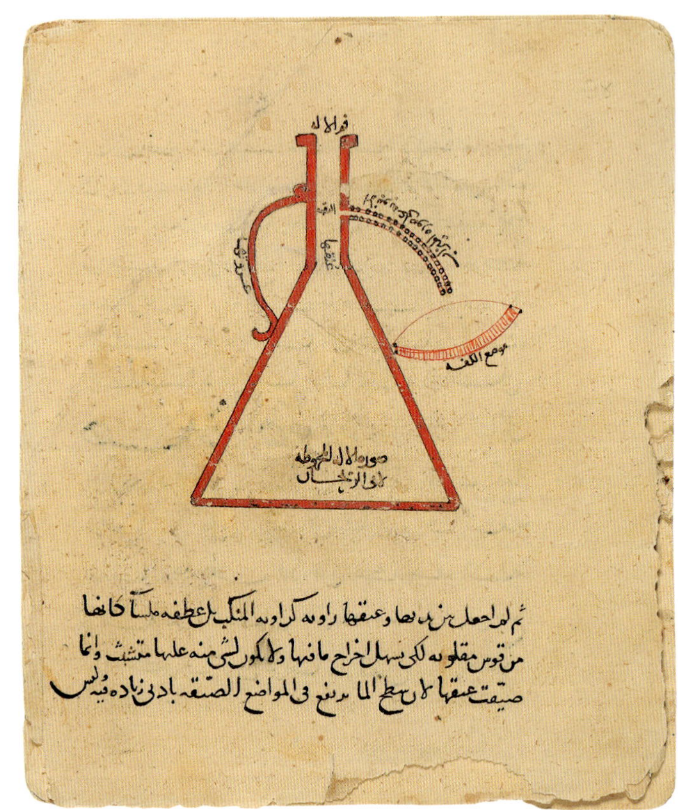

LJS 386
p. 98

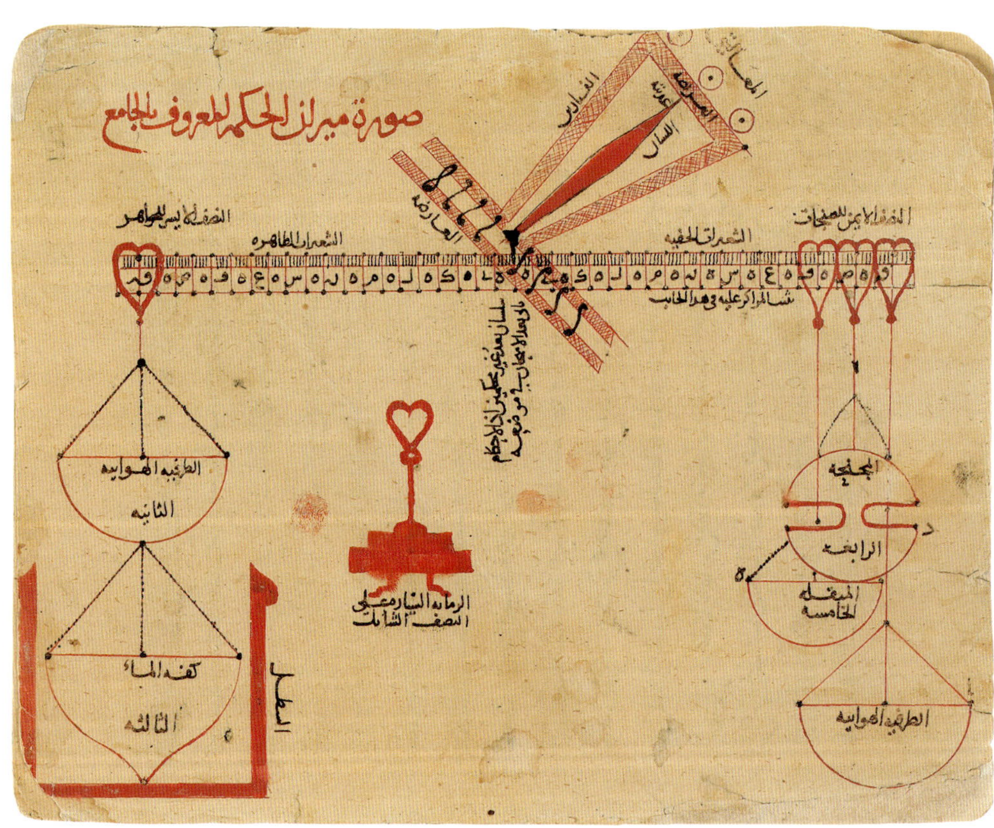

LJS 386
p. 192

MECHANICS AND ENGINEERING

1 LJS 386

Al-Khazini, *Kitab mizan al-hikmah*
c. 1270

The principle of hydrostatic balance goes back to Archimedes of Syracuse (*c.* 287–212 BC) and his famous bath: "Sitting down in the tub, he noticed that the amount of water which flowed over by the tub was equal to the amount by which his body was immersed" (Vitruvius, *De architectura*, IX 3). The technique passed into the Arabic tradition in the works of al-Razi (see LJS 404 [IX, no. 4]), al-Biruni (see LJS 478 [IV, no. 2]) and Omar Khayam (d. 1123), among others, with the particular application of determining the composition of alloys and the specific gravities of metals and jewels.

'Abd al-Rahman al-Khazini, a Persian astronomer and physician, wrote the present treatise ('Book of the Balance of Wisdom') in 1121. It comprises a historical introduction to theories of gravity and weighing in Greek and Arabic science, tables of densities of 50 substances (including metals, precious stones, solids and liquids) and accounts of various types of balance, including the "balance of wisdom", invented by Muzaffar ibn Isma'il and perfected by al-Khazini himself. Al-Khazini also made use of the conical vessel constructed by al-Biruni for determining specific gravities. Few manuscript copies of this work are known: this one can be dated to *c.* 1270 by its paper and script.

DESCRIPTION Paper, 98 folios, 195 x 150 mm, in Arabic, neat naskh script in black ink, headings in riqa' script in black ink; 26 diagrams and 18 tables in red and black ink. Unbound.
PROVENANCE Sam Fogg, cat. 22, no. 56
BIBLIOGRAPHY Sarton II 128; DSB I 213-14; EI IV 1186, VII 195-200

2 LJS 399

Al-Karaji, *Inbat al-miyah al-khafiyyah*
Iraq or Persia, 14 Dhu'l Qa'da 1084 / 20 February 1674

Abu Bakr Muhammad al-Karaji, mathematician and engineer, was resident in Baghdad and Persia; he composed this work ('The Search for Hidden Waters') around 1019 AD. It is a manual on hydraulics and water supply, including practical information on the construction of irrigation systems in the form of subterranean tunnels (*qanats*). According to al-Karaji, this was the most beneficial of crafts, since it helped the earth to flourish and men to attain order in their lives.

The work begins with a general description of the earth and the waters that are to be found in it – how to find them, what types and tastes there are, and how to clean contaminated water. It goes on to discuss springs and wells, drilling, the measurement of water and the construction and upkeep of *qanats*, including dealing with blockages.

DESCRIPTION Paper, 49 folios, 190 x 125 mm, in Arabic, nasta'liq script, black ink, rubrication and overlining in red; 14 large diagrams in black and red. Brown morocco binding, blind-tooled.
PROVENANCE Sam Fogg, December 2000
BIBLIOGRAPHY EI IV 529, 600; Krenkow

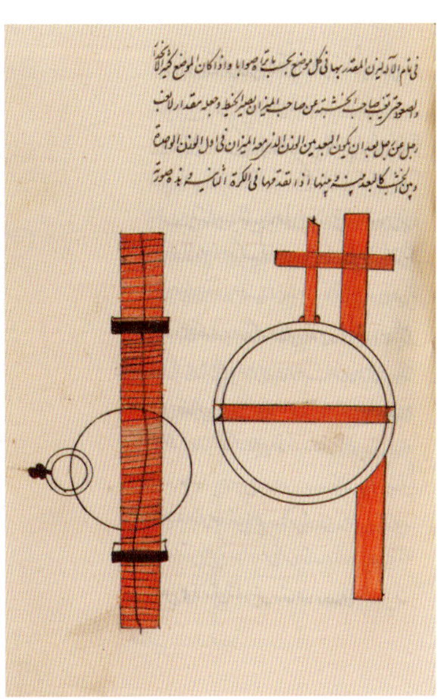

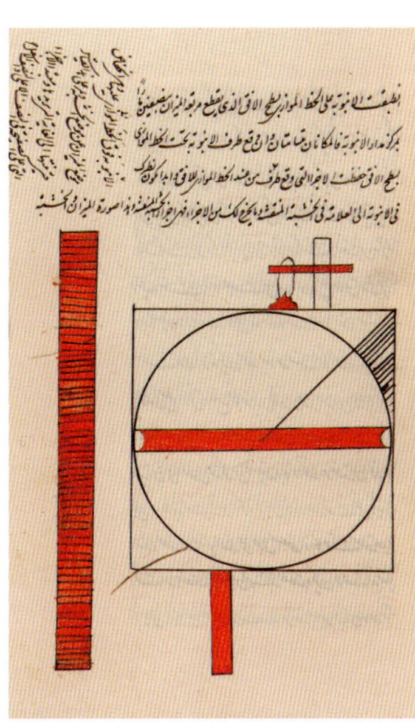

LJS 399, f. 32r   LJS 399, f. 35r

3 LJS 201

Evangelista Torricelli, Letter to Marin Mersenne
Florence, 9 January 1645

Torricelli (1608–1647) derived his renown from his proof that,
contrary to standard medieval belief, nature does not "abhor a
vacuum". He also made a significant contribution to
mathematics, especially geometry. In addition to this, he had a
particular skill in constructing glass lenses. In this letter he
offers to send one of his lenses to the French scholar Marin
Mersenne (1588–1649).

DESCRIPTION Paper, 1 folio, 275 x 201 mm, in Italian, cursive script,
brown ink. Tipped into red morocco binding.
PROVENANCE Sir Thomas Phillipps; W.H. Robinson, 1945; H.P.
Kraus, cat. 155 (1980), no. 89, and cat. 186 (1991), no. 156; John Stanitz,
ms. 32
BIBLIOGRAPHY DSB XIII 433-40

4 LJS 186

Adamus Adamandus, *Disquisitiones physicomathematicae*
Florence, 1668

This manuscript contains seven treatises by the Jesuit Adam
Kochansky (pseudonym Adamus Adamandus; 1631–1700).
Described as "physico-mathematical", they are concerned
with a miscellany of topics. The first discusses the motion of
fluids. The second argues for the impossibility of perpetual
motion. The third is a proposal for an underwater vessel,
shaped like a fish (apparently the subject of a demonstration
by the Florentine scholar Antonio Maria Salvini in August
1668); the fourth argues that "from mathematical principles, it
is demonstrated that the artificial flight of man is possible".
The fifth treatise proposes a method of long-distance
communication via telescopes and lamps, and the sixth
suggests modifications to the pendulum mechanism for more
accurate time-keeping. The last treatise is on geometry.

DESCRIPTION Paper, 89 folios, 213 x 156 mm, in Latin, cursive
script, three scribes, brown ink; pen-and-ink text illustrations and
plate laid in containing eight figures; engraved title cartouche.
Contemporary mottled calf binding.

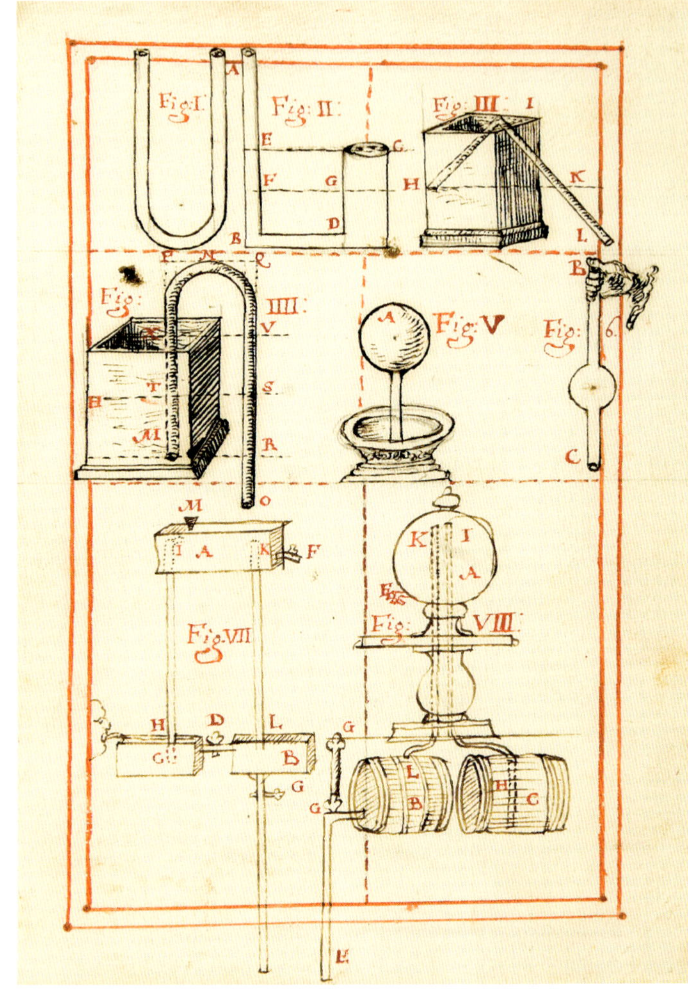

LJS 186
p. 1

PROVENANCE "Carolus Bono Crugius" inscribed on title cartouche,
partially effaced; Arturo Pregliasco, cat. 177 (1988), no. 78; H.P. Kraus,
cat. 179 (1988), no. 78; John Stanitz, ms. 17

5 LJS 178

Report on efforts to repair the aqueduct of Pantano
Rome, *c.* 1683

This is an extensive report on efforts made over a twenty-year
period to discover why the water of the aqueduct at Pantano
was hot and on occasion boiling.

DESCRIPTION Paper, 20 folios, 268 x 197 mm, in Italian, 1 column,
29 lines, brown ink, cursive script in a single hand. Disbound.

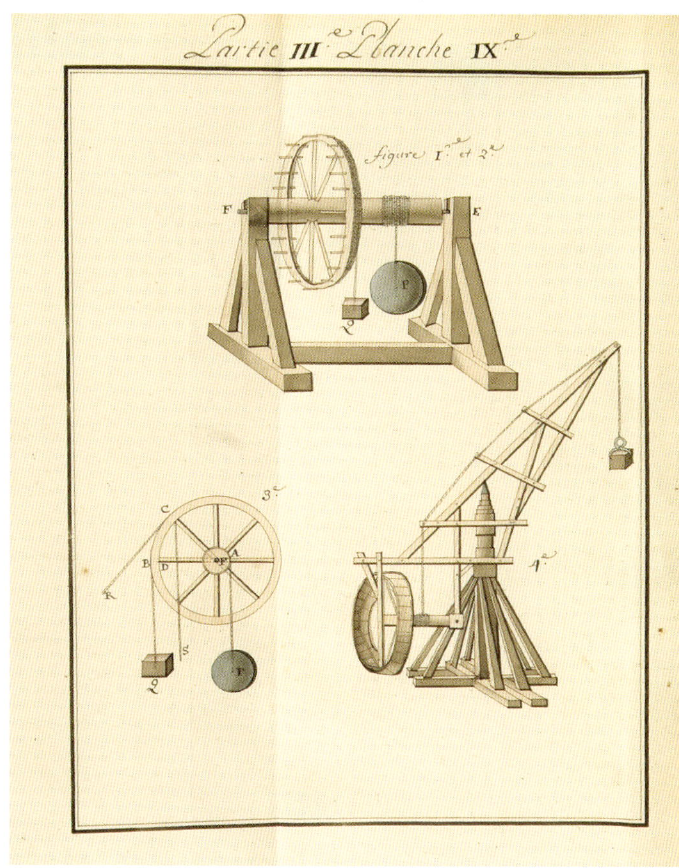

PROVENANCE Giuseppe Renato Imperiali; Frederick North, 5th Earl
of Guilford; his sale, Messrs Evans, 8 December 1830; Sir Thomas
Phillipps, ms. 21129; Robinson Brothers, 1945; H.P. Kraus, ms. 1010;
John Stanitz, ms. 9

6   LJS 176

Traité de mécanique
France, c. 1700

An illustrated treatise on mechanics.

DESCRIPTION Paper, 58 folios and 27 folding drawings,
262 x 185 mm, in French, fine professional cursive script, brown ink.
Original calf binding.
PROVENANCE Laurence Witten, no. 15173; John Stanitz, ms. 7

7   LJS 180

Letters on engineering and industrial history
France and England, 1727–1836

From an early reference to steel manufacturing in France (1727,
no. 6) to suggestions for improvements in candle production
(1836, no. 4), this collection encompasses more than a
hundred years of industrial development.

DESCRIPTION Paper, 112 folios, varying dimensions (mostly quarto),
25 manuscripts, ink, various cursive scripts, several hands. Disbound.
PROVENANCE Some letters are Sir Thomas Phillipps, ms. 18505,
18507 and 22927; Robinson Brothers, 1945; H.P. Kraus, ms. 836; John
Stanitz, ms. 11

8   LJS 190

Lectures on physics, statics and mechanics
Possibly Paris, c. 1770

This is an interesting text reporting a series of lectures that
draw upon the writings of Galileo, Gassendi, Musschenbroek,
Descartes and many others.

DESCRIPTION Paper, 163 folios, 263 x 191 mm, 25 lines, black ink,
cursive script, single hand. Disbound.
PROVENANCE Frederick North, 5th Earl of Guilford; his sale, Messrs
Evans, 8 December 1830, vol. 7, lot 286, to Thorpe; Sir Thomas
Phillipps, ms. 7552; Robinson Brothers, 1945; H.P. Kraus; John
Stanitz, ms. 21

9   LJS 163

Illustrated notebook of machinery
Germany, 1864

This illustrated notebook contains more than 16 0 full-page
drawings for various kinds of machinery, including sewing
machines, printing presses, cranes, turbines, pumps, and
water- and steam-powered engines and locomotives.

DESCRIPTION Paper, 191 folios, 254 x 182 mm, in German, brown ink,
cursive script. Green cloth, entitled *Skizzen* on upper cover.
PROVENANCE Howard Douglas Bode; Samuel Koslov; Christie's,
London, 12 November 1996, lot 376

NAVIGATION

10 LJS 473

L'arte del navegare
North-eastern Italy, possibly Venice, 1464–65

The manuscript, probably the original presentation copy, is a treatise on ships and navigation dedicated to the Doge and Senate of Venice in 1464–65. Venice at this period was economically dependent on trade by sea. The author begins his work with an overview of the habitable world, including accounts of cartography, topography and the construction of the compass. The second book then focuses on the designs of different types of ship. Book III is a discourse on the role of meteorology and astronomy in navigation; Book IV turns to maps, with a particular description of the shores of the Mediterranean, with distances.

DESCRIPTION Parchment and paper, 84 folios, 210 x 135 mm, in Italian, slightly sloping humanistic cursive minuscule, dark brown ink, headings and marginal notes in red; 2-line initials in red or blue, four larger illuminated initials; seven pages with diagrams, drawings or tables. 19th-century English blind-tooled dark brown morocco binding.

PROVENANCE Frederick North (1766-1827), fifth Earl of Guilford; his sale, Messrs Evans, 13 December 1830, lot 563; John Lee (1783-1866), F.S.A.; his sale, Sotheby's, 8 November 1888, lot 266; Sotheby's, London, 10 July 1968, lot 283; Sotheby's, London, 7 December 2004, lot 40

BIBLIOGRAPHY Saibanti

11 LJS 28

Battista Agnese, Portolan Atlas
Venice, *c.* 1535–38

This is an early work by Battista Agnese (1527–1564), one of the most distinguished sixteenth-century makers of portolans (nautical charts). Portolans, which developed from the beginning of the fourteenth century, were primarily made for sailors and as such concentrated on accurate representations

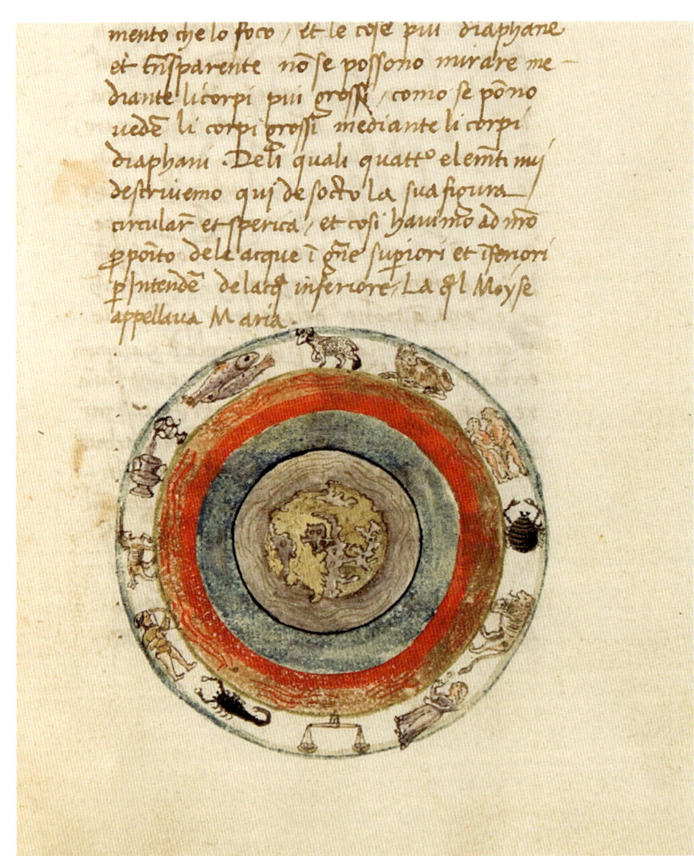

LJS 473
f. 8v

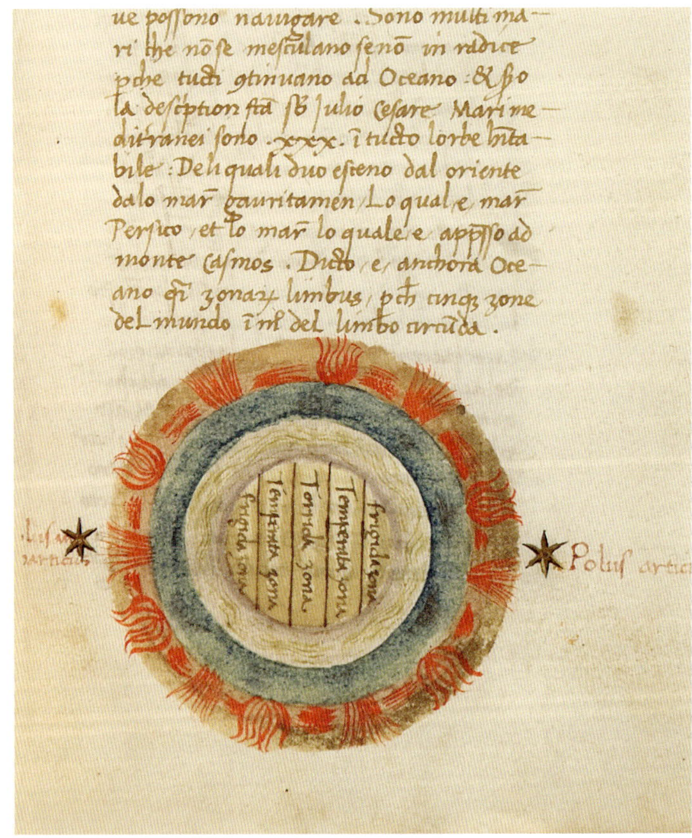

LJS 473
f. 12r

of coastlines superimposed with rhumb lines depicting compass directions. Agnese's work represents the late peak of this tradition, in which technical accuracy was matched by artistic skill.

The seven maps (five of which appear to be in Agnese's own hand; see overleaf) portray Britain and north-west Europe; Spain and North Africa; the Mediterranean (from northern Italy to Antioch); the seas of Marmara and Azov and the Black Sea; the Adriatic; the Aegean; and a world map. The world map includes the Straits of Magellan, discovered in 1520, and seven named towns in North and South America, although the west coast was still unknown at the time it was produced. This, and other inaccuracies which Agnese later corrected, date the atlas to among the first of Agnese's productions.

The first recorded owner of the present atlas was Tommaso Compeggio (1483–1564), diplomat and bishop of Feltre, who presented it to Paolo Giovio, humanist and bishop of Nocera, on 8 August 1541. The gift is recorded in an inscription in Giovio's hand.

DESCRIPTION Parchment, 398 x 285 mm, seven double-page maps in brown ink, rhumb lines in brown and red emanating from central compass roses, place names in small gothic bookhand, brown and red; polychrome colouring of coastlines and land-masses. Contemporary Venetian goatskin binding.

PROVENANCE Tommaso Compeggio (1483-1564); Paolo Giovio (1483-1552); J. Paul Getty Museum, 1983; Sotheby's, London, 6 December 1988, lot 38

BIBLIOGRAPHY Tooley 15-16; Wagner

12 LJS 345

William Bourne, *Inventions or Devises*
Gravesend, *c.* 1576

William Bourne's *Inventions or Devises* is a treatise on the use of machines for war by land and sea ("martiall affayres by seas and ships" and "devises of ordinance"). It was printed in London in 1578, dedicated to Charles Howard, Baron Effingham, a naval commander and later Lord Admiral. The present manuscript copy, however, is dedicated to William Cecil, Lord Burghley, who in the 1570s was Elizabeth I's Lord

LJS 345
pp. 112-13

High Treasurer. He had a particular interest in navigation, ships and military science.

Although lacking some of the devices that appear in the printed version, this copy includes twenty more devices overall, and has six more illustrations. Bourne also designed a submarine and a diving suit.

DESCRIPTION Paper, 120 folios, 200 x 150 mm, in English, neat secretarial hand, autograph emendations and additions in Bourne's secretary hand, autograph foliation and headings; autograph illustrations and tables. Speckled calf binding.

PROVENANCE An American collector; Christie's, London, 29 November 1999, lot 207

BIBLIOGRAPHY ODNB X 792

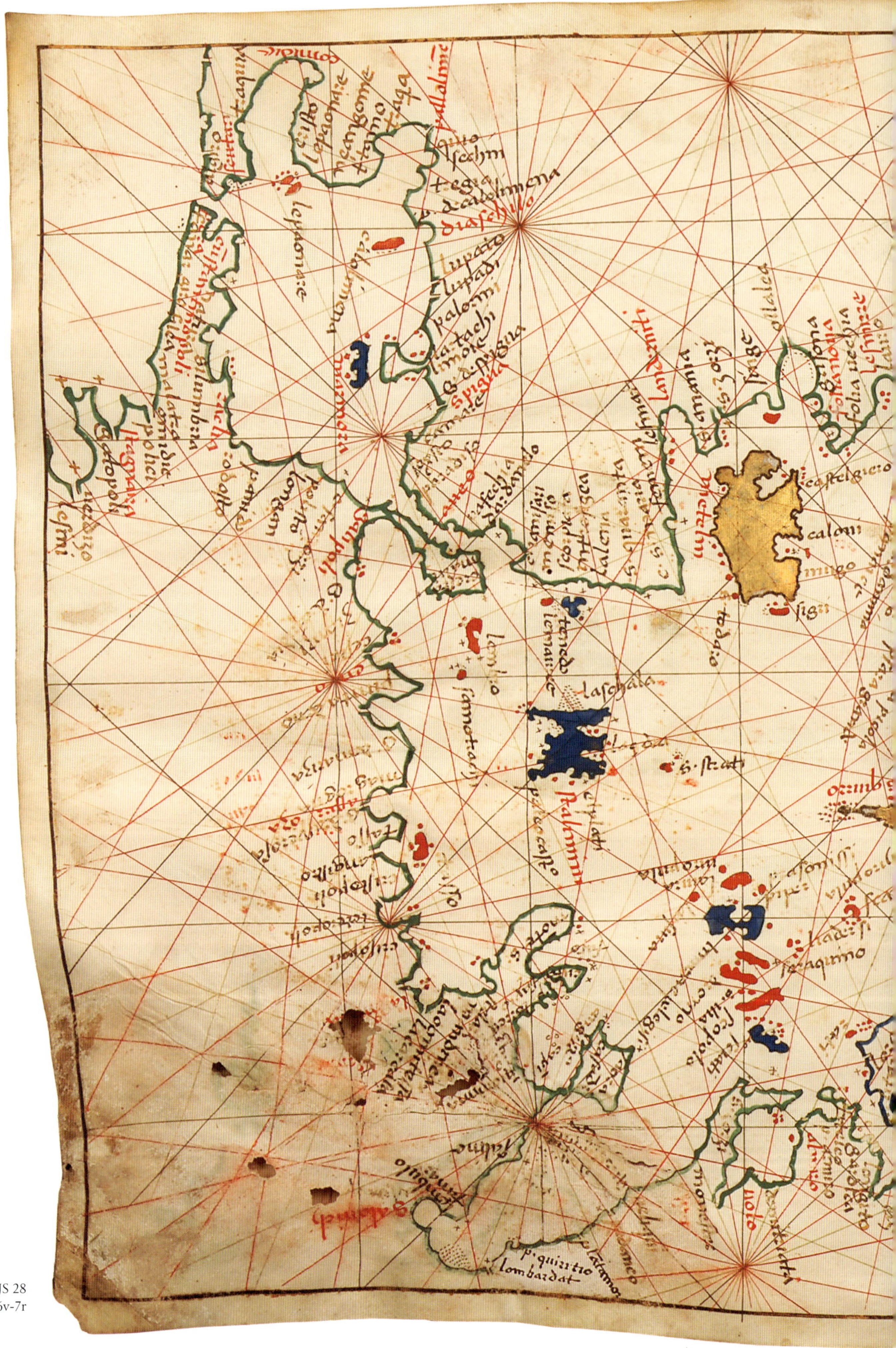

LJS 28
ff. 6v-7r

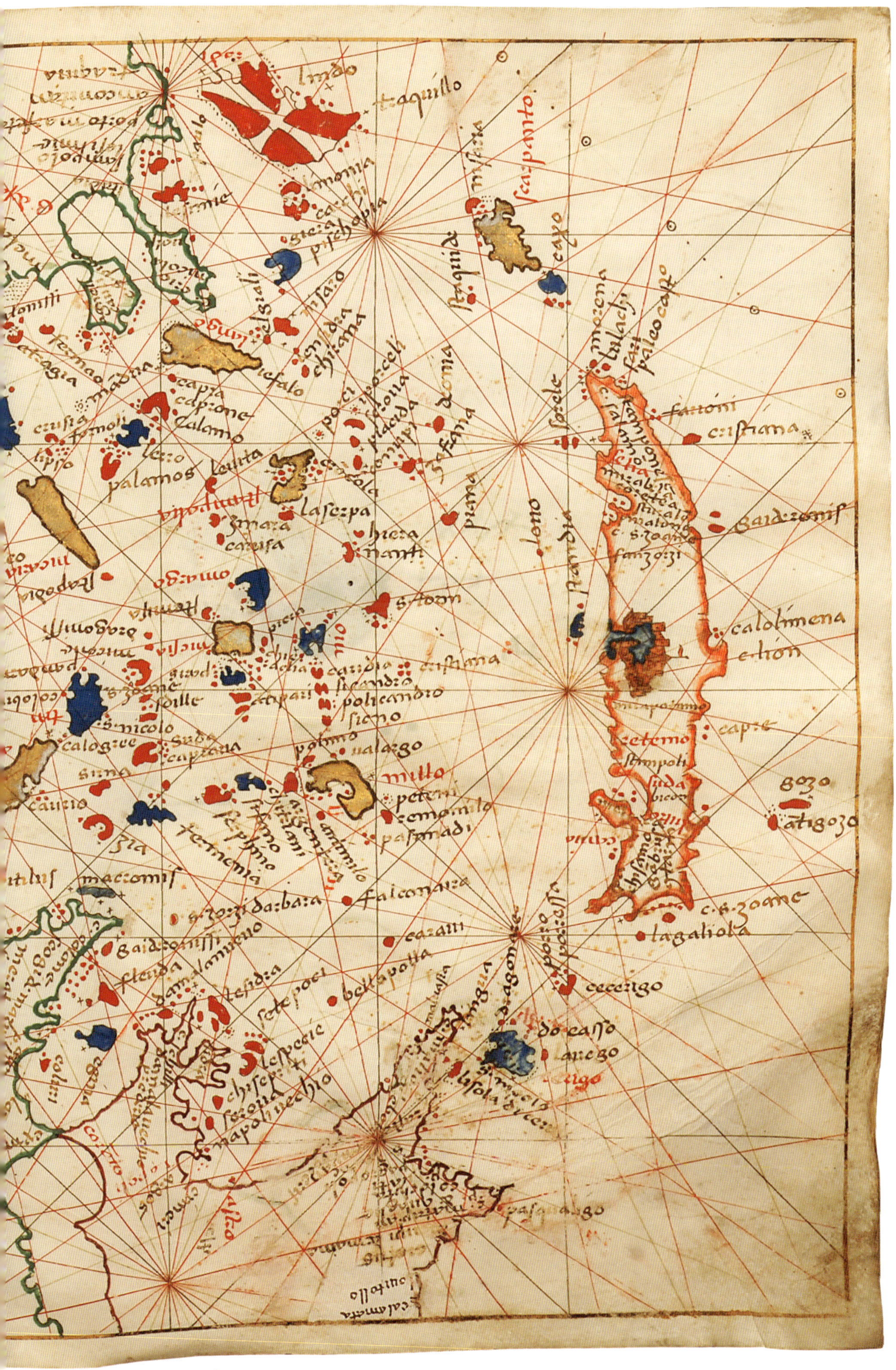
Lindo
traquillo
scarpanto
cauo
mezena
balacli
fazi pisco cauo
faroni
cistiana
Baldzronis
calolimena
e tion
capre
gozo
atigozo
c.s.zoane
tagaliola
cecengo
do casso
anego
ejgo
c.s.zoane
fanzozzi
retemo
stimpoli
suda
branda
torro
corno
piroa doma
scarfaria
chisiana
sechi
nona
polcandro
sieno
ualazgo
milo
petani
remonilo
pasinadi
falconara
cazani
boccauotta
setepoci
lespezie
chisetto
napolinechio
scandro
candia
cristiana
andia
chisiana
perissale
palamos leuita
lasezpa
smara carisa
hiera nanti
s.toon
policastro
pischopia
iazo
macomis
baldsronissi
damalauneio
stenda
fermia
trapadui
napoli
s.zoane
s.nicolo
calogrec
suna
cauro
macona
corno
canoni
calamia
pontello

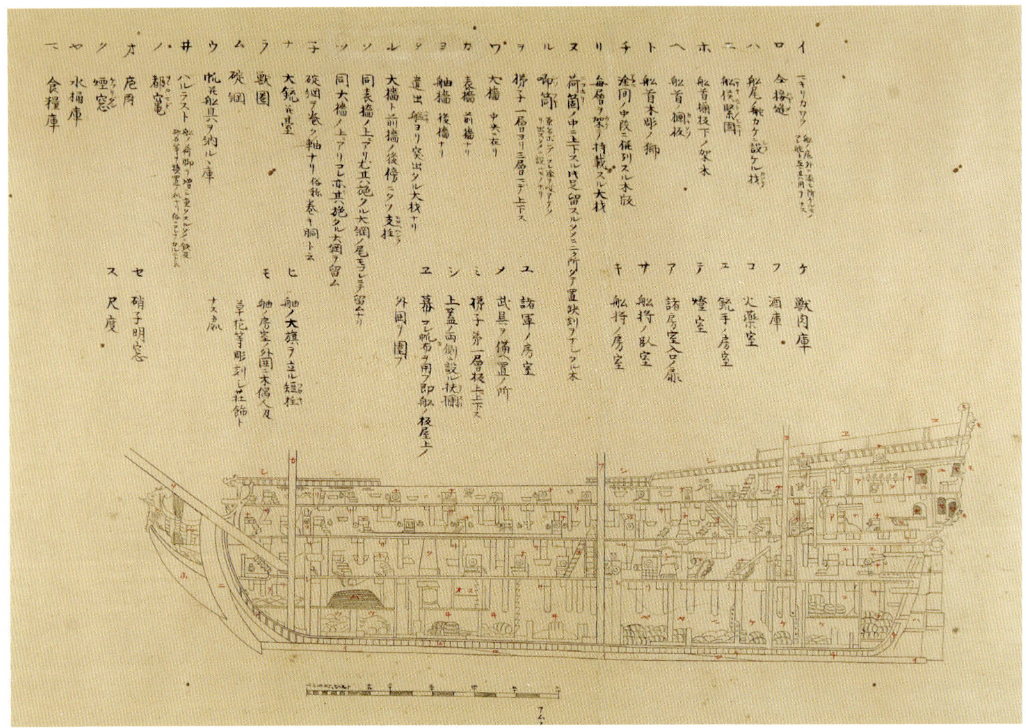

LJS 454

DESCRIPTION 2 folios, 37 x 894 cm, in Japanese
PROVENANCE Sam Fogg, 1999

15 LJS 222

Three codices on the construction of the Ganges canal
India, 1854

The manuscript contains a report on the planning, construction and management of the Ganges canal, compiled for the British engineer Sir Proby Cautley (1802–1871) in 1854. Among other matters it considers surveying, brick firing, bridge building and accounting. It includes corrections and notes, some in Cautley's hand, which were incorporated in the printed edition of 1860.

DESCRIPTION Paper, *c.* 2044 pages, 345 x 230 mm, in English, cursive script, black ink. Later half royal-blue morocco binding.
PROVENANCE Written under Cautley's direction in 1854; Asher Rare Books, cat. 27, no. 30; John Stanitz, ms. 53
BIBLIOGRAPHY ODNB X 584-85

13 LJS 319

Derrota destancias en navegacion en los distintos puntes del archipielago manila
Manila, Philippines, *c.* 1750

This is a set of sailing instructions, from Manila, typical of the manuals used by sailors in the eighteenth century. Distances are given in rhumbs, miles and leagues.

DESCRIPTION Paper, 4 folios, 314 x 215 mm, in Spanish, cursive script. Original bamboo scroll case.
PROVENANCE Martayan Lan, August 1999
BIBLIOGRAPHY Waters

14 LJS 454

'How to Pack a Dutch Merchant Ship'
Nagasaki, *c.* 1800

The cross-sections and their commentary illustrate the construction and compartmentalization of a contemporary European cargo ship.

16 LJS 192

John B. Whitehead and L.O. Grondahl, *Submarine Detection in an Alternating Magnetic Field*
Possibly Pittsburgh, 1919

This is an official report of experiments with submarine detection containing mounted photographs of the ships and devices involved and including a full theoretical discussion of the tests.

DESCRIPTION Paper, 94 ff., 280 x 224 mm, in English. Original full leather binding.
PROVENANCE Co-author Leo O. Grondahl's copy; Palinurus Antiquarian Books, cat. 30 (1992), no. 66; John Stanitz, ms. 23

ARTILLERY

17 LJS 254

Franz Helm (?), Treatise on artillery and gunpowder
South-east Germany, late 16th century

This text includes instructions for the preparation of gunpowder and the establishment of an arsenal, and has illustrations of different types of firearms and grenades. It appears to be a copy of an early recension of a work by Franz Helm, composed *c.* 1527–35.

DESCRIPTION Paper, *c.* 500 folios, 320 x 210 mm, in German, cursive script, brown ink, rubrics in fractura script; over 30 full-page and folding coloured plates. Limp parchment wrappers.
PROVENANCE Sotheby's, London, 21 May 1998, lot 40

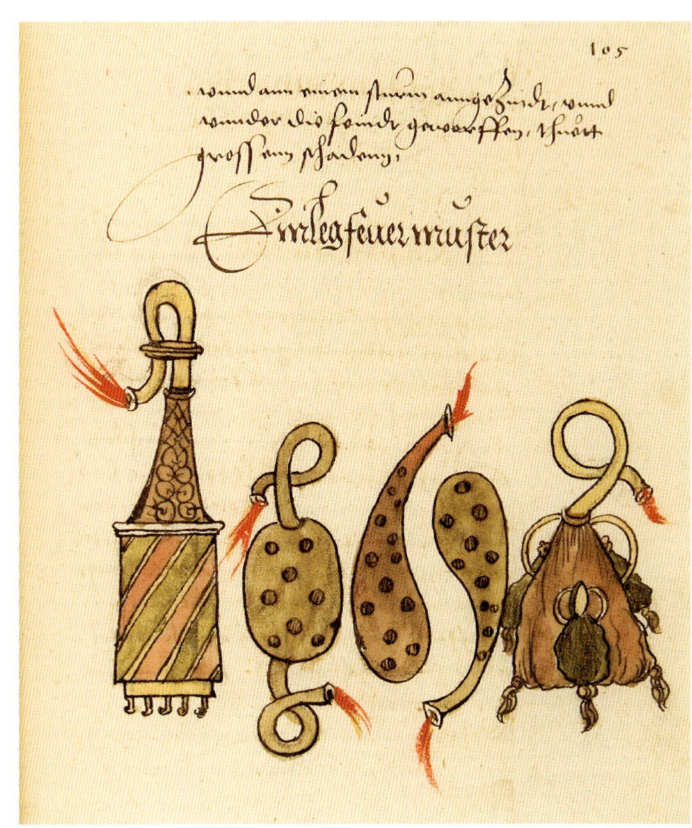

LJS 254
f. 105r

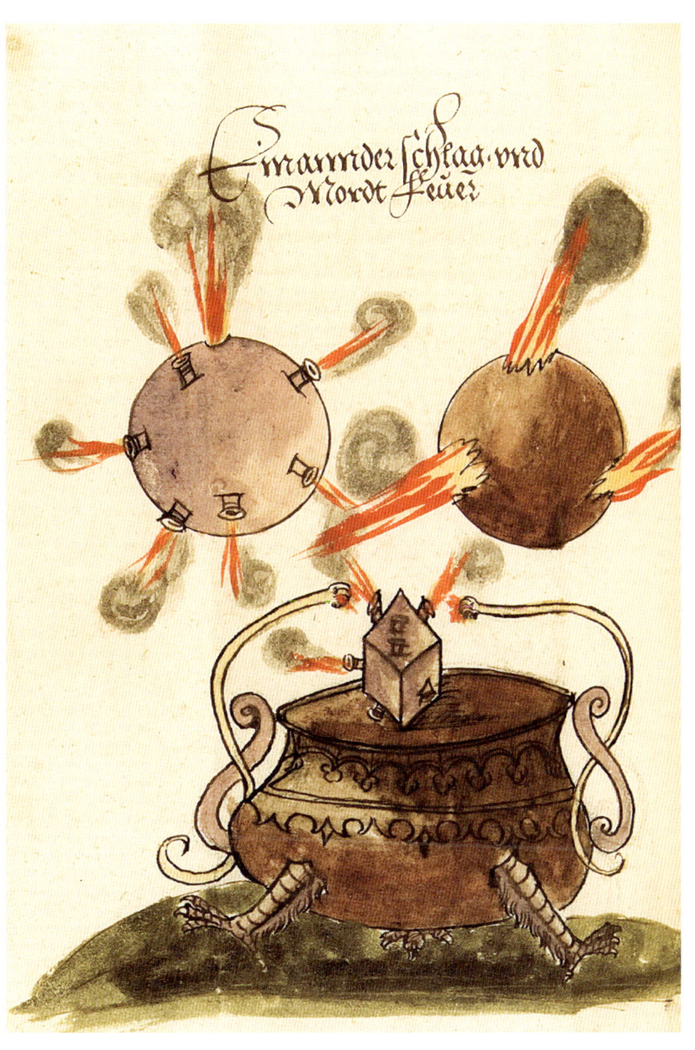

LJS 254
f. 125v

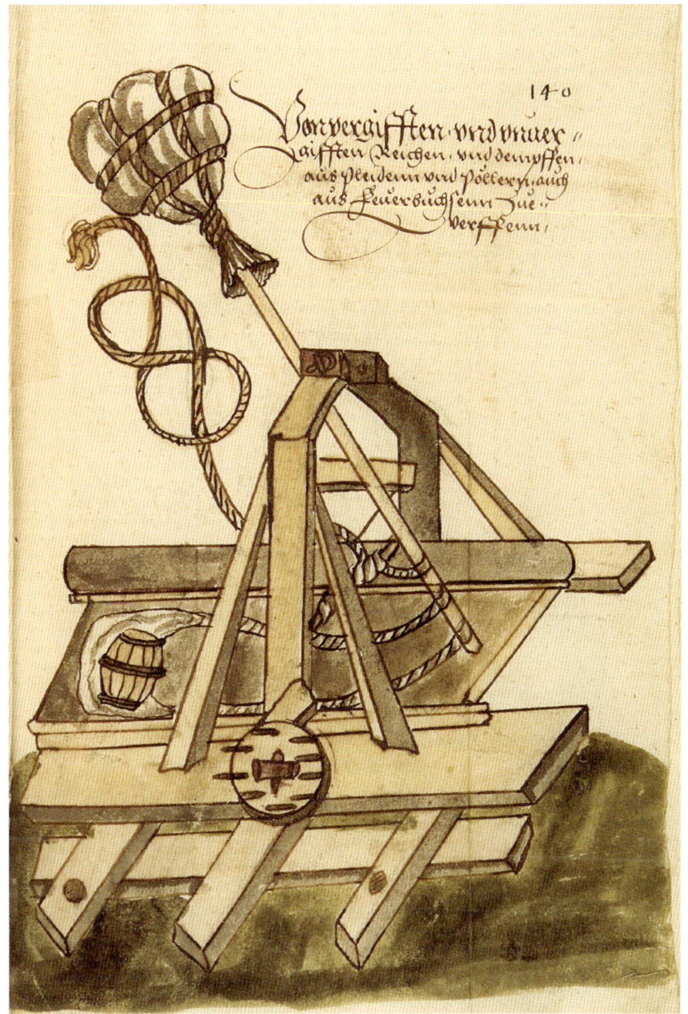

LJS 254
f. 140r

18   LJS 442

Instruction book for a cannon master
Bavaria, probably late 16th century

This practical manual for a "Büchsenmeister" (member of the
guild of cannon masters) contains instructions for making
gunpowder, mines, grenades, flares, smokescreens and booby
traps. The emphasis is on siege warfare. Several devices are
proposed for attaching to animals such as dogs or birds. A
copy of the privileges of the guild of cannon masters,
established in 1444 by the Holy Roman Emperor Frederick III
of Austria, is also included.

DESCRIPTION Paper, 132 folios, 310 x 192 mm, in German, neat
cursive script, grey ink, headings in red and black; two framed
frontispieces, 30 illustrations using black, blue and red ink and sepia,
lilac and grey washes over ink drawings. Contemporary leather
binding, stamped and gold-tooled.
PROVENANCE B. De Guard Duleireux, no. 124; Baron Valentin von
Ersdorff (?), 1731; Sam Fogg, November 2002

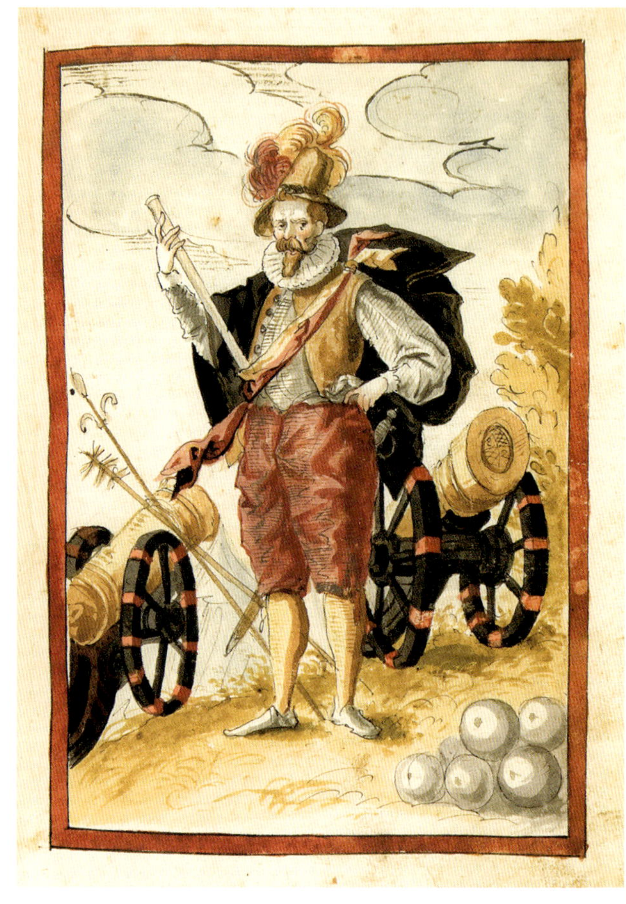

LJS 442
f. 1r

19   LJS 432

'Instructions for a bombardier'
Italy, possibly Rome, mid-17th century

This text, on the theory and practice of artillery in
seventeenth-century Italy, is structured as a dialogue of
question and answer between an instructor and a recruit. The
dialogue discusses different kinds of bombs, fuses, guns,
cartridges and mortars; it cites no printed authority and is
probably drawn from personal experience. It is copiously
illustrated with the devices in question. Various signs of
correction suggest that it was used in a practical context.

DESCRIPTION Paper, 165 folios, 260 x 190 mm, in Italian, cursive
script, probably two hands, brown ink; *c.* 114 ink and wash
illustrations. Contemporary stiff parchment binding.
PROVENANCE Martayan Lan, March 2002

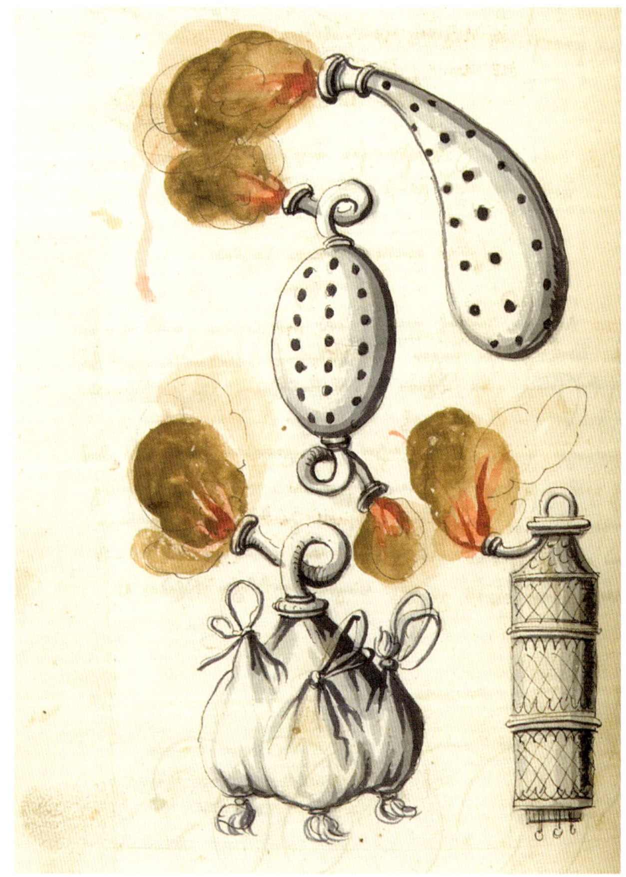

LJS 442
f. 66v

Daniel Krammer, 'Design and Construction of Fireworks and Ballistics'
Augsburg, 1661

Daniel Krammer was a gunsmith and pyrotechnician active in Augsburg. This is a work in two parts: the first section derives from a well-known work (probably Furttenbach's *Halinitro-pyrobolia* or *Büchsenmeisterey-Schul* of 1627 and 1643) and the second section presents a summary of Krammer's own research and experiments. It is notable for its illustrations, which not only depict the construction of cannons and barrels, but also show castles and towers, as well as Krammer and other figures detonating pyrotechnic devices.

DESCRIPTION Paper, 124 folios, 284 x 195 mm, in German, South German cursive hand, brown ink, two titles, two tables with watercolour borders; 63 large and 32 smaller watercolour illustrations. Contemporary parchment binding.

PROVENANCE "G.C. von A.", ms. 729; Mark Dineley; H.P. Kraus; Sotheby's, New York, 4 December 2003, lot 368

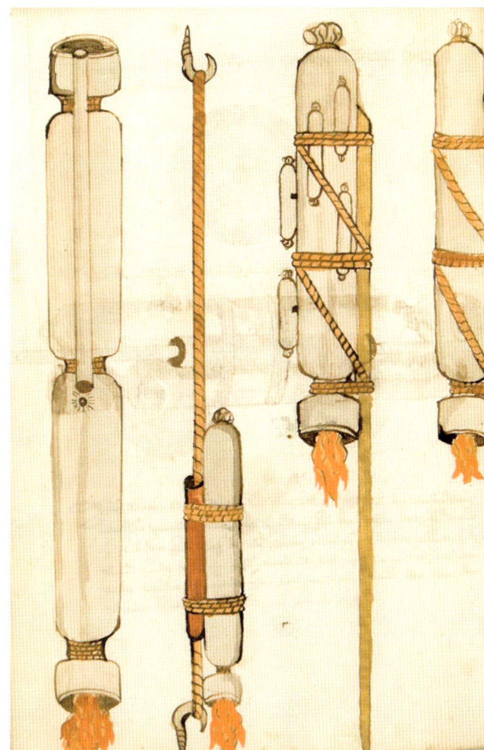

LJS 461, f. 52v

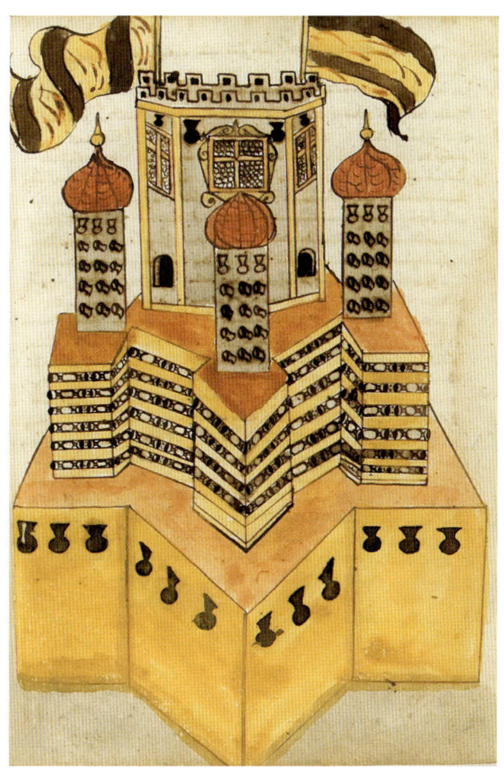

LJS 461, f. 76r

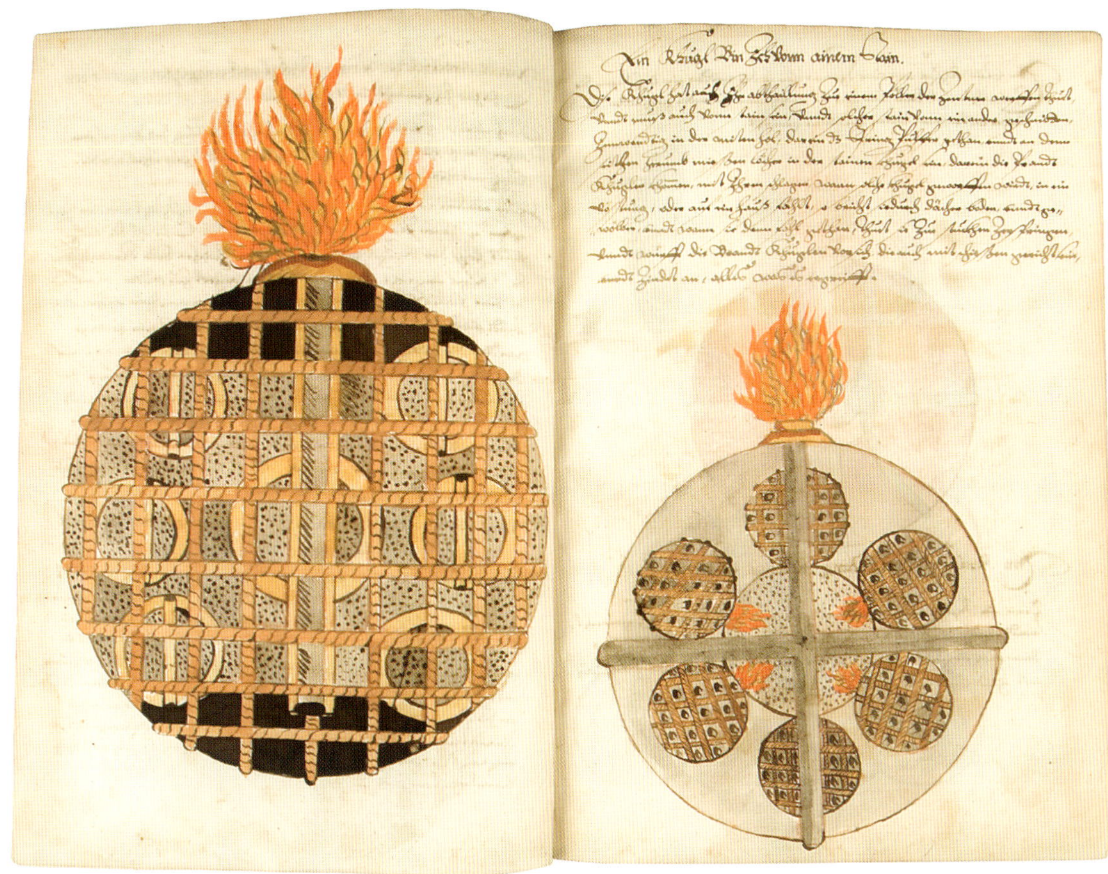

LJS 461, ff. 32-33v

21 LJS 22

Trattato di varie cose attenenti a guerra, mosini, ague, pesi,
mechaniche fortezze, et altro
Italy, 1687

This heavily illustrated manuscript surveys the variety of
machines necessary for offensive and defensive success in
war.

DESCRIPTION Paper, 99 folios, 311 x 225 mm, in Italian, cursive
script, black ink; 164 pen and ink drawings. Contemporary
parchment binding.
PROVENANCE Frederick North, 5th Earl of Guilford; his sale, Mssrs
Evans, 8-11 December 1830, vol. 2, lot 262, to Cochran; Thomas
Cochran; Sir Thomas Phillipps, ms. 5473; Swann Galleries,
6 December 1984, lot 200

22 LJS 219

Instruction pour les officiers de l'artillerie
France, after 1720

This lengthy and detailed treatise discusses not only the major
implements of war but also the construction and use of a
plethora of devices required for their construction and
implementation.

DESCRIPTION Paper, 422 folios, 282 x 210 mm, in French, cursive
script, black ink. Contemporary calf binding.
PROVENANCE "D.L. du Tronquet Beatrix / Officier d'Artillerie" (18th
century); F. Thomas Heller, New York; John Stanitz, ms. 50

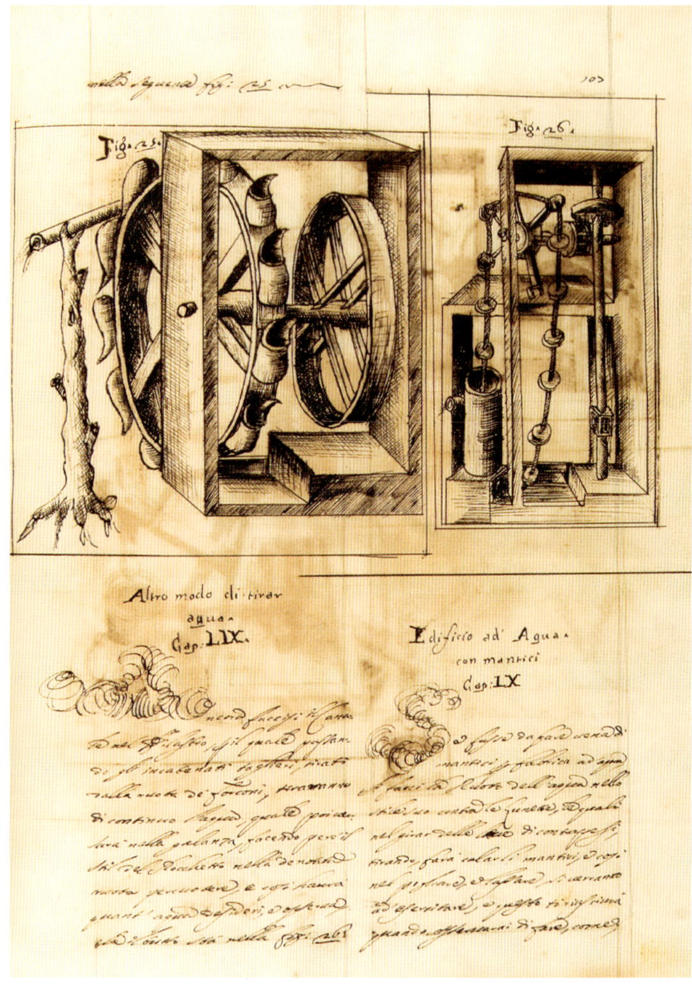

LJS
p. 1

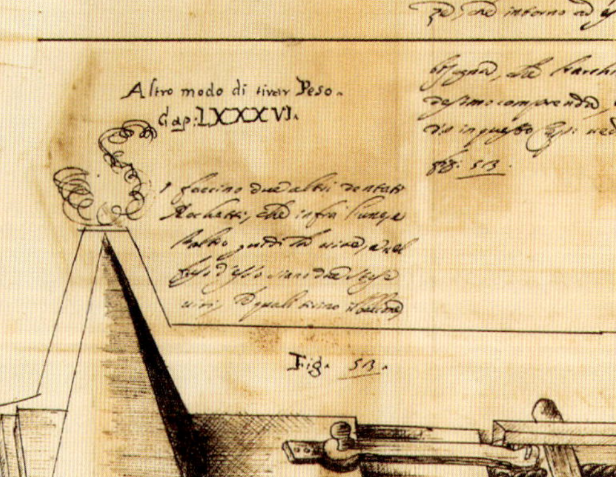

LJS
p. 1

VIII Agriculture and Animal Husbandry

The western literary tradition of works on agriculture was inaugurated around the eighth century BC by Hesiod's *Works and Days*. It was continued in Rome, with Varro's *De re rustica*, written around 37 BC, and Virgil's *Georgics*. Varro's work was used at the start of the fourteenth century by the Italian politician Pietro Crescenzio, who devoted his retirement to the composition of his 'Book of Useful Rural Matters' (LJS 265 [no. 3]).

Horses were vital tools for such activity. On a more elevated social plane, however, their function was also decorative (see LJS 356 [no. 6] and 239 [no. 7]). Aristocratic and royal interest in horses is represented by LJS 29 (no. 5).

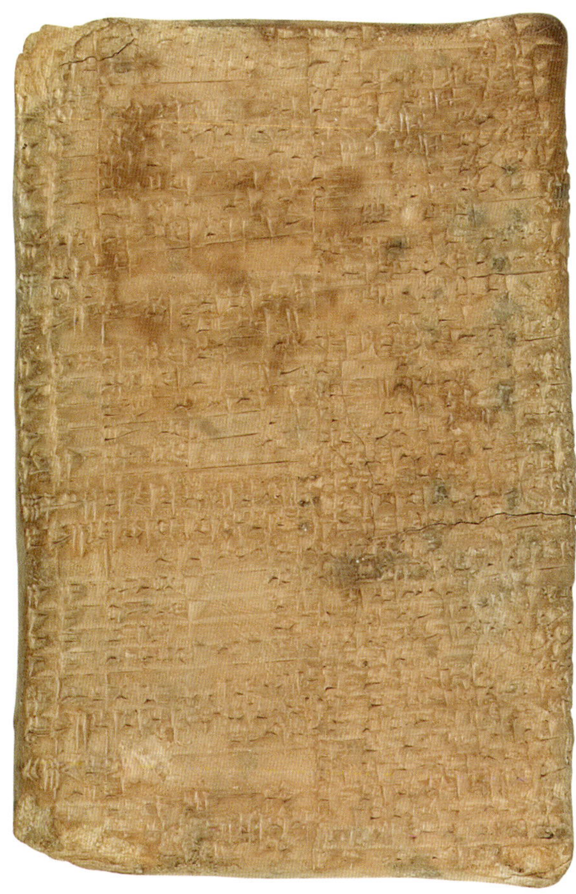

LJS 480

1   LJS 480

On the use of a ploughing team
Babylonia, *c.* 1900–1700 BC

The text of this clay tablet describes the use of a team of oxen hired for ploughing and other work in the fields. The tablet seems to have no close parallel and contains a word otherwise unrecorded.

DESCRIPTION Clay tablet, 135 x 85 mm, 130 lines, 4 columns, cuneiform script by a professional scribe.
PROVENANCE Sam Fogg, March 2002

2   LJS 467

Khawas al-manazil wa al-shuhur wa al-anwa'a
North Africa or Spain, 14th century

The anonymous author of this text uses astronomical observation to predict weather changes, which in turn provide information useful for farming, such as the best times to sow or harvest. The text was intended for use in Morocco. The calendar is described according to the solar year, with the European names of the months transliterated into Arabic, rather than according to the Islamic lunar year: the solar year was more practical when referring to seasonal variations.

DESCRIPTION Paper, 23 folios, 202 x 128 mm, in Arabic, andalusi script, brown ink. Later brown tooled morocco binding.
PROVENANCE Sam Fogg, June 2004

3   LJS 265

Petrus de Crescentiis, *Liber ruralium commodorum*
Italy (Rome?), *c.* 1465

Petrus de Crescentiis or Pietro Crescenzio (*c.* 1230–*c.* 1320) was active in city politics in northern Italy before withdrawing to his estate near Bologna, where he composed this work on husbandry around 1306. It is divided into twelve books, which discuss, among other things, the best location for a farm; plants and agriculture; threshing and granaries; viticulture; arboriculture (especially of fruit); plants, especially medicinal; meadows and woods; gardens; animals and hunting and fishing. The last two books comprise a summary of the work, in 52 general rules and with a monthly calendar of tasks.

Crescenzio harmonized Roman authors (Varro, Pliny,

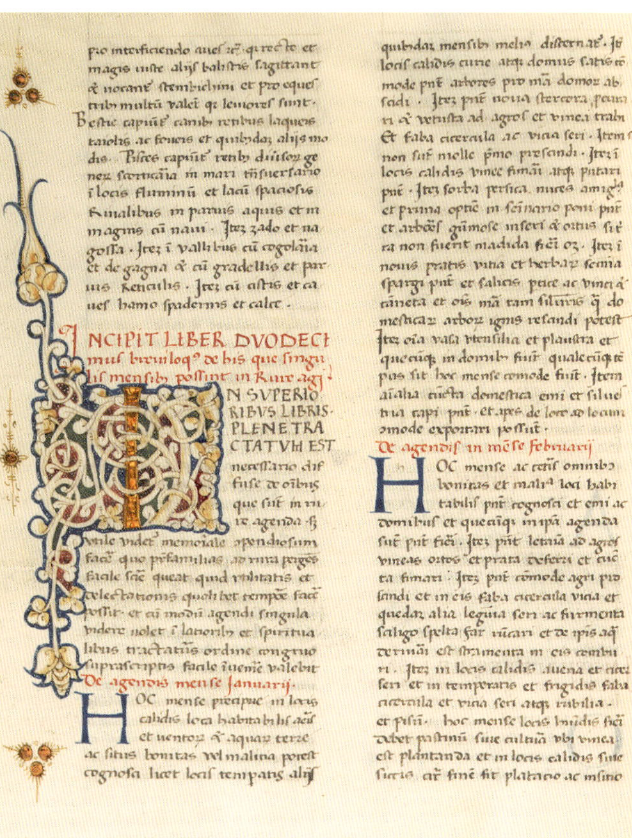

LJS 265
p. 168

Palladius) with medieval sources (Avicenna, Albertus Magnus) and with practical experience. The work circulated widely in manuscript and was first printed in 1471. It was translated into Italian (1st half 14th century) and French (1373 and 1413), and adapted into Spanish.

The beginning of each book in the manuscript is marked with a gilded initial entwined in white vine stems that spill into the margins, picked out with green and red in the interstices and surrounded with blue.

DESCRIPTION Parchment, 172 folios, 330 x 230 mm, in Latin, semi-humanistic script, black ink, chapter headings in red with initials in blue; two initials in gold on f. 1 with illumination in blue, green and red extending into margin, similar on f. 7 and at beginning of each book. Late 18th-century Italian red morocco binding, gilt, with arms of Pope Pius VI.

PROVENANCE Rebound for Pope Pius VI (Giovanni Angelico Braschi, pope 1775-99); Robert Hoe; his sale, Anderson Auction Company, 19 November 1912, Part IV, lot 2333; Sir Chester Beatty, small early book-label no. 44; Hermann Marx; sold Sotheby's, London, 19 April 1948, lot 32; Sotheby's, London, 3 December 1968, lot 26; Librairie J.M. Le Fell, June 1998

BIBLIOGRAPHY Richter; Sarton III 811-15

4 LJS 358

Commentary on a passage from Varro's *De re rustica*
Possibly Como, *c.* 1560

Varro's *De re rustica* was the earliest and main classical source of farming lore (see LJS 265 [no. 3]).

DESCRIPTION Paper, 5 folios, 305 x 210 mm, in Italian, cursive script, brown ink. Disbound.
PROVENANCE E.K. Schreiber, Spring List (2000), no. 58

5 LJS 29

Extratto da un libro de razza da cavalli del re ferrante vechio de aragona
Italy, 1541

This treatise on the anatomy, breeding and training of horses reflects the well-known passion for these animals of Ferdinand I of Aragon, King of Naples from 1458 to 1494, whose library included many books on horses and horse medicine. It is an otherwise unknown text claiming to be the synthesis of a book written by Ferdinand himself.

DESCRIPTION Parchment, 47 folios, 228 x 155 mm, in Italian, very fine upright cursive cancellaresco script with many calligraphic flourishes including multiple scrollwork on either side of the title. Original Venetian black morocco binding, gilt.
PROVENANCE Possibly commissioned by Philippe de Croy (1496–1549); vicomte Morel de Vindé; Jean-Baptiste Huzard (1755–1838); Louis-Charles-Henri-Adélaïde Mathevon, Baron de Curnieu (1812–1871); Etude Couturier Nicolay auction of the Collection of Baron de Curnieu, Hôtel Drouot, Paris, 25 February 1986, lot 144; Sotheby's, London, 5 December 1994, lot 85

6 LJS 356

Ornamental harnesses and bridle patterns
Italy and Prague or Austria, 2nd half 16th century

DESCRIPTION 2 volumes; vol 1: paper, 46 folios, 436 x 281 mm, in Italian, cursive script, brown ink; 56 full-page and 102 large black penwork illustrations. Limp parchment binding; vol. 2: paper,

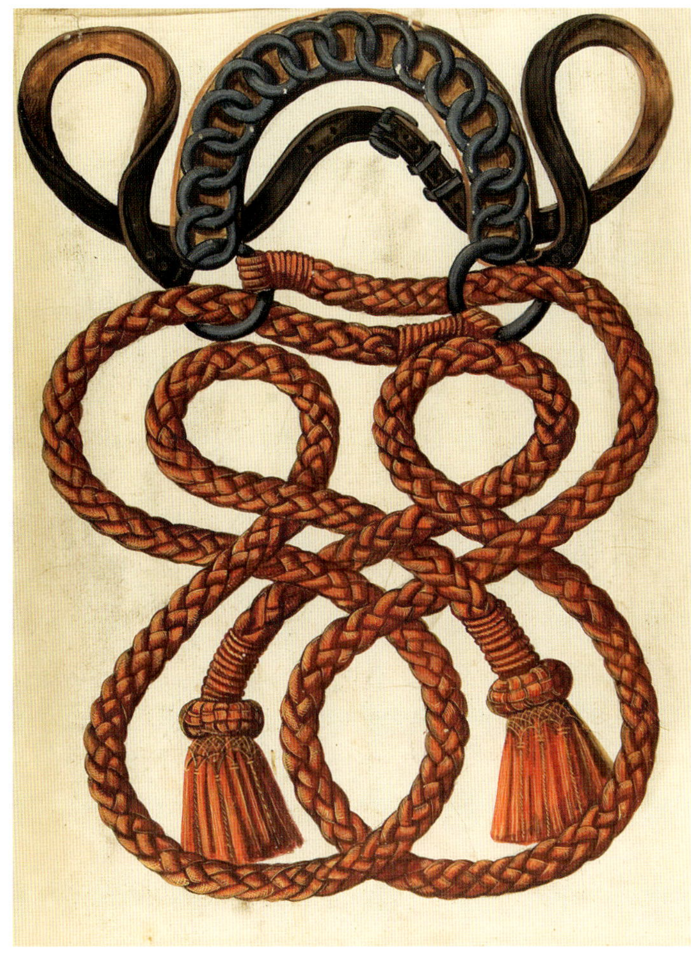

239
f. 4v

31 folios, 432 x 285 mm, 37 full-page illustrations with cross-hatch shading, one coloured. Half blind-rolled and stamped pigskin over green parchment binding.

PROVENANCE Armorial watermark of the Schrobenhausen family (vol. 2); Konrad Meuschel, Bad Honnef, Germany, February 1999

7   LJS 239

Veit Forster (?), Pattern-book of bridles, bits and straps
Upper Saxony, *c*. 1560

This manuscript may be a lost work of Veit Forster, whose pupil Mang Seutter published in 1584 a collection of engravings of cavessons, curbs and bits which stands among the finest illustrated works of the later sixteenth century. In that work Seutter praised Forster for having produced the first systematic collection of such full-scale drawings, and credited them as the inspiration for his engravings. Seutter's patron (and the earliest recorded owner of the present manuscript) was Marx Fugger, who became the head of the principal branch of the Fugger dynasty in 1560. From this position, Fugger indulged two great princely passions, horses and books. This manuscript, imposing in scale, is a fitting reflection of these two enthusiasms.

DESCRIPTION Paper, 174 folios, 505 x 350 mm, in German, gothic fraktura script, brown ink; painted frontispiece of man leading donkey; eight full-page coloured cavessons; 68 drawings of bits, staves and curbs in blue with silver, three full-page drawings of harnesses, 316 outline drawings of bits. Blind-stamped pigskin binding dated 1579.

PROVENANCE Marx Fugger (Augsburg, 1529-1597); Count of Oettingen-Wallerstein; Edwin Dloss (1853); Sotheby's, London, 11 December 1961, lot 173; G. Heilbrun; Paul Breman, cat. 1 (1970), no. 1; Bredford Libri Rari (Francesco Radaeli); Sam Fogg, February 1998

8   LJS 272

Drawings of bits and bridles
Germany, 17th century

DESCRIPTION Paper, 49 folios, 400 x 273 mm, 45 ink over pencil drawings. Brown paper board binding.

PROVENANCE Sotheby's, New York, 26 June 1998, lot 441

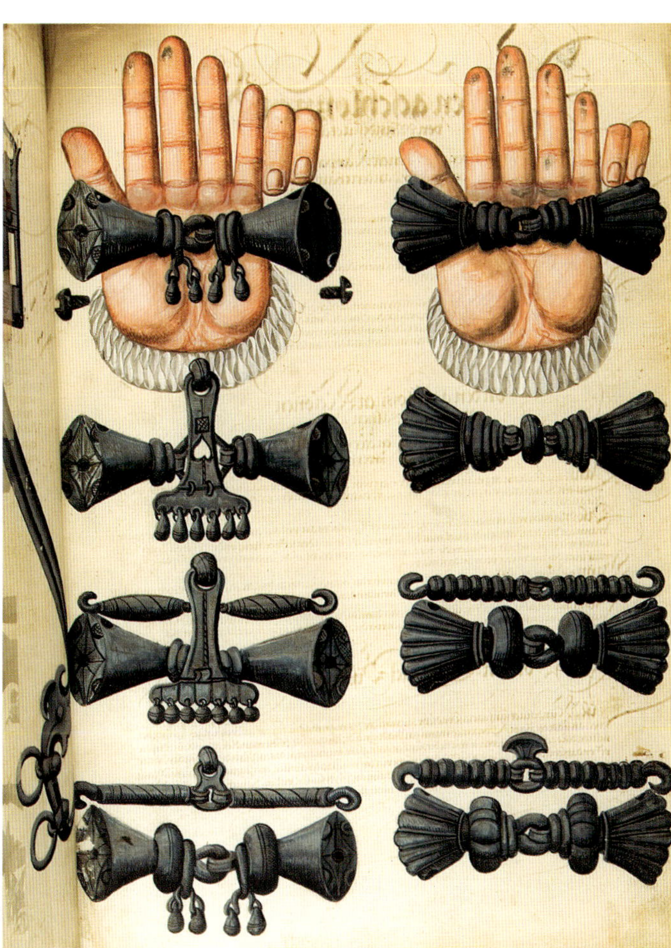

239
f. 7r

IX ORGANIZATION OF KNOWLEDGE

ENCYCLOPAEDIAS AND COSMOGRAPHIES

Readers of the Middle Ages turned to encyclopaedias and cosmologies to comprehend the scope and variety of the universe they inhabited. In the early modern era the universe was considered to be an orderly structure, hierarchically arranged and logically comprehensible. Encyclopaedias reflected these principles in their taxonomies; the modern method of ordering by the alphabet did not come into vogue until the eighteenth century. Encyclopaedias were commonly divided into sections such as God and creation, corporeal and incorporeal substances, the earth and the heavens, different types of animals, plants and minerals, and so on. Contrary to popular assumption it was not commonly held that the earth was flat. The geographical basis of most of these works followed the formulation of Pomponius Mela (see LJS 60 [no. 1]), who promulgated a spherical globe, divided into five climatic zones, of which only two were habitable; the entire race of humans inhabited the northern of these two zones.

One result of the belief in comprehensible cosmic structure was the idea that words, rather than being conventional, actually contained the essence or nature of the things they signified. This theory can be seen functioning in Isidore of Seville's *Etymologiae* (see LJS 184 [no. 2]). This chapter also contains, in a second section (LJS 45 [no. 13] *et sqq.*), a variety of other linguistic works, both dictionaries and grammars, from the Middle Ages and Renaissance.

In a third section, a selection of historical accounts, secular and sacred, is prefaced by a work which, rather than portraying the past of a people, reflected their hopes for the future, the Egyptian coffin-text commonly known as the 'Book of the Dead' (LJS 45 [no. 19]). The chapter concludes with two works on chess, one of them (LJS 267 [no. 28]) in fact a didactic work on society and morality.

1 LJS 60

Pomponius Mela, *De cosmographia*
Possibly northern Italy, late 14th–early 15th century

Pomponius Mela's *Cosmographia* (also called *Chorographia*), composed about 44 AD, aims to give "a description of the world … which consists largely in the names and places of peoples and their rather perplexing arrangement". It therefore begins with an outline of the terrestrial sphere and goes on to a more detailed description of the geography of European, Asian and African peoples. In Pomponius's view, the earth is spherical, its land mass surrounded by ocean, and divided into five zones: "Heat infests the inner zone, and cold the outer ones". Of the remaining two zones, "the antichthones inhabit one, and we the other".

Pomponius was an important source for the *Natural History* of Pliny (d. 79) and subsequently for the encyclopaedist Martianus Capella. The *Cosmographia* itself circulated widely in manuscript in the fifteenth and sixteenth centuries.

DESCRIPTION Parchment, 72 folios (many palimpsests), 170 x 115 mm, in Latin, northern Italian rounded script, rubrics in red, marginal annotations in red or blue, one 6-line initial in blue with red decoration, frame and marginal extensions; ten 2- to 3-line initials, alternating red and blue; five 2-line initials, black and red. 15th-century parchment binding.
PROVENANCE Inscription (f. 68v), "Antonio de Bonius" (?), dated 1450; Boncampagni Library; Narducci, ms. 3560; J. Halle, Munich, cat. 50 (1914), no. 20; Sam Fogg, February 1997
BIBLIOGRAPHY Sarton I 239; Romer; Ranstrand

Isidore of Seville, *Etymologiae*
Southern France or Catalonia, *c.* late 13th century

The *Etymologiae* ('Etymologies'; otherwise known as *Origines*, 'Origins'), written in the first half of the seventh century, became the model for the medieval encyclopaedia tradition. The work is structured thematically. It begins with a discussion of the seven liberal arts and goes on to include medicine, law and religion, geography, history and human games and activities. The encyclopaedia took its name from the numerous discussions of word origins contained in each section: for example, Isidore claimed that 'man' (*homo*) was derived from 'mud' (*humus*), an etymology justified by reference to Genesis 2: 7, "God created man from the mud of the earth". This and other such derivations were commonly cited throughout the Middle Ages.

The present manuscript contains the complete text of the *Etymologiae*, divided into twenty-one chapters instead of the usual twenty. It also contains some subsidiary material, which appears to be taken from Bede's *De temporum ratione*, a work on time and tides written in 725. There is no indication of provenance, but the script suggests southern France or possibly Catalonia. The first page has a historiated initial showing Isidore teaching, surrounded by a half-border of semi-bestial musicians and grotesques.

DESCRIPTION Parchment, 184 folios, 356 x 242 mm, early gothic script, brown ink, red rubrics, headings in blue and red; one historiated initial, decorated half-border, other initials in red and blue. Contemporary wooden boards, rebacked.

PROVENANCE Harrison Horblit; H.P. Kraus, cat. 155, no. 8; John Stanitz, ms. 15

BIBLIOGRAPHY Lindsay; Sarton I 471; ODCC 851-52

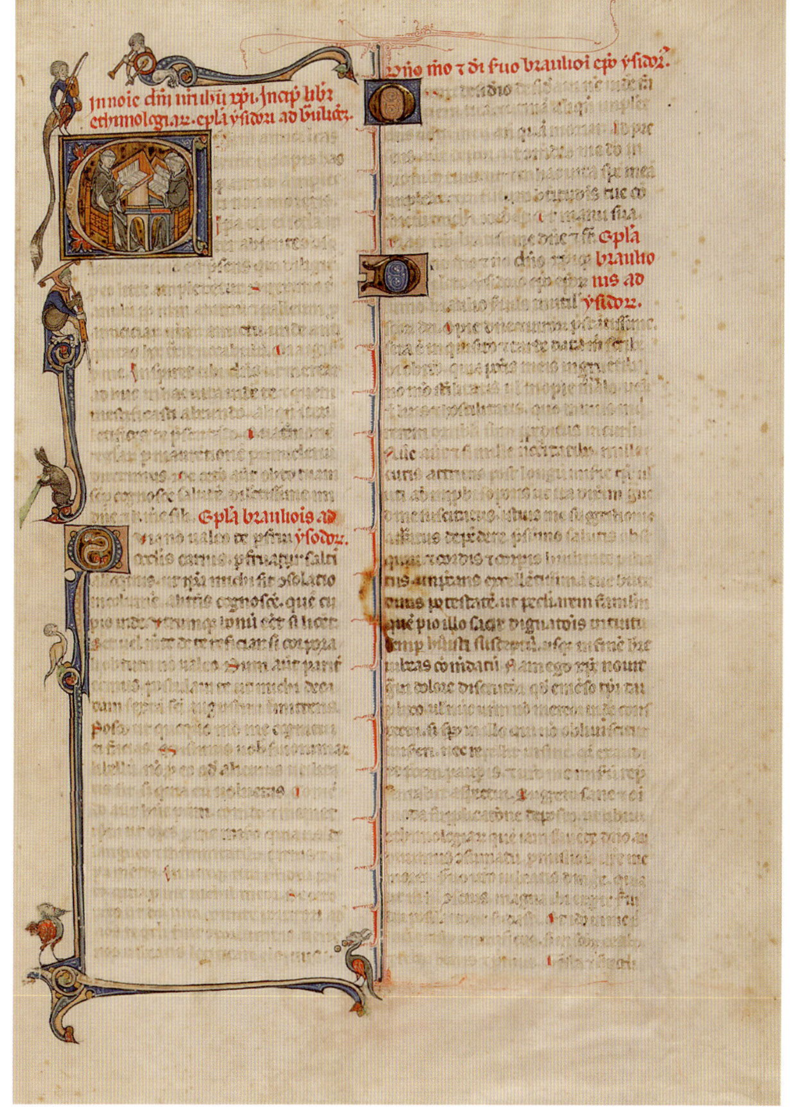

LJS 184, f. 1r

3 LJS 384

William of Conches, *De philosophia mundi*
France, 2nd half 12th century

William of Conches (*c.* 1090–*c.* 1154) was active as a teacher in
northern France. *De philosophia mundi*, written *c.* 1125, is a
short, pedagogically oriented summary of philosophical
knowledge. William defines philosophy as "the true
comprehension of things which are, both invisible and
visible". The work is divided into four books. The first book
considers God and creation, the second the stars and planets,
the third weather phenomena and the fourth the earth and
man. In the present manuscript part of the section on man,
dealing with procreation, has been deleted by an early reader
(ff. 15v–16r). William's philosophy was broadly influenced by
Platonism, absorbed especially through the *Commentary on the
Dream of Scipio* of Macrobius. He also made use of Boethius
and patristic sources such as Augustine and Bede.

The manuscript contains a number of astronomical
diagrams and two world maps. The first shows the world as a
circle, divided into two hemispheres: the southern one is
empty and the northern one contains Europe and Africa
(f. 13r). The second map shows the division of the world into
five climatic zones, described at the beginning of Book IV
(f. 15r).

Also included is part of an otherwise unknown text on the
Gospels attributed to William's contemporary Hugh of St
Victor.

DESCRIPTION Parchment, 21 folios, 207 x 145 mm, in Latin, small
early gothic script, brown ink, in two columns, some contemporary
marginal additions and corrections, deletions by an early reader; six
initials in red, 16 maps and diagrams. Modern parchment binding.
PROVENANCE Emil Hirsch, Munich (*c.* 1925); E.P. Goldschmidt &
Co.; Charles Singer; William Foyle; Christie's, London, 11 July 2000,
lot 7
BIBLIOGRAPHY OHCC 1744; Maurach

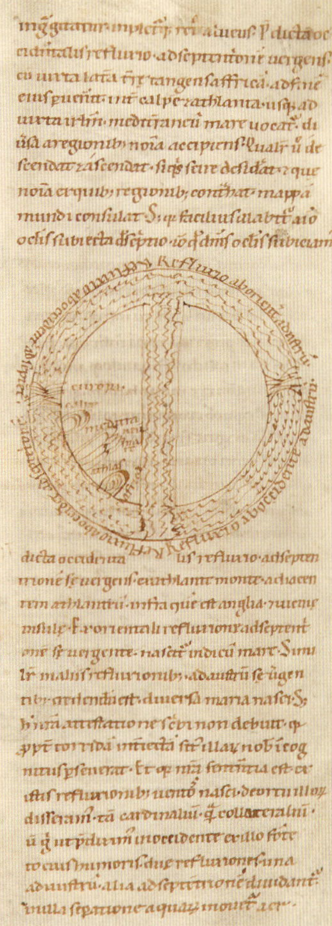

LJS 384, f. 13r   LJS 384, f. 15r

4 LJS 404

Al-Razi, *Jawami al-'ulum*
Persia, early 13th century

The *Jawami al-'ulum* (Totality of the sciences) is attributed to
the Persian philosopher Fakhr al-Din al-Razi (see LJS 440
[I, no. 6]). It presents a comprehensive summary of the
branchs of knowledge, beginning with the Qur'an, the Hadith
and Islamic history and followed by the trivium of grammar,
rhetoric and logic; medicine, anatomy and pharmacology;
gems and talismans; agriculture; geometry; geodesy and
weights; arithmetic and algebra; magic; theology, ethics and
politics.

DESCRIPTION Paper, 178 folios, 177 x 140 mm, in Persian, naskh
script, headings in red thuluth; 25 diagrams in red and black. Later
brown morocco binding, tooled.
PROVENANCE Sam Fogg, March 2001

5 LJS 23

Thomas de Cantimpré, Sections from the *Liber de natura rerum*
Northern France or Flanders, *c.* 1250–70

The *Liber de natura rerum* of Thomas de Cantimpré occupies a
central position in the medieval encyclopaedia tradition.
Written *c.* 1240, it drew on Isidore of Seville for its taxonomy
of the animal kingdom, and was an important source not
only for Albertus Magnus (for whom see LJS 234 [I, no. 9])
and Vincent of Beauvais (see LJS 124 and 16 [no. 11]) but also
for the Italian humanist Pier Candido Decembrio (1399–1477).
The present manuscript, which can be dated on stylistic
grounds to the third quarter of the thirteenth century, is one
of the oldest known copies of Thomas's work.

Included here are the sections on fish, insects, trees, herbs,
springs, precious stones, the seven regions of the air, the
seven planets, the movements of the air, the four elements and
"the stars and eclipses of the sun and moon". The copy thus
comprises most of Books VII to XX of the complete text.

DESCRIPTION Parchment, 56 folios, 185 x 134 mm, in Latin, gothic
script, brown ink, rubrication in red; 3- and 4-line initials in red and
blue with penwork decoration extending into margins; five
polychrome 8-line initials; three historiated initials with mythical
beasts. Modern paper covers.

PROVENANCE Sam Fogg, cat. 16 (1995), no. 57

BIBLIOGRAPHY Pyle; Boese; Thorndike II 372-98

6 LJS 264

Gauthier (or Gossouin) de Metz, *L'Image du monde*
France, *c.* 1400

The *Image du monde,* intended as a summary of all knowledge,
was initially composed in verse in 1245. An expanded version
was made in 1247 and a prose version around 1280. The poem
was translated into Hebrew possibly as early as 1273; the prose
version, meanwhile, was translated into English by William
Caxton in 1480. The present manuscript contains the text of
the earliest verse recension, comprising around 6,600
octosyllabic lines.

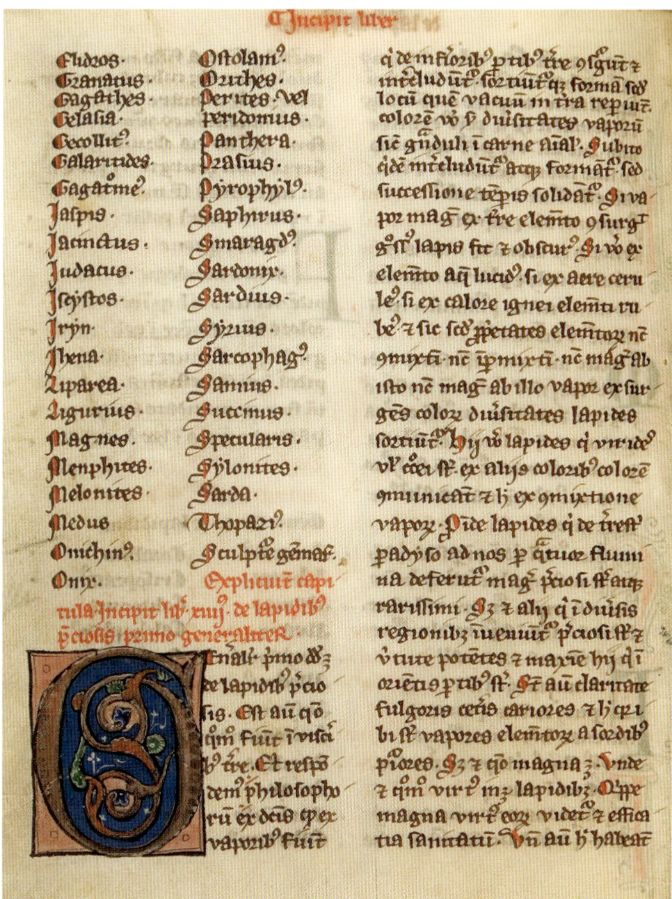

LJS 23
p. 60

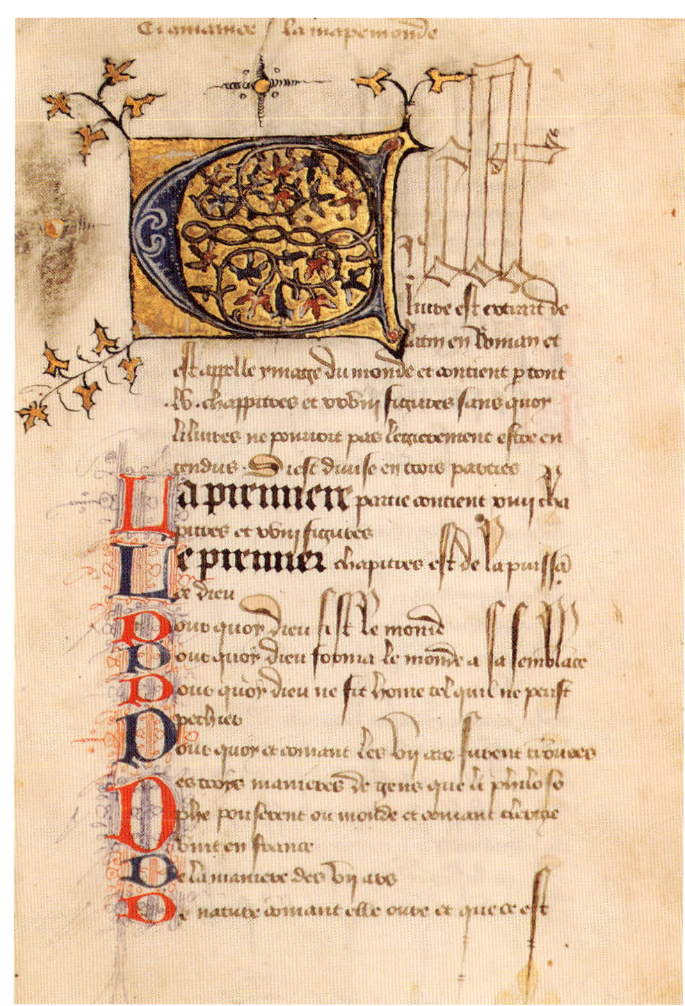

LJS 264
f. 2r

The text is in three parts: on the creation of the world and man; on geography, including the terrestrial paradise, the continents and the climatic zones; and on astronomy. Aside from the Bible, the author used classical works (presumably in Latin translation) including Plato, Aristotle and Ptolemy, and patristic sources such as Augustine, Bede and Gregory the Great, as well as other medieval encyclopaedias.

The text remained a popular vernacular source of knowledge for several centuries. In the sixteenth century the present manuscript was in the collection of Benoît le Court, a noted bibliophile of Lyons.

DESCRIPTION Parchment, 210 x 153, 126 folios, in French, bâtarde script in brown ink, red rubrics, decorated initials and section headers; 18 astronomical diagrams. 16th-century binding with central armorial medallion of Benoît le Court.

PROVENANCE Benoît le Court (1500-1566); Librairie Thomas-Scheler, 1998

BIBLIOGRAPHY Prior

7 LJS 55

Gauthier (or Gossouin) de Metz, *L'Image du monde*, and other texts
France (Lorraine?), 14th century

The first half of this manuscript contains the later prose recension of *L'Image du monde* (see LJS 264 [no. 6]). It is followed by the *Lucidarius*, a pedagogical dialogue by the theologian Honorius of Autun (early 12th century) explaining Christian doctrine, and by a French text on the moral sayings of the philosophers. The final folio contains an unknown medical text, on midwifery, possibly derived from Albertus Magnus's *De secretis mulierum*.

DESCRIPTION Parchment, 52 folios, 332 x 220 mm, in French and Latin, French gothic script, headings in red; large initial with floral decoration on first page, numeous other initials in red and blue with penwork decoration. Dark red velvet binding.

PROVENANCE H.P. Kraus, cat. 80 (1956), no. 117; Harrison D. Horblit, shelf number H12487 in pencil inside back cover; H.P. Kraus, cat. 155 (1980), no. 6; cat. 191 (1993), no. 41

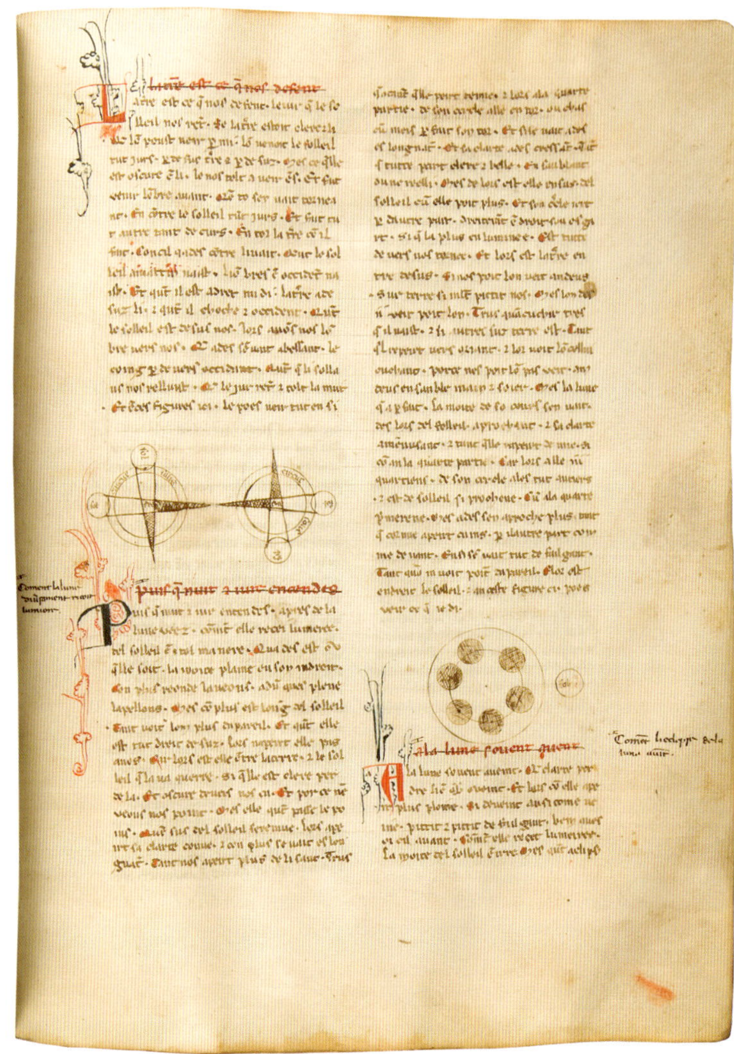

LJ f.

8 LJS 50

'The Wonders of Creation'
Persia, 1552

Cosmological texts, describing celestial and terrestrial phenomena, were popular in Arabic, Persian and Turkish literature from the thirteenth century onwards. The best-known of them was the *'Aja'ib al-makhluqat wa-ghara'ib al-mawjudat* (Prodigies of things created and miraculous aspects of things existing) of Zakariyya' ibn Muhammad al-Qazwini (*c.* 1203–1283). Al-Qazwini's sources have yet to be comprehensively studied; this manuscript contains a text in the same tradition but possibly composed earlier than al-Qazwini's work.

Its numerous illustrations depict constellations and signs of the zodiac, angels and other celestial entities, the winds and

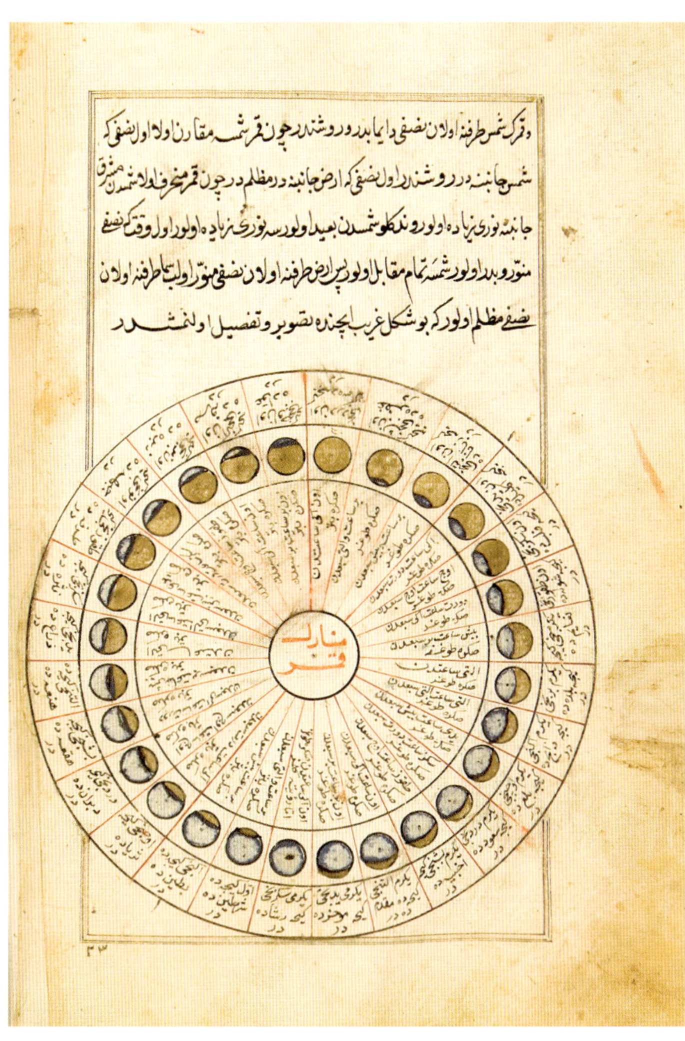

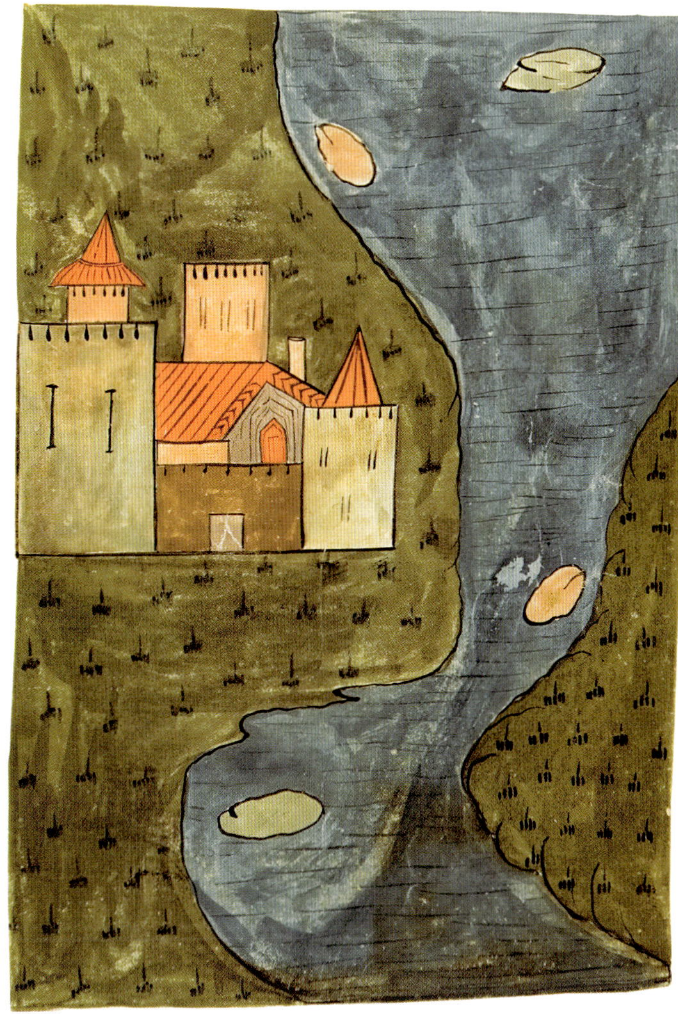

the multiplicity of terrestrial created life. This last section includes not only realistic portrayals of birds, animals and fish but also fabulous creatures, monsters and chimeras, existing on the margins of the known world. There are also many stylized illustrations of cities.

DESCRIPTION Paper, 162 folios, 250 x 170 mm, in Turkish (as used in Persia), naskh script, black and red ink; many charts and 148 miniatures. Contemporary leather binding.

PROVENANCE Edward Everett Ayer (late 19th century); Newberry Library, Chicago, ms. or. 551; Sam Fogg, June 1996

BIBLIOGRAPHY EI IV 864-67

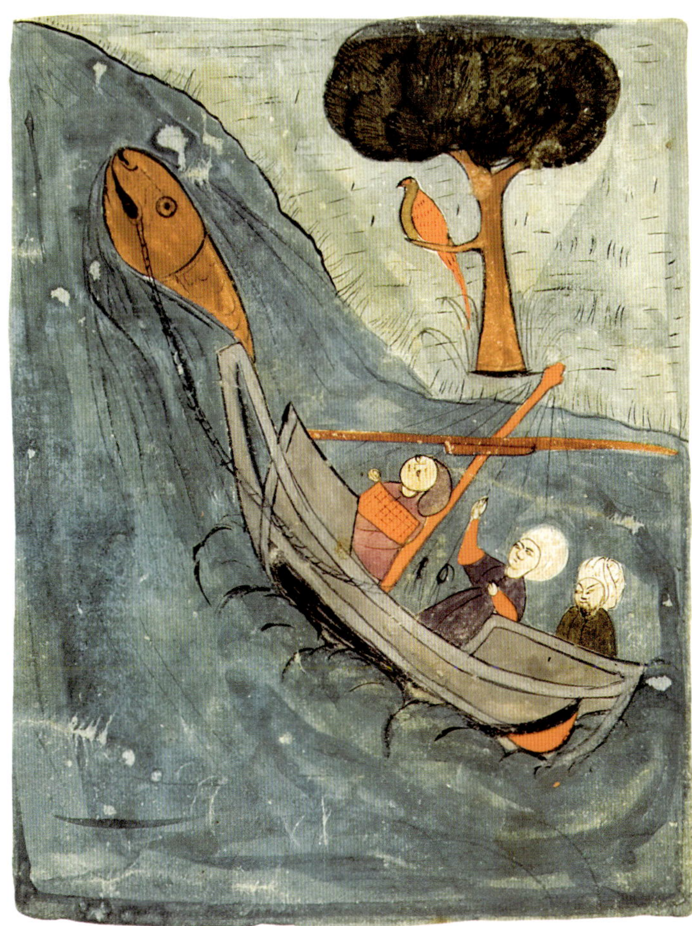

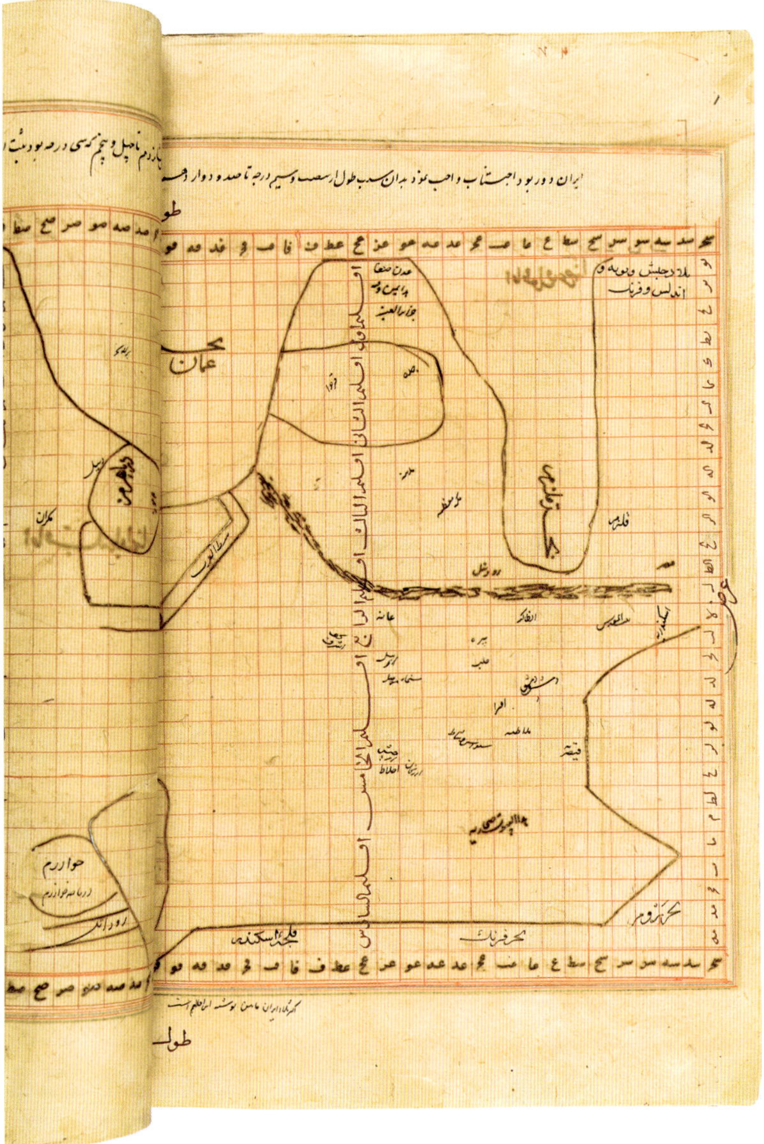

LJS 413, f. 178v

9 LJS 413

Al-Mustawfi, *Nuzhat al-qulub*
The Deccan, late 16th–early 17th century

The *Nuzhat al-qulub* (Heart's bliss) is a historical and
geographical work by Hamd Allah al-Mustawfi al-Qazwini
(*c.* 1281–*c.* 1339), of particular value as a source for facts about
the later period of the Ilkhanid empire. The author made use
of a large number of authorities, who are cited on ff. 3r–4v of
the present manuscript. A contemporary reader, writing in
the Deccan during the reign of Muhammad Qutubshah
(1611–26), has noted his responses to the work in the margin,
relating al-Mustawfi's text to his own knowledge of the
geography and fauna of India.

The text is divided into five parts. The introductory section
deals with the heavenly bodies and the earth's division into
longitude and latitude. There follow chapters on the division
of creation into minerals, plants and animals; on man; on
towns, kingdoms and valleys in Iran; and on the wonders of
the world. It includes a double-page map of the world
(ff. 178v–179r).

DESCRIPTION Paper, 252 folios, 313 x 252 mm, in Persian, elegant
nasta'liq script, headings and significant words in red, blue and
green, copious marginal annotations; two illuminated headpieces,
gold and polychrome. Brown morocco binding.
PROVENANCE Sam Fogg, March 2001
BIBLIOGRAPHY EI III 122

10 LJS 477

Florilegium
Probably England, possibly Oxford, *c.* 1250

The manuscript has major sections on natural history,
starting with a discussion of donkeys, and continuing with
Aristotle's *De animalibus,* Book VII. To this is attached a
prologue on animals and especially birds, featuring an
alphabetical aviary including the 'caladrius', a bird which can
foretell the death or recovery of a patient. These texts are
followed by notes on natural substances, solids, powders,
liquids, sulphur, gold, the four elements, silver, iron, copper,
lead, and so on. The structural outline includes very early
instances of Arabic numerals. The system of line numbering
suggests a provenance in Oxford.

DESCRIPTION Parchment, 71 folios, 195 x 140 mm, in Latin,
extremely small scholastic bookhand, dark brown ink, some
underlining in red, paragraph marks and some small initials in red;
10 pages with diagrams; very many contemporary marginal
annotations. Modern parchment over pasteboard binding.
PROVENANCE Possibly written at the Dominican Convent in
Oxford; Dr André Rooryck; Sotheby's, London, 5 July 2005, lot 50

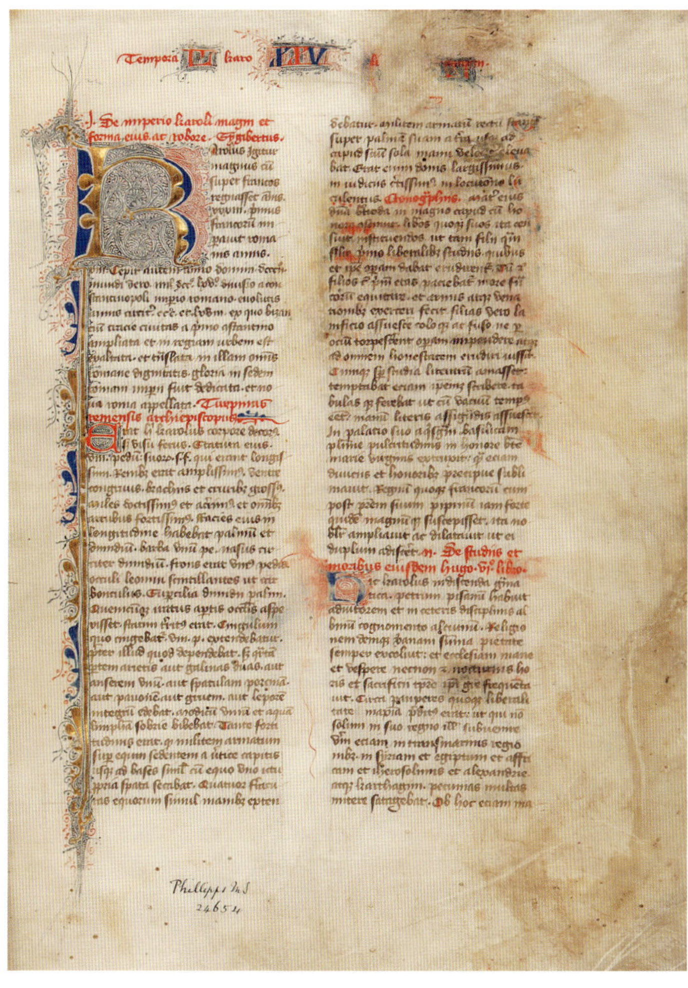

LJS 124
f. 3r

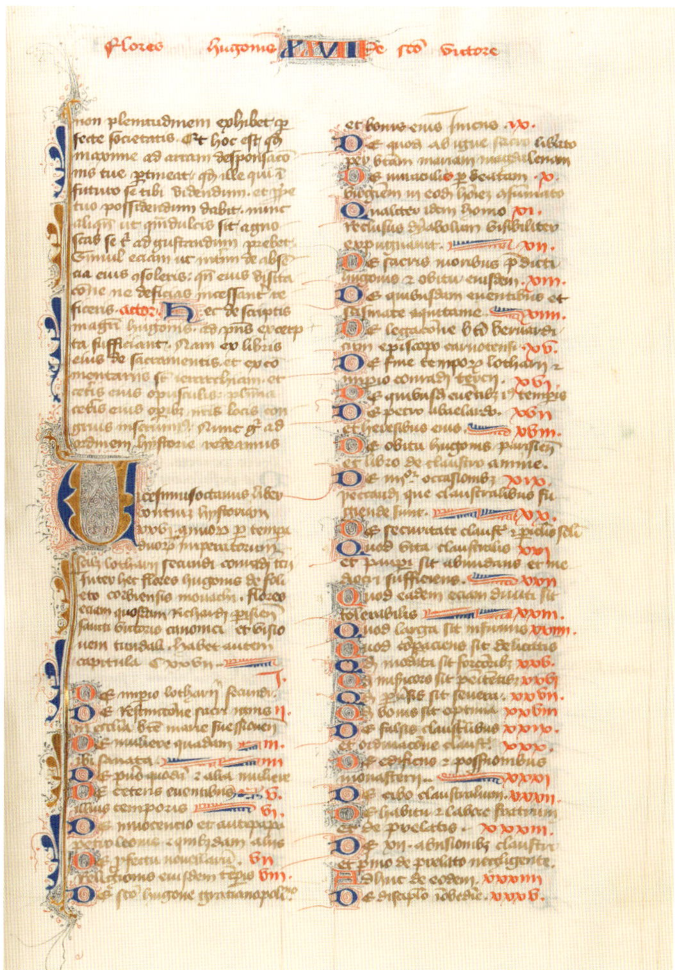

LJS 124
f. 148r

11   LJS 124 and LJS 16

Vincent of Beauvais, *Speculum Historiale*
Paris, *c.* 1400

Vincent of Beauvais (d. 1264), a Dominican friar, was commissioned by his order to compile an encylopedia of universal knowledge. The resulting work, the *Speculum maius*, which comprised three parts, *Naturale*, *Doctrinale* and *Historiale*, drew on written sources ranging from Antiquity to his own generation, and included the new Aristotelian learning of Albertus Magnus, Thomas Aquinas and others. Of the books of Vincent's encyclopaedia, the *Speculum Historiale* circulated most widely.

The half fleurs-de-lys device in blue and gold that appears in the present manuscript's borders suggest that it may have been made for a member of the French royal family, which would accord with the quality of the book's script and decoration. More recently, this manuscript has had a colourful history, having been owned by the notorious book thief Guglielmo Libri. H.R. Creswick, a later owner, gave several of its leaves away to friends; LJS 124 was given to Sir Irvine Masson, and others were presented to A.N.L. Munby and A.Y. Campbell (these are now Liverpool University Library, ms. F.4.14).

DESCRIPTION Parchment; LJS 16: 176 folios, 370 x 255 mm, in Latin, gothic semi-cursive bookhand. Pale brown morocco binding, by Douglas Cockerell & Son, 1980. LJS 124: 362 x 260 mm, 1 folio (earlier removed from the end of LJS 16).

PROVENANCE Possibly commissioned by a member of the French royal family; Guglielmo Libri (1803-1869); Sotheby's, 1 June 1864, lot 71; Sir Thomas Phillipps, ms. 24654; Sotheby's, 24 June 1935, lot 74; H.R. Creswick (1902-1988);
(LJS 124) Sotheby's, London, 7 December 1982, lot 53; Lawrence

Witten, cat. 18, no. 17; German private collection; Sotheby's, London, 20 June 1995, lot 87;

(LJS 16) apparently given by H.R. Creswick to Sir Irvine Masson; Sotheby's, London, 16 December 1957, lot 32; Francis Edwards; Sotheby's, London, 17 June 1997, lot 1

12 LJS 447

Al-'Umari, section from the *Masalik al-absar fi mamalik al-amsar*
Aleppo, 1710

Shihab al-Din ibn Fadlallah al-'Umari (1301–1349) was a Syrian historian and geographer. His 'Voyages of the Eyes in the Kingdoms of the Main Cities' was composed in the 1340s; it originally constituted an encyclopaedic work in over twenty volumes, although no complete copy is extant. The section in the present manuscript includes many illustrations of domestic and wild animals, birds, insects, marine animals, plants and herbs, possibly copied from European prints. The scribe was Gilbrail ibn Mikail al-Harmawi, a Christian from Aleppo.

DESCRIPTION Paper, 193 folios, in Arabic, naskh script, black ink, titled in red; 584 watercolour illustrations. Embossed brown binding.
PROVENANCE Christie's, London, 15 October 2002, lot 59
BIBLIOGRAPHY Sarton III 802-03

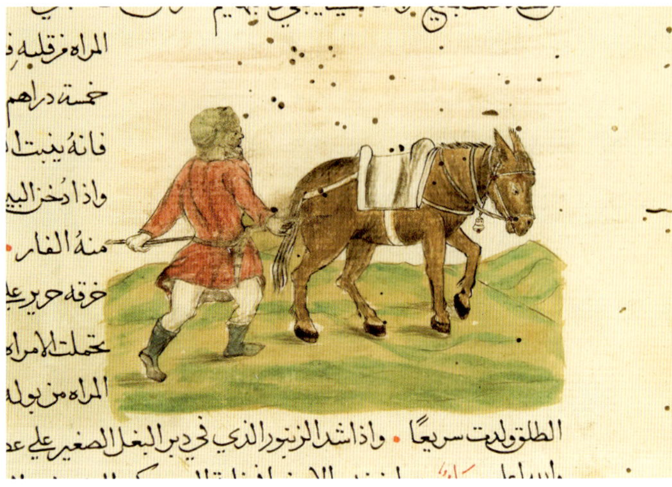

LJS 447
f. 2v

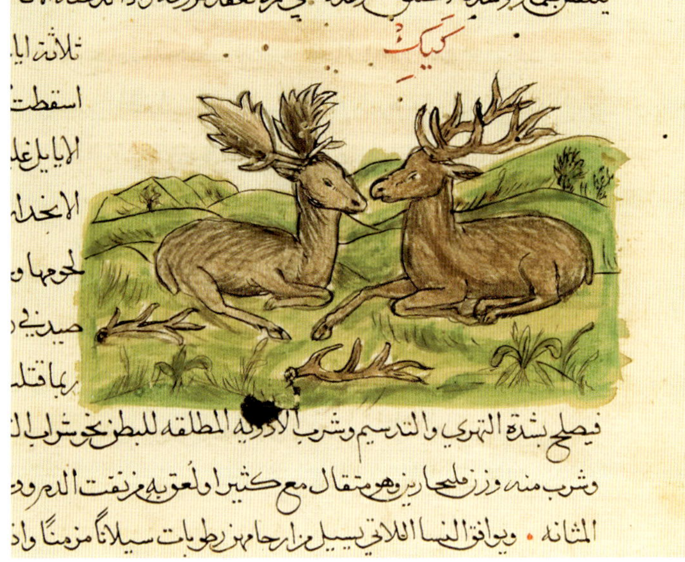

LJS 447
f. 7v

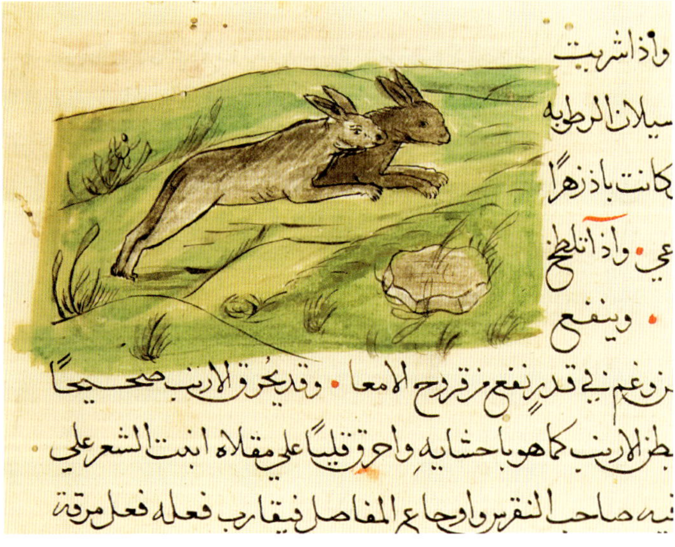

LJS 447
f. 8v

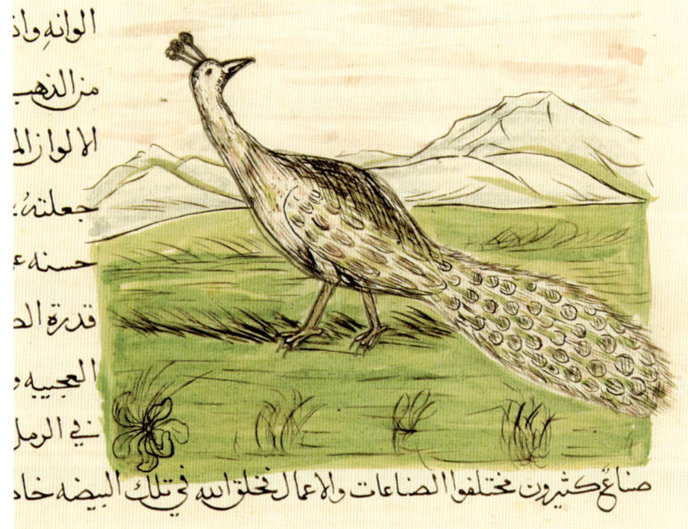

LJS 447
f. 22

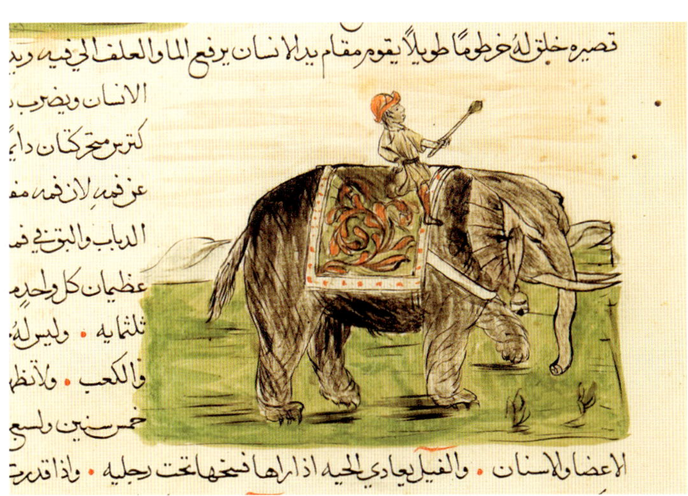

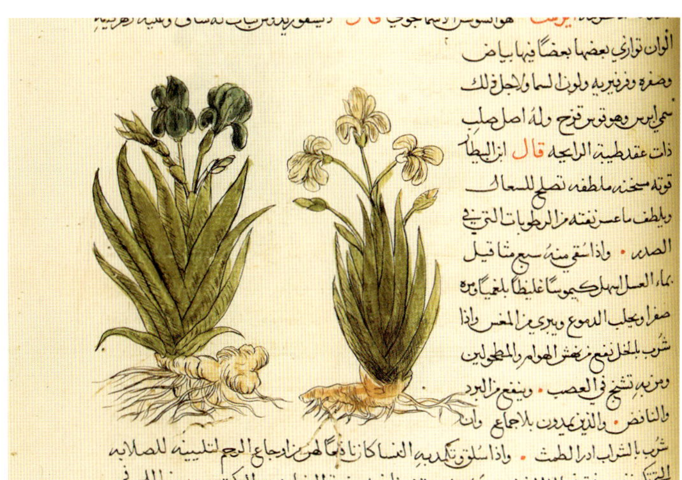

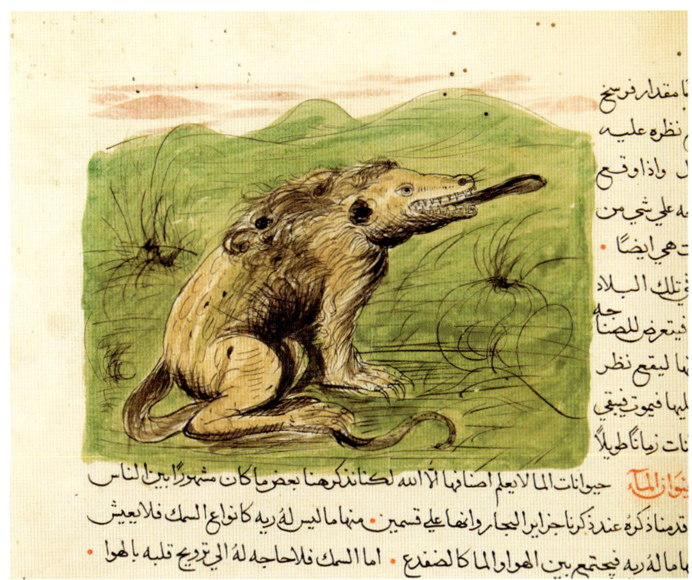

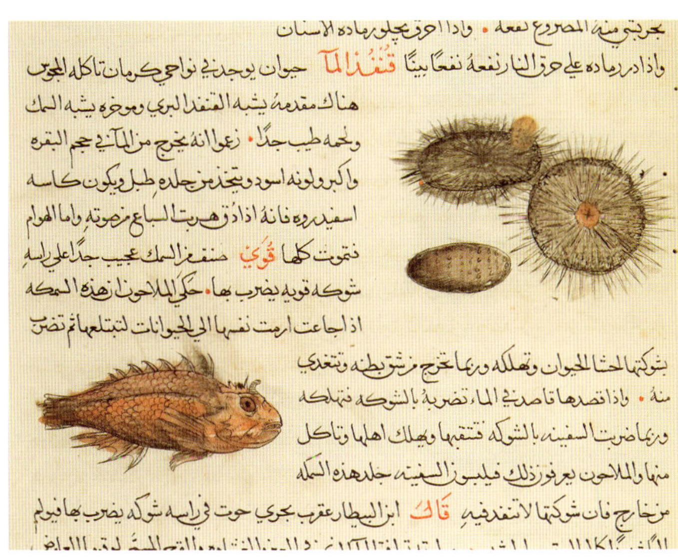

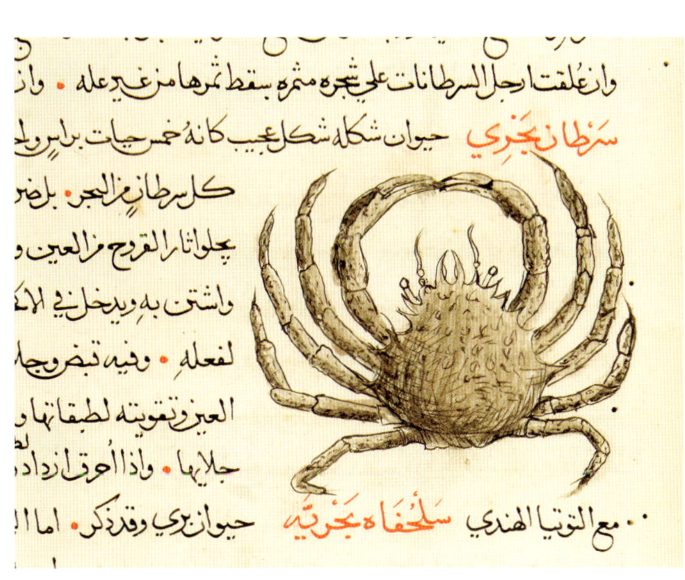

13   LJS 451

Commentary on Alexander of Villa Dei's *Doctrinale*
France, late 13th century

Alexander of Villa Dei's didactic poem on arithmetic, the *Carmen de Algorismo*, has already been cited (see LJS 462 [III, no. 17]). It was complemented by his poem on grammar, the *Doctrinale*. The *Doctrinale* considers nouns and their declensions, verbs and their participles, as well as syntax and rhetorical figures. Composed at the end of the twelfth century, it was a very popular work which was still being copied in the sixteenth century. The present manuscript is a commentary on the *Doctrinale*. It starts with a prologue discussing the curriculum and its division into trivium and quadrivium, and then proceeds to close elucidation of Alexander's text.

DESCRIPTION Parchment, 60 folios, 195 x 135 mm, in Latin, small gothic cursive script, brown or black ink, paragraph marks and 3-line initials in red, lemmata underlined in red; 4-line opening initial, red with penwork extensions and flourishing in red and black. 19th-century Germanic cloth-backed paper binding.
PROVENANCE Count Oswald von Seilern (1901–1967); Christie's, London, 26 March 2003, lot 4
BIBLIOGRAPHY Reichling; Galindo

14   LJS 452

Vocabularius ex quo
Germany, 15th century

The *Vocabularius ex quo*, composed around 1400, became the most widely diffused Latin-German dictionary of the fifteenth century. Its success is attested not only by 280 surviving manuscript copies but also by 48 incunable editions; in this process of transmission a number of different versions of the text evolved, some expanding it, others compressing it.

The *Vocabularius* was based on previous works, notably the

Breviologus and works by Johannes de Ianua, Hugucios of Pisa and Guilielmus Brito. The compiler criticized his forebears as being "rich in comparison and prolix in collocation, but obscure in understanding". The intention of the *Vocabularius* was to help "poor scholars" understand Scripture. A wide selection of proper names is included.

DESCRIPTION Paper, 194 folios, 218 x 134 mm, in Latin and German, cursive script, brown ink, catchwords; 2- to 3-line initials, red, and capitals touched in red (ff. 1-89); two 4-line initials, red flourished brown. 15th-century Germanic limp parchment binding, link-stitch sewing on rigid leather backplate.
PROVENANCE Wolfgang Täxer; Christie's, London, 26 March 2003, lot 11
BIBLIOGRAPHY Schnell (1986 and 1988-2001)

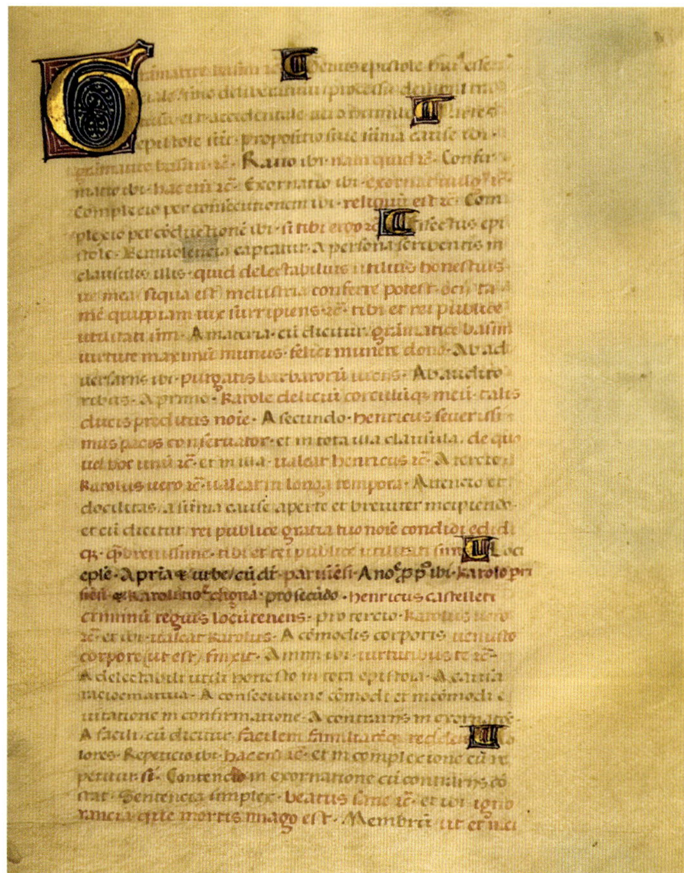

LJS
f. 1

15 LJS 242

Guillaume Tardif, *Basis grammaticae*
Paris, 1 January 1470

Tardif (*c.* 1440–*c.* 1500) was one of the foremost French
humanists of the fifteenth century. His *Basis grammaticae*, of
which this is the autograph, was written for his young pupil
Charles Mariette, godson of Louis XI's brother Charles de
Guyenne. The text is a basic introduction to Latin grammar
divided into eight parts, which consider nouns, pronouns,
verbs, participles, adverbs, prepositions, conjunctions and
interjections. It also includes conjugation tables for four verbs,
with some glosses in French for the verb *amare* (to love). The
second half of the manuscript contains a commentary, in
which Tardif explains his purpose – to give an account of Latin
grammar "purged of the vices of the Barbarians". This is the first
French humanist grammar; it was printed in the early 1470s.

DESCRIPTION Parchment, 20 folios, 198 x 143 mm, in Latin, French
humanistic script, brown ink, red rubrics, paragraph marks in gold,
2- to 4-line initials throughout in red and blue. 19th-century binding.
PROVENANCE Dedicated by the author to his student Charles
Marriette (Karoli Mariete), godson of Charles of France (brother of
Louis XI); E.K. Schreiber, New York, cat. 21 (1989), no. 94; Librairie
Thomas-Scheler, *Un Choix* (April 1998), no. 3
BIBLIOGRAPHY Bietenholz III 309-10; Beltran

16 LJS 406

Al-Sakkaki, *Miftah al-'ulum*
1 Safar 671 / 28 August 1272

The *Miftah al-'ulum* (Key to the sciences) of Abu Ya'qub Yusuf
al-Sakkaki (1160–1229) is a comprehensive treatise on
linguistics. It is divided into three "sciences", morphology (*'ilm
al sarf*), syntax (*'ilm al-nahw*) and stylistics and imagery (*'ilm al-
ma'ani wa'l bayan*). The first section includes remarks about
phonetics, which in this manuscript are accompanied by a
diagram (f. 6v) of the mouth, showing where different sounds
(*i.e.* labial, dental, gutteral, etc.) originate. The third section
includes a discussion of rhetoric, and was influential in later
rhetorical analysis.

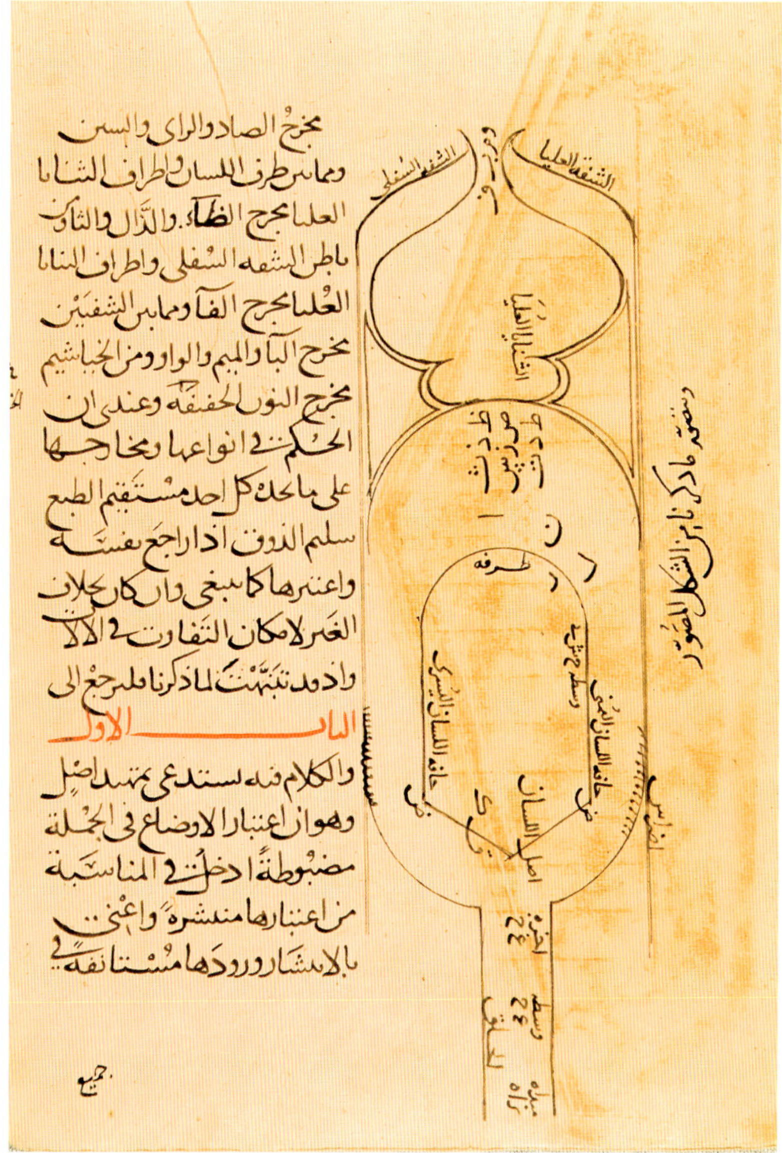

LJS 406, f. 6v

DESCRIPTION Paper, 301 folios, 258 x 182 mm, in an elegant naksh
script by the scribe Bihzad ibn 'Ali, brown ink, contemporary brown
morocco binding
PROVENANCE Sam Fogg, March 2001
BIBLIOGRAPHY EI VIII 893-94

17 LJS 394

Al-Jawhari, *Taj al-lughah wa-sihah al-'arabiyyah*
Mamluk Egypt or Syria, 14th century

This text, commonly known as the *Sihah,* by Abu Nasr Isma'il
al-Jawhari (d. *c.* 1009), was the standard dictionary of Arabic
from the eleventh to the fifteenth century. It was superseded
by al-Firuzabadi's *Qamus al-muhit* (see LJS 387 [no. 18]).

DESCRIPTION Paper, 203 folios, 260 x 170 mm, in Arabic, naskh
script, black ink, some words and phrases in red; opening folio with
gold, blue and red illumination. Brown card and leather binding.
PROVENANCE Sam Fogg, November 2000
BIBLIOGRAPHY EI II 495-97

18 LJS 387

Al-Firuzabadi, *Al-Qamus al-muhit*
Western Persia, *c.* 1400

Abu 'l-Tahir Muhammad al-Firuzabadi (1329–1415) led a
peripatetic life, journeying between Persia, Jerusalem, Cairo,
Mecca and Yemen, among other places. This work, entitled
'The Encompassing Ocean', a compact dictionary of Arabic,
was composed between 1368 and 1392. The illumination and
paper of this manuscript suggest a date of *c.* 1400, soon after
the work was completed and within the lifetime of the author.

Firuzabadi intended his dictionary to rival the *Sihah* of al-
Jawhari (see LJS 394 [no. 17]), and criticized the earlier work
accordingly. He was predominantly influenced by two other
lexical works, the *'Ubab* of al-Saghani (1181–1252) and the
Muhkam of Ibn Sida (d. 1066).

DESCRIPTION Paper, 480 folios, 232 x 165 mm, in Arabic, neat
naskh script, black ink, significant words in red, blue and gold,
copious marginal notes; chapter headings in gold, in illuminated
panels. Titlepage with central medallion, gold and polychrome.
Brown morocco binding, possibly *c.* 1500.
PROVENANCE Turkish ownership seals; Sam Fogg, cat. 22, no. 63
BIBLIOGRAPHY EI II 926-27

HISTORY AND SOCIETY

19 LJS 45

Book of the Dead
Egypt, *c.* 11th century BC

The 'Book of Going Forth by Day', popularly known as the
'Egyptian Book of the Dead', accompanied Egyptians on their
departure from this life; its intention was to aid them in the
next one. Typically, a papyrus roll was placed in the coffin
next to the mummified body of the deceased. There is no
single canonical recension of the work. Instead, each copy
comprises a personal selection from a large body of 'spells'
and other magical texts, made according to the circumstances

LJS

of the individual and the period. These spells derive from the
earlier 'Coffin Texts' which circulated from the end of the third
millennium BC to the middle of the second. By *c.* 1600 BC this
material had evolved into the 'Book of Going Forth by Day'.

A number of surviving copies include coloured
illustrations, showing the deceased alongside various gods, or
taking part in religious acts. The fragments preserved here
have eight such skilfully executed pictures.

DESCRIPTION Papyrus, nine fragments, from 142 x 80 to 59 x 65
mm, in hieratic, written horizontally in black and red ink, divided
into compartments by single or double lines; eight drawings,
outlined in black, infilled with black, red-brown, yellow and purple.
Inset into card pages, 19th-century red morocco binding.

PROVENANCE Clarence S. Bement (1843–1923), of Philadelphia, apparently bought from Maggs Bros, 1907; his sale, Anderson, 28 February 1923; Robert Walsingham Martin (1871–1961); Sotheby's, London, 18 June 1996, lot 60
BIBLIOGRAPHY Eliade V 6; Faulkner; Allen

20 LJS 17

Hystoires anciennes jusqu'à César
Bourges, *c.* 1470

This illustrated history of the world, from Creation to Julius Caesar, was compiled in the thirteenth century from diverse classical and early medieval sources.

DESCRIPTION Parchment, 355 folios, 326 x 225 mm, in French, small and rather clubbed bâtarde script, brown ink, headings in red, paragraph-marks alternately blue and burnished gold; 2- to 3-line illuminated initials at beginning of every chapter, one 4-line initial and 11 very large illuminated initials with partial borders; two coats-of-arms; 51 miniatures in colours and gold. Late 18th century French green morocco binding, gilt.
PROVENANCE Illuminated for Yves du Fou (d. 1488), of Fou-en-Poitou, knight, counsellor and chamberlain to Louis XI; William Beckford of Fonthill; Alexander Douglas, son-in-law of Beckford, 10th Duke of Hamilton (1767-1852), ms. 243; Duke of Hamilton sale, Sotheby's, 23 May 1889, lot 47; Lord Wardington; Heribert Tenschert, cat. 16 (1984), no. 10; Sotheby's, London, 26 November 1985, lot 107
BIBLIOGRAPHY P. Meyer

21 LJS 98

Jean Mansel, *La fleur des histoires*
French Flanders, *c.* 1450–60

The third volume of a monumental universal history by Jean Mansel (*c.* 1400–*c.* 1473), composed around 1450, with eight highly detailed miniatures of historical scenes.

DESCRIPTION Parchment, 223 folios, 415 x 282 mm, in French (some Latin phrases), calligraphic bâtarde script, grey-brown ink, headings in red, capitals touched in red, paragraph-marks and some line-fillers and small initials in alternately red or blue; 3-line chapter initials in blue or red with extensive penwork; five 4- to 6-line initials in red and blue, with penwork; one very large 6-line initial in red and blue with very extensive penwork in red and brown; eight large 3- to 7-line illuminated initials in a variety of Gothic designs; eight miniatures with illuminated borders. Parchment binding.
PROVENANCE Illuminated with Crévecour arms, and probably commissioned by Antoine de Crévecour (d. 1493), chamberlain of the Dukes of Burgundy; at least part of the Crévecour library was dispersed at the sack of Boulogne Castle by Henry VIII in 1544; scribbled names of Pierre Orillan and Pierre la Pierre (16th–17th century); Princes of Dietrichstein, at Schloss Nikolsberg, Moravia; Gilhofer and Ranschburg (Lucerne), 21 November 1933, lot 373; Sotheby's, London, 17 June 1997, lot 59

22 LJS 266
Generacion de Adam
North-west France, 1404–06

This is a genealogical history of the world, from Adam to the royal families of England and France, and including the popes up to Innocent VII.

DESCRIPTION Parchment, 45 folios, 352 x 185 mm, in French, bâtarde script, dark brown ink, rubrics underlined in red, paragraph marks alternately in red and blue; 2-line gold initials throughout, two 5-line illuminated initials, blue and red, illuminated border on f. 1 and one unfinished diagram. Contemporary blind-stamped calf binding.
PROVENANCE 15th-century inscriptions on flyleaf; Sébastien de Rosmadec, Marquis de Molac (d. 1693); Sotheby's, London, 23 June 1998, lot 53

23 LJS 36
Folio from Chronicle describing Jewish Wars
Italy, 12th century

Originally part of a large and beautiful manuscript, this as yet unidentified text concerns the conquest of Ptolemais by Alexander, son of Antiochus, as also described in the Book of Maccabees.
DESCRIPTION 1 folio, 397 x 260 mm, in Latin, Romanesque script, brown ink, one 2-line initial in red.

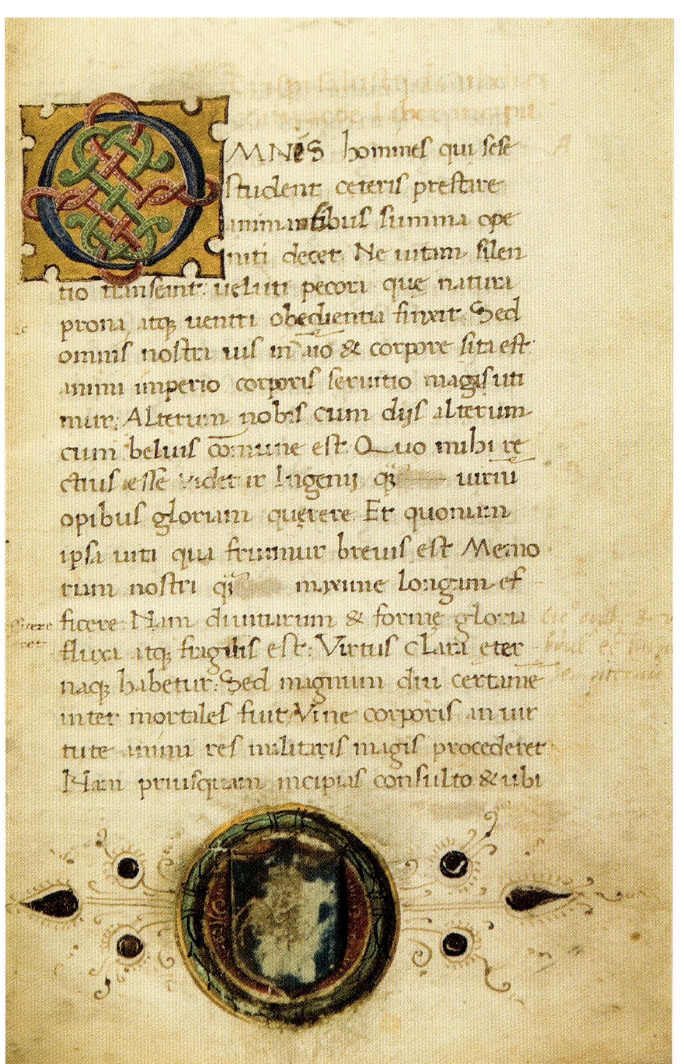

LJS 381
f. 1r

PROVENANCE Formerly used as a binding fragment; Sotheby's, London, 22 June 1993, lot 7(2)

24 LJS 405

Al-Mawardi, Treatise on government
North Africa, probably Egypt, mid-13th century

Abu al-Hasan al-Mawardi of Basra in Iraq (972–1088) was an important thinker in political science, known as Alboacen in the West. Here he outlines the good qualities of a ruler and the art of good government.

DESCRIPTION Paper, 75 folios, 225 x 155 mm, in Arabic, elegant 'Abbasid naskh script. Modern binding.
PROVENANCE Sam Fogg, March 2001

25 LJS 41

Book of Esther
15th century

This manuscript of the Book of Esther was originally part of a larger compendium of Hebrew biblical and liturgical texts.

DESCRIPTION Parchment, 16 folios, 87 x 65 mm, in Hebrew, semi-square Italian Sephardic script, brown ink; later elaborate foliate borders. Early parchment over pasteboard binding.
PROVENANCE Swann Galleries, 11 December 1988, lot 206A

26 LJS 237

Hegesippus, *De excidio Judeorum libri quinque*
Possibly Padua, *c.* 1460

An adaptation of Flavius Josephus's *Jewish War*, probably made in the fourth century.

DESCRIPTION Parchment, 185 folios, 292 x 203 mm, in Latin, humanistic script, brown ink, blank space left for rubrics, guide text written in gutter, with rubrics supplied for the beginning of Book I and the very end of the manuscript only, running headings in upper margin from Book II on; six decorated 5- to 8-line initials, the body of the letter in maroon, on a blue ground sprinkled with white within a gold border. 17th-century French tan morocco binding.

PROVENANCE Copied by Petrus Lomer; possibly Franz Joseph von Hahn, Bishop of Bamberg (see Visconti arms, added to frontispiece in the 18th century); William Ewart Gladstone, shelfmark MMI10; Christie's, London, 8 December 1982, lot 122; Israel; Amsterdam; Sam Fogg, February 1998

27 LJS 381

Sallust, *Catilinae conjuratio* and *Bellum Jugurthinum*
Padua, *c.* 1455–65

Two works, sharing the theme of the moral and political decline of Rome, by the historian Sallust (*c.* 86–35 BC).

DESCRIPTION Parchment, 160 folios, 178 x 113 mm, in Latin, humanistic script, black or brown ink, titles in red, extensive

contemporary and later annotations and corrections; 2- or 3-line
initials alternately in red and blue; 6-line initial panelled blue with
green and red interlace filling on burnished gold ground; 5-line
initial in gold on a shaped ground of white vine work, filled with red,
green, blue and gold. Contemporary Italian blind-tooled goatskin
binding.

PROVENANCE Mario Maffei of Volterra (1463-1537), and
descendants; Clemente Carilli of Volterra (17th century); Guiseppe
Antonio Saccardini of Volterra (1666); Christie's, 7 June 2000, lot 9

28 LJS 267

Compendium containing Jacobus de Cessolis, *Ludo scachorum*
Probably northern Italy, 1409

The manuscript opens with the *Ludo scachorum* of Jacobus de
Cessolis (late 13th–early 14th centuries). This work, which was
very widely read, uses chess as a metaphor for "the behaviour
of men and the duties of nobles". The present copy is
particularly notable for its illustrations of chesspieces
juxtaposed with representations of different strata of society –
kings, knights, a bishop portrayed beside a judge, and pawns
next to workers of various trades, including builder, carpenter
and scribe.

The text was translated from Latin into French in the
fourteenth century; in the fifteenth century, it was
retranslated into English by William Caxton. In 1474 it became
one of the first works to issue from Caxton's press.

DESCRIPTION Parchment, 175 folios, 190 x 122 mm, in Latin and
Italian, gothic rounded script, brown ink, by several scribes, a
palimpsest of a 13th-century (probably juristic) text; rubrics red,
capitals stroked yellow; 2-line initials in red; 11 ink drawings in first
text. 18th-century leather over pasteboard binding.
PROVENANCE Copied by Francis Gennay in 1409; Sir Thomas
Phillipps, ms. 4570; H.P. Kraus, cat. 153, no. 51; Irene and Peter
Ludwig, ms. XV 16; Jörn Günther Antiquariat, *Recent Acquisitions*
(Autumn 1997); J. Paul Getty Museum; Sam Fogg, June 1998
BIBLIOGRAPHY Köpke; Collet; Figgins

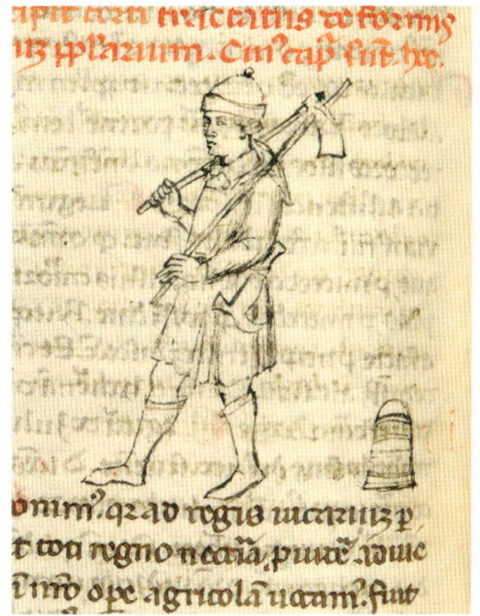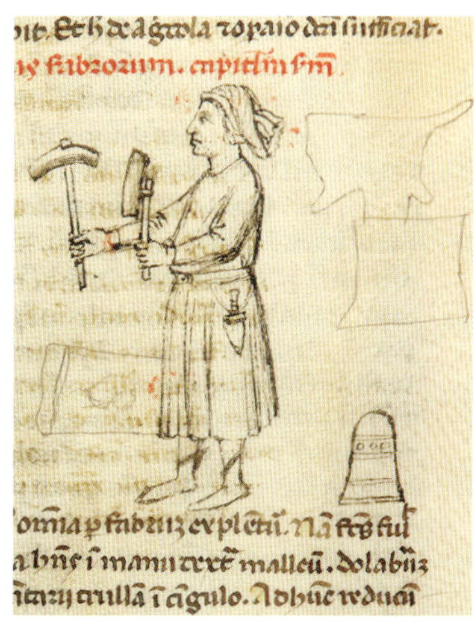
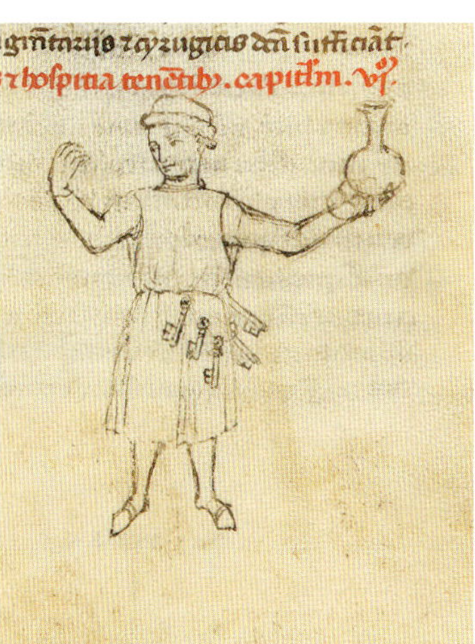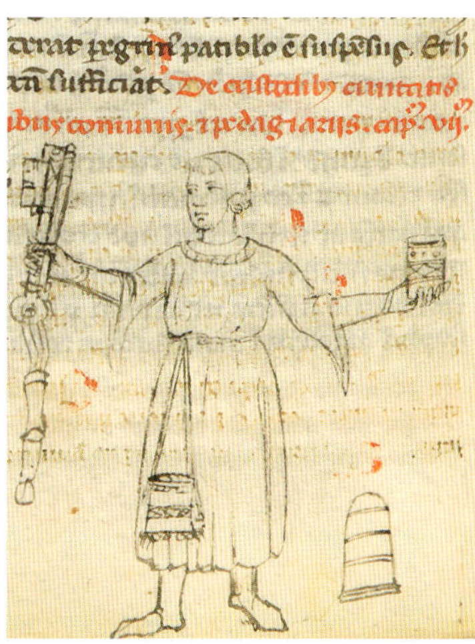

LJS 267, ff. 25r, 27r (above);
ff. 38r, 40v (below)

29 LJS 33

Chess scene, by 'the Spanish Forger'
France, *c.* 1900

A woman is beating a man at chess as another couple look on.
This painting, made on a folio from a 14th- or 15th-century
liturgical manuscript from which the original writing had
been scraped off, is the work of the celebrated 'Spanish forger',
who produced over 300 works purporting to be authentic
medieval paintings and miniatures.

DESCRIPTION Parchment, 187 x 134 mm, verso with four lines of
text and music in a 14th- or 15th-century Italian hand, two small
decorated initials.
PROVENANCE Sotheby's, London, 25 June 1985, lot 37

X WRITS AND CHARTERS

Whereas the previous chapters have focused on some of the high points of intellectual history, the manuscripts selected here constitute an intriguing record of culture at ground level. This material offers evidence of the mundane concerns which made the rarefied achievements of the previous chapters possible. Included here are documents of land use and sales, business accounts and regulations, legal issues and political appointments; there are documents from King Edward III of England, King Philip II of Spain and such Italian families as the Gonzaga and the Medici.

1 LJS 100

Debt record
Babylon, 21 Ayyaru, 27 [?] of the reign of Darius I (494 BC?)

This documents the business interests of a wealthy Babylonian family.

DESCRIPTION Clay tablet, 61 x 48 mm, 10 lines of cuneiform.
PROVENANCE Swann Galleries, 10 October 1989, lot 66

2 LJS 309

Collateral letter for a one-fifth share of a brewery
Meïdoum, Egypt, 201-200 BC

DESCRIPTION Papyrus, 1 folio, 255 x 92 mm, in Demotic and Greek, 30 lines of flamboyant Demotic script, confirmed by five witnesses, with 2-line subscription in Greek.
PROVENANCE M.R. Lambert; Louis Leconte; 1. Antiquariaat Forum and Les Enluminures, 20th Congress of the International Association of Bibliophiles, Paris 1997, no. 1; Sotheby's, London, 22 June 1999, lot 57

3 LJS 273

Land grant document
Benevento, 821

The text is a grant of level land in a place known as Murtula.

DESCRIPTION Parchment, single folio, 423 x 140 mm, in Latin, single column, 23 lines of text, brown ink, provincial chancery script, single scribe (with signatures of numerous witnesses).
PROVENANCE Maggs Bros., August 1998

4 LJS 275

Land sale document
Benevento, 823

The document confirms the sale of land with trees, vines, and orchards in a place called A lo Tuoro.

DESCRIPTION Parchment, single folio, 743 x 184 mm, in Latin, single column, 40 lines of text, brown ink, provincial chancery script, single scribe (with 12 signatures).
PROVENANCE Maggs Bros., August 1998

5 LJS 274

Land sale document
Salerno, 840

The document records the sale of land with a vineyard.

DESCRIPTION Parchment, single folio, 440 x 195 mm, in Latin, single column, 21 lines of text, brown ink, provincial chancery script, five signatures.
PROVENANCE Maggs Bros., August 1998

6 LJS 211

Charter granting land
Suffolk, *c.* 1201-05

This charter includes a very early record, possibly the earliest, of a windmill in Suffolk (windmills are thought to have been introduced into East Anglia in about 1185).

DESCRIPTION Parchment, single sheet with yellow wax seal attached, 111 x 167 mm, in Latin, 1 column, 17 lines, brown ink, chancery script.
PROVENANCE Sir Thomas Phillipps, ms. 27838; Sotheby's, London, 26 June 1974, lot 3057, and 22 June 1982, lot 29; Paul Grinke; Sam Fogg, cat. 16 (1995), no. 44; John Stanitz, ms. 42

7 LJS 54

Magister Contarini, Notarial formulary
Padua, *c.* 1230

Formerly unrecorded, this is one of the earliest of all extant Italian notarial formularies. It not only gives insight into medieval legal procedures but constitutes a significant historical source in recording the personal and business transactions of a wide variety of Paduan citizens and institutions of the first third of the thirteenth century.

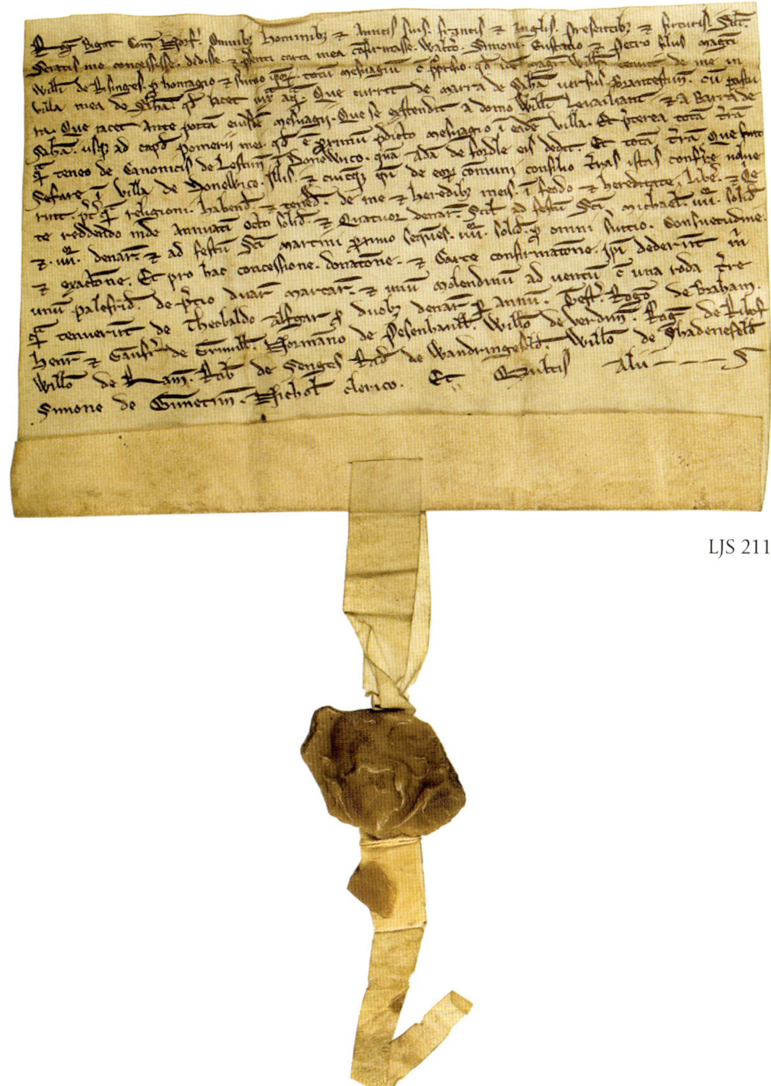

LJS 211

DESCRIPTION Parchment, 40 folios, 154 x 110 mm, in Latin, black ink, gothic script. 19th-century Italian gold-tooled diced-leather binding.
PROVENANCE Gabus, Geneva, 11 December 1989, lot 5253; Sam Fogg; H.P. Kraus, cat. 188 (1991), no. 6, and cat. 199 (1995) no. 112; H.P. Kraus, September 1996

8 LJS 115

Folio of a civil law text on contracts
Southern France, mid-13th century

DESCRIPTION Parchment, 1 folio, 178 x 125 mm, in Latin, black ink, proto-gothic script.

9   LJS 280

Raymond of Peñafort, *Decretales abbreviate Gregorii IX*
France, 2nd half 13th century

The *Decretales* was a codification of canon law compiled by the
Dominican scholar Raymond of Peñafort (1185–1274) on the
direction of Pope Gregory IX in the 1230s; this is an
abbreviated version.

DESCRIPTION Parchment, 147 of 163 folios, 210 x 154 mm, in Latin,
early gothic script, black ink. 15th-century sheepskin over wooden
board binding.
PROVENANCE St. Martin Major, Cologne; S. Ereilter, 1893; a German
ducal library; Sam Fogg, 1998

10   LJS 231

Statutes regulating taxation of commerce
Barga (Tuscany), 26 February 1346

These statutes regulate the taxation of internal and external
trade in a wide variety of products with particular attention to
defining weights and measures. They offer a unique witness
to the economic life of the fourteenth century in Tuscany.

DESCRIPTION Paper, 28 folios, 298 x 200 mmm, in Latin, gothic
cursive script, brown ink, several scribes. 16th-century vellum
binding over pasteboard.
PROVENANCE Neri ser Petri de Monte Alcino, 1346; Giannalisa
Feltrinelli; Pierpont Morgan Library, New York; Christie's,
3 December 1997, lot 210

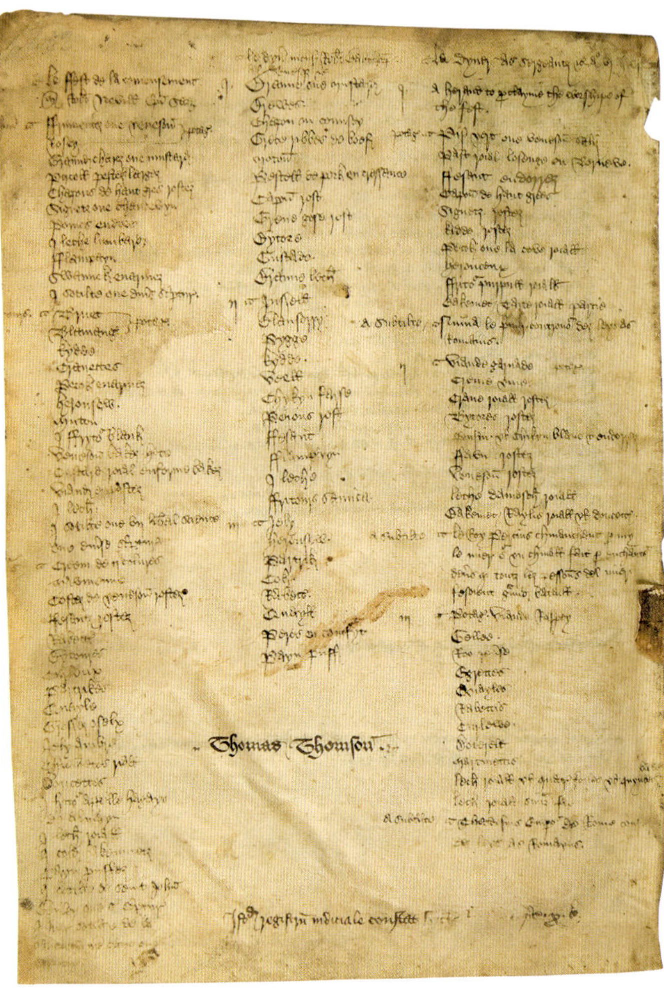

LJS
f. 21

PROVENANCE Sir Thomas Phillipps, ms. 30744; Sotheby's,
London, 30 November 1976, lot 867; A.L. Shane; Sotheby's,
London, 22 June 1999, lot 52

11   LJS 308

Grant by King Edward III of a licence to close a public road
Gloucester, 16 August 1347

This document grants to Robert de Burghcher permission to
close and to convert to cultivation the public road which ran
through the middle of his land at Stansted (now the site of an
airport) on condition that Robert should build another
appropriate road across his land.

DESCRIPTION Paper, 1 folio, 190 x 270 mm, in Latin, the Great
Seal of England (105 mm) on white wax suspended on a parchment
tab.

12   LJS 212

Account of maintenance expenses of fulling mills
Poligny, Jura, 1380

This account, part of what was once a larger collection, details
the parts of the mill machinery and plant as well as the costs
of transport, labour and the purchase of iron and nails.

DESCRIPTION Parchment, single sheet, 430 x 300 mm, in French,
black ink, chancery script. Disbound.
PROVENANCE Sam Fogg, cat. 16 (1995), no. 69; John Stanitz, ms. 43

13 LJS 342

Eight documents relating to
water rights in Milan
Milan, 1383–86 (with a decree of
1444)

These documents relate to the
illicit use of water and diversion of
waterways in the territory of Milan
compiled presumably as a
confirmation of the legal status of
these assets. Canals and waterways
of Renaissance Lombardy were of
the greatest importance for the
irrigation, trade and
communication of the Po valley.

DESCRIPTION Parchment, 45 folios,
187 x 138 mm, in Latin, cursive
humanistic script, brown ink.
Contemporary brown leather wallet
binding.
PROVENANCE Christie's, London,
29 November 1999, lot 8

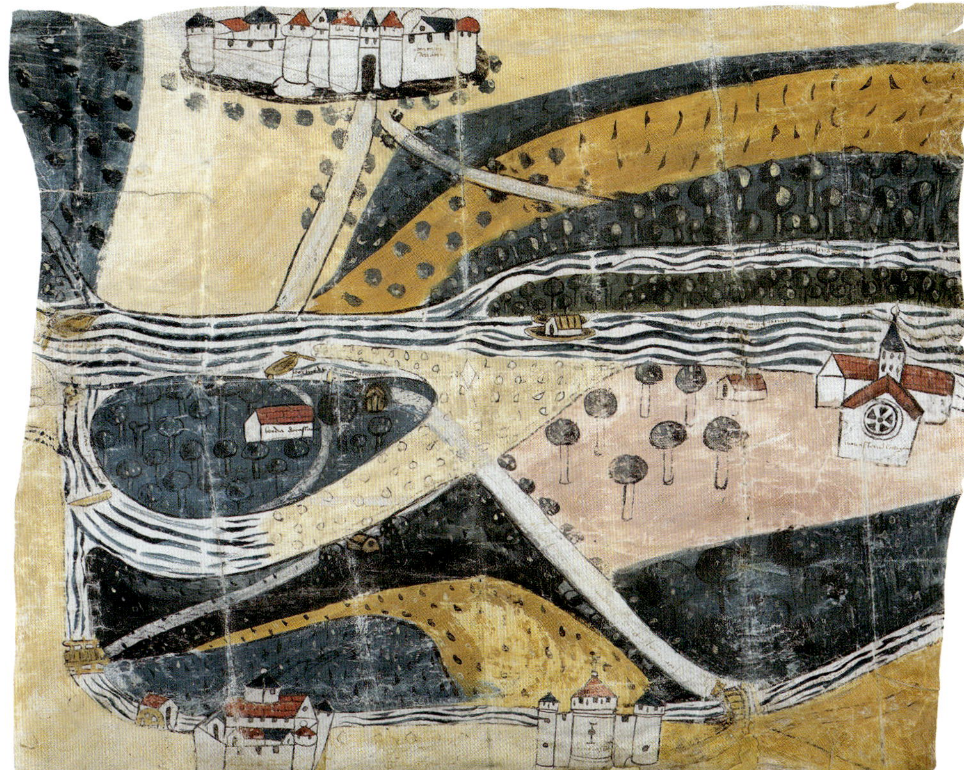

LJS 310

ms. 10349; Sotheby's, 5 June 1899, lot 32, and 27 April 1903, lot 957;
Christie's, London, 26 June 1996, lot 16; Sam Fogg, June 1996

14 LJS 61

Writs from the end of the reign of Richard II and the
beginning of the reign of Henry IV
London, 1407

This full series of royal chancery writs, ranging widely in
subject, is of central importance to any study of this historical
period. Three feasts are the subject of writs, one, for the
graduation of Robert Neville, involving 75 dishes featuring
many species that are today rare or endangered (f. 214v).

DESCRIPTION Parchment, 231 folios, 260 x 173 mm, in Latin and
French, main portion gothic cursive script. Late 15th-century calf
binding over wooden boards.
PROVENANCE Robert Nevill, Bishop of Salisbury (1427-37), or one of
his legal officers; Nicolas Fowle; Thomas Thomson; Revd Dr Adam
Clarke (?1762-1832); Sotheby's, 21 May 1838; Sir Thomas Phillipps,

15 LJS 310

Map of a district in Tarn-et-Garonne
Castelferrus, between 1460 and 1545

This large map appears to have been made for Jean Rollet,
seigneur of Castelferrus, for the purpose of illustrating the
prevailing water rights between Castelferrus and
Castelsarrasin. Its central feature is the Garonne river and its
watercourses, of which the bridges, mill, sandbanks and ferry
points are detailed. A variety of other features are also shown,
such as the monastery of Belleperche, several settlements of
different sizes, roads and farmland.

DESCRIPTION Parchment, 1 sheet, 630 x 700 mm, with text in Latin.
PROVENANCE Jean Rollet; Simon Finch Rare Books, cat. 8 (1991),
no. 68; acquired from a Swiss collector through Sam Fogg, July 1999

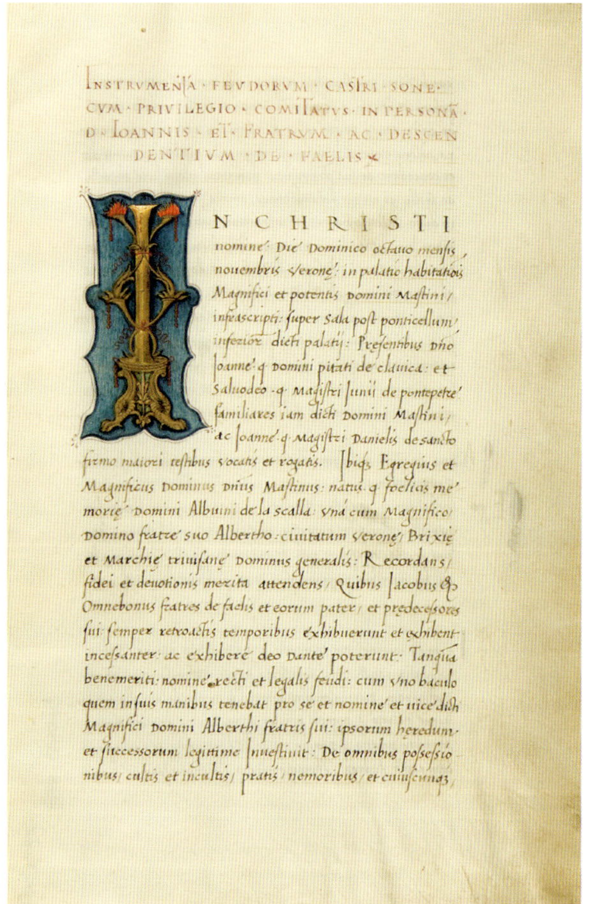

LJS 48
f. 3r

LJS 48
f. 13v

16 LJS 450

Compendium of legal texts
Italy, 2nd half 15th century

The manuscript consists of a collection of treatises on civil law assembled in Italy as reference material, including both Roman law and canon law.

DESCRIPTION Paper, 331 folios, 308 x 212 mm, in Latin, small cursive script, brown ink. Wooden boards on three leather bands, remains of leather to spine and inside covers.

PROVENANCE Christie's, London, 4 June 2003, lot 16

17 LJS 48

Decrees and grants relating to Giovanni Faella of Verona
Verona, 1504

The manuscript is of great beauty and elegance, and of considerable artistic interest, on account both of its illuminations, strongly influenced by Mantegna (who was still alive in 1504), and of its series of unpublished documents concerning the architectural heritage of the city of Verona.

DESCRIPTION Parchment, 26 folios, 305 x 187 mm, in Latin, superb calligraphic humanistic script, written by the imperial notary Francesco di Andrea Ruffo, signed with his notarial mark. Fine original Veronese binding of brown calf over wooden boards.

PROVENANCE Commissioned by Count Giovanni Faella of Sona; Menno Hertzberger International Antiquariaat, Amsterdam, 22 March 1961, lot 915; B.S. Cron, 1 July 1965; Alan Thomas, cat. 18 (1967), no. 4; Major J.R. Abbey, ms. JA 7387; Sotheby's, London, 20 June 1978, lot 2992; H. P. Kraus, cat. 159 (1981), no 9; Martin Breslauer, 1989; Christie's, London, 3 April 1996, lot 8; Sam Fogg, June 1996

18   LJS 59

Document concerning the duties, rights and obligations
of Paolo Nani (1496–1551) in his capacity as Podestà and
Capitaneus of Treviso
Venice, 25 May 1517

Treviso passed under Venetian power in 1388; the governor
(*podestà*) would be a Venetian patrician.

DESCRIPTION Parchment, 34 folios, 240 x 164 mm, fine calligraphic
humanistic minuscule, brown ink. Handsome contemporary binding.
PROVENANCE Victor Glm (?); private collection, Würzburg; Sam
Fogg, February 1997

19   LJS 238

Regulations for breadmaking
Winchester, 16th century

This gives the prescribed weights for five varieties of loaves of
different grades of wheat in an attempt to standardize
previous local policies and regulations for bakers in England.

DESCRIPTION Parchment, scroll (flattened), 437 x 338 mm, in
English, gothic cursive script, red and black ink. Housed in quarter
dark orange leather over blue boards.
PROVENANCE Sir John Fenn; Sir Thomas Phillipps, ms. 33859;
Sotheby's, London, 14 June 1971, lot 1448; Charles Sawyer; Mark
Landsberg; Bruce Ferrini; Sam Fogg, February 1998

20   LJS 416

Regulations for breadmaking
Rouen, France, 1518

The document traces 200 years of the history of milling of
wheat flour and the making and selling of bread and pastries
in Rouen.

DESCRIPTION Parchment, 28 folios, 210 x 150 mm, in French, very
fine clubbed semi-bâtarde script, dark brown ink. Contemporary
decorated morocco binding.
PROVENANCE Written for Pierre Tassel; Sotheby's, London, 5
December 1994, lot 87; Simon Finch Rare Books; Sam Fogg, April 2001

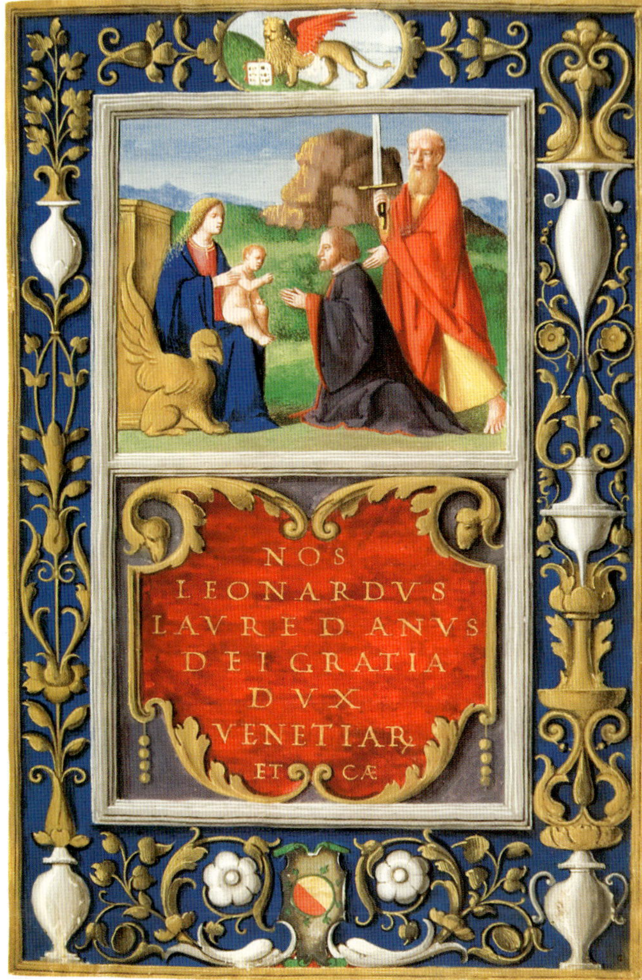

LJS 59
f. 1r

LJS 238

21 LJS 285

Francesco Gonzaga, Bank charter to Isaac de Massaran, Mantua, Italy, 24 May 1542

The charter licenses Isaac and two other shareholders from the Jewish community of Mantua to establish a money-lending bank with the same benefits, immunities, privileges and honours given to the other loan-bankers in Mantua.

DESCRIPTION Parchment, 347 x 440 mm, in Latin, elegant sloping italic script, with large red wax Gonzaga seal.
PROVENANCE Sotheby's, London, 1 December 1998, lot 66

22 LJS 19

Juan Garcia de la Puente, *Pleito de hidalguia*
Granada, 16 June 1542

The need for such 'litigation to prove noble status' is a reflection of the political climate of sixteenth-century Spain; see further LJS 20 (no. 25) and 21 (no. 30).

DESCRIPTION Parchment, 38 folios, 350 x 210 mm, in Spanish, rounded gothic script, dark brown ink. Outer bifolium used as wrapper.
PROVENANCE Sotheby's, London, 10 December 1980, lot 58

23 LJS 304

Commissions to Girolamo Priuli, Podestà of Brescia
Venice, 6 March 1574

The manuscript contains copies of the letters of appointment from the Doge (*Commissioni* and *Dogali*) to Girolamo Priuli as governor (*podestà*) of Brescia, and of the local laws, decrees and conditions. See LJS 59 (no. 18) for another such *dogale*.

DESCRIPTION Parchment, 210 folios, 225 x 165 mm, brown ink.
PROVENANCE Girolamo Priuli; Christie's, London, 2 June 1999, lot 43

24 LJS 349

Letter from Philip II, King of Spain, to officials in the Council of the Indies in Seville
Madrid, 6 November 1576

The letter is signed by Philip II, King of Spain (1556–98), officially ordering the admiral of the fleet to provide free passage on one of his flagships for Ochoa de Aguirre and his entourage to the new Kingdom of Grenada (Columbia).

DESCRIPTION Paper, 1 page, 298 x 203 mm, in Spanish.
PROVENANCE Sotheby's, New York, 7 December 1999, lot 271

25 LJS 20

Grant of nobility to Juan Gayton de Cuenca
Granada, 12 September 1578

This *pleito de hidalguia* claims emphatically that three brothers of the de Cuenca family were legitimate, of old Christian family and of pure blood, without Jewish or Moorish taint. See LJS 19 (no. 22) and 21 (no. 30) for other such *pleitos de hidalguia*.

DESCRIPTION Parchment, 67 folios, 321 x 226 mm, in Spanish, rounded Gothic script, dark brown ink. Contemporary parchment binding over pasteboards.
PROVENANCE Thorp, cat. 405 (1973), no. 28; Monsignor David McRoberts, 1973; Sotheby's, London, 24 June 1980, lot 86

26 LJS 383

Legal contract
France, 1592

The contract is drawn up between two French families.

DESCRIPTION Paper, 266 x 178 mm, in French, black ink, French notary script.
PROVENANCE Trobador's Art (Joel Cohen), 1 May 2000

27 LJS 379

Ferdinando I de' Medici, Document granting Jewish merchants the right to settle in Livorno and Pisa
Florence, 10 June 1593

The edict grants not only the right to settle but also unprecedented protections during a period of inquisition and expulsion of Jews. The promulgation of this edict led directly to the development of the city as a major Italian port and as an important centre of Jewish life in Italy.

DESCRIPTION Parchment, 12 folios, 257 x 200 mm, in Italian, large italic script, black ink. Contemporary Italian blind-ruled brown goatskin over pasteboard binding.
PROVENANCE Pietro Ginori Conti, ms. 10375; Christie's, New York, 19 May 2000, lot 229

28 LJS 346

Guiglielmo and Vincenzo Gonzaga, Edicts confirming privileges and amnesties for Jews in Mantua
Mantua, 10 November 1594

The manuscript is an official copy of the three edicts which allowed freedom to Jews to work as bankers, merchants and butchers in Mantua, confirming privileges and amnesties, as well as describing the many restrictions, in return for a payment of 4000 *scudi*.

DESCRIPTION Paper, 20 folios, 355 x 247 mm, in Latin and Italian, elegant chancery script. Old pink marbled paper binding over limp pasteboard.
PROVENANCE Sotheby's, London, 7 December 1999, lot 24

29 LJS 177

Documents pertaining to the history and condition of the Pontine Marsh
Italy, mostly Rome, 16th–18th century

This volume contains an impressive collection of documents concerning the Pontine Marsh project, including three manuscripts dating from the sixteenth century and engraved folding maps, dating from the eighteenth century, which delineates the locations of proposed drainage systems.

DESCRIPTION Paper, 600 folios, 292 x 215 mm, in Latin and Italian; 26 manuscripts, 10 printed booklets, three maps and one broadside; manuscript sections in ink in cursive scripts by numerous hands.
PROVENANCE Millini family archives; Colonna Biblioteca (according to Phillipps catalogue, p. 115); Frederick North, 5th Earl of Guilford (1766-1827); Mssrs Evans, 8 December 1830, lot 289, to Thorpe; Sir Thomas Phillipps, ms. 7636; Robinson Bros., 1945; H.P. Kraus, cat. 204 (1982), no. 74; John Stanitz, ms. 8

30 LJS 21

Grant of nobility to Juan de Mena Gutierrez
Granada, 14 April 1606

This *Pleito de hidalguia* (see LJS 19 [no. 22] and 20 [no. 25]) dates from the reign of Philip III.

DESCRIPTION Parchment, 52 folios, 316 x 212 mm, in Spanish, rounded gothic hand, dark brown ink. Contemporary Spanish dark brown morocco binding over pasteboard.
PROVENANCE Sotheby's, London, 11 December 1979, lot 28

31 LJS 314

East India Company, Petition to Shah 'Abbas II of Persia
London, 9 April 1660

This petition for a share of the customs of Gombroon, in the Persian Gulf, is striking witness to the power and confidence of the East India Company in the 1660s, when, under the fostering care of King Charles II, it grew into the great and formidable chartered company which would play such a significant role in British colonial history.

DESCRIPTION Parchment, 574 x 478 mm, in English, professional script, illumination. Modern morocco backed binding.
PROVENANCE Sotheby's, London, 15 July 1999, lot 31

CONCORDANCE

Note: The SDBM (*Schoenberg Database of Manuscripts*) column gives the number by which the manuscript can be found in the database. The SDBM does not include manuscripts of fewer than five folios or postdating 1600.

LJS	Section	Cat. no.	Page	SDBM	LJS	Section	Cat. no.	Page	SDBM	LJS	Section	Cat. no.	Page	SDBM
16	IX	11	137	359	115	X	8	147		211	X	6	147	22853
17	IX	20	143	1316	124	IX	11	137		212	X	12	148	
19	X	22	152	14977	163	VII	9	117		213	III	31	51	
20	X	25	152	14978	170	VI	9	113		214	VI	10	113	
21	X	30	153		171	V	35	99		215	IV	37	75	17405
22	VII	21	126		172	IV	32	73	17501	216	III	16	39	17555
23	IX	5	133	9730	173	III	26	50		217	VI	12	113	
24	V	18	89	9737	174	IV	25	69	1359	218	III	35	51	
25	I	4	15	1757	175	IV	19	63		219	VII	22	126	
26	IV	11	57	1205	176	VII	6	117		220	V	28	93	17559
27	III	18	41	614	177	X	29	153		221	III	32	51	
28	VII	11	118	14981	178	VII	5	116		222	VII	15	122	
29	VIII	5	128	427	179	I	24	26		223	I	20	24	17560
33	IX	29	145		180	VII	7	117		224	I	16	20	17561
36	IX	23	143		181	III	30	51		225	III	21	43	264
37	III	6	35	14985	182	IV	20	64		226	IV	26	69	17568
41	IX	25	144	14404	183	III	27	50		228	III	5	35	
42	IV	14	60	15014	184	IX	2	131	17495	229	I	13	19	17574
45	IX	19	142	15049	186	VII	4	116		231	X	10	148	144
46	V	41	106	15060	187	VI	11	113		232	III	22	45	164
47	II	2	28	15074	188	IV	41	78	17537	234	I	9	18	1992
48	X	17	150	297	189	V	14	84	17541	235	II	3	30	17582
49	V	15	85	15075	190	VII	8	117		236	V	26	92	17583
50	IX	8	134	15473	191	IV	36	75	1544	237	IX	26	144	1567
51	III	20	43	55241	192	VII	16	122		238	X	19	151	
54	X	7	147	14758	194	III	7	36	17503	239	VIII	7	129	17600
55	IX	7	134	17481	195	V	27	93	17549	242	IX	15	141	18457
56	I	15	20	10350	198	V	23	90	10594	251	III	23	46	18462
57	IV	24	66	15197	199	III	25	49		252	I	10	18	
59	X	18	151	17502	200	IV	18	62		254	VII	17	123	18463
60	IX	1	130	9943	201	VII	3	116		264	IX	6	133	18464
61	X	14	149	265	202	IV	42	79		265	VIII	3	127	18465
62	V	38	100	17512	203	I	21	24		266	IX	22	143	
63	II	8	33		204	IV	23	65	17554	267	IX	28	145	9873
64	IV	12	59	17527	205	IV	21	64		268	IV	1	52	18469
97	II	1	27	17529	206	III	33	51		269	III	4	35	
98	IX	21	143	215	207	III	34	51		270	III	4	35	
99	III	1	34		208	III	28	50		272	VIII	8	129	
100	X	1	146		209	III	28	50		273	X	3	146	
101	I	1	12	239	210	V	37	99		274	X	5	147	

LJS	Section	Cat. no.	Page	SDBM
275	X	4	146	
278	V	42	106	55272
279	IV	10	57	
280	X	9	148	18470
285	X	21	152	
286	III	9	37	18471
289	III	19	43	18472
293	III	10	38	18554
294	II	4	31	
295	II	5	32	18516
296	III	13	39	18547
299	V	8	81	18568
300	IV	33	74	18558
301	III	2	34	
302	III	3	34	
304	X	23	152	18559
308	X	11	148	
309	X	2	146	
310	X	15	149	
311	V	9	82	18560
312	III	14	39	18561
313	V	36	99	
314	X	31	153	
319	VII	13	122	
320	III	29	50	
322	V	2	81	4952
323	IV	17	62	
325	I	18	21	23732
342	X	13	149	18768
345	VII	12	119	18769
346	X	28	153	18780
347	I	2	14	6
349	X	24	152	
355	V	4	81	18781
356	VIII	6	128	18782
358	VIII	4	128	
359	V	7	81	13559
361	IV	22	64	66
379	X	27	153	13596
380	I	22	25	17061
381	IX	27	144	13599
382	VI	3	110	18085
383	X	26	152	
384	IX	3	132	30659
385	I	3	14	30735
386	VII	1	115	13775
387	IX	18	142	13780
388	IV	6	55	13778

LJS	Section	Cat. no.	Page	SDBM
389	V	33	94	13836
391	V	17	88	N/A
392	IV	4	54	30252
393	V	12	83	18797
394	IX	17	142	18798
395	V	21	90	N/A
397	IV	16	61	8235
398	V	13	84	18889
399	VII	2	115	
400	IV	38	77	18890
401	VI	7	113	
402	VI	8	113	
403	VI	4	110	20346
404	IX	4	132	20376
405	IX	24	144	20377
406	IX	16	141	20378
407	IV	5	55	20379
408	IV	8	56	20380
409	VI	1	109	20381
410	IV	7	56	20382
411	IV	39	77	20383
412	IV	3	54	20384
413	IX	9	136	20385
414	IV	15	61	
416	X	20	151	426
417	V	5	81	13712
418	II	7	33	14130
419	V	40	103	20388
420	IV	34	74	20389
421	V	25	92	9240
423	III	24	47	20390
424	V	22	90	20392
425	II	6	32	
426	V	3	81	20391
427	V	6	81	20393
429	I	19	23	20394
430	V	20	89	9032
432	VII	19	124	
433	V	34	97	20396
434	IV	40	78	20397
435	V	16	87	20005
436	III	15	39	28361
437	V	24	91	515
438	I	23	26	59661
439	I	5	15	59662
440	I	6	16	55516
441	VI	5	111	56022
442	VII	18	124	56023

LJS	Section	Cat. no.	Page	SDBM
443	IV	27	70	56026
444	V	11	82	56025
445	IV	35	74	56026
446	V	1	80	56027
447	IX	12	138	
448	VI	6	112	
449	IV	29	70	1637
450	X	16	150	
451	IX	13	140	33412
452	IX	14	140	33419
453	I	12	19	30981
454	VII	14	122	
455	VI	2	110	56028
456	I	8	18	39905
457	I	17	21	8744
458	V	29	93	56029
459	I	7	17	39868
460	III	6	35	39895
461	VII	20	125	
462	III	17	40	48380
463	IV	28	70	40553
464	III	11	38	56030
465	III	8	37	56031
466	IV	30	72	50032
467	VIII	2	127	56033
468	V	32	94	52429
469	V	10	82	52434
470	V	31	94	52455
471	V	30	93	52426
472	IV	13	60	52416
473	VII	10	118	40559
474	IV	9	57	56706
475	V	39	102	
476	IV	31	72	51300
477	IX	10	136	59740
478	IV	2	53	69446
479	V	19	89	76843
480	VIII	1	127	
481	III	12	39	75988
482	I	11	19	77521
483	I	14	19	76943

BIBLIOGRAPHY

Aiton, E.J., (ed.), 'Peurbach's *Theoricae novae planetarum*: A Translation with Commentary', *Osiris*, 2nd series, 3 (1987), pp. 5-43

Al-Daffa, A.A., and Stroyles, J.J., 'Nasir al-Din al-Tusi's Attempt to Prove the Parallel Postulate of Euclid', in their *Studies in the Exact Sciences in Medieval Islam*, Dhahran 1984, pp. 31-59

Algorismus: Trattato di aritmetica practica e mercantile del secolo XV, ed. G. Chiarini *et al.*, 2 vols., Banca Commerciale Italiana, Verona 1972

Allen, T.G., *The Book of the Dead or Going Forth by Day*, Chicago 1974

Annas, J., and Barnes, J., eds., Sextus Empiricus, *Outlines of Scepticism*, Cambridge 2000

Baldwin, S., and Barrette, P., eds., Brunetto Latini, *Li Livres dou Tresor*, Tempe, Arizona, 2003

Barker, A., *Greek Musical Writings*, 2 vols., Cambridge 1984-89

Beltran, E., 'Un manuscrit autographe de la *Grammaticae basis* de Guillaume Tardif', *Bibliothèque d'humanisme et Renaissance*, 61 (1999), pp. 495-508

Beullens, P., 'Supplement to the Aristoteles latinus: An Unknown Manuscript of Moerbeke's Translation of the *Metaphysica*', *Recherches de théologie et philosophie médiévales*, 69.1 (2002), 66-87

Bietenholz, P.G., ed., *Contemporaries of Erasmus: A Biographical Register of the Renaissance and Reformation*, 3 vols., Toronto 1985-87

Boese, H., ed., Thomas Cantimpratensis, *Liber de natura rerum: editio princeps secundum codices manuscriptos*, 2 vols., Berlin and New York 1973

Bond, J.D., 'The Development of Trigonometric Methods down to the Close of the XVth Century', *Isis*, 4.2 (1921), pp. 295-323

Bower, C.M., 'Boethius's *De institutione musica*: A Handlist of Manuscripts', *Scriptorium*, 42 (1988), pp. 205-51

Bower, C.M., ed., Boethius, *Fundamentals of Music*, New Haven and London 1989

Brams, J., 'Guillaume de Moerbeke et Aristote', in *Rencontres de cultures dans la philosophie médiévale: traductions et traducteurs de l'antiquité tardive au XIVe siècle*, ed. J. Hamesse and M. Fattori, Louvain-la-Neuve 1990, pp. 317-36

Brévart, F.B., 'The German Volkskalender of the Fifteenth Century', *Speculum*, 63 (1988), pp. 312-42

Cao, G.M., 'The Prehistory of Modern Scepticism: Sextus Empiricus in Fifteenth-Century Italy', *Journal of the Warburg and Courtauld Institutes*, 64 (2001), pp. 229-79

Collet, A., ed., *Le jeu des eschaz moralisé*, Paris 1999

Cooper, J., tr., and Baigent, M., ed., Placidus de Titis, *Primum mobile*, London 1983

DLF: *Dictionnaire des lettres françaises: le moyen âge*, ed. R. Bossuat *et al.*, Paris 1964

DSB: *Dictionary of Scientific Biography*, ed. C.C. Gillispie, New York 1970-80

Düring, I., *Ptolemaios und Porphyrios über die Musik*, Göteborg 1934

Eade, J.C., *The Forgotten Sky: A Guide to Astrology in English Literature*, Oxford 1984

Eamon, W., 'Books of Secrets in Medieval and Early Modern Science', *Sudhoffs Archiv*, 69.1 (1985), pp. 26-49

Ebeling, K. *Ragamala Painting*, New Delhi, 1973

EI: *Encyclopaedia of Islam*, 2nd edn, Leiden 1965-

EJ: *Encyclopaedia Judaica*, ed. C. Roth, Jerusalem 1972

Elgood, C., *A Medical History of Persia and the Eastern Caliphate*, Cambridge 1951

Eliade, M., ed., *The Encyclopaedia of Religion*, 16 vols., New York 1987

Farmer, H.G., *The Sources of Arabian Music*, Bearsden 1940

Faulkner, R.O., tr., *et al.*, *The Egyptian Book of the Dead*, San Francisco 1994

Figgins, V., ed., William Caxton, *The Game of the Chesse*, London 1860

Floridi, L., 'The Diffusion of Sextus Empiricus's Works in the Renaissance', *Journal of the History of Ideas*, 56 (1995), pp. 63-85

Galindo, M.A.G., *El Doctrinal: Una gramática latina del Renacimiento del siglo XII*, Madrid 1993

Gambino Longom, S., *Savoir de la nature et poésie des choses: Lucrèce et Epicure à la Renaissance italienne*, Paris 2004

Gandz, S., 'The Invention of the Decimal Fractions and the Application of the Exponential Calculus by Immanuel Bonfils of Tarascon (c. 1350)', *Isis*, 25 (1936), pp. 16-45

Grove: *The New Grove Dictionary of Music and Musicians*, ed. S. Sadie, 20 vols., London 1980

Halliwell, J.O., ed., *Rara mathematica: or A Collection of Treatises on the Mathematics and Subjects Connected with them, from Ancient Inedited Manuscripts*, London 1841

Hankins, J., *Plato in the Italian Renaissance*, 2 vols., Leiden and New York 1990

HMES: Thorndike, L., *History of Magic and Experimental Science*, 8 vols., New York 1923-58

HMI: *Encyclopaedia Iranica, The History of Medicine in Iran: Entries Extracted from Volumes I-XII*, New York 2004

Horsley, S., ed., *Isaaci Newtoni Opera quae exstant omnia*, 5 vols., London 1779-85

Hossfeld, P., ed., *Alberti Magni Physica, Opera omnia, tomus IV*, 2 vols., Westfalia 1987-93

HUM: Steinschneider, M., *Die Hebräischen Übersetzungen des Mittelalters und die Juden als Dometscher*, 2 vols., Berlin 1893

Inati, S.C., tr., Ibn Sina, *Remarks and Admonitions: Part I: Logic*, Toronto 1984

Iter Italicum, ed. P.O. Kristeller, 6 vols., London 1963-97

Jarcho, S., ed., *Tractatus simplex de cortice peruviano: A Plain Treatise on the Peruvian Bark ("The Stanitz Manuscript")*, Boston 1992

Jones, H., *The Epicurean Tradition*, London and New York 1989

Karpozilos, A., 'The Yale University Manuscripts of Andreas Darmarius', *Hellenika*, 26 (1973), pp. 67-71

Köpke, E., ed., Iacobus de Cessolis, *De ludo scachorum*, Brandenburg an der Havel 1879

Krenkow, F., 'The Construction of Subterranean Water Supplies during the Abbasid Caliphate, *Transactions of the Glasgow University Oriental Society*, 13 (1951), pp. 23-32

Kristeller, P. O., 'The School of Salerno: Its Development and its Contribution to the History of Learning', *Bulletin of the History of Medicine*, 17.2 (1945), pp. 138-94

Lacombe, G., *Aristoteles Latinus codices descripsit*, 2 vols., Rome 1939

LDS: *Libros del saber de astronomia del rey D. Alfonso X de Castilla*, 5 vols., Madrid 1863-67

Lindsay, W.M., ed., *Isidori Hispalensis Episcopi Etymologiarum sive Originum libri XX*, 2 vols., Oxford 1911

Lohr, C.H., *Latin Aristotle Commentaries*, 3 vols., Florence 1988-2005

Lopez, S.G., *Le passioni degli atomi: Montanari e Rossetti: una polemica tra galileiani*, Florence 1997

Luti, F., *Don Antonio de' Medici e i suoi tempi*, Florence 2006

Meyer, C., ed., *Boethius, Traité de la musique*, Turnhout 2004

Meyer, P., 'Les premières compilations françaises d'histoire ancienne', *Romania*, no. 14 (1884), pp. 1-81

Manzalaoui, M., 'The pseudo-Aristotelian *Kitab Sirr al-Asrar*', *Oriens*, 23-4 (1974), pp. 147-257

Marenbon, J., *Boethius*, Oxford 2003

Maurach, G., ed., William of Conches, *Philosophia*, Pretoria 1980

Morison, S.E., *Christopher Columbus: Admiral of the Ocean Sea*, Oxford 1942

Moyer, A.E., *The Philosophers' Game: Rithmomachia in Medieval and Renaissance Europe*, Ann Arbor, Michigan, 2001

Muntner, S., tr., Moses Maimonides, *Treatise on Poisons and their Antidotes*, Philadelphia and Montreal 1966

Noja, S., *Catalogo dei manoscritti orientali della Biblioteca Nazionale di Torino*, I: *I manoscritti arabi, persiani e turchi*, Rome 1974

OCIL: *Oxford Companion to Italian Literature*, ed. P. Hainsworth and D. Robey, Oxford 2002

ODCC: *Oxford Dictionary of the Christian Church*, ed. F.L. Cross and E.A. Livingston, Oxford 1997

ODNB: *Oxford Dictionary of National Biography*, ed. H.C.G. Matthew and B. Harrison, Oxford 2004

Perreiah, A.R., ed., Paulus Venetus, *Logica parva: Translation of the 1472 edition with Introduction and Notes*, Munich 1984

Perreiah, A.R., *Paul of Venice: A Bibliographical Guide*, Bowling Green, Ohio, 1986

Perreiah, A.R., ed., Paulus Venetus, *Logica parva: First Critical Edition from the Manuscripts with Introduction and Commentary*, Leiden 2002

PL: *Patrologiae latinae cursus completus*, ed. J.-P. Migne, 221 vols., Paris 1844-64

Prior, O.H., *L'image du monde de Maître Gossouin*, Lausanne and Paris 1913

Próder, I., 'Einige biographische Daten über Auton Ruprecht (1748-1814)', in *Papers delivered at the first 'Mineralkontor' International Conference on the History of Chemistry and Chemical Industry*, [n.p.] 1991, pp. 194-97

Pyle, C.M., 'The Art and Science of Renaissance Natural History: Thomas of Cantimpré, Pier Candido Decembrio, Conrad Gessner and Teodoro Ghisi in Vatican Library Ms. Urb. Lat. 276', *Viator*, 27 (1996), pp. 265-321

Ragep, F.J., *Nasir al-Din al-Tusi's Memoir on Astronomy*, 2 vols., New York, Berlin and Heidelberg 1993

Randles, W.G.L., *The Unmaking of the Medieval Christian Cosmos, 1500-1760*, Aldershot 1999

Ranstrand, G., ed., Pomponius Mela, *De chorographia libri tres*, Göteborg 1971

Reichling, D., ed., *Das Doctrinale des Alexander de Villa-Dei: Kritisch-Exegetische Ausgabe*, 1845, repr. New York 1974

Reif, P., 'The Textbook Tradition in Natural Philosophy, 1600-1650', *Journal for the History of Ideas*, 30 (1969), pp. 17-32

REP: *Routledge Encyclopaedia of Philosophy*, ed. E. Craig, 10 vols., London 1998

Richter, W., ed., Petrus de Crescentiis, *Ruralia commoda*, 4 vols., Heidelberg 1995

Rivolta, A., *Contributo a uno studio sulla biblioteca di Gian Vincenzo Pinelli*, Monza 1914

Romer, F.E., tr., Pomponius Mela, *Description of the World*, Ann Arbor, Michigan, 1998

Ryan, W., and Schmitt, C., eds., *Pseudo-Aristotle, The Secret of Secrets: Sources and Influences*, London 1982

Saccenti, M., *Lucrezio in Toscana: Studio su Alessandro Marchetti*, Florence 1966

Saibanti, C. de P., 'Arte del Navigare, manoscritto inedito datato 1464-1465', in *Imago et mensura mundi: atti del IX Congresso internazionale di Storia della Cartografia*, ed. C.C. Marzoli, 2 vols., Florence 1985, I, pp. 71-79

Sarton, G., *Introduction to the History of Science*, 3 vols., Washington, DC, 1927–48

Schmitt, C.B., 'The Recovery and Assimilation of Ancient Scepticism in the Renaissance', *Rivista critica di storia della filosofia*, 27 (1972), pp. 363-84

Schnell, B., 'Der *Vocabularius ex quo*', in *La lexicographie au moyen-âge*, ed. C. Buridant et al., Lille 1986, pp. 71-82

Schnell, B., ed., *Vocabularius ex quo*, 6 vols., Tübingen 1988-2001

Shiloah, A., *The Theory of Music in Arabic Writings (c. 900-1900)* (Répertoire International des Sources Musicales, B/X), Munich 1979

Singer, C. and D., *The Origin of the Medical School of Salerno, the First University: An Attempted Reconstruction*, London 1924

Smith, D.E., *The History of Mathematics*, 2 vols., Boston 1923

Smith, D.E., ed., *Le comput manuel de Magister Anianus*, Paris 1928

Smith, D.E., *Rara arithmetica*, New York 1970

Spink, M.S., and Lewis, G.L., eds., Albucasis, *On Surgery and Instruments: A Definitive Edition of the Arabic Text with English Translation and Commentary*, London 1973

Steinschneider, M., 'Medicinische Handschriften im Besitz des Herrn Halberstam', *Magazin für die Wissenschaft des Judentums*, 10 (1883), pp. 160-65

Struick, D.J., ed., *A Source Book in Mathematics, 1200-1800*, Cambridge, Mass., 1969

Swetz, F.J., *Capitalism and Arithmetic: The New Math of the 15th Century*, Illinois 1987

Thorndike, L., *The Sphere of Sacrobosco and its Commentators*, Chicago 1949

Tooley, R.V., *Maps and Map-Makers*, London 1970

Toomer, G.J., *Ptolemy's Almagest*, London 1984

Tzvi Langermann, Y., 'Peuerbach in the Hebrew Tradition', *Journal for the History of Astronomy*, 29 (1998), pp. 137-50

Ullmann, M., *Islamic Medicine*, Edinburgh 1978

Vuillemin-Diem, G., ed., Aristotle, *Metaphysica* (Aristoteles Latinus XXV 3), 2 vols., Leiden 1995

Wagner, H.R., 'The Manuscript Atlases of Battista Agnese', *Papers of the Bibliographical Society of America*, 25 (1931), pp. 1-110

Waters, David W., *The Art of Navigation in England in Elizabethan and Early Stuart times*, Greenwich 1978

Westman, R.S., 'The Melanchthon Circle, Rheticus, and the Wittenberg Interpretation of the Copernican Theory', *Isis*, 66 (1975), pp. 164-93

Whiteside, D.T., ed., *The Mathematical Papers of Isaac Newton*, Volume III, 1670-1673, Cambridge 1969

Worrell, W.H., 'Qusta ibn Luqa on the Use of the Celestial Globe', *Isis*, 35 (1944), pp. 285-93

Wright, O., 'A Preliminary Version of the *Kitab al-adwar*', *Bulletin of the School of Oriental and African Studies*, 58.3 (1995), pp. 455-78

Zinner, E., *Leben und Wirken des Johannes Müller*, Osnabrück 1968